National Communism and
Popular Revolt in Eastern Europe

National Communism

AND *Popular Revolt*

IN *Eastern Europe*

A SELECTION OF DOCUMENTS ON

Events in Poland and Hungary

FEBRUARY-NOVEMBER, 1956

Edited by PAUL E. ZINNER

Program on East Central Europe, Columbia University

COLUMBIA UNIVERSITY PRESS New York

24340

Foreword

IN 1956, AFTER YEARS of presenting to the world the appearance of disciplined conformity, the international Communist movement, in the Soviet orbit and abroad, was obviously being subjected to internal strains. While the decision by the Soviet leaders to make an attack on the "cult of personality" was certainly not the only cause of these strains—more likely it was itself a symptom of malaise—it is true that the more spectacular happenings of the year are associated with this question of "de-Stalinization."

At the important 20th Congress of the Communist Party of the Soviet Union, held in February, 1956, public criticism of Stalin was relatively circumspect and restrained—though the intent was clear—but in his secret speech, made before a closed session of the Congress, Nikita S. Khrushchev delivered himself of a bitter indictment of the late dictator.[1] Rumors of this speech began to circulate abroad in the early spring, and on June 4 the United States Department of State released a text of it. The marked repercussions which the public appearance of this report produced in the Communist Parties of Western Europe and the United States are the subject of *The Anti-Stalin Campaign and International Communism: A Selection of Documents* (edited by the Russian Institute of Columbia University; New York, Columbia University Press, 1956). The repercussions were also felt in the Communist Parties of Eastern Europe, although in some of them, notably the Polish Party, criticism of Stalinism and Soviet interference had appeared well before the 20th Party Congress.

The present selection of documents, a sequel to *The Anti-Stalin Campaign,* deals with developments, chiefly in Poland and Hungary, from the time of the 20th Party Congress through

---

[1] A translation of the proceedings of the 20th Party Congress, including the secret Krushchev report, will appear shortly as *Current Soviet Policies—II,* edited by *The Current Digest of the Soviet Press.*

the dramatic weeks of October and November: the establishment of the Gomulka regime in Poland, and the victory and
Soviet suppression of the Hungarian revolution.

It should be stressed, however, that it does not pretend
to be a history of these events, especially not of the Hungarian
revolution which swept quite beyond the limits of Communism.
The essential purpose of this volume is to document the vicis-
situdes of the international Communist movement, the debates
and frictions arising within it. The materials presented are,
with but few exceptions, from Communist sources. One will
not find here the voice of the Hungarian people in their anger
and defiance, only the voice of Communists—Polish, Hungarian,
Russian, and Yugoslav—in a time of crisis.[2]

Nor does the present work undertake to interpret these
recent events. Admittedly any selection of documents may
carry an implicit interpretation. In the present case, however,
the aim has been only to present what appear to be the most
important official or authoritative Communist statements,
speeches, and resolutions. For this reason the documents which
have been selected are presented in their entirety. Wherever
possible the translations have been made directly from the
original printed text. In some cases only the radio broadcast
was available. The function of the connecting narrative has
been to provide the chronology and a brief description of the
setting of particular documents. Documentary extracts have
been used in this narrative only for purposes of illustration.

Documents are often thought to be dull fare. Communist
documents are particularly repetitious and long-winded. Still,
the reader will find that a careful reading of this material has
its own reward: a surprisingly revealing picture of the state
of mind of various elements of the Communist movement in
this year of change and upheaval.

The early publication of these documents has been made
possible by a grant from the Ford Foundation. I wish also

---

[2] For a documented account of the Hungarian revolution which
presents the other half of the picture, and especially the broadcasts of
the unofficial radios during the period of active fighting, see *The Revolt
in Hungary: A Documentary Chronology of Events* (Free Europe Committee, 2 Park Avenue, New York).

to thank Professor Paul E. Zinner who has assumed the heavy burden of organizing and editing this volume—a task above and beyond his normal academic responsibilities.

December 14, 1956   HENRY L. ROBERTS
                                        Director
                                        Program on East Central Europe
                                        Columbia University

Preface

THE PUBLICATION OF THIS volume arises from the obvious international importance of the happenings in Poland and Hungary in 1956. As Professor Roberts says in his foreword, this selection of documents makes no pretense at being a narrative history. It does contain a certain amount of connecting text—which appears in a smaller type face—in order to provide a general sense of continuity and to present the major facts which make the content of the documents themselves more understandable.

The documents on Poland and Hungary, which make up the bulk of the volume, are presented in the broader setting of discussion or debate among Communists—with the Soviet Union and Yugoslavia by far the heaviest contributors—concerning the general problem of relations between the Soviet Union and other Communist states. This general debate influenced, and was in turn influenced by, Polish and Hungarian developments. It is therefore treated in two separate sections, one preceding and one following the sections on Poland and Hungary.

The selection of one document as against another was based on an estimate of its importance and authoritativeness. Thus, in the case of two documents of seemingly equal importance, e.g., a speech by the First Secretary of a Communist Party and a resolution adopted by the Central Committee of a Party, the resolution, though perhaps duller in tone, was chosen. Many documents deserving inclusion were omitted, not, I believe, through oversight—the material was carefully sifted—but through limitations of space.

In all but two cases the documents presented in full, as well as the quotations from documents in the connecting text, are based on original printed sources, for the most part the official dailies and journals of the Communist Parties in question. The two exceptions are the statement of the Government of the Chinese People's Republic of November, 1956, and excerpts from the *People's Daily* (November 2, 1956), organ of the Chinese Communist Party Central Committee. (Printed in Part Four, Chapter I.) The originals were unavailable, and broadcast versions had to be used without comparison with the Chinese language text.

Many of the documents relating to the Hungarian revolt, i.e., covering the period from October 23 to November 4 (Chapters VI-IX), are also based on broadcasts. For some days no newspapers appeared in Hungary, while for the rest, such newspapers as were published have not yet become available in this country. (Indeed, there is a question whether documentary evidence in such a period of turmoil will have been preserved.) During the crisis the only means available to the authorities for communicating with the population was by radio. Consequently, all official statements were broadcast in full and the more important ones were often repeated. These broadcasts directed at the Hungarian people were monitored. The translations appearing here are based on the original Hungarian language monitoring texts which were carefully examined for completeness. No garbled or incomplete texts were used except in one instance where, in a long and important document, the name of a person appeared doubtful. Some of the translations were prepared exclusively for this volume. In other cases where partial translations existed, they were used in checking against the Hungarian original, and were changed and completed prior to inclusion here.

As a matter of general interest to the reader it may be stated that all public statements by Messrs. Nagy and Kadar, the two main figures in the Hungarian crisis between October 23 and November 4, 1956, are included.

In the case of Poland, all of Gomulka's public pronouncements between October 20 and November 4 are also published in full, as are some other documents of significance. However, the coverage of the crisis in Poland is less complete than that of Hungary, because of the greater mass of Polish documents (and the greater length of almost every document). In the editor's opinion, the entire issue of *Nowe Drogi* (the Polish United Workers Party's theoretical journal) containing the minutes of the eighth plenary session of the Central Committee of the Polish United Workers Party, at which the turn to national Communism was made, is worthy of translation. Seldom has the world been treated to such frank and revealing self-examination by a Communist Party. This particular issue of *Nowe Drogi* (October, 1956) alone runs to 271 pages.

The always vexatious question of consistency in style, spelling, and capitalization was solved by means of a convenient rule of thumb. In the main it was decided to pay more attention to substantive meaning and faithfulness to the original language text than to mechanical consistency. Proper names, however, have been preserved in their original spelling, except for the diacritical marks on Hungarian names, which were omitted.

It is my pleasant duty to express deep appreciation and heartfelt thanks to the many hands who have contributed to the preparation of this volume in a variety of ways. The list is long indeed: Elaine Adam, Charles Andras, Alexander Dallin, Alexander Erlich, Matthew Fryde, Helen V. Gillespie, Leslie Laszlo, Joan Miller, Mark Neuweld, Anna Oren, Alex Peskin, Joseph Rothschild, Marija and Paul Shoup, Elizabeth Snapper, Alexander Urban, Elizabeth Valkenier, Vivian Weaver, Myra Zinner.

I should like to express special thanks to Professor Henry L. Roberts, Director of the Program on East Central Europe, for the active part he has taken in seeing the volume through to publication. Special thanks are also due to members of the staff of the Columbia University Press, William F. Bernhardt, Nancy Dixon, Eugenia Porter, and Henry H. Wiggins, who have been more than accommodating in handling the manuscript and editing and in juggling an incredibly tight schedule so as to ease the burdens on the editor.

I also wish to express thanks to *The Twentieth Century* for permission to reprint Lucjan Blit's translation of Adam Wazyk's "Poem for Adults" and to *The Current Digest of the Soviet Press* for permission to reprint several translations which first appeared in that publication.

While credit is properly shared by a large number of people, responsibility for the debit side of the ledger will be cheerfully accepted by the editor, on whom decisions with regard to selection of documents, organization, style, footnoting, and the connecting text ultimately rested.

December 15, 1956   PAUL E. ZINNER

Contents

PART ONE: *"Different Roads to Socialism"*

CHAPTER I

BACKGROUND

The twin and inseparable problems of the pattern of internal evolution of the Communist-dominated countries in Eastern Europe and
the precise nature of their relationship to the Soviet Union have
been in the forefront of interest ever since 1944 when—with Soviet
support—Communist Parties began to bid for power in Eastern
Europe. At first the evolutionary pattern of the East European
"people's democracies" was interpreted by local Communists as
following a path of "national exclusiveness" in accordance with
the traditions and particular conditions prevailing in any given
country. Early notions of "national exclusiveness" were aided and
abetted by a number of outstanding Soviet scholars, e.g., the late
I. P. Trainin, E. S. Varga, and L. A. Leontiev. Varga characterized
the emerging people's democratic states as representing a "social
order" which "differs from all hitherto known to us."[1] Trainin saw
the people's democracies as hybrid regimes combining features of
the proletarian (Soviet) and bourgeois type of "democracy" but
being really at variance with both.[2]

The concept of people's democracy, not fully worked out to be
sure, as that of a "third" or "different" type of social system was
justified by Lenin's dictum on the distinctness of the evolutionary
pattern of various countries, the "different roads to socialism."

In 1948, following the completion of the seizure of power in
Eastern Europe (the coup in Czechoslovakia in February, 1948)
and the first break in the outward solidarity of the Communist
countries (Yugoslavia's expulsion from the Cominform in June,
1948), an abrupt and drastic revision in the concept of people's
democracy took place. To some extent the revision was forecast

---

[1] See E. S. Varga, "Democracies of a New Type," *Mirovoye Kho-
ziaistvo i Mirovaia Politika,* 1947, No. 3, pp. 3-14. See also Samuel L.
Sharp, "New Democracy: A Soviet Interpretation," *American Perspective,* Vol. I, No. 6 (November, 1947).

[2] I. P. Trainin, "Democracy of a Special Type," *Sovetskoye Gosudarstvo i Pravo,* 1947, No. 1, pp. 1-15, and No. 3, pp. 1-14.

at the founding meeting of the Cominform in September, 1947. While Andrei Zhdanov, the chief Soviet spokesman at the meeting (the other was G. M. Malenkov), stressed that "the Soviet Union unswervingly holds the position that political and economic relations between states must be built exclusively on the basis of equality of the Parties and mutual respect for their sovereign rights,"[3] he also made it clear that the Soviet Union did not choose to abandon its task of guiding and instructing foreign Communists and that the East European Communists would do well to avail themselves of the rich experience which the Soviet Union had accumulated on its road to socialism.

The new theory of people's democracy was clearly enunciated by Georgi Dimitrov, leader of the Bulgarian Workers Party (Communist), in December, 1948, when he said that "in accordance with the Marxist-Leninist view, the Soviet regime and the people's democratic regime are two forms of one and the same power . . . i.e., the proletarian dictatorship."[4]

From then on the essential, or substantive, identity of the Soviet and people's democratic systems was stressed by Communist theoreticians and political leaders as well. The emulation of the Soviet pattern was supported by Lenin's dictum concerning the applicability of "bolshevik experience" anywhere at any time.[5]

The essence of the new theory and its practical implications were summarized by Klement Gottwald, leader of the Czechoslovak Communist Party, in the following terms:[6]

---

[3] See *For a Lasting Peace, for a People's Democracy,* organ of the Cominform, November 10, 1947. See also A. Ulam, *Titoism and the Cominform,* Harvard University Press, 1952, pp. 39-68.

[4] Dimitrov's remarks were reprinted in the Cominform journal, January 1, 1949, and in *Pravda,* December 21 and December 27, 1948.

[5] See, for example, P. F. Yudin, "On the Path of Transition to Socialism in the People's Democracies," *Voprosy Filosofii,* 1949, No. 1, pp. 40-59; B. S. Mankovsky, "Class Essence of the People's Democratic State," *Sovetskoye Gosudarstvo i Pravo,* 1949, No. 6, pp. 7-17; N. P. Farberov, *Gosudarstvennoye Pravo Stran Narodnoi Demokratii* (Public Law in the States of People's Democracy), Moscow, 1949. See also H. Gordon Skilling, " 'People's Democracy' in Soviet Theory," *Soviet Studies,* III, No. 1 (July, 1951), 16-33, and III, No. 2 (October, 1951), 131-149.

[6] *Rude Pravo,* January 22, 1953.

Lenin's teachings on the international applicability of the Bolshevik experience extends to the construction of socialist society as well.

It is, of course, natural that on our road to socialism, as in the other people's democracies, there should have been significant differences compared with the Soviet Union. It would have been stupid and dangerous dogmatism had we not observed these differences after 1945. On the contrary, because we observed them and exploited them we won our victory over the bourgeoisie in 1948.

On the other hand it would be criminal stupidity if we wanted to conserve some of these "differences" which were only of temporary nature and progressively tend to disappear.

Ever greater utilization of Soviet experiences and thus ever closer approximation of the Soviet example, this is one of the main laws of development of the people's democratic countries. Therefore every additional step along this line . . . marks . . . significant progress toward socialism. . . . Conversely, retaining the lower transitional forms and presenting them as unchanging "norms" . . . and rejecting Soviet examples and experiences finally leads to the denial and overturn of the very substance of people's democracy and to the restoration of capitalism.

Indeed, the development of the people's democratic regimes of Eastern Europe from 1948 to 1953 was marked by ever closer imitation of Soviet political, economic, and cultural organization and practice, and subordination of national aims to those of the "socialist camp" as formulated by the Soviet leadership.

While Stalin's death in March, 1953, did not bring any explicit reformulation of the notion of people's democracy in its wake, the relaxation of internal pressures in the Soviet Union was extended to the people's democracies as well. The response of these countries to the policies of the "new course"—associated with the premiership of G. M. Malenkov in the USSR from March, 1953, to February, 1955, and characterized, among other things, by greater attention to the needs of consumers—was not uniform. Hungary mapped out a fairly ambitious program of changes. Others, like Poland or Czechoslovakia, moved more cautiously. Simultaneously with these developments, intellectuals and students began to grope for greater freedom of expression. In this respect, Hungary and

Poland showed the most pronounced signs of ferment. The very fact that differences in individual country responses to the new situation were discernible might have been interpreted as an indication of possibilities for national initiative and departure, at least within certain limits, from a rigidly held pattern of behavior.

In the spring of 1955 the Soviet leadership of Party (Khrushchev) and Government (Bulganin) bid to restore friendly relations with Tito's Yugoslavia. The gesture, emphasized by the fact that the Soviet leaders journeyed to Belgrade for the purpose, carried with it implications of a possible acceptance and approval of a degree of national independence under Communist rule, less subordination to the direction of Moscow, and experimentation with indigenous variations in social organization within the framework of "socialist construction." The question was not whether the East European people's democracies would be accorded a status identical with Tito's Yugoslavia, but rather on what terms the differences between Tito and the Kremlin could be made up, and to what extent and in what form the patching up of these differences would modify the relationship between the people's democracies and Moscow.

The "Declaration of the Governments of the Union of Soviet Socialist Republics and the Federal People's Republic of Yugoslavia" issued in Belgrade on June 2, 1955,[7] stated as one of the principles from which the two governments proceeded to examine the questions of reciprocal concern: "mutual respect and non-interference in one another's internal affairs for whatever reason, whether of an economic, political, or ideological nature, inasmuch as questions of internal organization, difference of social systems, and difference in the concrete forms of socialist development are exclusively the concern of the peoples of the respective countries."

One of the aims of future contact, according to the Declaration, was "to assist and facilitate cooperation between public organizations of the two countries through the establishment of contacts, exchange of socialist experience, and free exchange of opinions." This stipulation pertained especially to contacts between the Communist Parties of the two countries. It was not followed by tangible results until June, 1956, when, on the occasion of Tito's return visit to Moscow, a "Declaration on Relations between the Yugo-

---

[7] *Review of International Affairs* (Belgrade), VI, No. 124 (June 1, 1955), 1, 2.

slav League of Communists and the Communist Party of the Soviet Union" was issued.[8]

In the wake of the Belgrade Declaration of 1955 signs of possible adjustment in the relations between the Soviet Union and the people's democracies came to light. The most important of these was in a *Pravda* editorial appraising the findings of a plenary session of the Communist Party's Central Committee which "heard and discussed a report by Comrade N. S. Khrushchev, on the results of the Soviet-Yugoslav talks."[9]

The course and results of the Soviet-Yugoslav talks [said *Pravda*] vividly express the foreign policy worked out by our Party and based on the firm principles of Leninism and on respect for the sovereignty and equality of all countries, large and small.

"Our experience," taught V. I. Lenin, "has formed in us the deep conviction that only tremendous attentiveness to the interests of the various nations eliminates the ground for conflicts, removes mutual distrusts, removes fear of any intrigues, and creates trust, particularly among workers and peasants speaking different languages, without which any peaceful relations between peoples and any successful development at all of everything which is valuable in modern civilization are absolutely impossible."

It is precisely tremendous attentiveness to the interests of various nations which is a most important feature of socialist internationalism, radically hostile to any manifestations of bourgeois ideology, including nationalism.

Soviet Communists consider it their sacred duty to set an example of the practice of the principles of socialist internationalism, as befits representatives of a multinational socialist country in which the national question has been solved consistently on the basis of Marxist-Leninist theory.

Relations between the Soviet Union and the people's democracies are built upon the granite foundation of socialist internationalism. The Communist Party has always willingly shared and still shares its wealth of experience with all fraternal parties,

---

[8] See Document 2 in this chapter.

[9] See *Pravda*, July 16, 1955, also a full translation of the editorial in *The Current Digest of the Soviet Press*, VII, No. 26 (August 10, 1955), 3.

and at the same time Soviet Communists are called upon to study assiduously and imitate all that is advanced to be found in the people's democracies in the sphere of management of the national economy, achievements of science, technology, and so on.

All nations will arrive at socialism, Lenin pointed out; that is inevitable, but not all will arrive there in exactly the same way. Each one will introduce its own features into this or that form of democracy, into this or that form of dictatorship of the proletariat, into this or that rate of socialist transformation of different aspects of social life.

The historical experience of the Soviet Union and of the people's democracies shows that, given unity in the chief fundamental matter of ensuring the victory of socialism, various ways and means may be used in different countries to solve the specific problems of socialist construction, depending upon historical and national features.

The question of "different roads to socialism" was next treated by *Kommunist,* the CPSU's theoretical journal (No. 14, September, 1955). Shortly afterward the tenets of the discussion were taken up by *Nowe Drogi,* the theoretical journal of the Polish United Workers Party (PUWP) (October, 1955). Under the title "For an Increase of Our Creative Effort and Ideological Work," the Polish journal said, among other things: "We have paid too little attention to that which is innate in our movement, in our historical road, in our methods of construction, in our struggle and slogans, to that which arises from the specific conditions in the development of our country and from our historical past. . . ." At the same time, *Nowe Drogi* sought to guard against misunderstanding of the meaning of national "specificity." It attacked "harmful confusion and ideological chaos . . . nihilistic tendencies to disregard the achievements . . . of the past ten years, particularly in the field of culture and morality," and censured "tendencies to revise our ideological principles, attempts at an allegedly creative 'supplementation' of Marxism . . . concepts of liberalism, solidarism, relativism, cultural autonomy . . . an autonomy conceived as being independent of the class struggle, of politics, and of the leading role of the Party."

CHAPTER II

THE GENERAL DEBATE, FEBRUARY-SEPTEMBER, 1956

The public documents of the 20th Congress of the CPSU, held in February, 1956, contributed little to an elaboration of the permissible content and limits of any deviation from a unitary pattern of development in the people's democracies. The general concept of "different roads to socialism," however, was authoritatively reaffirmed, but it applied more to the period preceding total seizure of power than to the period following it. The early evolution of the people's democracies (from 1944 to 1948) was cited by speakers such as Khrushchev and Mikoyan as an historic example of different (and for the most part peaceful) ways of development.[1]

The chief contribution of the 20th Congress was the official denunciation of the "cult of personality" which opened the way to reappraisal of Stalinist policies and the legacy of the Stalinist era. One of the aspects of Stalinism which came under review in the people's democracies was the nature of their relation to the Soviet Union.

On April 17, 1956, the Cominform was dissolved.

1. ANNOUNCEMENT OF THE DISSOLUTION OF THE INFORMATION BUREAU OF THE COMMUNIST AND WORKERS PARTIES, APRIL 17, 1956[2]

THE FOUNDING IN 1947 of the Information Bureau of the Communist and Workers Parties was a positive contribution toward overcoming the lack of coordination which developed among Communist Parties after the dissolution of the Comintern [in 1943] and was an important force in strengthening

---

[1] See *Current Soviet Policies—II*, a volume of documents on the 20th Congress and the anti-Stalin campaign in the USSR, to be issued by *The Current Digest of the Soviet Press* in the spring of 1957.

[2] See *Pravda*, April 18, 1956. Translation reproduced from *The Current Digest of the Soviet Press*, VIII, No. 16 (May 30, 1956), 6.

proletarian internationalism in the ranks of the international Communist movement and in further uniting the working class and all working people in the struggle for lasting peace, democracy, and socialism. The Information Bureau and its newspaper, *For a Lasting Peace, for a People's Democracy!,* played a positive role in developing and strengthening fraternal ties and mutual exchanges of experience among Communist and Workers Parties and in clarifying problems of Marxist-Leninist theory as applied to the concrete conditions in various countries and the experience of the international Communist and working class movement. This promoted the ideological, organizational, and political strengthening of the fraternal parties and an extension of the influence of Communist Parties among the masses.

However, there have been changes in recent years in the international situation: the extension of socialism beyond the boundaries of a single country and its transformation into a world system; the formation of a vast "peace zone" including both socialist and nonsocialist peace-loving countries of Europe and Asia; the growth and consolidation of many Communist Parties in capitalist, dependent, and colonial countries and their increased activities in the struggle against the threat of war and reaction, in the struggle for peace, for the vital interests of the working people and their countries' national independence; and, finally, the particularly urgent tasks today of overcoming the division within the working class movement and strengthening the unity of the working class in the interests of a successful struggle for peace and socialism. These changes have provided new conditions for the activities of the Communist and Workers Parties. The Information Bureau of the Communist and Workers Parties, in terms both of its make-up and the content of its activity, no longer meets these new conditions.

The Central Committees of the Communist and Workers Parties belonging to the Information Bureau having exchanged views on problems of its activity, recognized that the Information Bureau which they set up in 1947 had completed its function, and so by mutual agreement they adopted a decision to end the activity of the Information Bureau of the Communist and Workers Parties and its newspaper, *For a Lasting Peace, for a People's Democracy!*

The Central Committees of the Communist and Workers Parties which participated in the Information Bureau consider that in the struggle for working class interests, for the cause of peace, democracy, and socialism, each party or group of parties will, in the course of developing its work in conformity with the common aims and tasks of Marxist-Leninist parties and the specific national features and conditions of their countries, find new and useful forms of establishing links and contacts among themselves. The Communist and Workers Parties will undoubtedly continue, at their own discretion and taking into account specific conditions of their work, to exchange opinions on general problems of the struggle for peace, democracy, and socialism, of defending the interests of the working class and all working people, of mobilizing the masses for the struggle against the danger of war, and at the same time will continue to take up problems of cooperating with parties and movements oriented toward socialism and with other organizations striving toward strengthening peace and democracy. All this will reinforce to a still greater degree the spirit of mutual cooperation among Communist and Workers Parties on the basis of the principles of proletarian internationalism and will strengthen the fraternal ties among them in the interests of peace, democracy, and socialism.

(Signed)

Central Committee of the Bulgarian Communist Party
Central Committee of the Hungarian Workers Party
Central Committee of the Italian Communist Party
Central Committee of the Polish United Workers Party
Central Committee of the Rumanian Workers Party
Central Committee of the Communist Party of the Soviet Union
Central Committee of the Communist Party of Czechoslovakia
Central Committee of the French Communist Party

The significance of the dissolution of the Cominform was evaluated in *Pravda* (April 18, 1956) under the title "An Important Decision." The *Pravda* article repeated in substance the main points of the official announcement.[3]

A joint declaration of the Yugoslav League of Communists and the CPSU, issued on June 20, 1956, further clarified the principles governing the relations between the two Parties.

2. DECLARATION ON RELATIONS BETWEEN THE YUGOSLAV LEAGUE OF COMMUNISTS AND THE COMMUNIST PARTY OF THE SOVIET UNION, JUNE 20, 1956[4]

DURING THE OFFICIAL visit of the Government Delegation of the FPRY [Federal People's Republic of Yugoslavia] to the Soviet Union, from June 1 to June 23, 1956, Josip Broz-Tito, General Secretary of the YLC, Edvard Kardelj, Secretary of the Executive Committee of the Central Committee, YLC, and Members of the CC, YLC, Jakov Blazevic, Veljko Micunovic, Koca Popovic, and Mijalko Todorovic, as representatives of the Yugoslav League of Communists and of the Socialist Alliance of the Working People of Yugoslavia; and N. S. Khrushchev, First Secretary of the CC, CPSU, Members of the Presidium of the CC, CPSU, N. A. Bulganin, K. Y. Voroshilov, A. I. Mikoyan, and V. M. Molotov, and alternate member of the Presidium of the CC, CPSU, D. T. Shepilov, as representatives of the CPSU, exchanged opinions, in a spirit of comradely sincerity and candor, on relations and cooperation between the YLC and CPSU.

In the course of the conversations they agreed upon the following:

1. The Belgrade Declaration of June 2, 1955, placed relations between the two socialist countries on a healthy footing, and the principles formulated in it are finding ever broader application in their mutual cooperation.

---

[3] For a full translation of the article see *ibid.*, pp. 6-7.

[4] See *New Times*, No. 26, June, 1956, Special Supplement.

2. Cooperation between the two countries and the general development of their relations since the signing of the Belgrade Declaration, and also the contacts established between their political and other public organizations, have created favorable political conditions for cooperation also between the CPSU and the YLC.

Proceeding from the foregoing, bearing in mind the concrete conditions of development of the modern socialist movements, and guided by the internationalist principles of Marxism-Leninism, the delegations of the YLC and CPSU have agreed on the need and value of continuously developing existing contacts between the two parties for cooperation in further strengthening our socialist countries and promoting their prosperity, for cooperation in the international labor movement on a wide range of questions concerning the present development of socialism, and also for the development of peaceful coexistence and cooperation between the nations of the world, regardless of difference in social and political systems, in the interests of the peace, freedom, and independence of the peoples.

The representatives of the two parties proceed from the premise that continued development of contacts and cooperation between the CPSU and YLC, as the leading parties in countries where the working class is in power, and as parties which share the common aim of building a complete socialist society in their countries and ensuring human progress and durable peace, will undoubtedly facilitate further cooperation between the USSR and FPRY and the promotion of enduring friendship between their peoples.

3. Believing that the path of socialist development differs in various countries and conditions, that the multiplicity of forms of socialist development tends to strengthen socialism, and proceeding from the fact that any tendency of imposing one's opinion on the ways and forms of socialist development is alien to both—the two parties have agreed that their cooperation shall be based on complete voluntariness and equality, friendly criticism, and comradely exchange of opinions on controversial questions.

4. With the above as a basis, cooperation between the YLC and CPSU will develop primarily through comprehensive mutual acquaintance with the forms and methods of socialist construction in both countries, free and comradely exchange of experience and opinions on questions of common interest for the development of socialist practice and for the advancement of socialist thought, and also on questions concerning peace, rapprochement, and intercourse between nations, and human progress generally.

5. The present material and spiritual reconstruction of the world, which finds expression in the tremendous growth of the forces of socialism, the upsurge of the national-liberation movement, the increased part played by the working class in the solution of concrete questions of international development, poses a number of momentous tasks before the international labor movement. From this follows the need for scientific analysis of developments and of the basic material and social factors and trends in the present-day world. For these reasons the two parties have agreed that guided by the principles of Marxism-Leninism, they will do everything to encourage—both in their relations and in the international labor movement generally—mutual cooperation and exchange of opinions in the field of socialist scientific thought.

6. With regard to concrete forms of cooperation between the YLC and the CPSU, the delegations have agreed that it will be carried out through personal contacts, written and oral communications and exchange of opinions, through exchange of delegations, information matter, and literature, as well as through personal meetings of party leaders, when necessary, to discuss pressing problems of common interest, and generally through all forms of constructive comradely discussion.

7. The representatives of the CPSU and YLC consider such cooperation to be a component part of their contacts with other Communist and Workers Parties, and also with the socialist and other progressive movements of the world.

8. The CPSU and YLC believe that the promotion of durable peace, security, and social progress requires broad

cooperation between all progressive and peace-loving forces, which is making itself increasingly felt in diverse forms and on a world scale. This cooperation is an essential need of modern social development. Such contacts must be equal, frank, democratic, and accessible to world public opinion. They should serve as a means of reciprocal information and consultation on diverse problems of general interest, and should foster closer understanding, based on tolerant explanation of the positions and views of the parties. This presupposes freedom of action for each and every participant in this cooperation, in conformity with the conditions of their development and their general progressive aims.

The representatives of the YLC and the CPSU are confident that cooperation between the workers' movements of the FPRY and the Soviet Union, based on these principles and forms, will serve the interest of their peoples and of socialist construction in their countries. They are confident that by such cooperation they will contribute to a general rapprochement between socialist and other progressive movements of the world, which will likewise serve the interests of world peace and human progress.

For the Central Committee of the YLC	For the Central Committee of the CPSU
JOSIP BROZ-TITO, General Secretary	N. KHRUSHCHEV, First Secretary

Moscow, June 20, 1956

Less than ten days after the publication of the Yugoslav-Soviet declaration on Party relations, riots broke out in Poznan, Poland. While the riots were put down without spreading to other areas, they seem in retrospect to have marked an important turning point in the internal evolution of Poland[5] as well as in relations between the people's democracies and the Soviet Union. On July 16, *Pravda* dealt with this subject at length.

---

[5] See Poland, Chapter II.

3. EDITORIAL: "THE INTERNATIONAL FORCES OF PEACE, DEMOCRACY, AND SOCIALISM ARE GROWING AND GAINING IN STRENGTH," *Pravda*, JULY 16, 1956[6]

THE 20TH PARTY CONGRESS occupies an especially important place in the eventful history of the postwar period. At this Congress the Party, which leads 200,000,000 people toward Communism, mapped out a comprehensive program of action, which gave a tremendous uplift to the creative forces of the Soviet people, and which has substantially altered the international situation.

After the 20th Party Congress, the enthusiastic labor of the Soviet people, inspired by the idea of Communism, has led to new and significant achievements in the Soviet Union in all fields of the political, economic, and cultural life of the country. Our international relations are also developing successfully. Upon the initiative of the Soviet Union and with her active participation a relaxation of tension in the relations between states has been achieved. Positive results have been achieved in the regulation of a number of unresolved international problems. The position of the peace-loving forces has been considerably strengthened, and effective prerequisites for a lasting peace have been created.

The 20th Party Congress not only proclaimed that the forces of peace are sufficiently great at the present time to prevent a war but it also mapped out a concrete program to achieve the great and noble goal of consolidating peace. The realization of this program will give mankind the opportunity to avert a new and even more destructive war. The theoretical theses, advanced by the Congress, on peaceful coexistence of states with different social and economic systems, on the possibility to avert war in the present era, and on the diversity of forms of transition of different countries to socialism contribute to a strengthening of the unity of action of all progressive forces and to a further consolidation of the position of the world socialist system.

---

[6] A condensed translation of the article appears in *The Current Digest of the Soviet Press*, VIII, No. 29 (August 29, 1956), 3-5.

The broad masses of the people not only in the socialist countries, but in the capitalist countries as well, have welcomed and supported the program of peace and of international cooperation, which was proclaimed by the 20th Party Congress. They accepted this program as their own and began fighting for its realization. The tremendous and ever increasing influence of the decisions of the 20th Party Congress on the international situation is causing alarm and rage in the camp of the enemies of the working class. Trying to weaken somehow the beneficial influence of these decisions on the international atmosphere, they have concentrated all their efforts on discrediting the program of peace and cooperation proposed to the people by the 20th Party Congress. But the more stubbornly they have been occupied with this thankless task, the clearer have become the true, antipopular designs of the imperialist forces.

U. S. statesmen, who aspire to leadership of the entire capitalist world, have seized upon the past errors and shortcomings connected with the cult of J. V. Stalin in the USSR, which were condemned by the 20th Party Congress and have already been rectified by the Party Central Committee. Having cast aside diplomacy, the U. S. State Department has become the headquarters for the propaganda campaign which it has launched against the cult of personality. The aim of this campaign is to cast aspersions on the great ideas of Marxism-Leninism, to undermine the trust of the working people in the world's first socialist power, the Soviet Union, to sow dissension in the ranks of the international Communist and workers' movement.[7]

The facts show that in this case we are not dealing with an ordinary propaganda campaign such as those which the State Department organized in the "cold war" years. It is a question of a broadly conceived new political plan on which reactionary U. S. circles place great hopes.

---

[7] The reference is to the release of an English text of Khrushchev's secret speech at the 20th Congress on the "cult of personality." For a full text of the speech see *The Anti-Stalin Campaign and International Communism,* Columbia University Press, 1956, pp. 1-89.

Realizing that in present conditions the idea of restoring capitalism cannot find any substantial number of supporters in the people's democracies, the henchmen of the American monopolies are choosing a more artful way. Using their network of agents, relying on the remnants of the defeated exploiting classes which are hostile to Communism, and trying to draw into their network certain people who are honest but not well-tempered politically, they are trying to arouse chauvinistic sentiments, to destroy the bonds among socialist countries, and to sow strife. Acting in this way, the imperialists count on weakening the socialist countries so that they can proceed to extensive subversive operations against the rule of the people and the socialist system.

Analogous tactics are also planned by the imperialist ideologists with regard to the Communist Parties in the capitalist countries: They are striving to undermine the international ties of the international workers' movement. That same Dulles, the rabid enemy of Communism, is ready to swear that he is not against Communist Parties in general, but only against their being "linked too closely" with the Communist Party of the Soviet Union.

Apparently Dulles and his accomplices are incapable of understanding that their false "solicitude" for the "independence" of the people's democracies and Communist Parties can only put the supporters of peace, democracy, and socialism on the alert against hostile intrigues. Despite all this, however, we would make a grave mistake if we were to underestimate the enemy's maneuver. It should not be forgotten that in some places there are still opportunist elements on which the enemies of the working people undoubtedly rely. It should also be remembered that among people who are not politically mature and who are extremely gullible there may be some who will rise to the bait of the bombastic words about "national Communism," about the fact that the international bonds among Communist Parties have become "superfluous," etc.

I

The world socialist system is a stable, indestructible commonwealth of many countries. The countries which now comprise the world socialist system broke with capitalism as a result of a long and arduous struggle for the liberation of the working class and the peasantry from their oppressors. The Communist and Workers Parties have led and are leading the peoples of these countries along the true path of social and national liberation, gaining inspiration from the ideas of Leninism, that eternally living and developing teaching which is transforming the world.

Before World War II such countries as Poland, Rumania, Hungary, Bulgaria, and Albania had a weak industry and a backward agriculture. These countries were ruled by fascist and semi-fascist regimes, which oppressed the working people cruelly. Foreign monopoly concerns dominated their national economies. The construction of socialism gave these countries, and other people's democracies as well, the opportunity to do away once and for all with the economic backwardness of the past, to build up heavy industry, and to secure the growth of national culture.

It is significant that the once backward countries of Eastern Europe, having entered the path of socialism, are almost completely catching up with the advanced states of Western Europe in the development of the most important branches of heavy industry.

Socialist construction in the Chinese People's Republic developed at a roaring tempo, and the alliance of the working class and the peasantry is becoming steadily stronger and stronger. China's industrialization plans, until recently called castles in the air by many bourgeois "prophets," are being over-fulfilled. The agricultural cooperatives plan is being fulfilled successfully.

All this speaks for a new and significant advance on the path toward socialism in all people's democracies and for a continuing strengthening of the world socialist system.

The Communist construction in the Soviet Union and the socialist construction in the people's democracies form a unified process of the movement of peoples toward a new life.

It is completely natural that small and large socialist states have established fraternal, friendly relations based on a community of political and economic development, on unity of ultimate aim. Communist and Workers Parties, which carry aloft the banner of Leninism, the banner of friendship among peoples, are playing the decisive role in uniting the socialist countries.

The decisions of the 20th Party Congress have assumed historic importance in strengthening the entire socialist camp. The newspaper *Jen Min Jih Pao,* the organ of the Chinese Communist Party Central Committee, wrote in an editorial:

The 20th Congress of the Communist Party of the Soviet Union is an historic event of world importance. Creatively applying Marxism-Leninism, the Congress pointed out to the Soviet People the way to the successful building of Communism, contributed to the further development of the struggle of all peace-loving people for peace, for averting a new war. The Chinese people, who are building socialism, will make a new contribution, together with the Soviet people and the peoples of other countries, to the noble goal of fighting for peace and the progress of mankind.

The great idea of the struggle for peace and for the progress of mankind, for which the countries of Socialism are fighting, finds ever wider support throughout the world. And it is not an accident that the peoples who only recently freed themselves from the colonial yoke, as well as the peoples who are fighting for their national independence and freedom, find a common language with the countries of the socialist camp. They are united by the interests of the defense of peace and democracy and of the struggle against imperialist aggression and reaction.

The decisions of the 20th Party Congress were supported unanimously at recent congresses of the Korean Workers Party and the Albanian Workers Party, at conferences of the Czechoslovak Communist Party and German Socialist Unity Party, and at plenary sessions of Communist and Workers Parties Central Committees in other people's democracies.

Progress in the political and labor activity of the masses, the true makers of history, can now be observed in all socialist countries. The consistent, principled struggle against the cult of personality and its consequences makes it possible to develop in every way the activity and fighting efficiency of all Communists, to adhere strictly to Leninist norms of Party and cultural development, to rectify violations of socialist justice, and, in general, on the basis of the development of socialist democracy, to give scope to manifestations of the inexhaustible, unlimited creative force of the broadest masses of the people.

It is since the 20th Party Congress that the struggle for the creative application of Marxism in conditions peculiar to each country has become more intensive in fraternal Communist and Workers Parties of the people's democracies. Lenin had already foreseen that, given unity and community of paths in the fundamental and main respects, transition to socialism in various countries would not be exactly the same, that each nation would introduce its own specific features into some form of democracy, into some variant of the dictatorship of the proletariat, into some tempo of socialist transformation of various aspects of public life.

Creatively applying Marxism-Leninism in the conditions of their own countries, free people, under the leadership of Communist Parties, are moving toward one goal, toward Communism. It is impossible to move separately or haphazardly toward such a great goal. The working people of all socialist countries are marching toward this aim in unison, grasping each other firmly by the hand. No one will succeed in destroying this unity. The necessary consideration of national peculiarities not only does not lead to estrangement among the countries building socialism but, on the contrary, contributes to their solidarity.

However, certain U. S. circles just cannot understand the historical law of the strengthening of the socialist system in the Soviet Union, people's China, and the people's democracies.

They still have not abandoned their dreams of bringing back the "good old days" when American, British, French, and German capitalists ruled China, Poland, Hungary, and other countries which have now embarked on the path of independent development.

The imperialists calculate that in an atmosphere of further development of socialist democracy and expansion of criticism and self-criticism in these countries, their agents will succeed in sowing their poisonous seeds. For example, the discussion which took place in Hungary in the Petofi Circle was used for these purposes.[8] Certain elements which opposed the policy of the Hungarian Workers Party and which had succumbed to the external influence of imperialist circles tried, under the guise of discussion, to spread their anti-Party views, thus playing into the hands of the enemies of people's Hungary.

Free people recognize the enemy even in his new mask, they are exposing him and making him harmless. At the same time, we must not close our eyes to the fact that wherever mass-political and ideological-educational work is poor, the enemy's network of agents hastens to take advantage of this for its own purposes. We should also remember in this connection the recent events in Poznan.[9]

Everyone now knows that this provocation was the work of enemy agents. The American press did not even consider it necessary to conceal the existence of a direct link between the Poznan events and the overseas centers which direct the "cold war." As has already been reported, the New York *Journal-American* stated on June 30 with cynical frankness that the "Senate has decided to allocate within the framework of aid to foreign states the sum of $25,000,000 for financing secret activity behind the iron curtain like that which led to the riots in Poznan."

The provocateurs who were active in Poznan crudely played on the temporary difficulties of growth which Poland is experi-

---

[8] See Hungary, Chapter II, Document 1.
[9] See Poland, Chapter II, Documents 1-3.

encing. In the people's democracies there are still certain difficulties connected with the profound reorganization of the entire national economy, with the necessity for large capital expenditures, with the liquidation of the devastation caused by war and the Hitlerite occupation. There were also individual errors, in planning, for example, which sometimes led to disproportions in the development of individual branches of the national economy. These errors are being successfully corrected. But the enemies of the working class are trying to use these difficulties and shortcomings for their antipopular purposes, particularly where the political work of the Communist and Workers Parties is weakening. Many people who succumbed to the enemy provocation in Poznan obviously did not realize who was inciting them. This could happen only because some people in the people's democracies do not understand that as long as class forces hostile to the socialist system still exist in these countries, they can in certain circumstances actively oppose the people's democratic system, attempting to attract wavering, unstable elements, the more so because hostile foreign circles are trying and will continue to try to organize various provocations. The workers, peasants, and intelligentsia in the people's democracies, guarding their achievements, will undoubtedly take this lesson into account and will be able to curb the enemies of the working class, the criminal network of imperialist agents.

The failure of the Poznan provocation, a provocation which has been unanimously condemned by the Polish people, has caused despondency among those who are still dreaming of restoring the old regimes in the people's democracies. In this connection it is significant that the British bourgeois press is transparently condemning Dulles, who in his recent speeches has again been repeating his former plans for a forcible change of the social system in the people's democracies. It is emphasized in London that escapades such as that in Poznan are hopeless and that they represent merely a "futile waste of forces."

Even such undisguised adventurers as the not unknown General Bor-Komorowski,[10] who played a fateful role in the 1944 Warsaw uprising, have been forced to reckon with the stability of the popular democratic system. Bor-Komorowski described the Poznan provocation as "hopeless." And does not the return to Poland of two Prime Ministers of the émigré "government" and hundreds of prominent émigrés bear witness to the fact that even the stubbornest opponents of the popular democratic system are losing confidence in the possibility of restoring the old institutions?

It is high time that the imperialist gentlemen understood that the friendship of the socialist countries, which is an historic victory of the people, is firm and unshakable. It ensures the national independence of the socialist countries, consolidates their international position, and gives them the possibility of developing uninterruptedly their national economy and raising the standard of living of the working people.

Relations among the socialist countries are firm because they are founded on principles of fraternal friendship, equality, noninterference in internal affairs, and many-sided mutual aid. The imperialist policy of threats, oppression, and various provocations leads only to the still greater consolidation of the socialist countries.

Comrade Mao Tse-Tung wrote, characterizing the growth of the forces of socialism:

At present the Soviet Union has achieved such power, the Chinese People's revolution won such a great victory, the governments of the people's democratic countries have scored such great successes, the movement of the countries of peace against oppression and aggression has attained such scope, and our front of friendship and solidarity has become strengthened to such an extent, that it is possible to say in full confidence that we are not afraid of any kind of imperialist aggression. We will crush every imperialist aggression. All underhanded provocations will end in disaster.

---

[10] Military Commander of the Polish Home Army which engaged the Germans in prolonged but futile struggle in the summer of 1944 while Soviet troops stood by "regrouping" without offering assistance.

Relying on mutual aid and support and overcoming the difficulties of growth, the socialist countries are marching confidently along the path of strengthening the world socialist system, along the paths of consolidating peace throughout the world.

The peoples of these countries are rallied around the Communist Parties and the people's governments, who are tested and well tempered in the fight for socialism; they are united by an unshakable resolve to guard reverently and to defend their great conquests. They give a firm rebuff to the provocations of the enemies of socialism. The collective leadership, which has emerged in these countries and which has risen from amongst the masses of the people, enjoys the complete support of the working peoples; basing itself on this support, it skillfully organizes the creative, constructive labor of the workers, the peasants, and the working intelligentsia, who are building the socialist society. The stability of the people's democratic system and the radical changes in the international situation in favor of the forces of peace and democracy condemned to failure all attempts by the reactionary forces to undermine the socialist construction in the people's democracies and to turn them back on the path of capitalism.

II

The world is now on the eve of a sharp new development and consolidation of the democratic movement, of strengthening the unity of the ranks of the working people in their struggle for a better future. The decisions of the 20th Party Congress have opened up majestic prospects for uniting all forces which support peace and socialism. An immense role belongs to the Communist Parties in this regard.

Having gone through the severe test of war, having been steeled in the struggle against fascism, having grown still stronger during the postwar period in the struggle for peace, freedom, and national independence, the Communist Parties of several capitalist countries have gained tremendous historical experience. The working people recognize the Communists as the steadfast defenders of the interests of the people. Communists have become an important force in the parliaments of France and Italy. The attempts of imperialist reaction to isolate the Communist Parties, to restrict their activities, and even to drive them underground have not made any headway.

The unconquerable striving for unity is strengthening among all sectors of the working masses. The unity of the working class, including workers who follow the Communists and those who follow the Socialists, is essential for the success of the struggle for peace among people and for securing the vital interests of the working class and of all workers.

The real possibility of establishing unity among all democratic forces and the growth of the influence of the Communist Parties cause extreme alarm among the enemies of the working class, all reactionaries, the "cold war" advocates, and the protagonists of a crusade against Communism. It is precisely for this reason that in the capitalist countries the reactionary forces are now placing their main hope on disrupting the international workers' movement. This is the direction of the main thrust of all the forces of imperialist reaction.

The enemies of the working class cherish the dream of dividing the Communist Parties, of weakening their international relations, primarily their relations with the Communist Party of the Soviet Union, of isolating individual centers of the international workers' movement in order then to try to attack them.

On what do the politicians and ideologists of the imperialist reaction place their hopes?

First, they think that if such international working class organizations as the Comintern and Cominform have ended their activities, then international solidarity is weakening and contacts among fraternal revolutionary parties, adhering to positions of Marxism-Leninism, are being destroyed.

Second, they hope that the Communist Parties, which based their activity upon the national peculiarities and conditions of each country and which express the national interests of the

people, might forget their great duty to international proletarian unity, forget that the working class of each and every
country is interested in strengthening international unity.

These calculations of imperialist reaction will inevitably fail.

Only hopeless, confused individuals within the ranks of the
workers' movement, who are capable of losing their way among
three pine trees and who can never see the forest for the trees,
only opportunist elements who have forgotten the main goal of
the working class, can forget international proletarian unity in
their activity. The entire experience of life and of the class
struggle has taught the working class to value the profound
meaning of proletarian solidarity. This idea has been for a
long time an immutable principle of proletarian philosophy.

The Marxist parties of the working class in all their activity
have been guided, and are now guided, by the principle of
international proletarian unity. Marxism-Leninism teaches that
the national interests of the working people, correctly understood, cannot contradict their international socialist interests.
In his well-known article "National Pride of the Great Russians,"
V. I. Lenin emphasized with very great force that the interest
of the Great Russians' national pride, correctly understood,
coincides with the socialist interest of the Great Russians and
of all other proletarians.

Forgetting international ties would, in the final reckoning,
lead to grave difficulties for the national interests of the working people. It could not be otherwise, for a very important
result of all recent history is the conclusion that proletarian
internationalism is the sharpest weapon of the working class
and of all the working people in the struggle against any oppression, in solving the tasks of the conquest of freedom and
national independence for the people, for building socialism
and communism.

Proletarian internationalism is a great slogan of the Marxist
parties, consistent with their entire philosophy and expressing
their policy. From the time the *Communist Manifesto* by Marx
and Engels was published, the call "Workers of the world

unite!" has been for more than a century one of the most important slogans of the labor movement, whose strength and power lies in its unity and solidarity.

The fundamental community of interests of all workers' Marxist parties in their struggle for the interests of the working class and of all working people against the threat of a new war, against the antipopular forces of monopoly capital, and against colonial oppression is the granite base of proletarian internationalism. Strengthening international links is an historical necessity both for the Workers Parties of socialist countries and also for Marxist parties of all capitalist countries; it is a pledge for the further successful development of the entire international workers' movement.

At present, the imperialists, who are forging military blocs, entangling weaker capitalist countries in a system of enslaving financial dependence, and are putting into operation such levers as the powerful mechanism of international monopolies, are trying to unite all reactionary forces in a single anti-Communist front. Under such conditions ideological unity and international solidarity of all Marxist revolutionary parties of the working class attain special significance. Both fraternal Communist Parties and the Communists of the Soviet Union deeply understand this.

The Communist Parties of capitalist countries are giving an ever more decisive rebuff to the diversionist intrigues of imperialist circles, are disclosing step by step the slanderous campaign which the enemies of the working class are now conducting in their attempt to disrupt the international workers' movement.

The June 30 resolution of the Communist Party Central Committee "On Overcoming the Cult of Personality and Its Consequences" is very important for this struggle, which is of historic importance.[11] The newspaper *L'Humanite,* organ of

---

[11] This was the CPSU's reply to a number of "erroneous views" which developed among Communists in consequence of the release of Khrushchev's secret speech at the 20th Congress. See *The Anti-Stalin Campaign,* pp. 275-306.

the French Communist Party, correctly calls this resolution "a very important new contribution to the activity of the international workers' movements in the interests of peace and socialism."

In the June 30 resolution of the Communist Party Central Committee, the present stage in the history of the workers' movement is illumined by the bright light of Marxism-Leninism. The slanderers who opposed the Soviet Union and Communism have been dealt a crushing blow. They have now begun to run about aimlessly like hares on a road in the glare of bright headlights. The enemies of the working class cannot conceal their confusion.

Communist Parties of capitalist countries are raising still higher the glorious Marxist-Leninist banner of proletarian internationalism. The French Communist Party Central Committee warmly approved the Soviet Communist Party Central Committee resolution. Comrade Palmiro Togliatti, Secretary General of the Italian Communist Party, has called for "unconditional approval of the actions which have been and are being taken by the Communist Party leaders for the complete overcoming of the consequences of the cult of personality both in the Soviet Union and in the international labor movement." The recent talks in Moscow of delegations of French, Italian, Belgian, and British Communist Parties with the leaders of the Soviet Communist Party took place in a cordial atmosphere, in a spirit of sincere friendship and mutual trust among the fraternal parties. These meetings aid the unity and fraternal solidarity of the Marxist parties of the working class of various countries and strengthen ties and cooperation among them.

A resolution of the Indian Communist Party Central Committee declared that the June 30 resolution of the Communist Party Central Committee gives a true account of the machinations of the enemies of the working people and stresses the necessity for loyalty to the scientific ideology of Marxism-Leninism and to the cause of proletarian internationalism.

The idea of international solidarity in the struggle for peace and socialism, which is capturing the minds of the masses of the working people, is becoming the great historic force of the present. That is why the intrigues of the enemies of the working class are doomed to failure and why they will not succeed in disrupting proletarian internationalism.

The concluding lines of the June 30 resolution of the Communist Party Central Committee, which are permeated with deep trust in the forces of Communism, resound with tremendous force and confidence today:

Let the bourgeois ideologists concoct fables about the "crisis" of Communism, about "confusion" in the ranks of the Communist Parties. We are used to hearing such invocations by enemies. Their predictions have always burst like soap bubbles. These ill-starred prophets have come and gone, but the Communist movement, the immortal and life-giving ideas of Marxism-Leninism, have triumphed and continue to triumph. And so will it be in the future. No malicious, slanderous attacks by our enemies can halt the invincible course of mankind's historical development toward Communism.

The *Pravda* editorial was supplemented by statements and additional articles stressing the unity of the "socialist camp" and warning against attempts to disrupt it, e.g., M. A. Suslov at the Congress of the French CP (*Pravda,* July 20, 1956); N. S. Khrushchev in addressing the East German delegation in Moscow (*Pravda,* July 18, 1956); N. A. Bulganin and G. K. Zhukov, visiting in Poland in connection with the 12th anniversary of the country's liberation (*Pravda,* July 22 and 26, 1956).

A journey undertaken by A. I. Mikoyan during the second half of July, in the course of which he participated in a Central Committee meeting of the Hungarian Workers Party (HWP)[12] and had conferences with Tito and the Bulgarian and Rumanian Communist leaders in their respective countries, also appeared to have as its object discussion of the relations among the Communist Parties.

In September, animosity between Yugoslavia and the Soviet Union flared up briefly in connection with the treatment by certain Communist newspapers, including *Pravda* (August 31, 1956), of the trial of former supporters of the Cominform.

---

[12] See Hungary, Chapter III.

4. ARTICLE: "IN WHOSE DEFENSE?" *Borba,* SEPTEMBER 8, 1956

IN THOSE DIFFICULT, critical, and fatal days of 1948 when the Yugoslav Communists and all the peoples of Yugoslavia had unanimously backed the position of their leadership, there were a number of people in our country, partly weaklings, cowards, and waverers and partly morally corrupted persons, careerists, and speculators, who came out for Stalin's campaign against socialist Yugoslavia.

Thus there was formed an emigration of a special kind, with an exactly determined purpose.

This emigration, a typical product of Stalin's policy, inevitably possessed all of its characteristics since both the origin and fate of that emigration were closely connected with it. It is therefore indisputable that not only the political aspect of that emigration but its role as well is inseparable from the character and role of Stalin's policy.

The persons included in that emigration—who ended up there either because they were misled, or because they were guided by speculative and careerist motives—were partly victims of Stalin's policy and partly an instrument and device of Stalin's aggressive campaign against socialist Yugoslavia. It logically follows that the attitude toward that emigration cannot therefore be isolated from the attitude toward Stalin's policy, i.e., one cannot have one attitude toward Stalin's policy and another separate attitude toward that emigration.

The humanitarian aspect and the treatment of these individuals is quite something else again. In that respect Yugoslavia has already displayed such generosity as can rarely be encountered anywhere else in the world. Naturally, those persons who have committed grave criminal deeds cannot and must not remain unpunished. However, even for those individuals the possibility exists of one day becoming useful citizens of our country, because, as is well known, all our laws and all our policy are imbued with deep humanitarianism.

But as far as the political treatment of former Cominformists is concerned, and this is what is most essential in the whole affair, one can have no doubts whatsoever that those persons were both victims and tools of a policy which has been altogether compromised and is a complete failure.

Simply because of this it is difficult to believe that even today, in certain countries, one comes across attempts at political justification of these former Yugoslav Cominformists.

Now that Stalin's policy toward Yugoslavia and the international workers' movement has definitely been condemned and the attitude of the Yugoslav leadership has been given full satisfaction and recognition, it is more than amazing that someone should even raise the question of the role of former Cominformists and voice suspicion with regard to the correctness of Yugoslavia's attitude toward them.

Unfortunately, such strange conceptions were also reflected in the columns of certain foreign newspapers. Indeed, incomplete and inaccurate information was published on recent trials of some former Cominformists who had trampled over the laws of our country. In those reports no mention at all was made of the grave criminal acts because of which those persons were sentenced to imprisonment. Those newspaper reports instead presented these condemned persons as political emigrants, particularly stressing the fact that they had voluntarily returned to their country. In an indirect way suspicion is voiced as to the validity of the sentences pronounced against these persons. It is also characteristic of those reports that they create the impression that all former Cominformists who return to Yugoslavia are being arrested and tried.

The facts, of course, are quite different. Of former Cominformists who have returned to Yugoslavia since the normalization of relations with the USSR and Eastern European countries, only 16.6 percent were sentenced. This means that only those persons who were guilty of the most serious criminal acts against their own people and country were sentenced, those who were guilty of such criminal acts as major offenses against the FPRY committed while abroad, intelligence-diversionist activities in our own territory, participation in intelligence services and other hostile activities upon their return to the country, as well as various types of grave criminal offenses.

Our Cominform emigration was clearly informed by us that all those who had committed criminal acts would have to appear before the court and would be subject to the laws which apply to all citizens of our country. The purpose of our law, furthermore, is to allow those persons who have committed criminal acts to become, by means of an amnesty, constructive citizens of our socialist country.

It is difficult indeed to understand how it is possible that certain circles abroad continue to protect former Cominformists politically and try to justify their behavior. Undoubtedly, everybody who takes such an attitude toward this matter is also indirectly attacking the entire policy of the leadership of the Yugoslav League of Communists, thus proving that they still take the anti-Yugoslav position of the Cominform.

Even more worthy of condemnation are the writings to be found in the newspaper *Il Lavoratore* [organ of the Vidali group which heads the CP in Trieste], which, in defending former Yugoslav Cominformists, went so far as to call them "champions of the international Communist movement." We were not in the least surprised that Vidali's paper was the first to produce such a thesis.

If the former Yugoslav Cominformists who were engaged in hostile activities against their own country are fighters for Communism, as is claimed by Vidali, then this means that the Yugoslav Communists, headed by their leaders, are enemies of Communism and that the whole new orientation of the international workers' movement which was definitely established by the 20th Congress of the CPSU is contrary to the interests of socialism. Or it is just the opposite. For, obviously, both things cannot be true at the same time. Only one or the other is possible.

From all this it clearly follows that the attitude toward the Cominform emigration is far from being an unimportant, subordinate matter. No! And by his attitude toward it one can see how and what somebody is really thinking about international cooperation, the relations between socialist countries, and the international workers' movement.

Hence attempts made to justify the actions of former Cominformists cannot mean anything else but to be behind the times. And in essence, consciously or unconsciously, continuing to hold the old Stalinist position.

On September 19, N. S. Khrushchev, First Secretary of the CPSU, arrived on a suprise visit in Yugoslavia.[13] On September 27 Tito, also unexpectedly and without explanation, accompanied Khrushchev to the Soviet Union. There they held conferences with other Soviet leaders and at least one leader of a people's democracy, Erno Gero, who joined the talks on September 30. Tito returned to Yugoslavia on October 5. The subject of the talks had centered on relations among the Communist Parties.[14]

In the meantime, events in Poland and Hungary, set in motion by the 20th Congress of the CPSU, were moving toward a climax.

---

[13] A brief announcement of Khrushchev's impending departure, without further explanation as to purpose, was made in *Izvestia*, September 18, 1956.

At about the same time, a memorandum of the CPSU Central Committee was reported to be circulating among the East European Communist Parties (except the Yugoslav) warning them in effect that the Yugoslavs, while friendly and progressive, were tainted with social democratism and should not be followed as a valid, Marxist-Leninist model of socialist construction. Though the memorandum has so far not come into the public domain, its existence was reported by the New York *Times*, September 24, 1956, and was alluded to by Yugoslav spokesmen who have learned about it.

[14] See Tito's speech at Pula, Part Four, Chapter II, Document 4.

PART TWO: *Poland*

CHAPTER I.

THE ANTI-STALIN CAMPAIGN; FIRST PHASE: FEBRUARY—JUNE, 1956

The exposure of past, Stalinist misdeeds at the 20th Congress of the CPSU had immediate bearing on Poland. For it helped to set straight the historical record of the fate of the Communist Party of Poland whose leadership was in overwhelming numbers liquidated in 1938 on charges of having served the interests of German espionage agencies. Announcement of the rehabilitation of the CPP was first made in the pages of *Trybuna Ludu,* the central organ of the Polish United Workers Party (PUWP) on February 19, 1956. The announcement was reprinted in *Pravda* two days later.

1. STATEMENT ON THE WRONGFUL LIQUIDATION OF THE COMMUNIST PARTY OF POLAND IN 1938, *Pravda,* FEBRUARY 21, 1956[1]

IN 1938 THE Executive Committee of the Communist International adopted a resolution on dissolving the Communist Party of Poland in view of an accusation made at that time concerning wide-scale penetration by enemy agents into the ranks of its leading Party *aktiv.*

It has now been established that this accusation was based on materials which were falsified by subsequently exposed provocateurs.

After examining all the materials on this matter, the Central Committees of the Communist Parties of the Soviet Union, Italy, Bulgaria, and Finland, together with the Central Committee of the Polish United Workers Party, have come to the conclusion that the dissolution of the Polish Communist Party was groundless.

---

[1] Translation reproduced from *The Current Digest of the Soviet Press,* VIII, No. 8 (April 4, 1956), 27.

Even the above-mentioned Executive Committee resolution stressed the glorious revolutionary past of the heroic Polish proletariat and noted that thousands of Polish Communists were giving themselves and their lives to the cause of serving the working class and defending the working masses' vital interests.   Under the difficult conditions of fascist terrorism the Polish Communist Party led the struggle of Polish working people and peasants against the oppression of the capitalists and landlords, for the social and national liberation of the working people.   The Polish Communist Party received and continued the glorious traditions of the joint revolutionary struggle of the Polish and Russian proletariat, consistently taking the stand of proletarian internationalism, of close cooperation with fraternal Communist and Workers Parties, with the international revolutionary movement.

Even after the dissolution of the Communist Party, Polish Communists actively struggled against the fascist dictatorship of the capitalists and landlords, against the impending threat of the Hitlerite aggression, utilizing all existing organizational forms of the mass workers' and peasants' movement.

After the Hitlerite army attacked Poland, the Polish Communists together with the left-wing socialists led the Polish people's antifascist liberation struggle.

The Polish Workers Party, set up in 1942 by prominent leaders of the Polish Communist Party, led a wide partisan movement of workers, peasants, and intelligentsia against the Hitlerite plunderers and was the founder of the Krajowa Rada Narodowa [National Council of the Homeland].[2]   The struggle of the people's democratic forces, headed by the Polish Workers Party, led under conditions of the Soviet Union's historic victory to the establishment of the Polish People's Republic.

In December, 1948, the Polish Workers Party united with the Polish Socialist Party on a Marxist-Leninist platform and formed the Polish United Workers Party, which is now a militant, monolithic Marxist-Leninist Party, the leading force in

---

[2] Wartime underground organizations.   Together with the Union of Patriots, an organization of Polish Communists and left-wing socialists

the struggle of the working people of people's Poland for the building of socialism.

> Central Committee of the Communist Party of the Soviet Union; Central Committee of the Polish United Workers Party; Central Committee of the Italian Communist Party; Central Committee of the Bulgarian Communist Party; Central Committee of the Communist Party of Finland.
>
> (Published in the newspaper *Trybuna Ludu*, Feb. 19, 1956.)

On March 12, 1956, Boleslaw Bierut, First Secretary of the PUWP, died of an illness he contracted while attending the 20th Congress of the CPSU in Moscow. He was buried in Warsaw on March 16. On March 20, the Central Committee of the PUWP held its sixth plenary session. It was attended by N. S. Khrushchev, First Secretary of the CPSU, who had journeyed to Warsaw along with other Soviet leaders to be present at the last rites of Bierut. At the Central Committee session Edward Ochab was elected First Secretary of the PUWP. On the following day, Khrushchev departed from Warsaw.

In the meantime the anti-Stalin campaign in Poland gathered momentum.

One of the strongest attacks repudiating the past was made at the 19th session of the Council of Culture and Art which convened on March 24-25, 1956. Polish writers, artists, and philosophers had voiced criticism of the conditions affecting them before. *Trybuna Ludu,* commenting on the Council's session, summarized past developments in the following terms:[3]

> In order to understand, in order even to begin to analyze this rejuvenating shock which is taking place these days in the Polish arts, one should recall three dates, three symbolic . . . stages.
>
> In January of 1949 at the Congress of Writers in Szczecin a unity of literary men in Poland was proclaimed under the aegis of socialist realism. The same unity was accepted at that time on behalf of every branch of the arts.

---

in the Soviet Union, it was the nucleus of the Polish Government formed in Lublin under Soviet auspices in 1944.

[3] J. A. Szczepanski, "With a Full Voice," *Trybuna Ludu,* April 8, 1956.

In October of 1951 a conference was held in the hall of the National Council in Warsaw between the writers and the Party leadership, which demonstrated the unity of views of the leaders of the Party building socialism with that of the artists who wanted to participate as much as possible in the construction of socialism.

And then in April of 1954, the 11th Congress of the Council of Culture was held and it proclaimed the bankruptcy of the practices of contemporary cultural policy in Poland, sharply attacking administrative and bureaucratic manners of guiding the arts, clearly indicating the necessity of loosening and breaking up the tight and iron armor in which socialist realism was riveted and which halted and to a certain extent made impossible the development of artistic creativity.

Critical attitudes which developed in the atmosphere of the "new course" found pungent expression in a "Poem for Adults" by Adam Wazyk. The poem, published in *Nowa Kultura,* the official organ of the Polish Writers' Union, on August 19, 1955, appeared to strike a responsive chord in the Polish public and in other people's democracies where its contents became known. Because of the interest it aroused, it is reproduced here in full:[4]

2. "POEM FOR ADULTS" BY ADAM WAZYK

1

I jumped by mistake on the wrong bus;
people sat as usual returning from work.
The bus swept down a strange road,
through Holy Cross Street. You are no longer a Holy Cross!
Where are your antique shops, your bookstalls and students?
Where are you, the dead?
Even your memory fades.

Then the bus stopped
at a little square which had been dug up.
The back of an old four-story house
stood waiting its fate.

---

[4] The translation reproduced here is by Lucjan Blit. Reprinted with permission from *The Twentieth Century,* No. 158 (December, 1955), pp. 504-511.

I got off at the little square
in a working class quarter,
with memories shimmering from the grey walls.
People were hurrying home
and I dared not ask where I was.
Was I not here as a child, visiting the chemist?

I went home,
like a man who had gone out to buy medicine,
and returned twenty years later.

My wife asked: Where were you?
The children asked: Where were you?
I was silent, trembling like a mouse.

2
The squares, like cobras, hold their beauties high;
the houses flaunt themselves like peacocks.
Give me one fragment of old stone.
Let me find myself back in Warsaw.

I stand like a mindless post
under the lamps in the square,
I praise, I wonder, I curse,
with cobra, with abracadabra.

  I let myself go, like a hero,
  beneath the compassionate columns.
  What do I care for these Galluxa puppets
  painted as if for the coffin!

Here young people buy ices!
Oh, here all are young,
their memories hold only ruins;
the girl will shortly give birth.

Here tawdriness takes hands with compassion:
what has grown into stone will endure.
Here you will learn your letters,
future poet of Warsaw.

It is natural for you to love them.
I loved other stones,
grey and great
ringing with memories.

The squares, like cobras, hold their beauties high;
the houses flaunt themselves like peacocks.
Give me one fragment of old stone:
let me find myself back in Warsaw.

3
"Today our skies are not empty"—*from a political speech*
It was dawn. I heard the whistling of jets.
They are expensive, and yet we must. . . .
When we no longer want to talk about the earth we know
then we say: The sky is not empty.

People walk here uncaring in rags,
our women soon grow old.
When we no longer want to talk about the earth we know
then we say: The sky is not empty.

Over the ocean in the clouds seethes
the apocalypse; here the passer-by kneels down . . .
when we do not want to talk frankly about the earth,
the kneeling man says: the sky is not empty.

A legion of boys releases doves,
a girl knots a scarf . . .
when we do not want to talk frankly about the earth,
then we say: The sky is not empty.

4
From villages, from little towns, they go in wagons,
to build a foundry, to conjure up a town,
to dig out a new Eldorado.
A pioneer army, a gathered mob.
They crowd each other in barracks, in hostels, in huts.
They plunge and whistle in the muddy streets:
the great migration, dishevelled ambition,

on their necks a little string—the Cross of Czestochowa.
With a storehouse of oaths, with a little feather pillow,
bestial with vodka, boasting of tarts,
a distrusting soul—wrenched from the bonds,
half-awake and half-mad,
silent in words, singing snatches of song—
is suddenly thrust out from mediaeval darkness.
A migrating mass, this inhuman Poland,
howling with boredom in December evenings . . .
from rubbish baskets swinging on ropes
boys run like cats on the walls;
from the women's hostels, those lay monasteries,
sounds of lust and travail.   The duchesses
will be rid of their issue—the Vistula flows near by.
The great migration builds new industry,
unknown to Poland but known to history,
is fed on great empty words, lives
wildly from day to day in despite of preachers—
amid coal fumes is melted in this slow torture
into a working class.
Much is wasted.   As yet only dross.

5
And it happened this way: a brown column
of smoke burst from a burning mine,
a gallery is cut off; of the agony below
no one will tell; the black tunnel is a coffin.
The saboteur had blood, bones, hands.
A hundred families mourn, two hundred families;
they write in the papers, or they do not write.
Only smoke wreathing the air hangs over all.

6
In the railway station
Miss Jadzia in the buffet,
so charming when she yawns,
so charming when she pours . . .
LOOK OUT! THE ENEMY OFFERS YOU VODKA!

Here you'll be poisoned for sure,
Miss Jadzia'll make off with your boots,
so charming when she yawns
so charming when she pours . . .
LOOK OUT! THE ENEMY OFFERS YOU VODKA!

Don't go, boy, to Nowa Huta,
You will be poisoned on the way,
be warned by this ominous poster,
in your stomach you have a People's fish:
LOOK OUT! THE ENEMY OFFERS YOU VODKA!

7

I will never believe, my dear, that a lion is a little lamb,
I will never believe, my dear, that a little lamb is a lion!
I will never believe, my dear, in a magic spell;
I will never believe in minds kept under glass;
but I believe that a table has only four legs,
but I believe that the fifth leg is a chimera,
and when the chimeras rally, my dear,
then one dies slowly of a worn out heart.

8

It is true,
when these farthing boredoms
howl down the great aims of education,
when the vultures of abstraction pick out our brains,
when students are enclosed in text books without windows,
when language is reduced to thirty incantations,
when the lamp of imagination is extinguished,
when good people from the moon deny us our taste,
then truly
oblivion is dangerously near.

9

A drowned man was fished out of the Vistula.
A note was found in his pocket:
'My sleeve is right,
my button is wrong,

my collar is wrong,
but my half-belt is right.'
They buried him under a willow.

10

In the newly painted street of fresh built flats,
mortar dust floats in the air, a cloud covers the sky,
steamrollers flatten the road,
transplanted chestnuts are greening, they rustle in the dusk.
Under the chestnuts run children, big and small,
from the half-demolished frames they take wood for the kitchen.
Fifteen-year-old little whores go down the planks to the cellars,
they have plaster smiles, they smell of mortar.
Nearby the radio plays in the darkness, unearthly dance music.
Night is coming, hooligans play as hooligans will.
How difficult it is to fall asleep in the years of your childhood,
    among the rustling chestnuts . . .
Float away into darkness, you dissonance!
I wanted to find joy in the newness,
I wanted to tell of a young street, but not that one.
Have I lost the gift of seeing, or the gift of convenient blindness?
I am left with a short note, with these verses of a new grief.

11

Racketeers enticed her to a quiet hell
in a retired villa out of town—
she escaped, and wandered through the night, drunk.
She lay on the pavement till morning.
She was thrown out of the Art School for want of a socialist
    morality.
She poisoned herself once—they saved her.
She poisoned herself twice—they buried her.

It is all very old. Old are the twisters
of socialist morality.

The dreamer Fourier beautifully prophesied
that the sea would flow with lemonade.
And does it not flow?

They drink sea-water,
and cry—
Lemonade!
They return quietly home
to vomit
to vomit.

12
They ran to us, shouting:
A communist does not die.
It never happened that a man did not die.
Only the memory abides.
The worthier the man,
the greater the pain.
They ran to us, shouting:
Under socialism
a cut finger does not hurt.

They cut their finger,
they felt pain.
They lost faith.

13
They cursed the routinists.
They taught the routinists.
They shamed the routinists.
They called in literature to help—
a five-year-old snotty-nosed child,
who needs educating,
who needs to educate others—
Is this routinist an enemy?
Routinist is not an enemy.
Routinist should be taught.
Routinist should be enlightened.
Routinist should be shamed.
Routinist should be convinced.
He should be educated.

They turn people into feeding bottles.
I heard a clever lecture:
'Without appropriately distributed
economic incentives
we will not achieve technical progress.'
These are the words of a Marxist.
This is the knowledge of the law of realism.
The end of utopia.

No story will be told of the routinist,
but there will be novels about the troubles of the inventor,
of the fears which disquiet us all.

This is a naked poem,
before it is clothed
with vexation, colors and the smells of this earth.

14
There are people overworked,
there are people from Nowa Huta
who have never been to a theatre,
there are Polish apples which Polish children cannot reach,
there are boys forced to lie,
there are girls forced to lie,
there are old wives turned away from their homes by their hus-
    bands,
there are the weary dying of tired hearts,
there are people slandered, spat upon,
there are people stripped in the streets by common bandits,
for whom the authorities still seek a legal definition,
there are people who wait for documents,
there are people who wait for justice,
there are people who wait very long.

We make demands on this earth,
for the people who are overworked,
for keys to open doors,
for rooms with windows,
for walls which do not rot,

for hatred of little documents,
for holy human time,
for safe homecoming,
for a simple distinction between words and deeds.

We make demands on this earth,
for which we did not throw dice,
for which a million perished in battle:
for a clear truth,
for the bread of freedom,
for burning reason,
for burning reason.

We demand these every day.
We demand through the Party.

Wazyk's poem was sharply condemned by spokesmen for the Party and the Government.[5] Subsequently, criticism of existing conditions by writers became more muted, though not altogether stilled.[6]

The 20th Congress of the CPSU revived attacks on the past and gave impetus to fresh demands for greater creative freedom.

Jan Kott, speaking before the 19th session of the Council of Culture and Art, characterized developments in literature since 1949 as having led to ever greater distortions of the truth:[7]

We have been trying to explain reality and not to learn the truth; to explain and justify at any price, even the price of truth. Thus modern history became a great mythology before our eyes. . . . Whenever the facts stood in the way, the facts were changed. If genuine heroes were obstacles, they evaporated.

Literature which was not allowed to speak about crimes, literature which had to keep silent about trials which shocked men's minds and which were the daily reality for years, literature which

5 See, for example, *Poprostu*, September 4, 1955; *Trybuna Wolnosci*, September 21, 1955 *Tygodnik Demokratyczny*, October 19, 1955; *Zycie Literackie*, October 30, 1955.

6 Wazyk himself did not publish again until April 8, 1956, when several of his poems were printed in *Nowa Kultura*.

7 Jan Kott, "Mythology and Truth," *Przeglad Kulturalny*, Vol. V, No. 14, April 5/11, 1956.

had a sealed lip and wandered ever further and deeper into lies, created a more and more fictitious vision of reality. The false theory of the mechanical rotting of art in bourgeois society in the imperialist epoch was accompanied by a theory of the automatic flourishing of art in socialist society. . . ."

An equally harsh appraisal of the past was made by Antoni Slonimski.

3. "For the Restoration of the Citizen's Right," Report by Antoni Slonimski before the 19th Session of the Council of Culture and Art, March 24-25, 1956[8]

After the address of Mr. Kott, who in the name of the bankrupt party was settling with the creditors, I would like to press several personal claims.

The history of philosophy knows few periods in which intolerance has so greatly increased as that of the last few years. The persecution of critical thought at the beginning of the Renaissance or later, in the seventeenth and eighteenth centuries, appears to have been almost idyllic when compared to the times we have recently witnessed and which, we can add with relief, are passing.

It would be meaningless to speak about problems in Polish art and science during the last ten years without mentioning the real cause of many of our misfortunes. It is not in Marxism that we find the source of this state of affairs, but rather in departure from the theses of Marx and Engels. The first of these criminal deviations and departures from the Marxist classics was the 1936 convention of Soviet writers. It was then that, basing himself on Gorky's flighty opinions and exploiting his authority in letters, Zhdanov created the theses of socialist realism. He then distributed this precision tool for destroying art to officials who for the past twenty years have carried out the destructive procedure with zeal and application sharpened by fear.

---

[8] *Ibid.*

There were even some who attributed this failure of Soviet art to the original sin of the revolution. Historical truth negates this view. The first decade following the October revolution [of 1917] brought great achievements. Soviet films moved and enraptured millions of movie-goers in the whole world and had a tremendous influence on the development of film making in the West. In literature, then, there was Mayakovsky and Yessenin, Tolstoy and Sholokhov.

It is worth while to consider why it was that numerous axioms of socialist realism, though contrary to centuries of experience and common sense, survived that long and partially even into our days. Only recently many of these truths became the prey of satirical papers and cabarets. But it is discouraging that they lasted that long and met with so little protest.

The writers were haunted not only with an "ism," but also with the positive hero and typicality. They were told to believe that Don Quixote was typical, that Dante's wandering in Hell and Gulliver's travels to the Lilliputians were events typical of their time, that Robinson Crusoe's adventure was an example of colonial imperialism, that Hamlet was really an exposé of the nasty methods used to gain power in a feudal system (pouring poison into the ear), that the pessimism in Mickiewicz's sonnets was directly connected with the grain crisis in Odessa. Then in a small school it was taught that only a progressive work can be beautiful. There could always be found a magician to prove that Notre Dame was not beautiful or, if more convenient, that it was a progressive work.

We would be guilty of simplification if we presumed that all these, at times completely contradictory, literary directives were accepted only for reasons of opportunism or for the sake of peace. I am willing to admit that the trumpeters as well as the rank-and-file of this literary Salvation Army had faith or, more often, wanted to have faith, for it is human nature to manufacture an ideological or rather ideo-nonlogical superstructure for one's own comfort. However, fear was a very important factor during that sad period and to pass over this in silence would be to surrender again to hypocrisy. If it was not fear of immediate liquidation, of being accused of espionage, it was the deeply demoralizing fear of losing one's job, prestige, and privileges.

Brecht enthusiasts participated in condemnations of Brecht adherents, only to shake their fists fiercely a few months later at those who did not like Brecht. One can find some excuse for people who believed that things must be so, but it is not easy to forget the deeds of eager beavers, and those who favored foul play. Not long ago a talented poet of the younger generation, Mandalian, recalled that in those days, too, the older poets wrote schematic and declaratory poems. He also cited a fragment from one of my poems, though possibly he did not know that the ending had been struck out by the editors of *Nowa Kultura,* and was restored by me only in the second edition of my poetic works. The verses in question were: "But protect their banner the masses will, and the tightly-clenched fist into a brotherly palm will bloom."

This small morsel from the literary kitchen shows what the administration of art was like. This stanza, by no means schematic, was eliminated without my knowledge; there was a certain binding doctrine to the effect that the clenched fist would always remain clenched and that the element of hatred would forever accompany the ideal of socialism. Even though, during that period, I was in a better situation than my younger colleagues—I did not have to attain a place in poetry under the conditions of such warped cultural life—nevertheless I suffered serious losses especially as a dramatist and publicist.

At first I thought that these sacrifices made by the artists were to some degree necessary and that one had to subordinate oneself to the higher political reasons for that great cause, which the building of the basis of socialism and the strengthening of popular rule in our country undoubtedly was. However, not long after my return to Poland I became convinced that these sacrifices not only were unnecessary but decidedly harmful both for our literature and for socialism.

The harm wrought by the period of fear and cynicism was especially painful with regard to education and our attitude to our cultural past. We remember how some eager beavers eliminated Zeromski, Wyspianski, Norwid, from the history of our literature.[9]

Is it possible that writers who officiated at these doings should continue to occupy positions of influence and leadership in the Polish Writers' Union?

The attitude toward world literature and the cultural achievements of our interwar period was wrapped in lies. Even now one hears voices that in that period only the cheap novels of Zarzycka were being published in editions of hundreds of thousands.

It should be recalled that during that period Kruczkowski published *Kordian and the Boor,* and Broniewski wrote his best poems. It should be recalled that the entire glorious theatrical career of Leon Schiller occurred during the interwar years, that the best Polish stage designer, Wladislas Daniszewski, worked with distinction for the Polish stage during those days. We know and must state bitterly that Schiller was brought to ruin in People's Poland and Daniszewski was not shown at international expositions. I limit myself to the activities of Polish artists of the extreme left and to members of the Communist Party.

Our colleagues, Stande, Wandurski, Bruno Jasienski, died but not in Polish prisons.[10]

If we want the truth about the last decade it does not mean in the least that we underestimate its impressive achievement in spreading culture. Not without pride, we can mention the editions of our classics and of the masterpieces of world literature.

---

[9] Outstanding Polish poets and writers of the prewar and interwar period.

[10] Polish poets and writers who were imprisoned in the Soviet Union.

When we see what great possibilities we had and still have, we should be all the more critical and ruthless in talking about our errors.

We are now leaving the period of fear and cynicism. Discussions are animated and passionate, but we still have a lot to undo. The 20th Congress, which contributed so greatly to the task of clearing the poisoned atmosphere, unfortunately did not give us much in the field of literature. There, they saw salvation of literature through decentralization and through sending writers into the field. I would gladly send a few of our writers to the devil, but I do not think they would return from that visit with Dante's tercets.

Those changes for the better which we observe from the time when literature left the period of fear and began slowly to rid itself of cynicism, are not to everybody's liking. Here and there appear bereaved orphans and widows of Beria, the supporters of the big stick policy whose existence and influence was possible in the period of politico-literary blackmail.

One of our pressing tasks should be to limit the Writers' Union to appropriate functions. It is imperative that this Red Salvation Army renounce its drum beating and public confessions; that it abandon its joyful criticism that binds no one, and cease its pastoral activity of soul-saving. I see an improvement of our cultural life and writing not in these or other organizations but in the reinstatement of the citizen's basic freedoms. Freedom of speech guaranteed by the Constitution cannot be a plaything in the hands of anonymous officials. We must give back to words their meaning and integrity. During the times when schematism was forced upon literature, the editorials in our press gave an unparalleled example of this [practice]. Even to this day, there can be found that conglomeration of liturgy and thieves' jargon into which our publications were turned. We must clear the road of all leftovers and of the whole mythology of the era of fear. This is the opinion of the Polish writers.

Unfortunately, new myths are appearing in place of old. Now they say that the responsibility for the past belongs to the cult of personality.   This I found formulated by the chief Marxist theorist, Professor Schaff.   Let us follow this formula to the end.   First of all, it is not to the cult of personality, but the individual himself.   It is not the individual but the system which permits the individual to conduct such dangerous activities.   Only a true democratization of public life, restoration of public opinion, and the return from fideism to rational and unfettered thought can save us from Caesarism.

An improvement in cultural relations cannot come without far-reaching changes in our public life.   In order that literature may serve the cause of socialism, it must come to believe in socialism.   Despite everything, this faith has not been shaken. Our just cause needs not only clean hands but also clear thinking.   We are emerging from medieval darkness.   There are in Poland young forces, healthy minds and characters who have been waiting for this moment of change.   Today, they must be allowed to speak out.[11]

Meanwhile the leadership of the PUWP also sought to evaluate the applicability of the lessons of the 20th Congress of the CPSU to Poland, to define the scope of the anti-Stalin campaign, and in this context to come to terms with one of the legacies of the Stalinist period in Poland, the case of Wladyslaw Gomulka (erstwhile First

---

[11] Polish writers continued to speak out.   Zbigniev Florczak, for example, hailed the 20th Congress of the CPSU for giving an "entirely new interpretation" to history, and urged that the Poles "should at last realize that we are living in an independent state."   (*Nowa Kultura,* April 8, 1956.)   Julian Przybos and Henryk Markiewicz directed their fire on "socialist realism," comparing it with a big stick "created for the needs of officials of the propaganda bureau and for lackeys and panegyrists" and going so far as to imply that Lenin's theses on literature (contained in the pamphlet *Party Organization and Party Literature*) were merely a "tactical step at a given stage of the revolution" and not an ideological program for a new art of high principles.   Others also joined in the chorus of criticism with which the Polish Communist leaders tried to cope and for which they were finally taken to task by V. Ozerov in *Literaturnaia Gazeta,* the organ of the Soviet Writers' Union.   (September 30, 1956.)   A partial translation of Ozerov's article appears in *The Current Digest of the Soviet Press,* VIII, No. 39 (November 7, 1956), 7-9.

Secretary of the Party) and other Communists who had been jailed for "deviationist" views after 1949.

4. "THE LESSONS OF THE 20TH CONGRESS OF THE CPSU," ARTICLE BY JERZY MORAWSKI, SECRETARY OF THE POLISH UNITED WORKERS PARTY, *Trybuna Ludu,* MARCH 27, 1956

THE 20TH CONGRESS has been for us all—those who took part in it and those who became acquainted with its materials through the radio and the press—an important experience. It is an experience because it has fulfilled our expectations. It has answered the questions which for many years have preoccupied millions of people. It has drawn up vast prospects of the struggle for peace and a better life for the working people. This Congress is a landmark between two epochs.

At the 20th Congress new, bold ideas were put forward regarding international problems, regarding the problem of the defense of peace and of the perspectives of a peaceful transition to socialism. We know that even before the Congress Soviet foreign policy was developing in a new and bold way, achieving great successes. To attain such results it was necessary, however, to overcome all that had previously hampered the development of this policy. It was necessary to revise certain old, unjustified opinions and certain old, erroneous moves. And this was done by the leadership of the CPSU.

On the basis of a profound analysis of the present alignment of forces in the world, the Congress has given an answer to the question preoccupying the largest sections of the people: Is it possible to safeguard peace? It is known that up to now there existed in our propaganda a certain obscurity on this matter. We called on people to increase their efforts for peace. We told them that the forces of peace were superior to the forces of war. But at the same time the thesis that wars were inevitable in the era of imperialism hung over our heads like an ominous fate.

The Congress has shown that there is no fatal necessity for wars. The forces of peace throughout the world have grown to such a degree that in spite of the existence of imperialism and of the drive to war resulting from its nature, an outbreak of war can be prevented and peace safeguarded and preserved.

Of course, this is only a possibility, only an opportunity. This opportunity must be turned to advantage.

Poland, with her economic potential, which is already considerable, her vast traditional and new international contacts, has no small role to play here.

Up to now we have not been fully utilizing our possibilities to exercise influence upon and establish contacts with various social groups in capitalist countries, as well as with the governments of many of these countries. We can substantially develop our diplomatic, economic, and cultural contacts, both with many countries of Western Europe as well as with the Middle East which is awakening to independent life. Following the setting up of our diplomatic missions in Burma and Indonesia, we should enliven our cooperation not only with those countries but also with all Southeast Asia. Also, the first attempts at establishing contacts with the countries of Latin America are auguring good results.

Now as never before we can and we should enter the international arena, and strengthen our initiative in foreign policy, in international trade, in social and political, cultural and scientific contacts which are being developed both by state authorities and by various social organizations.

This is linked up with the necessity of training numerous cadres possessing knowledge of the language and culture of various countries, of experts in various branches of international trade and cooperation. This is also linked up with the need for intensifying, in comparison with the present situation, the propaganda of international problems in our community, for fostering a still deeper and more thorough knowledge of various countries and of international relations, for liquidating misunderstandings and prejudices held by a part of the population concerning, for instance, our exports to various countries, and so forth.

In doing so, we should not forget, of course, that the defensive strength of our camp is a factor most efficiently curbing the schemes of war adventurers. Our people understand this. A certain Polish contribution has already been made to the defense of peace. We shall continue to strengthen our defensive strength. We shall cooperate, to the best of our capacity, in strengthening the unity and cohesion of the entire socialist camp as the safest guarantee of Poland's security and of the maintenance of peace.

Another range of problems on which the Congress shed new light concerns the evaluation of the roads of transition to socialism.

The bourgeoisie has always represented the Communists as bloodthirsty people, advocates of an armed insurrection and civil war, regardless of conditions and of the situation. Communists say: To bring about a social revolution without recourse to violence, without the ruin and disorganization resulting from a bloody upheaval, would be very much to our liking. The working class, said Lenin, prefers to take power into its hands by peaceful means. Whether it will succeed in doing so depends on the degree of resistance of the bourgeoisie.

The 20th Congress has pointed out that the present alignment of forces in the world makes possible a peaceful transition to socialism in a number of countries by utilizing the parliament, by gaining a majority in it by the working class in alliance with other progressive forces of society, forming a revolutionary government, and expropriating the exploiters by parliamentary means with the support of organized forces of the working people—that is, by way of a peaceful achievement of basic social and political transformations making possible the construction of socialism.

It is known that as early as in the April Theses of 1917 Lenin spoke of the possibility of overthrowing the bourgeois regime by peaceful means, through gaining the majority in the Soviets. But then came the July events—the bourgeoisie applied bloody terror against the revolutionary movement and the peaceful way of gaining power was no longer possible.

Another example of the possibility of a peaceful accession to power by the people's masses was the period characterized by the formation of popular fronts in the thirties, for instance in Spain, where the working class and its allies gained the majority in the parliamentary elections and formed a popular front government. In response to this, fascism, with the aid of foreign intervention, unleashed civil war and drowned in blood the revolutionary upsurge of the people's masses.

After World War II, owing to the smashing of Nazism by the Soviet Union and to the paralyzing thereby of the attempts at resistance on the part of militant reactionaries, the prerequisites were created for the peaceful taking over of power by the working masses in the European countries of people's democracy. This is especially clearly evident in the example of Czechoslovakia.

In our country too—as a result of the victorious national liberation struggle, as a result of the smashing, owing to this victory, of all attempts at the restoration of the rule of Polish fascism—the prerequisites were created for a peaceful development of our revolution, although this revolution was not devoid of important elements of civil war and cost us tens of thousands of victims.

In speaking of the Polish road to socialism we put a different content in this notion than did the Gomulka group.

The attitude of the Gomulka group was opposed to the program which was being hammered out by the Party, a program of revolutionary transformations in the economy, in culture, and in education. The Gomulka group tried to detach the Polish working class movement from the revolutionary traditions of the Communist Party of Poland. It intended to build up the unity of the Polish working class by rejecting its revolutionary attainments—the Social Democratic Party of Poland and Lithuania and the Communist Party of Poland— and by whitewashing at the same time the nationalist and reformist traditions of the right wing of the Polish Socialist Party.

The Gomulka group propounded the theory of a "Polish road to socialism." It was not the slogan itself that was false, but the class content which the Gomulka group put into this slogan—holding up the process of revolutionary transformations, freezing the alignment of class forces in the countryside, holding up the process of basic transformations not only in the economy, but also in culture, science, and education.

In its essence this was not a variation of the Soviet road but its contradiction, and objectively it signified an outright negation of the road to socialism.

Marxism-Leninism and our Party tell of the particular and specific character of each country's road to socialism. This is also valid for our Polish road.

Wherein reside, then, the distinctive features of the Polish road to socialism in comparison with the Soviet road? They consist mainly in different forms and ways of accomplishing the revolution. Suffice it to recall that our revolution was born out of the national liberation struggle, that in the first stage it maintained the bourgeois double-track system of local administration—councils on the one hand, and the offices of wojewodas and starostas on the other.[12] Suffice it to recall the road of the development of the Party of the working class, which in our country, unlike the Soviet Union, was formed through the merging of the Polish Workers Party and the Polish Socialist Party. At the same time other political parties continued to exist. Our forms of the collectivization of agriculture are different from those in the Soviet Union and, in perspective, the manner of liquidating capitalist elements in the countryside will also be different. Different is our way of regulating relations with the church, and so forth. The Polish revolution was able to follow this road—it was able to develop its own distinctive features— owing to a large degree to the new alignment of forces in the world, brought about, above all, by the existence of the Soviet Union.

---

[12] Appointed officials heading the provincial and district administrations respectively.

The putting forth by the 20th Congress of the thesis of the possibility in the present conditions of a peaceful road to socialism does not entail any conciliation between revolution and reformism.

What we want is fundamental transformation of social relations, the overthrow of capitalism and its replacement by the socialist system. Reformism is a policy of concessions and reforms effected within the framework of the bourgeois system, intended to "correct" or "mend" capitalism, instead of radically liquidating the sources of class exploitation and oppression.

The point, however, is—and to this problem the 20th Congress devoted much attention—how to reject reformism and wage an ideological struggle against it while sparing no efforts to achieve rapprochement and cooperation between Communists and Socialists on the basis of any possible common actions in order to build up and consolidate the united front of the working class. Other progressive forces, too, for instance in peasant organizations and in Christian Democratic parties, can and should be induced to cooperate in broad. popular, and democratic anti-imperialist and antiwar fronts.

Listening to the deliberations of the Congress, we were aware how deeply these ideas affected the attending delegates from capitalistic countries, for answers were provided to many problems preoccupying these parties. Unusually important and far-ranging perspectives for the wide development of our movement on an international scale were drawn.

We have abandoned the false theory, once put forth, on social-fascism, a theory which, as a matter of fact, characterized Social Democracy as a peculiar variety of fascism. This theory led to the isolation of Communists confronted by the aggressive activities of fascism and wrought in its time much damage to the international working class movement.

True, it was overcome in the period of popular fronts, but even later, on more that one occasion, relapses of sectarianism and suspicion made themselves felt, as well as the alienation from us of the forces with which one could and should cooperate, and among which one could and should look for allies of the revolutionary movement and of the working class. Experience teaches that without the support of the Party by the workers masses, without the support of the working class by the nonproletarian sections of working people, victory is impossible.

The directives concerning the new Soviet Five-Year Plan adopted at the Congress are also of great international significance. What is involved here are not only the impressive plans in the field of the expansion of the national economy of the USSR, the rapid tempo of the further forward march, which, as the American daily, the New York *Times,* stated, "alas departs considerably from the leisurely pace at which the countries of the free world are moving forward."

What is involved here also is the direction of the Five-Year Plan, the striving, based on the development of the whole national economy, to overcome ever more effectively the disproportions between industry and agriculture, to raise as rapidly as possible the living standards of the working population, to create the conditions for a further and more rapid development of culture and education—for an all-around increase in the standards of living of the Soviet People.

Of tremendous significance for the Soviet Peoples, as well as for the peoples building socialism in the people's democratic countries, for the working masses struggling against exploitation and oppression in capitalist countries, are the decisions of the 20th Congress concerning working hours, norms and wages, housing construction, expansion of social and educational facilities, and so forth. Together with the Soviet people, we rejoice at the fact that the decades of their selfless toil will bring ever more abundant fruit. For the whole world this signifies great optimism and faith in a better future which socialism is opening up for mankind.

The workers in Poland correctly see in that our own prospects also.

In discussions on that subject among workers the right voices predominate which argue that we must earn that future by increasing production and a higher labor output.

This does not mean that we cannot now solve some economic and social problems which had existed for a long time but nonetheless had not been dealt with owing to delays in our economic policy and the slow functioning of the bureaucratic apparatus in many sections of our administration.

Let's take, for example, the matter of wages. We have the category of the lowest paid workers who earn less than 500 zlotys a month.[13] This problem can and should be solved by raising these lowest wages, which will be done this year already.

Let's take the matter of raising the living standards. At first our Five-Year Plan envisaged an increase of some 25 percent in real wages for workers and employees. Now, after a discussion of the Plan in enterprises and after the great campaign to extract the reserves which our economy contains, it seems possible to plan an increase of some 30 percent in real wages.

In addition to the matter of increasing wages for the lowest paid workers, the questions of regulating wages in some sectors of the economy, of reform in the wage system that would increase the basic wage in relation to overtime pay and premiums, of raising the wages of some categories of workers in state administration, in education, and in health service (that was especially neglected in this respect) are also important.

Proposals are also being prepared for raising pensions during this and the next year, at least for those who had worked the last ten years in People's Poland, and who in many cases receive very low pensions. It is difficult to determine now whether in the next two years we will be able to give raises to all.

Let's take the matter of shortening the working hours. This matter will also be taken up by our economic organs. But it is clear that the possibility of shortening the working day to less

---

13 The official exchange rate of the zloty to the dollar is 4:1.

than eight hours is now even more limited here than in the Soviet Union. Therefore, changes in this direction will take place at a slower tempo. Of course, this is connected with the productivity of labor. But in Poland not only the possibility of shortening the working day to less than eight hours is concerned. We have the problem of an eight-hour working day which is systematically violated in many enterprises. A big effort on the part of our Party, trade unions, and the economic apparatus is essential in the near future to make sure that all enterprises strictly observe the eight-hour day.

A number of suggestions for the direction of our economy are being made. Work on removing excessive centralization in the direction and administration of economy has only begun and is proceeding slowly. For example, the proposed decree on widening the powers of enterprise directors has been under consideration for months, but to this moment it has not been passed. Similar delays occur in a number of other areas.

It is imperative that work on the solution of these problems proceed much more energetically.

At the same time, as we remove excessive centralization in the direction of the economy, we shall aim to improve effectively and genuinely the role of the Party organization in enterprises and to strengthen its influence on the life of the enterprise. The activity of trade unions should be strengthened. They should fight much more courageously and energetically for full observance of collective agreements, for a better fulfillment of workers' needs. The influence of local Party organizations on the state of the economy in their territory should also increase. For that it is not enough to change the relationship of the economic administration to Party organizations. Party organizations should also fulfill their duty. We must draw conclusions from what was said at the CPSU Congress on the insufficient connection of Party work with economic work. In this respect we have even more to make up. The relation of Party work to economic activity has always been not only weak but, above all, often incorrect, fitful, and superficial. Part of our cadres, and especially Party workers, are insufficiently prepared for these tasks. We have paid too little attention in Party teaching and propaganda to problems of political economy in industry and agriculture. Even less attention is being paid to a mastery of technical problems, technological progress, agronomy, and so forth. Before we can speak seriously about a better relation between Party work and industrial and agricultural economy we must devote all our energy to the removal of this negligence. We must approach these matters basing ourselves on learning, on our scientists, on the practical experience of our best engineers, efficiency experts, shock workers in industry and agriculture. Without doubt we can quickly effect basic improvements in this sphere of our work.

The 20th Congress was able to put forth new and bold ideas concerning the defense of peace and the possibilities of a peaceful transition to socialism. And it was able to trace new and vast perspectives of the further development of the USSR not only because of the fact that the might of the USSR has increased to date but because changes in the international situation as well had created the indispensable prerequisites. In order to put forth these tasks it was also necessary to break with all that which previously hampered policy, all that which hindered people and prevented them from fully developing their initiative. It was necessary to free people from old habits and clichés which used to arise in the past, and which, if not rejected in due time, constitute obstacles to the development of new, more active, and more effective forms of struggle.

It is generally known that, for more than two and one-half years already, the CPSU leadership has been working in this direction and has attained great success both in the international arena and in the internal development of the country. Suffice it to recall the plenary meeting of the CPSU Central Committee devoted to problems of agriculture and technical progress, the conference devoted to problems of building, the decisions on the increase of the prerogatives of local authorities in economic matters, and so forth.

The struggle for the elimination of old clichés and petrification, for the development of the initiative of the masses, for the development of critical and creative thought, which is being waged by the CPSU, is closely linked to the struggle undertaken by the CPSU with the greatest energy against that which gives rise to clichés and petrification, to the lack of criticism and the lack of the initiative of the masses, that is, with the struggle against the cult of personality.

How did the cult of Stalin come about? How could it happen that in a country basing itself on the Marxist-Leninist ideology, that is, an ideology which rejects all cults and all irrationalism, the cult of personality could develop in such dangerous proportions and could become such a burdensome influence on the life of the whole socialist camp?

After the death of Lenin, a sharp ideological struggle was waged against departures from and distortions of Leninism, as well as against the propagators of those distortions—the Trotskyites, Bukharinites, and bourgeois nationalists—and for the realization of the Five-Year Plans, for the industrialization of the country, for the collectivization of the Soviet countryside, and so forth. This was a struggle to insure the socialist development of the land of the Soviets. If during these years the anti-Leninist trends—of the Trotskyites or Bukharinites—had won out, the revolution would have been endangered, would have become impotent and helpless before imperialist aggression.

In this struggle Stalin played a great role. This became the foundation for the rapid rise of Stalin's prestige and popularity which Stalin abused in later years, putting himself above the Party leadership and the Party itself, and applying repressions instead of ideological struggle against adversaries, and later on against everyone who did not agree with his views.

The need for thorough research into the history of this past period in order to restore the historic truth about the Soviet nation, about the Party, about all that was great and creative during that period, as well as about the profound distortions, damage, and crimes which sprang from the cult of personality and from Stalin's errors was pointed out at the Congress. This will also create the possibility of a more profound analysis of the historical process and the whole complex of social and political conditions which contributed to the formation of the cult of personality.

The development of the revolution under conditions of its being besieged by hostile imperialist states, a revolution which in the shortest possible time had to transform backward, peasant Russia into a powerful, industrial state or perish, assuredly played not the smallest role in this respect. The transformation of Russia could be achieved only by way of tremendous sacrifices. It required severe and iron discipline. Stalin knew how to impose this discipline. But later on he abused his power, ceased paying any attention to the collective body, began to put himself above the Party.

The collective character of the Party leadership was steadily reduced and finally liquidated. This is manifested for example by the fact that only one congress of the Party took place between 1934 and 1952. For years on end no plenary meetings of the Central Committee were convened.

Then came the war with all its consequences, which even further strengthened the cult of Stalin. Stalin's contribution, as we know today, was intertwined during this period with heavy errors which cost the lives of many human beings. These painful losses were caused by the fact that the danger of Nazi invasion was not detected in due time, that indispensable precautionary measures were neglected, and that during the war a number of operations were carried out at Stalin's orders despite the opinion of military experts.

But we know about this today. Then Stalin was surrounded by a nimbus of "infallibility." He described himself as a commander of genius.

The cult of personality, which was developing before the war, and still more so during the years of the war, went together with the infringement of Leninist principles of Party life, led to the violation of the principles of democracy within the Party and in social life, to the stifling of criticism, to discrepancy between word and deed.

The cult of personality could not but cause, and did cause, the weakening of control over various organs of authority—both collective control from above on the part of the Party leadership, and of social control from below, coming from the people's masses.

In these conditions, degeneration of the security organs could and did occur. The security organs became independent of Party authorities and were utilized to consolidate the personal power of Stalin over the Party.

In this situation, many honest activists of the CPSU, who opposed Stalin in various matters, fell victim to the repression. Later on, repressions were used mechanically and blindly ever more often against Communists and simple Soviet citizens who seemed suspect. Methods of provocation were used; false accusations were forged; abuses took place during investigations in order to bring about the condemnation of the accused. As a result, many honest people were imprisoned, sent to penal camps, or shot.

The CPSU is, at the present time, reviewing these cases on a wide scale and is rehabilitating those who were condemned although they were innocent.

During this period also, and with the aid of false and fabricated accusations, the decision of the Comintern on the dissolution of the Communist Party of Poland was brought about.[14] Almost all leaders and activists of the Communist Party of Poland, then residing in the Soviet Union, were arrested and sent to camps.

A further provocation was, as late as after the war, the so-called Leningrad affair, in which, on the basis of forged documents, many leading activists of the Leningrad Party organization were accused of hostile activity and arrested. A similar provocation was the so-called doctors' affair [plot].

---

[14] See Document 1 in this chapter.

The pressure of these criminal methods was felt also beyond the borders of the USSR, causing distortions in the security organs of a number of people's democratic countries, leading to provocation on a big scale in the case of Yugoslavia.

One must say that these practices found their "justification" and support in the erroneous, anti-Leninist theory which Stalin was developing, the theory of the sharpening of the class struggle in the period of the construction of socialism.

Stalin formulated this theory in an extensive way at the March Plenum of the CPSU Central Committee in 1937, stating that, as the class enemy is losing ground under his feet in a country which is building socialism, he is passing to ever sharper methods of struggle, to diversion and terror. Of course, one cannot question the fact that the class enemy does not hesitate to use any means in the fight against socialism, but as experience shows, the stronger socialism is, the narrower becomes the social basis of the enemy and the more limited are his possibilities of action. This does not mean that the class struggle is dying away. The enemy does not yield; he only changes his methods and forms of struggle. In accordance with concrete conditions and our policy, breakdowns and new upsurges in this struggle can occur, but the alignment of class forces which is changing in favor of socialism cannot but influence the scope and character of this struggle.

This is taught by the experience of each of the countries building socialism. This is what our Polish experience has also taught us. It was difficult to reconcile the theory of the sharpening of the class struggle, invented by Stalin, with experience derived from life, with the objective evaluation of facts. And all attempts at imposing and applying this theory against life, against the facts, were bound to lead to distortions.

The narrow-minded and false identification, included in the theory, of espionage and sabotage activity, which constitute one of the forms of activity of the enemy, with the class struggle in general, that is, with a very many-sided struggle between opposing social forces in the field of economy, ideology, politics, and so forth, also led to distortions.

Stalin's morbid suspiciousness and his growing despotism, allowing not even the least objection, found expression in this theory. With the aid of this theory he wanted to justify the application of drastic measures of repression not only with regard to enemies and political adversaries but also with regard to persons representing merely different views.

Let us compare Stalin's theses pronounced in 1937 (that is, one year after his announcement that the Soviet Union had already built socialism) with Lenin's declaration of February, 1920 (that is, when the civil war raged in Russia and when the threat of Pilsudski's aggression hung over the country). Lenin said then in explaining the terror used by the Soviet authorities against the White Guards:

Terror was forced upon us by the Entente's terroristic activity, when the powerful states of the world sent their hordes against us and did not stop at anything in their fight against us. We could not have survived even two days had we not answered ruthlessly, that means through terror, the attempts of officers and White Guardists. However, we were forced to apply terror by the terroristic methods of the Entente. Immediately after a decisive victory, even before the close of the civil war, right after the seizure of Rostov we renounced use of the death sentence and thus we gave proof that we stand on our own program as promised. We hold that the use of force is dictated by the task of stifling exploiters, stifling large landowners and capitalists. When this task is completed, we will renounce all extraordinary means. We have proven that in practice.

The question is sometimes put as to why the leadership of the CPSU did not earlier, during Stalin's lifetime, take up the struggle against the distortion of Leninist norms and the mistakes committed by him.

As the cult of personality was developing, as Stalin placed himself ever more above the collective leadership of the Party and the Party itself, and as he started to make personal decisions on many issues, many Soviet comrades certainly found themselves confronted by a difficult dilemma: whether to take up the struggle or wait. But in the circumstances, when a stubborn fight was being waged for a correct Party line, when an enormous effort was indispensable to build up the country— and Stalin adopted a correct attitude in actual problems of socialist construction—the dangers stemming from the growing cult of personality were not yet fully visible. And later on, under conditions of fanaticism and terror against any attempt at opposition, which were the direct result of the cult of personality, could a struggle against the cult of Stalin be real and effective?

The point was not to save one's own life; the point was to save the revolution.

During the years 1934 to 1941, when the imperialists were preparing aggression against the Soviet Union with ever greater intensity, when any action against Stalin would have plunged the country into chaos and disorder, this could mean only one thing: to open the gates to the enemy, to open the road to imperialist aggression, to facilitate this aggression. Was it possible to take such a decision? Or was it rather necessary to grit one's teeth on seeing all the damage arising from the cult of personality, and, with a feeling of responsibility for the cause of the revolution, to fight and work for the growth of the strength of the socialist state, counting on the dynamism of socialism, on the strength of the Communist idea which can force its way through all distortions brought about by the cult of personality?

We know that the correctness of such a decision has been confirmed by history, that the hopes have been fulfilled.

In spite of the damages, distortions, and losses which arose in the atmosphere of the cult of personality, the land of the Soviets marched forward and radiated all over the world the greatness of its achievements. Industry was being built and education was being spread; the whole economy and social structure of the country was thoroughly transformed, and social- ism was built. Stalin had no small share in all this. But these transformations were not the work of an individual. They were the work of the Party, the work of millions of Soviet people who with admirable selflessness were implementing the Five-Year Plans, and then gave their toil and blood to crush the fascist invader and to defend the first country of socialism. It was they—the Soviet peoples and the Communist Party—who were the decisive factor in the liberation of Europe from the yoke of fascism. It is to them that the Polish nation owes its survival and the decisive assistance in the regaining of independence, and later fraternal help in postwar years.

In spite of the distortions and losses, the general balance sheet of the past period is victorious. Socialism triumphed in the USSR; one-third of mankind took up the work of socialist construction. The revolutionary movement in all countries, the liberation fight of the nations against imperialism, as well as the forces of peace in the world, have grown to unprecedented might.

How much greater will be the scope and might of the struggle for peace and socialism owing to the overcoming of the cult of personality and of all its harmful consequences?

We are all impressed by the vast prospects and the revolutionary strength which emanate from the 20th Congress of the CPSU. We are all impressed by the uncompromising attitude and courage which was shown by the leadership of the CPSU when they put forth in such a full and sharp manner the problem of the struggle against the cult of personality.

At the reception given for the foreign delegations during the Congress, Comrade Khrushchev said that the struggle against the cult of personality was by no means over. This struggle should last until all the remnants of the cult of personality are eradicated from the whole of the social life, from science and education, from literature and art.

We know that this is a difficult and complicated struggle.

Each of us speaks about this matter with bitterness. We were ourselves under the influence of the cult of Stalin. We developed this cult ourselves. The distortions arising from the cult of personality, from the infringement of the Leninist norms of Party life, went deep into life. They went deep into the life of our country as well. Stubborn, petrified bureaucracy, suppression of criticism, disregard for the needs and views of the people—these are only some of the phenomena which could become rampant in the atmosphere of the cult of personality and of the infringement of the principles of Party democracy. It is only too often that we can still meet the harmful consequences of this atmosphere—commandeering, intimidation, disregard for collective will. In this atmosphere servility and obsequiousness develop, as well as an automatic attitude of obedience to all "orders from above," an attitude of concealing truth, lack of independent thinking and initiative.

Owing to the struggle taken up by the CPSU against the cult of personality and all its consequences, the atmosphere in the Party and in the whole life of the Soviet Union had radically changed, as the delegates to the Congress pointed out. A true Party atmosphere was created, an atmosphere favorable for normal work. It has been a long time since political life in the Party developed with an intensity equal to that of the present. The militancy and initiative of Communists have grown. Their sense of responsibility for their own tasks and for the cause of the whole Party has become greater. Now, said the delegates, it can be said that work is really going on better.

Among the delegates to the Congress we noticed not only the feeling of great relief, as if they had been relieved of a great burden, but also a sense of tremendous inner force and self-confidence, a conviction that everything which was only an intention at the Congress would be implemented. This militant spirit prevailing at the Congress is undoubtedly an outcome of the great transforming work done by the leadership of the CPSU over the past two and one-half years.

How was this expressed in the development of Party work?

Delegates pointed out three basic problems.

First—restoration, from top to bottom, of the collective principle in Party work. At the Congress people mentioned with approval that the Central Committee strictly honors conditions favoring genuine collective work in the entire Party and shows an example of it itself. The meetings of the CC take place regularly. Consultations of the *aktiv* are frequent; there are opportunities for sincere statements, for sincere Party criticism of errors without any regard for the person involved. Care is taken to strengthen the cohesiveness of the collective on the basis of a principled ideological position, on the basis of reciprocity that will not permit either mutual amnesty or mutual ill-will.

Second—delegates pointed to the considerable effort already made in the Party to restore and develop intra-Party democracy. In this sphere also the Central Committee gives an example and renders help to the local Party organizations. People approved of the fact that the Central Committee widely draws the central and territorial *aktiv* into participating in discussion and work on various problems, that the meetings and deliberations of territorial activists take place regularly in the CC, that the territorial *aktiv* is being more frequently invited to the plenary sessions of the Central Committee.

At the same time, systematic and ample information for Party members and activists about all the more important matters on which the CC was working and about its more important decisions was being assured. This gives every Party member an opportunity to experience problems of the entire Party, hastens the improvement of the political education of Communists, and activates them.

There was also talk about strengthening the ties between the leadership of the Party and the "hinterland" through visits of the members of the Presidium of the CC CPSU to Party organizations and their direct meetings with workers and collective farmers. All this contributes to the creation of a new atmosphere in the Party, permits the strengthening of intra-Party democracy.

Third—the delegates stressed especially the fact that the Party leadership arouses the local organizations to a critical appraisal of their own work, introduces creative anxiety, encourages uninterrupted search for ways to improve Party work. They referred to the report in which the Central Committee called on the Party to develop general criticism and self-criticism, to fight with determination against self-complacency and conceit. In that report Comrade Krushchev said:

We would have avoided many shortcomings, against which we are struggling these days, if at other times in some Party circles the tendency to self-complacency and embellishing the actual state of affairs had not become widespread.

Struggle against all attempts at varnishing [dressing up] things and for courageously facing the truth and speaking the truth—this is what characterized the Congress.

Owing to the fact that the leadership of the Party listened to voices from local organizations, that it consulted Party activists, that it critically analyzed the state of affairs in various branches of the economy and of Party work, it was able to concentrate on the most important problems, to adopt a number of well-known, momentous decisions in the field of economy and politics, in the domain of Party and social life in the Soviet Union.

This does not signify that the struggle against various shortcomings and hampering factors in the development of Party and social life has been concluded. This is a difficult and complex process which is going on and will go on. The 20th Congress not only was the summing up of achievements, but, above all, it mapped out the road to the future.

The direction pointed out by the Congress is clear. It points toward the democratization of life, toward a speedier growth of cadres, toward the development of a genuinely Communist atmosphere in all Party life.

The appraisal of the results of the work of the CPSU in the course of the past two and one-half years, as well as the tasks defined at the 20th Congress, provide us exceptionally valuable and important material from which to draw conclusions, although we have achieved a certain improvement in our work after the Third Plenum.[15] This improvement, however, is insufficient and cannot satisfy us.

---

[15] Held in January, 1955.

The decisions of the Third Plenum, which undoubtedly were a great achievement of our Party in the struggle for the restoration of Leninist principles in Party life, were being implemented by us with the necessary energy and impetus required by this problem only in the first months after the plenum. Later on, there was a visible weakening of this struggle. One must simply admit that we had done too little to assure that the decisions of the Third Plenum would reach all the Party organizations; in many instances they were wholly or partly forgotten. We could not achieve this, namely, that the entire Party *aktiv,* in all spheres of our life, could with sufficient energy and conviction realize in its sector of work the decisions of the Third Plenum. That is why it is understandable that we now hear voices saying, "We need a Third Plenum for economy, we need a Third Plenum for the life of trade unions, for the work of youth organizations, for the work of people's councils," and so forth. Of course, we do not speak here of a plenary session. These voices convey the thought and desire that the spirit of the Third Plenum, enriched by the ideas emanating from the 20th Congress, penetrate every sphere of our life. We must, consequently and finally, overcome everything that slows us down in the development of the democratization of our life, in the development of criticism in our cadres, in the development of collective work in the leadership of our Party, and the methods of Party work from top to bottom.

In the justified struggle we conducted against elements of the so-called black pessimism and negation of our achievements, the main task—struggle for further democratization of our life— was often forgotten. At the same time we were not as energetic as we should have been in fighting the suppression of criticism and in reacting to critical voices. Our work was also burdened with some symptoms of defensiveness. What is important is that we were not merely insufficiently aggressive in removing obstacles along our path. What is more important is an offensive in the real sense of the word—the development of the Party's attack, meeting and settling the problems which life poses.

We have already spoken about a number of delays and short-comings in our economic life. The situation in culture and ideological work is similar. Often we were not the ones who first criticized existing shortcomings and weaknesses. Often this criticism was made by someone else or even against our will. At times criticism was made from a hostile standpoint which put us in a defensive position, even though we should lead the way in the struggle for the improvement of our work.

All this contributed to the fact that in the period which followed the Third Plenum a partial slow-up in the realization of its decisions took place. We did not succeed in developing either critical passion or creative enthusiasm to such a degree as our Soviet comrades did. Therefore, we should at present embark with all the greater energy on the task of overcoming the lag and shortcomings in our work, rallying the forces of the whole Party in the struggle for a more rapid development of the economy, for insuring a speedier improvement in the living standards of the working people, for an energetic and correct implementation of the decision of the Fifth Plenum of our Party concerning agriculture,[16] for imbuing all our activity with greater enthusiasm and militancy.

An indispensable condition for the implementation of these tasks is the strengthening of the leading role and mobilizing powers of our Party organizations.

The main effort in the work on the strengthening of the basic Party organizations should be directed to the development of Party democracy, unhampered discussion, and criticism of persons and institutions without regard to the post or rank. Only by following this road shall we overcome the bureaucratic tendencies which weigh upon Party life and hamper its development.

To this end we should, among other things, keep our Party members far better informed than before. Party members should be better informed about what the Party leaders are thinking and doing, so that the whole Party may become

---

[16] Held February 8-9, 1956.

politically more active. As we know, the dissemination of such information, particularly by word of mouth, was poorly organized among us. We can detect a difference between information and publicity in papers and magazines and oral information, to the detriment of the latter. The pronouncements of our numerous speakers and agitators are still often characterized by primitive schematicism, omission of difficult problems, and empty phraseology. But how can we have different results if we neglect to work with this *aktiv,* if we do not inform it systematically about different matters? This should be done by those comrades who themselves are best informed.

As for the social composition of the Party, there is a need, as great as was mentioned at the 20th Congress, to regulate it in such a way that only the best people—first of all, workers directly involved in production and peasants—would join. We do not want to depart from the task of numerically increasing the Party ranks, especially in the countryside. But we should, as was done at the 20th Congress, put greatest emphasis on the matter of quality, level of development, and ideology of the people who make up the Party organization.

We should seriously take up the matter of the quality of work of our Party *aktiv* and apparatus. When I use the term "Party apparatus" I know that it is not a particularly happy expression. At once it evokes comparisons with some more or less efficiently functioning office machine and not with associations of political workers, organizers of the masses. But we are not concerned with terminological comparisons. What matters is the actual situation, the practice in which some Party workers in reality often only fulfill orders, collect reports, and control administration.

We are being seriously confronted with having to train quickly and raise the qualifications of those Party workers who deserve to remain in the Party apparatus. The extent to which they were provided with teaching, correspondence courses, and the like in the past constituted only a beginning, although we have had visible improvement in this field. At the same time we should exchange some of the workers in the Party apparatus for people with higher qualifications, with better ideological and general background, as well as professional training in industry and agriculture.

The 20th Congress considered the reduction of personnel in the Party apparatus. For example, in the Central Committee of the CPSU the number of members was reduced by one fourth during the last two years. We should follow in their footsteps. Among Party workers surely what matters is not quantity but quality.

Our most important task in this sphere is to change the work of the *aktiv* and the Party apparatus in such a way as to liquidate increasingly bureaucratic methods of action so that our colleagues from the *aktiv* and from the Party apparatus can increasingly become genuine Party workers who can think politically, show initiative, are courageous in criticism, factual in stating problems, and are known to the masses.

The 20th Congress permits us to draw many useful conclusions for our Party propaganda. We should struggle much more energetically than hitherto for the improvement of our propaganda, for its liberation from the bonds of dogmatism. We must eradicate signs of schematism and clichés for good, we must fight to give propaganda a creative character, to bring it closer to life and to the people. We must render it into a task which aids people to think more and more independently, strengthens in them the feeling of responsibility for the present —whose cocreators they are—makes it easier for them to live better and with more culture, to work better and more effectively. Certainly we can obtain a substantial improvement in our Party propaganda while we are working on the materials of the 20th Congress.

The interest taken in the Congress by the Party and the nation is tremendous. It can be safely said that millions of people in Poland are actively reading and discussing materials from the Congress. That is why it is not necessary to relate literally or to summarize the Congress materials. It is necessary to start with the people a lively conversation about the problems touched by the 20th Congress, to answer thousands of questions and doubts which people have in connection with the 20th Congress. It would be incomprehensible if during such a momentous turn of events there were no questions and doubts. What is important is that people in Poland should master in the best possible manner this strong ideological weapon which the 20th Congress has given, that the ideas of the Congress should be creatively applied in Poland, that this wide offensive should be developed in accordance with the possibilities which have arisen. Let us imbue the people with the sense of this splendid revival, of this revival in the Communist movement, which the 20th Congress of the CPSU brings with it.

After the Third Plenum a phrase came into use. It stated that "the reeducation of the Party" is indispensable. We are conscious of that. We know that it is a difficult and complex process that will require much time and stubborn effort. Is it not clear that the 20th Congress of the CPSU with its great treasure of theoretical and political thought gives us new possibilities for a quicker, much quicker than before, education of Party members into real members of the Polish United Workers Party and Communists?

"The resolutions and recommendations of the 20th Congress" were again taken up by Edward Ochab, First Secretary of the PUWP, in an address before a conference of the Party *aktiv* of Warsaw.[17] He acknowledged the "painful and bitter truth about the mistakes of Joseph Stalin, in whom we [*sic*] saw the example of revolutionary virtues [and about whom] there were ardent words not only in our mouths, but in our hearts too," and admitted that:

> Together with the difficulties, shortcomings, and errors of our economic policy, there have been deviations weakening the alliance of the working class and peasants and the confidence of the masses in revolutionary legality. There have also been deviations

---

[17] *Trybuna Ludu,* April 7, 1956. Portions of Ochab's address were printed in *Pravda,* April 8, 1956.

in the activities of the security apparatus, which were a subject
of resolutions passed by the Third Plenum.[18]

While admitting past wrongs, Ochab tried to set a limit to permissible criticism and called attention

to the fact that some comrades seem to be losing their sense of
balance and are beginning to lose their sense of proportion
between justified criticism and actions from positions which
cannot be of advantage to the Party. There are people who in
public—and not through the Party—and in the press, come out
against the Party. This shows an unhealthy, anarchistic tendency,
the loss of a feeling of Party responsibility, and a confusion of
ideas.

Finally, Ochab dwelt at some length on a problem of special
importance to the Party, the case of Wladyslaw Gomulka and other
Communists who were purged between 1949 and 1953:

Obviously it has not been easy to perceive at once all the
machinations of Beriaism which for a number of years influenced
our security organs, cleverly utilizing sophistries that all methods
were admissible when dealing with an enemy, fabricating, in a
provocative fashion, accusations against honest people, including
meritorious members of the Party, about hostile activities against
People's Poland.

In the year 1954-55 the Party leadership has done much to
effect the release and rehabilitation of persons accused without
foundation, but the question as to why the rehabilitation proceedings in regard to a number of people were delayed in an
unfounded manner must be answered.

Undoubtedly the delay was influenced by the realization of
the Third Plenum of the theory that the authority of the Party
could suffer if it were made public that high Party organs, even
the Party leadership, had made accusations against people whose
real guilt had not been proved. It is clear that the Party's
authority suffered much more because of the insufficiently energetic rehabilitation process in cases where the basic accusations
once formulated by the investigating officers and the public pros-

---

[18] Even before the the Third Plenum met in January, 1955, the
Ministry of Public Security was abolished (December, 1954) and Stanislaw Radkiewicz, the Minister who had held the post since 1945, was
transferred to head the Ministry of State Farms.

ecution collapsed in the face of new facts revealing the grim methods applied by men of the type of Rozanski.

Filled with grief, we think not only about cases of groundless arrests of our Party comrades whom we have fully rehabilitated, but also about unjustified arrests of people whom we fought with justice as purveyors of nationalistic and opportunistic views, but whom we unjustly accused of diversionary activity and consented to their being arrested, by yielding to the theories on the unavoidable transformation of an opportunistic deviation into an imperialist fifth column and by succumbing to a spy complex.

Of great importance to the socialist development of the Party, to the Leninist education of the Party, was the struggle against the opportunistic and nationalistic deviation represented by Wladyslaw Gomulka. The Party declared a struggle against Gomulka's tendencies at a moment when the Party and the working class faced the task of the further development of socialist construction in Poland and the initiation of the socialist reconstruction of the countryside. This was also the period when the historic task of the realization of the political unity of the working class, the unification of the Polish Workers Party and the Polish Socialist Party on the basis of Marxism-Leninism, had to be dealt with.

Gomulka countered the Party line with a nationalistic appraisal of the traditions of the Polish workers' movement, maintaining that in the historical conflict between the nationalistic right wing of the PPS[19] on the one hand and the internationalistic SDKPIL (Social-Democratic Party of the Kingdom of Poland and Lithuania) and the CPP on the other hand, the PPS was right. He represented the striving to make a break with revolutionary tendencies of the heroic CPP and rejected Marxism-Leninism as the ideological basis of the future united Party. He tried to infuse the concept of a Polish road to socialism—correctly used by the Party—with a foreign content, which meant essentially the abandonment of the development of socialist construction in Poland.

When the Party took up the task of propagating cooperative farms in the countryside and the socialist reconstruction of the countryside, when in defense of the village poor it took steps to limit kulak exploitation, Gomulka came out against that policy of the Party, seeking to maintain the then existing social and economic structure in the country.

---

[19] Polish Socialist Party.

In an open and sharp ideological struggle, the Party defeated Gomulka's views. Gomulka was completely isolated. He did not submit to the will of the Party and increasingly adopted anti-Party positions. This is the political aspect of the correct struggle of the Party against Gomulka.

But it is worth declaring with great emphasis that Gomulka's arrest in 1951, which took place in the atmosphere created by Beriaism, in the atmosphere of the Rajk trial, was unjustified and without foundation. The accusations of diversionary activity advanced against him not only harmed him, but also misled public opinion. The struggle against abuses on the part of security organs started by the Party has led to Gomulka's being cleared of the accusations made against him. Gomulka has been cleared of these accusations and released. It must be stated clearly, however, that the correction of the injustice done to Wladyslaw Gomulka does not in any way change the correct content of the political and ideological struggle which the Party has conducted and continues to conduct against the ideological conceptions represented by Gomulka.

The Third Plenum of the Central Committee of our Party, noting the abuses which have taken place in the security service, has emphasized the necessity of correcting all the wrongs committed as a result of these abuses. As a result of a careful analysis of the investigation material, the appropriate authorities have released from arrest several dozen people whose innocence has been determined. As the same time, Party rehabilitations of those among them who previously were Party members and whose exclusion from the Party has turned out to be unfounded has taken place. In this connection the Party Control Commission, in the year 1954-55, restored Party membership rights to thirty-six comrades. At the beginning of last month, full Party rights were restored to comrades Szczesny Dobrowolski, Josef Kuropieska, and Waclaw Komar.

Comrade Komar was arrested on suspicion of antistate activities on the basis of accusations and materials which, in the course of investigation, have been proved to be unfounded and fabricated in a provocative fashion.

The then chief, as well as several officers, of the Chief Board of Intelligence of the Polish Army, who are responsible for the so-called case of Comrade Komar, have been released from their posts and criminal proceedings have been started against them.

In 1954 Comrade Komar, together with other groundlessly accused officers—Comrade Leder, Comrade Flate, and others— was released from custody and proceedings against him were quashed as being without foundation. Accusations made against Comrade Komar on Party grounds were fully withdrawn in connection with Comrade Komar's complete rehabilitation, including the return of his Party card.[20]

Problems relating to the Party membership of a score of people whose rehabilitation proceedings have not yet been concluded are still being considered by the committee appointed on the basis of the resolution of the Politburo.

I should like to deal shortly with the case of the former Deputy Minister of National Defense, Marian Spychalski, who was arrested on the accusation of criminal activities in the Polish Army and of diversionary activities. It was ascertained in the course of the investigations that no proofs of plotting or diversionary activities of Spychalski existed. On the other hand, he is undoubtedly responsible for breaking Party and Government directives. In this situation, the organs of justice did not regard a trial of Spychalski as justified. He has recognized his guilt toward the people's authorities and has been released from prison.[21]

I wish also to inform the comrades that, of those sentenced in the trial of Tatar and Kirchmayer and other former Sanacja officers,[22] the sentence imposed on Kirchmayer and Mossor has been reduced as an act of mercy and a break in the sentence has been granted them because of ill health. Those sentenced in that trial have made complaints about the behavior of investigation authorities and have requested a review of the trial. The complaints of the prisoners are now the object of detailed inquiries on the part of the public prosecution.

In several cases which followed the trial of Tatar and Kirchmayer, the violation of principles of the rule of law during investigation proceedings has been determined and, by a judgment of

---

[20] General Waclaw Komar was appointed to head the police forces under the Ministry of the Interior in August, 1956.

[21] General Marian Spychalski returned to high post in October, 1956, when he was appointed Deputy Minister and a short while later Minister of National Defense, replacing Soviet Marshal Konstanty Rokossowski.

[22] Sanacja was the name given to the Pilsudski regime in Poland.

the Supreme Court, the sentences have been canceled and over twenty officers released and rehabilitated.

Such, in short, is the present stage of the painful and difficult problems connected with the liquidation of the effects of Beriaism and the violation of the socialist rule of law. The directives of the 20th Congress give us an example of how, in a resolute and determined fashion, one must put forth before the Party difficult and painful problems if this is necessary for the determination of historical truth and for the Leninist education of Party members.

In April a series of personnel changes in the Government took place. They affected Stanislaw Radkiewicz (former Minister of Public Security and since December, 1954, Minister of State Farms), Stefan Kalinowski (Prosecutor General), Stanislaw Zarakowski (Military Prosecutor General), Henryk Swiatkowski (Minister of Justice), Wlodzimierz Sokorski (Minister of Culture and Arts), and Stanislaw Skrzeszewski (Minister of Foreign Affairs), all of whom were dismissed. At the same time, two former security officials, Roman Romkowski (former Deputy Minister of Public Security) and Anatol Fejgin (former Director of the Tenth [investigating] Department of the Ministry of Public Security), were arrested and it was announced that they would be tried on charges of violating socialist legality. (Another change carried out on March 30 involved Edmund Pszczolkowski, who was released from his post of Minister of Agriculture in order to head up the Committee for Public Security, created in December, 1954, when the Ministry of Public Security was abolished. Wladyslaw Dworakowski, the former head of the Committee on Public Security, was assigned to work in the Central Committee of the Party.)

Amid these personnel changes, the Sejm [National Assembly] met. Speaking before it, Joseph Cyrankiewicz, Chairman of the Council of Ministers, outlined the range of measures the Government contemplated introducing into Polish political and economic life.

5. ADDRESS BY THE CHAIRMAN OF THE COUNCIL OF MINISTERS, CYRANKIEWICZ, BEFORE THE SEJM, APRIL 23, 1956[23]

MAY IT PLEASE the house, at the opening of the present session of the Sejm I would like to discuss briefly a few matters which

---

[23] *Trybuna Ludu,* April 24, 1956.

seem rather important among the whole list—one can say, among a whole sea—of problems with which at present our Party, the whole nation, and, of course, the Polish Sejm are concerned.

It is an undeniable fact that the present session of the Sejm takes place in an atmosphere of unusual increase in political activity in Poland. It is obvious that one of the signs of this activity can be found in the proceedings of the various Sejm committees during the past few weeks. Those who listened to these proceedings or read reports on them have been deeply convinced that the new spirit in debates, discussions, criticism, and creative search has penetrated Polish parliamentarianism, just as it has penetrated the entire Polish nation.

This fact is proved by the sharp and pointed criticism made in the committees, the depth of the analysis made there. This also shows that there is an ardent desire to fulfill the duties which the Constitution places on the deputies of the Polish People's Republic and the Sejm.

If here and there one meets with accusations that this or that statement was based on incomplete knowledge of all facts and the whole matter, then what can we who are responsible for the work of the Government say if we did not know how to supply the deputies during the previous period with all the facts and information in our possession, facts and information which we often overjealously and unjustly guarded?

We can only say that our duty in the future will be to supply the Sejm, in accordance with the right principle of deepening the *nonsecrecy* of our political and economic life, the maximum of facts and the maximum information. At any rate, this does not concern only the nonsecrecy of political and economic life because this problem, the problem of nonsecrecy, is concerned, to a large degree, with the means of informing the entire nation. In the case of the Sejm, it is, in addition, concerned with the fact that if some collective body is to make these or other decisions—and the Sejm is called upon by the Constitution to do that—then all members of this collective must possess the facts and all elements for decision. Otherwise, all the decisions of such a body become mere formalities; it becomes a rubber stamp, a tribute paid to form, without consideration for the contents proper in the legal role of a law-giving body.

Therein probably lies the key of the problem of forming true collective decisions in all state organs, as well as in the Party, and not excluding the Council of Ministers. Collective decision does not depend on the number of participants or on the frequency with which this or that body meets. It can hold daily and well-attended meetings, and it will not be a collective body making decisions if it confirms or has to confirm this or that motion without each member having all the facts and elements from which the motion originates; that is, facts and elements for reasoning, for assuming real coresponsibility for matters, for discussion, on this or that decision.

Clearly, all this concerns the Sejm. But there still exists a matter decisive for the fulfillment of the Sejm's role; that is the necessity of frequent sessions, and moreover of sessions devoted to problems, and also the necessity of better organizing the Sejm commissions' work, both in making material more quickly available to them and in meeting more frequently. Then this will have sense. But as we know, this concerns not just the Sejm. It surely concerns the people's councils[24] on all levels whose meetings still have a formal character. It also concerns the Council of Ministers. We want to make and are making a serious effort, and with determination we are changing the previous state of affairs.

We already spoke about the sources of the previous state of affairs at the Third Plenum; the 20th Congress of the CPSU covered the matter completely, revealing the causes of distortions. It is clear, and I wish to emphasize this point, that subjective reasons for this exist and have grown as a result of our own attitude and our bad habits. Here, too, a determined struggle is required. Later, when I shall speak about the excessive centralization and about the jungle of instructions, I would like to say a few more words on that subject.

---

[24] Local government bodies.

In so far as the role of the Sejm, the role of Sejm discussion, and the work of the Sejm are concerned, the demands voiced by members of Sejm committees are certainly justified. Yet even in the future, when the amount of information supplied to it is as complete as possible, inadequate opinions or extreme proposals may be voiced in the discussion by individual participants. Then in any case the decisive part will be played by their growing individual and collective sense of responsibility for matters under discussion on which a decision is required.

That is why there is probably no one in Poland who has not the good of our Republic at heart, the good of continued, better building of socialism in Poland—which we all desire—who does not follow with joy this process of rapid maturing of our people's parliamentarianism and its growing up to the requirements of people's democracy in the best meaning of this term.

I think about this matter at this time both as a representative of the Government and as one of the deputies. There can be no doubt that these positive, favorable, and necessary phenomena which have recently taken place in the Sejm are directly connected with the great wave of political activity embracing our whole country. Only against the background of this wave and in relation to it are these phenomena understandable, and that is why they are obviously far from being some sort of preelection fever. On the contrary, they are undoubtedly a reflection and an expression of lasting transformations.

I repeat: lasting, because we still meet very frequently with fears, arising out of a basically subjective understanding of historical development, that this is some kind of "spring" proclaimed voluntarily, or a renaissance, or whatever one may call it, and that equally voluntarily somebody might decree the conclusion of this period. Without any doubt, conscious of the irreversible nature of this process of democratization of our life, of the inevitability of its continued development, we shall mould this process, this difficult and frequently painful and yet creative process, founded on faith in the sound common sense of the masses and on the best and most resolute understanding of our ideology, in a more conscious fashion. We will develop and deepen it without succumbing to the temptation to let nature take its course, taking full advantage of this splendid vitality of the increased activeness, criticism, and sense of political responsibility of the widest masses.

Essentially, the deep political activation of Polish society began during the time of our Party's Third Plenum, that is around February of last year.

Does it follow from that, however, that we all—Party leadership, the entire Party, the Government, the entire administration, and the great masses of the Polish nation—could properly shape and develop that process during the time that followed the Third Plenum? Surely not! On the Party's side, we shall take up these matters and evaluate that period at the Plenum of the Central Committee.[25] First of all we shall draw conclusions for our present and future work. We shall also evaluate the realization of the Third Plenum's decisions by the Government and by the state organs.

Undoubtedly, the evaluation of what caused the slowing down of political activation of the widest masses and also of the Sejm and the territorial representatives of the nation—the people's councils on all levels—is closely and substantially connected with that.

Without any doubt, we are at the start of a new, historical process of democratization of our political and economic life. It must be stated emphatically that this has assumed a particular and decisive form since the 20th Congress, and this is a completely understandable matter. The 20th Congress has become a turning point in the development of the countries of socialism, in opening new perspectives for different forms of struggle for socialism and different forms of building socialism all over the world.

------

[25] See Chapter III, Document 2.

The recognition of the role and decisive influence of the 20th Congress of the CPSU for all Communist and Workers Parties does not conflict, it is clear, either with the independence of these Parties or with the differences in historical conditions in which every one of these Parties conducts its struggle for power, or when the power is won, for socialism.

The role of the 20th Congress clearly stems from the importance that the existence and victorious advance of the first socialist state, of the first Leninist Party, building Communism in the Soviet Union, had and has for the prospects of building socialism, for the very building of socialism, for the struggle of the working masses to gain power and for the struggle to consolidate this power, for the further progress of socialism throughout the world.

The fact that no pseudoparliament of landowners, capitalists, and Sanacja bureaucrats, which represented pre-September Poland, is at present holding its debates in this hall, in this old, prewar building; the fact that as a result of the victorious war against Nazism our nation has been able, on the basis of the Russian Revolution, to carry through its own revolution; the fact that during the eleven years that have elapsed since the war we have been able at a great cost, true, and by the toil of the whole nation, to make good to no small degree the centuries-long retardation in our economic development (even if we were unable to avoid a number of mistakes about which we speak today openly and about which we shall speak while assessing the Six-Year Plan); the fact that today, while evaluating the present international situation and the prospects of its further development toward international *détente,* we can more calmly than before look into the future of our national existence which is unbreakably linked with the cause of peace and security; the fact that today we are able to deal in such an incisive way with our errors and to search for the best methods of combating them and overcoming the obstacles; the fact that in Poland today such a broad and sharp discussion is going on in the struggle to overcome all that has been hampering us in our onward march—all this is undoubtedly the result and proof of the close bond linking our revolution with the common stream of transformation and progress sweeping the whole world.

The first sources of this stream burst forth during the October Revolution; further life-giving sources are today spouting in all countries engaged in socialist construction and are breaking through the layer of obstacles and resistance in numerous countries of the entire world.

The phrases of "satellite countries," "satellite parties," coined by limited and hostile minds, are nonsensical. In point of fact, what we are witnessing is a converging of tributaries stemming from national sources to one great river of social transformation running throughout the world and whose beginning dates back to the Russian October Revolution.

That is why the 20th Congress of the CPSU is a turning point for us all which has laid bare the unhealthiness and the distortions that bothered our system against the background of the exaggerated cult of Stalin, against the background of the dictatorship of the individual, which broke the norms of democratic rule, norms inseparably linked with the very sense of the socialist system.

Our revolution is returning to the Leninist road; it is tearing off the crust of distortions which grew during the thirties and forties. It is strengthening the political activity of the widest people's masses, so characteristic in the epoch of the Great October. Without this activity there would have been no revolution, the main characteristic of which was drawing millions of people into the political life, into active politics.

The slowing down of this activity, its incomplete, often half-hearted formal expression, could not fail to stamp its sign on the whole period of which I have spoken, as well as on the various spheres of life. Experience has shown that the call for political activation alone is not enough; that this should not be a campaign, a short action, that it must not be just a façade. Political activation can be based solely on drawing the widest people's masses into the process of ruling the state and the construction of socialism.

And although political development in Poland took a somewhat different course than in the Soviet Union, it is clear that the harmful distortions connected with the cult of personality have also had effects here, on our work.

Through its analysis of the past and its directives for the future, the 20th Congress made possible and facilitated, also in Poland, the deduction of proper conclusions from the past and of proper lessons for the future.

The reaction of the Polish nation to the proceedings and decisions of the 20th Congress shows that it understood rightly the meaning of the event. The healthy wave of criticism, the increased volume and the basic direction of discussions at Party and non-Party meetings, the discussions in the press—the whole great debate, in which practically all of us are participating—proves that a never-ending, national conference of political activists on the problems of socialism is taking place.

A characteristic feature of this discussion is the fact that it is accompanied by unprecedented intensification of political thought, as well as the fact that the political activists taking part in it are much more numerous than ever before. Simply, the time has come when every enlightened citizen becomes an activist, and not this or that man put forward by this or that body. I think that a measure of the maturity of our nation can be found in the range of these discussions, the mass character of this singular political debate.

Here and there in this debate improper words and incomplete thoughts, awkward formulations, and hasty conclusions can be heard. Could it have been otherwise? Can one expect that such a shock can be absorbed in twenty-four hours, that it can be expressed readily in correct, reasoned, faultless political formulae? It is not the single words or statements nor the unfortunate expressions that are authoritative but the general direction of the debate and the atmosphere it has created.

It is quite clear that this does not absolve anybody from the duty to oppose false opinions in sincere, quiet discussions, in polemics, and to oppose attempts to undermine our basic ideological principles.

Of primary importance, however, is the fact that there is taking place a deep process of political activation of society in which the people become increasingly active and increasingly conscious in the creation of the system which we are building.

Never before, despite all the pain of the present stocktaking of the past, of the distortions of the past—never before has socialism been so strong in Poland as it is now. Never before has it had such deep roots in the consciousness of the masses. Never before has it been to such a degree the unequivocal aim of the aspirations of the people, an aim realized by all. We remember, of course, that in contradistinction to the Soviet Union, in our country the debate is taking place in a class society, in a society where class antagonism still exists and where the class enemy is undoubtedly still active, the class enemy who could not be true to his nature if he did not count on profiting from this process and did not make endeavors in this direction.

It is turning out, however, that in this new atmosphere the enemy's activity is probably more difficult than before. Not only because the objective social processes connected with the building of socialism have already advanced so far that the enemy's base of action has eminently shrunk. This, of course, is of exceptional importance. But also important is the fact that, in the atmosphere marked by political activation—when in the course of this great debate our political armor is becoming more perfect, the maturity of the masses is certainly growing at a double rate, while complexes and grievances are being revealed (and thanks to this can be overcome)—the enemy is finding it increasingly more difficult to operate, more difficult than at the time when much discussion was taking the shape of an undercurrent, as it were.

Of what importance are such or other insinuations, slanders, gossip, whispering campaigns, and intrigues at a time when all of us are openly exposing and baring all shortcomings and errors, indicating their sources, when we are searching for these sources and have started to remove them with determination?

Of course I do not want to imply that we should ignore the class struggle taking place in Poland. Certainly not. I only want to state that we are today better armed to conduct it more effectively than in the past despite the fact that the false theory about the sharpening of class struggle commensurately with the development of socialism reigned among us.

We must add that the first attempt to deal with that theory in Poland was the Third Plenum, at which distortions in the security organs and the ideological sources of these distortions were discussed.

Overestimating the enemy's strength is as harmful as underestimating it. The application of Marxist analysis is always better than directing oneself by *a priori* hypotheses, which have not been and are not being tested in action.

Since we are talking about our political opponents, let us briefly consider their evaluation of the events taking place in Poland for this purpose. I shall take one émigré opinion.

On the whole, the émigré politicians, involved in the comic struggle of the two émigré governments, are not distinguished by shrewd or incisive political thought—quite the contrary. Nevertheless, in the opinions of people not directly involved in this comic strife, one can at times find interesting statements. Among those one can count the article of Mr. Juliusz Mieroszewski, in the April, 1956, issue of the Paris *Kultura*.[26]

Evaluating the course of recent events in Poland, the author reaches very significant conclusions. Here are some characteristic sentences from his article:

"I watch with anxiety the course of the 'thaw' in Poland," writes Mr. Mieroszewski. Why with anxiety, we ask. Mr. Mieroszewski answers:

"There is a struggle for the widening of freedom so that one can be a better Communist." Not a bad diagnosis. Truly, the fight which we proclaimed against the survivals from the epoch of the cult of personality, the fight for democratization

---

[26] A publication of a group of Polish political exiles.

of our political life, for that which Mr. Mieroszewski calls the widening of freedom, is conducted in Poland so that we can be better Communists, so that we can better build socialism. And Mr. Mieroszewski feels anxious about this. And not only about this; he feels even more anxious about the fact that even non-Marxists in Poland take the same stand as the Marxist. I cite:

Even those who would like to "reform" Marxism and choke with the ferment which for years had no way of expressing itself, even those who with characteristic speed want to utilize the "thaw" in order to discard all that oppresses them—never and in no way transcend the limits of "People's" Poland. Speaking simply, these people believe that something will result from that discussion. Things are bad, there is a housing shortage and thousands of other shortages, but something will result from that. From that and not from anything else.

Thus, Mr. Mieroszewski with his diagnosis takes away hope from the émigré reaction for an excessive exploitation of the process which is taking place among us.

It would be difficult to find a more precise expression of the bankruptcy of the entire Polish reaction. Until recently it deluded itself that in Poland people with non-Marxist views— and there are *very* many of those—are against socialism, but they cannot express it. And today, Mr. Mieroszewski writes, these people participate freely in the "thaw" as he calls it, and it is clear that they believe only and exclusively in a People's Poland. They want to improve it in this or that way.

Today in Poland the term "thaw" naturally evokes increasingly more compassionate smiles. The time for meteorological discussions have passed. Analogies and metaphors based on the four seasons of the year are out of date. This year spring is late, frost comes daily in April, and in no case can we apply these occurrences to the political life of the same month. The process of restoring Leninist norms to the political life of our Party and our country simply continues. This indicates a striving for a consistent democratization of our life, for the liquidation of all consequences and remnants of the preceding period, the period of the cult of Stalin, and of all negative phenomena connected with that period, such as "Beriaism," hampering the freedom of the development of culture and art, hampering the initiative of the people's masses, the bureaucratization of many of our state institutions. This is the direction of our march forward, clearly seen by ever broader circles of the community. This is a direction from which there is no turning back, which is not a "thaw," the direction of the further construction of socialism and of consolidating the principles of Marxism-Leninism.

In connection with this line of development toward fuller democratization of our life there is also the problem of the Sejm. The Constitution describes with sufficient precision the role of the Sejm. But it would be naive to deny that the Sejm, despite some effort, has not properly discharged its constitutional functions, or discharged them only in a fragmentary way. It is not accidental that the Sejm began to fulfill that role only during the recent period, during these days. It is one more proof that the democratization of political life is a slow, hard process wherein society and institutions mature. Today we have conditions enabling this process to proceed with increasing speed. The Sejm is without doubt more fully assuming the role allotted to it in the Constitution.

Discussion in the Council of Elders on the proper role of the Sejm was a very weighty event which can aid us in searching for the right solutions to the cooperation of the Government with the Sejm. For we must admit that in these matters we do not have any experience or any Polish parliamentary traditions. Although Polish parliamentarianism has a centuries-long existence, we must admit our shortcomings in this field due to historically understandable circumstances. The period of the partitions put an end to all state institutions, and the interwar period surely did not favor the formation and development of democratic institutions. Sanacja destroyed with particular fury Polish parliamentarianism. And even if Polish parliamentarianism did have a tradition behind it, it could not be mechanically copied in People's Poland. Our state, being a people's democracy, has a different class structure. The people's representatives have entirely different functions to fulfill. These functions are no less than in the classic lands of parliamentary democracy. On the contrary, the abolition of the class rule of the bourgeoisie created the proper conditions for a real development of representative institutions. But—I stress—only conditions. For it would be a mistake to think that the mere fact of the existence of a new class setup predetermines that a perfect popular democracy—perfect also in its parliamentary expression—will arise any day.

Today we are beginning to work out proper forms and proper practice. We want the Sejm really to become what a constitutional Sejm should be: the supreme legislative organ, supervising the activity of all lower state organs. We have seen in the practice of Sejm committees of the latest period that considerable efforts are now being made to enable it to fulfill this role.

I realize that this does not depend solely on the will of the Sejm and of the deputies, although the importance of the proper attitude on the part of the deputies should not be taken lightly. It is they who are above all responsible for carrying out their duties to the Sejm and to the electors. But if the Sejm is to function appropriately, it is necessary for the other state organs to adopt the right attitude toward it.

Above all this concerns the correct attitude of the Government toward the Sejm. It has to be said that in the past these matters did not look well, and this was not the fault of the Sejm. Without doubt too large a part of the legislative processes took the form of issuing decrees. The Sejm was called for short, too short, and too infrequent sessions, and in these conditions it had to limit itself to endorsing decrees without being able to analyze and discuss them fully. This, I think, was a subject of concern expressed at yesterday's Sejm committee. Obviously there have been and will surely continue to be cases demanding that decrees be issued quickly, but it would be contrary to the truth to say that decrees in the past were issued in this matter in such cases only. Without doubt, in the future it will be necessary to put an end to the practice followed to date whereby the vast majority of legislation took the form of decrees undiscussed by Sejm committees, although recently we made some efforts to base certain decrees on a wide expression of opinion. It should be the rule in principle that laws are passed by the Sejm, and the issuing of decrees the exception only when it is really required by the work of the state.

It is clear that an equally important factor in strengthening the rule of law is the performance by the Sejm of functions of control over organs of the executive authorities, control over the actions of the Government. But here, too, if the Sejm is to fulfill this important function, deputies have to have access to sources of information, and in this matter things were not well in the past. In general, we did not favor and did not facilitate providing the Sejm with required materials, or these were not provided to a sufficient extent. And there were even cases of obstructing efforts to find the relevant information. The Government intends to put an end to these evil practices. Cooperation with the Sejm will be, and must be, imperative for all state authorities.

The case is similar with regard to intervention on the part of deputies. These were frequently treated as troublesome importunities, disturbing the proper course of official events. Not infrequently the duty of replying to complaints was neglected in an inadmissible manner, and contrary to binding principles. Deputies' statements were treated lightly. An end must be put to these evil practices, and the Government will see to it that deputies' inquiries are treated by state organs to which they are directed in a correct manner. This also applies to interpellations made by deputies.

The strengthening of the rule of law continues to occupy and must naturally occupy the center of the attention of the Government. On the whole we have already carried out the reform of problems of security and the administration of justice since the Third Plenum. After the revelation of serious distortions in the organs of security and information, they have been reorganized and reduced in size. The leadership of the Ministry has been placed in the hands of a collective organ—the Public Security Committee.

Owing to the fact that the most serious distortions in the course of the past years took place in the field of investigating methods and that the problem of insuring that this sort of practice should not recur is arousing understandable and justified concern in the community, particular attention was paid to the verification and selection of the cadres and to the working out of a system guaranteeing strict observance of the rule of law and preservation of the rights of persons under investigation. Proper supervision by prosecutors has also been insured in this field. May I recall the regulations adopted here, modifying the previous ones in this direction.

The effectiveness of these means is the subject of daily concern of the supervising authorities and of the Government. There is no doubt that in the future, too, the vigilant reaction of public opinion to each violation of binding laws and civil rights can be of great assistance.

The Government is determined to carry to the end the investigation concerning those guilty of breaches of the rule of law, of applying illegal investigating methods, and of concocting trials. Those guilty will be handed over, together with evidence, to the organs of justice and will suffer deserved punishment.

This will be not only a just settling of accounts with the past but at the same time a warning for those who could at any time be tempted to violate again the rule of law and civil rights guaranteed by the Constitution. Permeated with a new spirit, the organs of public security are carrying out a hard and selfless struggle against the enemy, and we must all remember that. The diversionary and espionage centers have not weakened at all. A proof of this is the continuous sending to Poland of agents, spies, and diversionists, as well as the fact that they are being caught.

During 1955 organs of security liquidated a number of espionage networks. A total of 123 agents of foreign espionage were arrested, some of whom had been sent to Poland from espionage centers abroad. Their court trials are known from the press.

In 1955 the organs of security also liquidated the remnants of armed gangs and underground groups, whose terrorist and diversionary activities, although small, have been prolonged over many years, and whose activities and the failure to apprehend them was felt by citizens of some parts of the country.

Many murderers of past years have been apprehended, such as those who killed Semezyk, a member of the executive of the Polish United Workers Party district committee; Szymczakowski, an activist of the Poznan province Committee of the Polish Youth Union, murdered in June, 1955; Wiosua, the leader of the Siemiatycze district people's council. Recently there have been many cases of persons who have been in hiding because they had committed various crimes and offenses giving themselves up to the authorities. This is an expression of confidence that the authorities will deal with them justly if they give up their criminal past. There is no doubt that thanks to the reorganization that has been carried out, the security organs, with the support of the nation, scrupulously observing the principles of socialist legality and under control in this respect, will more effectively carry out the difficult and selfless struggle against espionage and terrorist activities aimed against People's Poland. An important step on the road leading to the just administration of justice is the draft bill on amnesty which has been submitted to the Sejm and which will be debated during this session.[27] This bill is an expression of our conviction that with the progress and development of socialist construction, with the strengthening of our people's state, we can decrease repressive means against those who once during the period of sharp class struggle worked against the revolution, against the people's rule. These

---

[27] The bill was passed and according to official Polish sources tens of thousands of people were affected by it.

persons, for the most part, have undoubtedly undergone a change of heart and we should make it possible for them to return to normal life. They will find themselves even today in the midst of a community which is more apt to educate them into good citizens.

The amnesty is of a very wide scope, corresponding to our appraisal of the strength of the people's state and the possibilities of exercising influence through it by political and educational means.

Yesterday, deputies voiced concern whether those freed as a result of the amnesty would find adequate conditions, whether they would be surrounded with adequate care. The Government is calling into being a special commission which will be composed of the Minister of Labor and Social Welfare, of representatives of the Prosecutor's Office, of security authorities, and of the Ministry of Justice. This commission, together with its counterparts in the provinces, will be responsible for this work—a rather difficult work affecting a great number of people leaving prison. To prevent any misunderstandings I would like to underline that the amnesty does not signify that we wish in any way to slow down the rehabilitation process with regard to persons who in the past have fallen victims to provocations, lawlessness, violations, and undeserved abuse.

We have already carried out the revision of a whole list of such cases. Imprisoned persons have been released and rehabilitated. A number of cases in courts have been dismissed, and a number of others are under consideration and will be dealt with in the near future. Everyone who has a valid reason has the possibility of demanding rehabilitation. I should like to emphasize here that the tasks of reviewing certain cases must also be carried out with greater precision than before on the spot, in the provinces where such cases exist, although they perhaps may not be covered by the articles pertaining to the most serious cases, those with which the Warsaw organs of justice were dealing. In any case it must be stressed that the organs of justice will do everything to restore honor and civil rights, and, if humanly possible, to compensate people who were unjustly sentenced and unjustly subjected to reprisals for the wrongs done to them.

The foremost place among economic tasks now facing us is undoubtedly occupied—and we all feel this—by the problem of raising the living standards of the working masses in Poland. We have recently made some steps in this field by increasing the lowest wages and by the increase in pensions now being introduced. These, however, are the first steps which eliminate immediately the most serious of the sore points. We realize that there are numerous groups of employees and workers who during the Six-Year Plan did not experience at all, or only to a minimum extent, an increase in living standards, and there are those whose wages lagged behind the movement of prices. We will seek to include these groups, first of all, in the proposed increase in earnings. It must be realized, however, that this problem is not a simple one.

Work is at present in progress on the Five-Year Plan. This work is being carried out by a fairly wide Party and state *aktiv,* and is supplemented by the extremely valuable discussion and numerous proposals put forward by hundreds of enterprises which have been brought into the drafting of the Five-Year Plan. At the foundation of this plan lies the striving to raise the living standards of the country, on the basis of the further development of industrial and agricultural production. We want to achieve in the five-year period—and the plans are redrafted in this direction—an increase in the average real per capita income of the agricultural population. It is not an easy task. At the same time we lay down foundations for a considerable increase in the housing program.

During this drafting of the Five-Year Plan we must use as a basis the experiences of the Six-Year Plan, and a critical appraisal of the achievements and mistakes committed during the drafting and implementation of this plan, mistakes which, as we well know, had a negative influence on the increase in agricultural output and the pace of increase in the standard of living.

The key matter in this deliberation is the assurance of correct proportions in the development of all the sections of the national economy, and the elimination of those disproportions which now appear and are the source of our serious difficulties.

The most serious disproportion which is now hampering the implementation of our tasks lies in the insufficient agricultural output. The tasks in the increase in agricultural production and the socialist reconstruction of the countryside decided upon at the Fifth Plenum of the Central Committee of the Polish United Workers Party are the basis of the new Five-Year Plan for the development of agriculture.

As for the development of industry—here the basic tenet of the plan is naturally the strengthening of the raw material supply for our industry, the fullest utilization of the production potential created during the Six-Year Plan; that is, savings in investments, development of production potentials with the help of technical progress. The new Five-Year Plan must, of course, be based to a considerably greater extent than the previous one on technical progress. Guided by these principles we envisage the highest pace of increase in investments in agriculture, the housing program, communal and social building. A comparatively slower pace is envisaged with regard to the investments in industry, which are to insure a growth in the output of means of production and in production of the means of consumption.

With such plans, the personnel of industrial enterprises, engineers, and technicians will face tasks of extreme responsibility. To a large degree the successful fulfillment of the Five-Year Plan for the development of industry will depend on their initiative, resourcefulness, and discipline.

In making up the plan we have difficulty, among other things, in finding full assurance for its fulfillment. Therefore we amass economic reserves while fulfilling the plans. For the lack of supplies, or their insufficient amount, is being very painfully felt today. Take for example the February frosts, when the low level of coal reserves in the beginning of the year created a difficult situation in many sectors—railroads, industry, and the population. Already in the current year we want to increase coal reserves in industry, transportation, and shops. But at the same time we must remember that during the cold weather we have used too much coal in industry and transportation and that forced us to decrease this year's planned export by at least a million tons. It is clear that if we are to increase our reserves when the balance is so slight, each enterprise has to fight systematically to save coal and to make up the amounts used in excess last February. Naturally, the fulfillment of plans for coal extraction is also indispensable.

What other difficulty do we have to face in making the Five-Year Plan? The payments on loans made during the previous period for economic development fall due during the time of this plan. The implementation of our present tasks will demand incomparably better management, full utilization of all reserves, and a stubborn struggle in every field of life for the best economic results. The tightening of economic cooperation with the countries of the socialist camp and the coordination of planning can become a fairly important factor in the implementation of our tasks, a factor of great assistance to us. What we say about saving and finding reserves applies also to a struggle, better conducted than hitherto, with the growth of bureaucracy in industrial administration, construction, transport—a struggle to make the overgrown administrative apparatus smaller. This year, as announced already by Comrade Ochab at the meeting of the Warsaw *aktiv,* we are carrying out an adjustment of wages, which will cover 3.4 million workers and employees and will mean for them in a year an increase of 5 billion zlotys.[28] We have already adopted decisions on regulating wages of agricultural workers engaged in field work. As I have already mentioned, we have decided to raise the minimum monthly wage to 500 zlotys for 200 work hours. A number of further decisions on wages will be taken up by the Council of Ministers before the end of the year. Projects for wage regulation are being prepared with the wide participation of trade unions and economic activists.

---

[28] See *Trybuna Ludu,* April 7, 1956.

I would like to announce that the indispensable steps to put an end to the system of overtime, still excessively used in industry, will be undertaken. In accordance with the resolutions of the Fifth Plenum, the Government adopted a number of measures to increase the interest of peasants in the expansion of agricultural production. The increase in the prices paid for livestock has encouraged peasants to expand stockbreeding and is increasing the income of peasant farmers. The reduction in certain excessively burdened districts of compulsory deliveries from the harvest of 1956 should also contribute to the economic development of these areas.

An important role in the development of the productivity and earning power of the producer cooperatives, I think, should also be played by Government decisions assuring preferential treatment for producer cooperatives in the computation of compulsory delivery obligations, reduction in payments made by cooperatives for POM [State Machine Station] services, and stockbreeding premiums. These decisions, adopted on the basis of resolutions of the Fifth Plenum, are expressions of the Government's concern for providing assistance and creating incentives for the continued struggle for the transformation of the Polish countryside to socialism.

The increased production assistance, both for producer cooperatives and for individual farms, should contribute to an increase in agricultural production, particularly in connection with the previously discussed incentives.

So one could say that during the current year the state appropriates means—modest when we consider our needs, but substantial when we consider our economic capacity—for the improvement of workers' and employees' wages, for the improvement of the peasants' income, and for the creation of incentives to raise agricultural production, so indispensable to assure a food supply for the cities.

In decisions on raising wages and on the necessary incentives for agriculture, we are assuming that resources allocated to these purposes will in fact be made available in thousands of work establishments in accordance with the guiding lines of this year's plan, and that the economic campaigns in agriculture will be correctly executed on producer cooperatives, on state farms, and on individual farms. We furthermore base ourselves on the second assumption that we cannot permit expenditures on other aims to exceed the planned limits, on purposes undoubtedly important but not more important—unless somebody can prove they are—than the problem of raising wages.

This was what the Government had in mind when it submitted the draft budget, drawn up along these lines. The economic aims which I have briefly discussed are most certainly completely realistic, but at the same time they are not easy, and they will demand a great mobilization of the entire community and will require a change in the climate of opinion within our whole economy. What factors can contribute to an improvement in this climate? For one, the steady perfecting of material incentives through the correct determination of wages and premiums which so far have often been shaped in an improper way. We have to tackle this with exceptional energy if we wish to break both resistance and bad habits.

The second element in this change in the climate of our economy should be improving, the struggle for improving, at all levels of the economy, the system of management, the drastic cutting of excessive bureaucratic staffs, and the reliance in this struggle on the initiative of the masses.

It seems that the matter of initiative is one of the key questions of our life. The past period, the period which was in considerable part one of administering people, bossing them about, a period often of inflexible hierarchies, in which every higher level was infallible in relation to the lower level, this period did not favor the development of the initiative of the masses, but stifled it, nullified it. People sometimes talked and criticized, but lost all desire to act because they did not see any results. This also had a deadly influence on the development of economic processes, because here the bureaucratization of the administration, the ossification of minds produces singularly dangerous results, although they are dangerous everywhere. Against this background, the cult of incompetence arose, thoughtlessness and conservative approach grew, criticism and a sense of responsibility disappeared, servility, fear of taking decisions, the desire to play it safe flourished, and this centralization also had its sources from below; that is, people who themselves did not want to make decisions tried to get an alibi from the highest rung. Of course, at times this reached even the Government's Presidium. It reached, if we must go into details, grotesque proportions. It reached the point, as our fellow delegates testified at one commission, when cookies, tarts, and cakes were being authorized by a hierarchy of officials who in no case could have any knowledge in this field. It results from that attitude: "I must have it O. K.'ed." I read with joy in the minutes of that commission that the matter of the cookies did not reach the Presidium. But it might have.

We must liberate people from fear of adopting decisions, and strengthen in them the feeling of responsibility for the decisions adopted. We must return to the initiative of the masses, give them an opportunity for expression, and we must create a climate for its development. Here lies also the immense importance of the great invigorating flow of discussion which is now spreading in Poland, from the point of view of our economic life. Political consciousness is an integral part of the development of the initiative of individuals and masses. Political activation of the greatest masses will bring a rich harvest in the economic sector, for it is there that people create daily in their work these values. The man who feels an increasingly greater personal responsibility for the policy of the whole state will surely feel increasingly responsible for his assigned work, for his shop, office, workroom, for his creative literary workshop.

Here is where the understanding of our efforts—in this case economic efforts—lies. Only a politically conscious man, who has the opportunity to speak up, to criticize, and who knows that this criticism will not be a voice in the desert, only such a man can show the proper initiative, be a socialist worker, in the real sense of the word, a real co-worker in the material enrichment of his people's homeland.

The open character of public life is an integral part of democratization. We will strive and are striving to widen the scope of information available to every citizen. We will inform the press and radio in a better, wider, and perhaps speedier manner about the decisions, ventures, and plans of the Government in order to enable public opinion to obtain a better picture in matters of home and foreign politics, as only a well-informed citizen can carry out his civic duties in a more responsible and efficient way. The responsibility for properly informing the country lies, of course, chiefly with the press. It must be stated that despite some slips or mistakes the press is carrying out this task better and better and has made considerable progress, especially in recent times. This can be measured by the steadily increasing interest in the press and the immense growth in the numbers of its readers.

Undoubtedly it is necessary to continue the effort of the Polish press and writers on public affairs in the field of informing and shaping of public opinion, in the sphere of struggle for the democratization of our life in the field of just and severe criticism of shortcomings, mistakes, and distortions, doing all this in a more mature and universal manner. We know that the criticisms in the press do not always find the right response on the part of the organs of state administration and the economic apparatus. The Government will try to make press criticism more effective. The Government will seek to make available to the press sources of information within the widest possible limits, will fight unjustified resistance, will liquidate attempts on the part of various organs to hide themselves behind falsely interpreted official secrecy, because in this field, too, we have committed a great many mistakes by widening unnecessarily the scope of this secrecy. I think that for the purpose of establishing closer contact between the work and the plans of the Government, on the one side, and the press, radio, and public opinion, on the other, it would perhaps be desirable to introduce regular press conferences attended by the Chairman of the Council of Ministers—of course, if the press representatives express a wish for this.

A very urgent problem which has been often raised at meetings of the Council of Ministers and of the Sejm committees, illustrated with incredible examples, is the excessive centralization of management in the administrative and economic apparatus. There is such an excess of orders issued by all of them that there are few people who can make head or tail of them. Undoubtedly, in the work of the Government, the State Economic Planning Commission, the Ministry of Finance, and other ministries of functional character, in previous years serious shortcomings and distortions emerged, consisting in excessive centralization and bureaucratic overgrowth of their activities. Similar tendencies have occurred to a varying degree in the other ministries. They have also assumed a very acute character in relations between ministries, as well as in relations between central boards and enterprises, between ministries and people's councils.

These harmful tendencies have found particular expression in the overdeveloped, uncoordinated activity in the realm of administrative regulations. The number of the Presidium's decisions, orders, dispositions, circulars, and all kinds of administrative acts issued by various ministries, especially by the State Economic Planning Commission, Finance Ministry, and construction ministries, has grown to tremendous proportions. The too frequent changes in these rules—and these have not always been changes for the better—have not been followed by appropriate codification, which would have at least annulled the preceding rules, reconciled those that conflicted, and introduced appropriate simplification. It is clear that the evaluation and legal control of the issued rules had been and is failing. The rules are too detailed and do not leave any room for the development of initiative.

In the central office in Warsaw everybody thinks himself wiser than in the provincial office and wants to give a prescription and to lead by the hand. In the provincial office everybody things himself wiser than in the county office and does the same. That is a malady of which we have not yet been cured.

Frequently these regulations are not adapted to local conditions. Finally, and this is the most serious error, such regulations are not properly elaborated and not tried out previously in some work establishment or in some province or district so as to have some practical experience behind them. Indeed, excessive centralization and bureaucratic distortion constitute no doubt a counterpart to the distortions, errors, and shortcomings ensuing from the infringements of the principles of democracy, from the inadequate democratization of social life, and from inadequate bonds between the state apparatus and the masses. However, it would be a search for a new alibi if every bureaucrat now started to explain in connection with all his previous work—for instance, a man who explained in manuals that a door was an opening through which one went out and that a window was an opening through which one looked out, or a man who issued regulations explaining how to stop a taxi cab, how to stand on the pavement, how to lift a hand and which hand—if everyone of them now explained that all this was connected with the cult of personality. Perhaps it is simply ordinary stupidity and we must look for that. And this door should be the opening through which they make their exit from the state apparatus. (*Applause.*)

Now, no doubt, selection could and should be better, for in view of the openness and in the face of sharp criticism, the chances of the overzealous and pliant people are smaller than during last year. The question arises—how were we fighting against this? Undoubtedly, during the past year, several measures aiming at an improvement of this situation have been adopted. The commission set up by the PUWP Central Committee and by the Council of Ministers has submitted several projects aimed at transferring some of the authority exercised at present by the Presidium of the Government, the State Economic Planning Commission, the Ministry of Finance, and by the State Staff Allocation Commission, and at transferring some of the authority exercised by the Government and by individual ministries to the provincial people's

councils. Certain changes and simplifications have been carried out in the methodology of planning, especially in agriculture. The same applies to reduction in the volume of the
centrally prepared reports and statistics. There was such a
commission. Results are still inadequate, particularly in view
of the fact that statistics—as the statisticians themselves admit
—are a kind of hydra, which, if cut off, grows twice as big
elsewhere. In the recent period, the Central Committee and
the Council of Ministers have adopted a decision on changes
in the authority of directors of enterprises, stressing the principle of one-man management and at the same time directing
management to rely more on the staff, giving them certain
rights which they did not possess before and for which they
had to apply to central boards, banks, ministries, and so forth.

Summing up, one must say that the results achieved are
unsatisfactory and that our work in the above-named directions
is lagging a great deal behind the requirements of life and
does not as yet constitute an answer to the justified and ever
sharper voices of criticism. It must be stated that the present
situation creates much better premises and conditions for further changes, for an increase of the powers of local people's
councils, for a bolder and wider restriction of the excessively
built-up administrative apparatus of all types. What are the
premises on which we can base ourselves in our further activity?
First, they consist in the release of the initiative and control,
so far restrained, in the rank and file, in the working masses,
in Party, trade union, and National Front organizations. This
creates new conditions for increased independence in ministries,
people's councils, enterprises, and working associations. Far
better results will be brought by thoroughgoing mass control
from below, by control on the part of the community, Party
and trade unions that will improve with experience, than were
brought by bureaucratic and often excessive controls from
above, controls bristling with a multitude of detailed regulations that—one must readily admit—was despite all this, and
maybe because of it, most often ineffective. The second element

which must help to speed up our work and assist us in our struggle is the growing role of the Sejm, as well as of the people's councils and Sejm committees. This will greatly augment the responsibility of executive organs—of the Government, various ministries, the presidiums of the people's councils, the state apparatus—toward the organs of people's rule and public opinion. Now we shall embark upon new work in these domains aiming at exploiting the ever larger number of proposals submitted during discussions in the committees of the Sejm.

On the basis of a detailed questionnaire, we are now working on considerably extending the rights of the district people's councils. The present fairly considerable extension of the rights of the provincial councils has not been adequately utilized to step up at the same time the part played by the district, municipal, and parish councils. Here the provincial councils, capable of applying correctly several proposals aimed at transferring certain rights to them from the central offices, did not display the same zeal and enthusiasm for the suggestions submitted concerning the transfer of certain rights to lower levels. This is one of our ailments. As far as the provincial councils are concerned, at the earliest date new changes will be adopted which will widen their rights.

Work is also in progress on improving the methods of planning, alongside the development of new methods and forms for long-term planning.

No doubt the inadequate results achieved with regard to the reduction of report writing now compel us to undertake in strict cooperation with GUS [Central Statistical Office] and the Ministry of Finance measures aimed at restricting so-called intra-ministry reporting and to put right the problems of finance and accounting where we have to deal with immense overgrowth, with equal treatment for large and small work establishments, and standardization which cost us so many extra jobs.

This month we are carrying out an analysis of the implementation of the Government's decision on economies in administration, a decision adopted last year. On the basis of this analysis we shall undertake further work and further decisions.

Of course, I shall not enumerate here all directions in which the battle against bureaucratic overgrowth must develop, the battle for the widest possible democratization of activities, for a concrete implementation of the principles of democratic centralism but at the same time for the decentralization of management, for the maximum self-government of the regions, for maximum initiative and control on the part of the masses, for the removal of all regulations which hamper the initiative and the self-government of the local bodies. In this battle for the codification of regulations and for putting the domain of management in order, the Government commission for the improvement of administration will welcome the assistance and cooperation of the delegates. It appears to me that this should be one of the conclusions issuing from the discussions now in progress.

The next problem, which is a painful one and which is the subject of continuous concern of the Government, is the battle for improving the state apparatus, for reducing its numbers and its costs. It must be said that the employment index in the state administration was in 1950 some 10 percent lower than at the end of 1955. In state administration the job index, which in 1950 was 5.5 percent of the total labor force, is today 3.87 percent. This is not only a percentage, for we shall not operate only in percentages. It is also an absolute number.

In this connection the expenditure on state administration in the total budget expenditure amounted in 1951 to 9.3 percent and in 1956 it will amount to 3.9 percent. Some 40,000 jobs were eliminated from the state administration apparatus in 1954 and in 1955/56. I speak only about the state apparatus because in the economic apparatus we have not yet reached the end. In the economic apparatus the general estimate also amounts to 40,000 jobs. Altogether there are 84,000 jobs.

This amounts to an economy of 600 million zlotys per year. This is not adequate, but it shows that it could be much more if we had not undertaken this fight even to such an extent.

Obviously, one could say that the decision of the Second Congress of the Polish United Workers Party[29] on the reduction of the size and cost of administration is being realized, together with other efficiency measures which also aid us. Nevertheless, there is still serious overstaffing in the administrative apparatus, there still exist tendencies to build it up without any reason. This results also from a lack of coordination in organizational work. It is imperative to deal with the still-existing reserves in establishments and to lower administrative costs further by simplifying the organization of the apparatus, decentralizing, which is meant to serve the same purpose, simplifying the method of planning, about which quite rightly such a great deal has been said in the committee stage, simplifying accountancy in enterprises, simplifying the technique of budget services by reducing the number of central boards and provincial boards and widening the rights of directors. Another task facing us is the merger of certain ministries and the introduction of the same simplifications at the central level without any fear. The administration and the Government face very many important tasks, which will call for intensive and properly controlled work by all ministries, for the assistance of the Sejm committees, and for the controlling bodies taking a greater interest than before in these affairs, in the problem of organization, in the problems of establishment, and in the battle against the overgrowth of our personnel. With regard to the ethics of the state apparatus, the Government is greatly concerned with the battle against corruption and abuses in our economic life, which result in the sapping of a part of our national revenue by parasitic elements, to the detriment of the toiling masses. This is illustrated by large numbers of cases taken at random.

---

[29] Held in March, 1954.

We have exposed several flagrant abuses at places where socialized industry joins with private initiative. We have brought to light several matters in commercial activities and cases of bribery in their financial apparatus. With regard to all these problems, we had to deal, on the one hand, with capitalists of larger or smaller caliber and, on the other, with corrupt employees in various links of our economic and state apparatus, as well as with criminal negligence and lightheartedness on the part of the heads of some state enterprises and institutions.

The scope of these affairs is considerable and losses of the state—and thus of the community—amount to hundreds of millions of zlotys per year. We have had several instances in the smelting industry, in the Lenin Foundry, in the Bierut Foundry, and in other foundries. The losses, according to available data, amount to 18 million zlotys in one year.

Recently an instance was discovered in the metal works in Skarzysko. They had their own joiners' shop in which they cemented the drilling machines, which they passed on to men belonging to private enterprise. This was called an auxiliary cooperative. They reduced the staff of the joiners' shop by half and paid over 4 million [zlotys] for the production of the cases. Another extensive affair was that of the profiteer Driadon of Krakow, who corrupted several links of our apparatus. As a result of various machinations, he bought large consignments of leather at state prices and profited from this business to the extent of several million zlotys. No doubt liberalism, lack of supervision, and the blindness of many of our economic organizers provided fertile ground for these abuses. The same is true in regard to lack of adequate control on the part of social organizations. Particularly great damage has been done in this domain by incorrect treatment of the auxiliary artisan cooperatives as part of the socialized economy. These cooperatives, which after all nobody wants to liquidate, instead of providing service to the community, were a hiding place for many capitalistic elements. They have practically switched their entire activity to the fulfillment of orders from enterprises and state institutions, naturally getting appropriate profits from this. Were we without any blame in this? No, for our regulations have hampered our enterprises in regard to the possibility of executing certain services within their own realm. Until the end of 1955 the regulations for the administration of the independent plant fund did not allow the consignment of work to individual artisans or to one's own employees. In this situation, state enterprises subcontracted work to auxiliary cooperatives, paying much higher prices for services rendered. We were biting our own tails. And that's not all. There were cases where auxiliary cooperatives engaged for this work workers from the same enterprise for which they were doing it. Thus they acted as middlemen between the directors and the workers in that factory and made money on it. Because of the detection of abuses and shenanigans, the Government, in addition to introducing penal and disciplinary proceedings against those responsible, has carried out several measures of a general nature aimed at limiting links between socialized economy and private enterprise. Does this mean that we are planning to oust or liquidate private enterprise, that we are urging a witch hunt against the petty capitalist elements, or that we intend to discontinue issuing licenses to a certain number of private owners, service points, production enterprises, merchants, stall-owners? This is by no means the case—although in certain areas this has been sometimes misunderstood. We do, however, want the existing private enterprise to be switched over to a path required by our economy, that is, we want this enterprise to be active in the field of services for the population, in the field of delivering goods to the market which supplement the output of socialized industry. But where this area linked to the economic apparatus of socialist industry exists, where there is danger of bribery, and where profits from the socialist sector are being pumped into the pockets of the speculators, we do want to oust private enterprise by limiting the supplies of private firms and auxiliary cooperatives to exceptional cases and to genuinely justified dimensions.

We have passed in that field a series of bills and directives. We will not get rid of these dangerous abuses unless an increasingly better organization of social control by works councils which would review such orders comes into being. This form of control should not, of course, impede the operations of the enterprise when such an order is economically very necessary. We are also dealing with another manifestation which must be talked about, that is, with serious abuses in commerce, causing damage both to the state and the consumer. The first of these are the problems connected with deficiencies, which are of a relatively large scope. Unfortunately, the procedure in effect at present does not favor the battle for the liquidation and curtailment of deficiencies, for the same procedure is being used in connection with great abuses, in which losses amount to several thousands and sometimes to several hundred thousands [zlotys], and to small deficiencies as well. These things are dealt with in overly protracted court procedures. Also, the effectiveness of the methods of repression is hardly perceptible. This problem will be on one of the next agendas of the Government. The battle against great deficiencies must be especially sharp. The existence of corruption which has been established by the state control organs also pertains to our state apparatus. For instance, out of 563 cases of tax assessment examined by control agents, it was revealed that 236 had been lowered to the amount of 16 million zlotys. Unjustified liberalism in the assessment of taxes on prosperous enterprises and the failure to make use of tax information by the department is in contrast with the frequently very high and often excessive rate of tax assessments on small artisans. This policy has often led to the liquidation of useful service agents. The Finance Ministry must step up control over its regional branches.

It would not be irrelevant in dealing with this problem to refer to the development of criticism from below and to the development of control from below if I said that the manifestations of petty bribes and abuses committed by officials have occurred in various offices in commerce in the GS, purchase apparatus, etc. These trifling and isolated cases are dangerous in their mass character and must be met not only by the resistance of the top echelons of the state and economic apparatus but also primarily by resistance from below through an increased surge of initiative on the part of the masses against the background of increased criticism. This battle will be effective only if we can fall back on the active support and initiative of the toiling masses.

From above, the Government intends to set up a Government commission comprising the Ministers of State Control, Internal Affairs, and Justice with the Public Prosecutor and the Ministers of Finance and Commerce for a transitional period in order to step up the struggle against corruption and abuses. This commission will work out effective methods of combating these abuses and coordinating the campaign for cleansing our state apparatus and protecting the interests of the toiling masses.

Citizen deputies, all our peaceful work, all our efforts, their direction and pace, our numerous tasks, and the possibility of their implementation—all this as we know is always conditioned by the international situation.

Even a glance at the international situation allows the assertion that it is much more favorable than in the past year. The very fact that the words and slogans of the Cold War resound so much less frequently from the columns of the press and from the lips of the politicians and that the words "peaceful coexistence" can be heard so much more often is eloquent in itself.

Without the danger of becoming overoptimistic, one can express the view that a clear relaxation in international relations has occurred and that there has been a clear easing of tension. All the necessary prerequisites exist for the complete liquidation of the Cold War and for leading mankind on a path of peaceful coexistence of all countries, irrespective of the political and social differences which divide them. Needless to say, this goal is in line with the most vital interests of our nation.

If we acknowledge today the undoubted fact of the relaxation of international tension, we must assert at the same time that it results first of all from the consistently peaceful policy of the Soviet Union and of the remaining countries of the peace camp. The determined battle for peace we have waged has already been crowned with success to such an extent that the other side—that is, the countries which until recently have stuck determinedly to the policy of the Cold War—has adopted the platform of discussion and negotiation. The principle that—in view of the existence of nuclear and thermonuclear weapons—war threatened incalculable consequences and that, therefore, it should be erased from the arsenal of means of settling international disputes, which was stated in the Geneva Declaration of the Heads of the Four Great Powers, is undoubtedly a great achievement. It testifies that the ruling political circles of the West are aware of the danger of the adventurous policy of the continuation of the Cold War and of attempts to transform it into an armed war. It is to be hoped that attempts to conduct international policy by the method of driving the world to the brink of war's abyss will be given up.

The past year was undoubtedly a period of an intensified offensive by the forces of peace. The great moves of Soviet diplomacy, characterized by boldness of conception, the courage to settle problems by drive and imagination, are arousing ever more universal respect and recognition by world opinion. It is increasingly difficult for extreme reactionary quarters to disseminate propaganda aimed at undermining faith in the sincerity and peaceful character of the Soviet political moves in the international arena. It is increasingly difficult for statesmen and politicians attempting to resist the new spirit in international relations, to proclaim their obsolete conceptions openly. They are afraid of the reaction of public opinion in their own countries.

However, one should not underestimate tendencies and efforts, apparent in the most aggressive imperialist circles, toward a further implementation of the position of strength policy. However, the atmosphere prevailing throughout the world today does not favor this sort of tendency and stimulates those who desire a genuine improvement in international relations, who want to see coexistence become a constant and universal fact.

Such positive moves toward a weakening of international tension must include the statements made by French Premier Mollet and Foreign Affairs Minister Pineau. We welcome these statements with particular joy in view of the fact that they were uttered by politicians of a country with which we are linked by traditional and profound bonds of sympathy and by a common political fate in the past, of a country with which we would like to maintain relations which would not only be correct but also friendly and cordial. This is in conformity both with the Polish *raison d'état* and with Polish national sentiments.

Of course we desire the best possible relations with all countries, regardless of their social system.

Today Poland maintains relations with forty-four states and, at an early date, we shall establish relations with four more countries. Our active foreign policy has become a factor in the battle for the consolidation of peace.

As for our bonds with countries in the West, we are linked with many of them by old and cordial bonds, bonds frequently established in the most difficult hours of the common battle for freedom and the common battle against the enemies of freedom. The Polish nation is proud of the participation of Polish soldiers in battles against the Nazi and fascist barbarians, fought together with the armies of our Western allies. It is proud of the participation of the Polish airmen of the famous 301st and 303d Squadrons in the Battle for Britain. It is proud of the part played by Polish sailors in the Battle of the Atlantic. The period of the Cold War had a detrimental effect on Polish-British relations, but there are no obstacles to prevent them from becoming friendly.

This is also true of our relations with the United States, which go back to the birth of the American Republic. We have behind us the common history of battles against Prussian militarism in two world wars. These great traditions cannot be erased by a few years of tense relations resulting from the Cold War. We hope that in the forthcoming period, when the idea of peaceful coexistence will be victorious, relations between our countries will assume a friendly character.

We want to take a most active part in the shaping of international relations on the plane of peaceful coexistence. That is why we are prepared to strengthen economic and cultural relations with all countries which want to eliminate discrimination in trade relations. We want to establish manifold bonds of economic exchange as well as a more lively cultural exchange and cooperation in the field of science and art. We want the mutual knowledge of our countries, of their social relations, technical achievements, and attainments in all fields to become ever more profound.

We have feelings of warm sympathy for the peoples of Asia and Africa who aim consistently at independence from imperialism and complete political and economic sovereignty.

We want to establish normal diplomatic relations with all those countries which so far do not maintain such relations with us. We are also supporting every international initiative aimed at settlement of existing controversial issues.

The entire Polish community is following the visit of the Soviet statesmen to London with special attention.[30] We regard it as a manifestation of the same concern of the Soviet Government for the weakening of international tension which is characteristic of Soviet policy. We have considered and still consider that the harmonious cooperation of the Five Great Powers constitutes the cornerstone of world peace. We fully share the view held by Soviet statesmen that it is not our purpose to drive a wedge between the friendly countries, but we want rapprochement with one of the powers to become a bridge leading to rapprochement with others. Similarly, a bitter disappointment awaits anyone who hopes that he will succeed

---

[30] The reference is to the visit of N. S. Khrushchev and N. A. Bulganin to England in April, 1956.

in driving a wedge between any of the people's democracies and the Soviet Union. No one will succeed in weakening the coherence and compactness of the countries belonging to the camp of peace and socialism, for this provides a guarantee for further victories of peace throughout the world.

The Polish Government and the Polish people are in harmony in appraising the great efforts of Soviet diplomacy and hope that the best possible results will be achieved by the London talks, that these talks will become a step forward along the path leading to the establishment of an effectively functioning collective security system, and that they will pave the way to disarmament and the elimination of atomic and hydrogen weapons from the arsenal of the means of war, once and for all. We realize that this is the only path leading to the consolidation of peace and we know that once international security is insured effectively, the solution of even such a difficult and complex problem as the German question will be possible.

We are aware of the weight of the German problem, as direct neighbors of Germany and direct victims of every aggressive paroxysm on the part of German imperialism and militarism. We are determinedly opposed to a revival of these evil forces, which augur new disasters and calamities for Europe and the world, for the East and the West. We shall make every possible effort to establish an all-European collective security system and to reduce armaments so as to prevent the growth of revived German militarism and to liquidate all military blocs which are dividing Europe.

We have full sympathy for the efforts of the GDR [German Democratic Republic] which lead toward this goal. We welcome its economic, political, and cultural achievements.

We appraise positively the development of our relations with the countries of northern Europe. Our entire camp is permeated with the desire to consolidate peace. These desires constitute firm bonds uniting us with the Soviet Union and with the people's democracies. The many-sided development of political, economic, and cultural cooperation became the basis of further rapprochement with Yugoslavia. Friendship with the Soviet Union is the cornerstone of our policy, the expression of a correctly understood Polish *raison d'état,* and the expression of the ideological communion binding us with the homeland of the revolution. The most recent events, such as the 20th Congress, have deepened this ideological communion still more. All the attempts of the enemy intended to sow ill-will toward the Soviet Union are doomed to failure and are rejected with indignation by the broadest masses of the Polish nation. Friendship between our two nations, two lands, and two states is primarily based on the feeling of a community of goals and strivings, desire for an all-around reconciliation, mutual understanding, mutual respect, and close cooperation. How accurately Lenin formulated these principles of mutual relations between countries! On them we are building and we shall build friendship, cooperation, and alliance so that the two nations may become even closer, even better acquainted, and even more strongly united in the common march toward common goals, which are peace, socialism, and the flowering of a universal culture. These principles guide all countries of our camp. On this basis we are also building friendship and cooperation with the great Chinese people and the brotherly countries of people's democracies. Citizen deputies, addressing you on behalf of the Government, at the threshold of the budget debate, I believe that at this moment the most important feeling animating us is the desire to fight better than before in order to raise the level of the work of the state; to fight for this purpose against all distortions which have hampered our work; to make good all errors and wrongs done; to wage a merciless battle to eradicate arbitrariness and violation of legality; to guard and guarantee legality vigilantly in the future; to make every possible effort leading to the implementation of our political and economic tasks, to the securing of a steady—even if slow— progress of prosperity; to fight for a real strengthening of our state; to secure its safe development in the international arena. May our work in all these sectors create the necessary conditions for the further development of the patriotic zeal, of the civic consciousness, of the feeling of responsibility and activity which is becoming so greatly intensified at present—responsibility on the part of the millions-strong toiling masses, true creators of a new life, the millions-strong masses of the Polish people engaged in victoriously building socialism. (*Applause.*)

On April 29, Edward Ochab, writing in *Pravda* on Lenin's rules and principles of Party life, returned to the theme of the anti-Stalin campaign in Poland.[31]

In recent times in Poland as well as in other brotherly nations a great deal has been written and said in the pages of the Communist press and in Party meetings about the necessity of strict adherence to Lenin's rules of Party life. . . . One of the most important principles of Leninism is the collegiality of leadership on all levels. . . . There were many, many incidents in the past of openly breaking this fundamental principle in the PUWP, too; these did the Party considerable damage. Even now we have incidents of only superficial adherence to this principle. . . .

Lenin frequently pointed out that the real goal of intra-Party democracy is the freedom of criticism, as long as this critique does not affect the Party's unity of action. One must at the same time carefully watch out for any abuses of the freedom of criticism which might harm the Party or which could be used against the Party's unity. In some organizations of the PUWP there occur instances of ideological instability on the part of one or another group of Party members; there are attempts at abusing freedom of criticism for the purpose of shaking the Party's unity of action or for the purpose of attacking the Party's political line.

The Party, of course, has sufficient strength to conquer these outbursts of instability and to oppose anti-Party expressions, at the same time, unfailingly, to bring about Lenin's rules of Party life and to create proper conditions for the cultivation of constructive criticism from below.

The resolutions of the 20th Congress of the CPSU had a tremendous impact on Poland and on the rest of the world. The working masses are espousing these resolutions. The matter of

---

[31] The article was reprinted in *Trybuna Ludu,* April 30, 1956.

the cult of personality and its serious consequences often result in bitter experiences. But this matter does not overshadow, for the Polish working people and in particular for the working class, other fundamental problems of the 20th Congress. The historic and decisive 20th Congress, imbued with the spirit of Lenin, shows to the millions of the masses, to all working humanity, Lenin's road to the victory of peace, democracy, and socialism.

The 20th Congress is being discussed among the petit-bourgeoisie of Poland and of certain other nations in a different manner, in an anti-Party manner, resulting from the political unsteadiness of these elements and resulting also from the pressure of hostile bourgeois propaganda, which wants to focus the attention of the masses primarily on the mistakes of Joseph Stalin and which wants to undermine confidence in the proper political road of the CPSU.

Certain newspapers in Poland failed to guard themselves against this unsteadiness, too. In certain broad discussions, which for the most part are fruitful and constructive, there appeared opportunistic, harmful, and sometimes bluntly anti-Party sallies and utterances, which were not resisted properly by the various editorial staffs. These facts create serious resentment among the working people. . . .

The Polish nation and especially the Polish working class know how to resist slanderers and opportunists, know how to uncover anti-Soviet sallies hostile to Poland, even if these are masked with lofty phrases.

The 20th Congress of the PUWP was enlivened by the struggle to realize Lenin's rules on Party life, a struggle on two fronts: first of all against bureaucratic stiffening, against schematism and declarationism, against any attempts to suppress criticism or to commandeer the masses, and at the same time against middle-class unsteadiness and its lack of principles, against attempts to undermine Party discipline and the unity of the Party's rank and file, and particularly against any attempts to undermine the friendship between the Polish and the Soviet nations. . . .

On May 6, *Trybuna Ludu* printed a communiqué stating that the Politburo of the PUWP had "critically evaluated the activities of Comrade Jakub Berman in the fields over which he exercised control. Consequently, Jakub Berman resigned from his post as member of the Politburo and Deputy Premier of the Government."[32]

---

[32] Berman's fall from high office was the most important change yet at the top level of the Party hierarchy. He had played an eminent role in Party and Government affairs ever since 1945 and was considered by many the *éminence grise* of the Party, its chief ideological expert, and simultaneously its watchdog over security matters. A particularly sharp attack on him was made by Leon Wudzki at the eighth plenary session of the Central Committee of the PUWP in October, 1956, at which Wladyslaw Gomulka was reelected First Secretary and Poland's new course of "national Communism" was chartered. (See Chapter V. For Wudzki's remarks, see *Nowe Drogi*, X, No. 10 [October, 1956], 59-64.)

CHAPTER II

RIOTS IN POZNAN AND THEIR AFTERMATH, JUNE 28-JULY 18, 1956

On June 17 an International Fair opened in Poznan. On June 28 workers of the ZISPO factory (locomotives and heavy machinery) and other plants staged a demonstration which turned into a riot and finally a pitched battle between the rioters and armed detachments of the police. The riots were quelled the following day, by which time a Government delegation headed by Premier Cyrankiewicz had arrived on the spot.

1. BULLETIN ON THE POZNAN INCIDENTS, *Trybuna Ludu,* JUNE 29, 1956[1]

DISORDERS WERE PROVOKED in Poznan on June 28.

For some time imperialist agents and the reactionary underground have been trying to use the economic difficulties and shortcomings at several Poznan enterprises to incite outbursts against the people's rule. It is no accident that the enemy selected Poznan, where an International Fair is in progress, as the place of provocation. They intended to cast a shadow on the good name of People's Poland and to impede development of peaceful international cooperation.

On June 28, enemy agents succeeded in provoking street disorders. Matters went so far that several public buildings were attacked, with casualties resulting.

Relying on the politically conscious part of the working class, the authorities gained control of the situation and restored order to the city.

---

[1] The bulletin was reprinted in full in *Pravda* on June 30, 1956. The translation here is reproduced from *The Current Digest of the Soviet Press,* VIII, No. 26 (August 8, 1956), 10.

Representatives of the Government and of the Polish United Workers Party, led by Jozef Cyrankiewicz, Chairman of the Council of Ministers, came to the scene of the events.[2]

The organizers of the destruction, a broad and carefully prepared provocative-diversionary action, will be punished to the full extent of the law.

In view of the Poznan events, all workers and patriotic forces of the people must be particularly vigilant against all antistate attempts and demonstrations inspired by the enemies of People's Poland.

The Poznan provocation was organized by the enemies of our fatherland at a time when the Party and Government are greatly concerned with eliminating shortcomings in the life of the workers and making our country more democratic. Every patriot and every honest person in Poland must realize this.

The Government and the Central Committee of the Polish United Workers Party are convinced that every attempt to provoke disorders and to act against the people's rule will be duly rebuffed by all the workers and citizens to whom the welfare of the country is dear.

2. "PROVOCATION": EDITORIAL IN *Trybuna Ludu* ON THE POZNAN INCIDENTS, JUNE 29, 1956

WE ARE PUBLISHING above the bulletin of PAP[3] concerning the disturbances in Poznan. Groups of provocateurs, taking advantage of discontent which arose among crews of certain factories in Poznan over economic difficulties, have caused antistate demonstrations and bloody street riots. There have been casualties, both dead and wounded.[4]

---

[2] Other members of the delegation were Edward Gierek, a secretary of the Central Committee, and Wiktor Klosiewicz, Chairman of the Central Council of Trade Unions.

[3] Polish Press Agency.

[4] The final figures given by Polish authorities were 53 dead, including rioters and police, and over 300 wounded.

Let us think. Who, and for what purpose, could have wanted at precisely this moment and just in Poznan, where the 25th International Fair is taking place with many foreigners participating, to create this sort of incident? Who could have wanted now more than ever—when the labor and the great toil of the Polish working class and of the entire nation is being displayed briefly at this Fair and is being acknowledged by the entire world—to strike at this effort?

Our economic situation is not easy. It is fraught with hardship. Many problems remain to be solved. We are burdened by many issues, the resolution of which had been delayed. Many justified demands of the working people await action.

The Party and the Government have undertaken serious attempts with the intention of correcting all phases of our life. In these attempts the great majority of the society participates more actively than ever before.

The political activity of the widest masses has increased. A great state-wide debate is taking place on the matter of correcting and improving our country, politically and economically, as well as on the matter of the widest possible democratization of our life.

Not only is a debate being held. The Party and the Government have already carried out many important political changes. An unusually broad amnesty has been proclaimed and carried out. Concrete steps have been undertaken to safeguard individual constitutional freedoms and socialist self-government. Wage regulations have been introduced within the means of our present possibilities. Reforms in the administration of our economy are being discussed and prepared.

A turnabout in the economic situation cannot, of course, take place from one day to the next. There are no magic formulae. Improvements require time. But only the blind or the enemy can deny the obvious fact: we have begun a great work of improvement.

The enemy and well-organized nests of agents chose precisely this moment, disregarding the intentions of the working people of Poznan, to incite riots for purely provocative purposes.

If the people, the Party and the Government want improvement; then the road to this improvement should be blocked with a bloody provocation. Thus thought the enemy.

If the people, the Party, and the Government want democratization of all the phases of our life, then this process of democratization should be halted by a bloody scandal. Thus thought the enemy.

If the people, the Party, and the Government want to improve the economic situation and increase production, on which the improvement of the standard of living of each of us depends, then the work of the national economy should be disturbed. Thus thought the enemy.

Those who caused the disturbances were not bent on correcting that which was wrong or on improving the standard of living. The provocateurs wanted to worsen the situation in every phase. Because the worse it is for the Polish working class and for Poland, the better it is for those who hate the people's rule and who dream of restoring the capitalistic-bourgeois "order."

We would be blind if were not to notice still another characteristic of this provocation, a characteristic which is closely linked with the activity of certain foreign circles.

A splendid majority of the society supports the foreign policy of the government, a policy dedicated to the defense of peace and of the permanence of our borders, a policy of friendship with the powerful Soviet Union and with the entire socialist camp, a policy of making closer ties with nations and governments, which although different from us in many respects, nevertheless desire peaceful coexistence. The ice of the cold war is quickly melting. The role of Poland and her significance in the world is greater than at any other time. Poland's foreign policy has become more active.

Therefore this policy should be halted and the international situation of Poland should be hampered at all costs—at a cost of a bloody provocation. Thus thought and thinks the enemy.

Was it so long ago that one of the American fanatics of the cold war, one of the praisers of the reactionary anti-Polish Wehrmacht, and one of the assassins of Karol Swierczewski strongly urged on the pages of the New York *Herald-Tribune* an uprising in Poland and in other socialist countries by massive counterrevolutionary action?

Let us take stock of all the above-mentioned facts and we will have an answer to the question: Who, and for what purpose, wanted to create bloody disturbances just today and just in Poznan?

The authorities supported by the conscientious part of the workers' class and by the healthy, patriotic strength of the Poznan community have mastered the situation in Poznan. Those guilty of the bloody provocation will be punished to the fullest extent of the law.

The Party, the Government, and the entire nation will not deviate from the road upon which we have entered. Let us not cease our efforts in developing still further and still more effectively the democratization of our life. We shall not lessen but increase our efforts to complete improvements in our nation, to better our economy in order to increase production in industry and agriculture. For this is the only road leading toward an improvement of the standard of living of each of us—the only road of strength and development in Poland.

Provocation will not succeed.

We shall defend against the maniacal plans of the internal and foreign reaction our most precious possession, Poland, which we raised from the depths of the destruction of war with the unlimited toil of the entire nation. We will immobilize the murderous hand which is attempting to inflict damages for which the entire nation must pay.

But in order that this hand may not strike at Poland, a mobilization of watchfulness, common sense, and action is necessary. A conscious counteraction against the provocateurs must be undertaken by:

The Party

The Working Class

The People.

The enemy wanted to unleash an action aimed at the most vital interests of the working class and of all the working people, an action aimed at Poland.

We shall carefully distinguish between groups of provocateurs and the Poznan workers. But all who think and feel Polish, all to whom our hard-earned possessions are dear, all who want improvements and democratization of our life, all who represent the huge majority of the people declare an unrelenting fight against those who aim at our paternal home.

3. Proclamation of the Chairman of the Council of Ministers, Cyrankiewicz, to the People of Poznan, June 29, 1956[5]

Citizens, inhabitants of Poznan, workers, intelligentsia, youth!

I am talking to you with great pain because this our beautiful city, known for its diligence, patriotism, and love of order, became the ground of murderous provocations and bloody riots which have shaken the conscience of every honest inhabitant of Poznan, of every Pole, and which the entire society has most energetically condemned.

We are talking among ourselves frankly and there is no need to hide the fact that the murderous provocateurs have taken advantage of unquestionably existing grievances and dissatisfactions in certain factories caused by economic difficulties and various, frequently annoying, situations. If all this has been brought about by the grievances that have come to light in a great number of factories of Poznan, grievances which have been caused to a great extent by mistakes and by an incorrect application of existing regulations, then, of course, these mistakes shall have to be and will be immediately corrected. The more so as the decisions to correct them had already been made by the Government and the Party a few days ago, when workers'

---

[5] *Trybuna Ludu,* June 30, 1956.

delegations were received by the representatives of the Government and their justified demands were positively acted upon.[6]

This did not prevent the provocateurs from organizing a demonstration on Thursday, which they had prepared for a long time with the aid of alien organizers. Imperialist centers concentrated their entire attention on Poznan, the city of International Fairs, because they wanted Poznan to become the scene of riots during the Fair. No one is so naive as not to see that. Such things are not accidental. The enemy thus sought to exploit the dissatisfaction of a portion of the workers and laborers of Poznan, caused by the difficult material conditions of the working population and particularly that of the workers. For it is obvious that these conditions were not such as we would have desired them to be.

The Central Committee of the Party and the Government have worked out a plan of action which will permit a gradual

---

[6] A 27-man delegation from the ZISPO works went to Warsaw earlier in the month to negotiate with various Government departments in order to obtain redress for some of their economic grievances. The results of this mission have not been reliably disclosed. While the Government eventually claimed that the workers' demands were heeded, the dismissal of the ministers directly involved in the talks soon after the riot could be interpreted as a sign of their dereliction in this matter.

As to the economic causes of unrest, Edward Ochab, First Secretary of the PUWP, had this to say at a plenary session of the Central Committee on July 19 (*Trybuna Ludu,* July 20, 1956):

"An analysis of these events and of their background reveals that an important role in them was played by the callousness and bureaucratism of the authorities, both central and local.

"As a result of ill-considered measures taken during the past months the wages of some groups of ZISPO workers declined. It must be said that this happened against the intentions of the Party and the Government. Owing to changes made in work norms during 1953, to a revision of norms in 1954, and partly to a revision of the organization of work in 1955, a rise in labor productivity of nearly 24.6 percent was achieved in the ZISPO works. This, however, was not properly reflected in the rise of wages.

"As a result of the elimination of progressive piecework rates in the second half of 1955 earnings began to diminish. About 75 percent of the workers were affected. Contrary to binding regulations, the income tax of shockworkers was assessed at excessively high levels."

increase in the standard of living of the masses. Special attention is being given especially to those working groups whose
incomes are particularly unsatisfactory. We do not want to
promise anything. Promises make no sense and with promises
you cannot improve the standard of living. But we will do
what we can, given our means, to raise the standard of living
since the entire society and particularly the workers and peasants
are toiling for it. We want to devote our efforts to this goal.
But were the provocateurs concerned with this? They were
naturally concerned with the very opposite. Whereas the
workers of Poznan undoubtedly intended to voice their grievances, which was their right, provocateurs and imperialistic
agents had something entirely different in mind. They want
to hinder us in meeting these grievances. In this they will be
unsuccessful. They would also like to create anarchy that
would hamper the progress of the processes of democratization
of our life, which the imperialistic agents fear most. So then
it is no wonder that these intentions of troublemakers have
proved a flash in the pan at a moment when they were recognized by the enormous majority of the working class which
withdrew and cut itself off from the next phase of demonstrations, from murky displays of agents and provocateurs, who
stepped forth with arms in hand and attacked public buildings.
The issue then became not just the matter of often justified
criticism on the part of the workers, not the matter of presenting more or less justified claims, the fulfillment of which may
or may not yet be possible in our present circumstances. The
issue centered on an armed uprising against the people's rule,
organized by provocateurs attacking public buildings, attacking
members of the militia and the security forces. It was then
that the workers, with the exception of misled individuals,
naturally rallied to the defense of the people's and their own
rule.

Then in certain places of the city, on various roofs, provocateurs had set up machine guns which aimed equally at defenders
of order and the peaceful population and caused casualties.

This had as much to do with the workers as they have to do with an imperialistic agent who would like to cause Poland's downfall and then duplicate such tragedies as the heroic population of Poznan endured under Hitler's invasion.

This, of course, will not happen because Poland is different today and different is the system of international forces, forces of peace and progress which induce all to peaceful coexistence and cooperation and drive warmongers to madness. Naturally, this did not disturb the dark elements of provocation in their useless attempts to change the course of history with the aid of murderous shots.

One must underscore the fully responsible and patriotic behavior of the militia, the army, and the members of the security forces who avoided using their weapons until the last moment when they were shot at by the aggressors who became more audacious as a result of the restraint of the authorities.

The authorities were forced to use extreme measures in the defense of life and property of the citizens and to restore peace. The majority of troublemakers, some with arms in hand, was halted, and against them criminal investigation will be initiated.

The fact that during the riots heroic soldiers, militiamen, and members of the security forces who defended the posts assigned to them, as well as workers of Poznan who braved the aggressors together with the militia and the armed forces, were killed, fills us with deepest sorrow and pain. The deaths of innocent citizens who happened to have been at the places of fighting also fill us with sorrow and pain. Imperialistic centers and the reactionary underground hostile to Poland are directly responsible for the incidents and are burdened with the blood spilled in Poznan.

The bloody incidents in Poznan shall not weaken or halt attempts of the Party and the Government to democratize our life, to achieve our aims in developing the national economy and culture, of which a quicker improvement of the standard of living of the working population is the greatest concern. The Party and the people's rule count, in these attempts, on the full support of the entire society of workers and the working intelligentsia of Poznan. We hope that all the working people of Poznan will conscientiously live up to their responsibilities. Every provocateur or maniac who will dare raise his hand against the people's rule may be sure that in the interest of the working class, in the interest of the working peasantry and intelligentsia, in the interest of the struggle to raise the standard of living of the people, in the interest of further democratization of our life, in the interest of our Fatherland, the authorities will chop off his hand. On the other hand we shall always greet with gratitude each sign of healthy and patriotic criticism of our imperfections, mistakes, and shortcomings.

We shall struggle together toward further democratization of our life, linked, of course, with the growing sense of responsibility to our country on the part of the masses as well as of each citizen individually.

Citizens of Poznan! In this difficult and painful moment which we share with you, I appeal to you in the name of the Party and the Government, in the name of the people's rule, to support completely the people's rule in our striving for the removal of the grievances which we are able to remove even today, and to help in the removal of other ills which we can remove tomorrow with a joint effort as part of our goal to improve our economy and to raise the standard of living of the broadest masses.

Let us work together and let us consider calmly what should be done in order to restore fully the good name of the city of Poznan and the respect which Poznanians enjoy in all of Poland, so that in the future the industriousness, fastidiousness, and patriotism of Poznanians can contribute still more to the development of our country.

The reaction of official media to the Poznan riot in the Soviet Union and the people's democracies was one of unanimous condemnation of the events as an example of "new machinations of the imperialists." The conclusion was drawn that "vigilance" against the class enemy from within and subversion by agents from abroad could not be relaxed. The response of the Soviet Union to the riots was contained in a long editorial in *Pravda* on July 16, 1956. (See Part One, Chapter II, Document 3.) The immediate Soviet reaction was recorded in a dispatch from *Pravda's* Warsaw correspondent.

4. SOVIET REACTION: "POLISH PEOPLE BRAND ORGANIZERS OF PROVOCATION," *Pravda,* JULY 1, 1956[7]

AS HAS ALREADY been reported, hostile agents carried out a crude provocation in Poznan. Imperialist and reactionary Polish underground agents, taking advantage of certain economic difficulties, incited serious disturbances and street disorders in the city. Several public buildings were attacked, resulting in casualties.

It is no accident that Poznan was selected as the place of provocation because of the International Fair now in progress there. The enemies of the Polish people tried to cast a shadow on the growing might of People's Poland which the fair clearly reflects in order to impede the development of peaceful international cooperation between Poland and other countries.

The hostile provocation failed. The politically conscious section of the Poznan working class helped the authorities to gain control of the situation and to reestablish order in the city. The Polish Press Agency reports that by 7:00 A.M. on June 29 the majority of the workers from the striking enterprises returned to their jobs. Streetcar and bus services have been resumed in the city. The workers express their indignation over the infamous activities of the diversionists who tried to organize a demonstration against the people's rule. Preliminary investigation of the case of the arrested saboteurs and bandits reveals their ties with the reactionary underground.

On June 29 Jozef Cyrankiewicz, Chairman of the Council of Ministers of the republic, who is in Poznan, delivered a radio address to the Poznan workers. He stated that the bloodshed

[7] Translation reproduced from *The Current Digest of the Soviet Press*, VIII, No. 26 (August 8, 1956), 10-11.

in Poznan lies on the imperialist centers and the hostile reactionary underground, the direct organizers of the events. However, Jozef Cyrankiewicz stressed that the Poznan events will not impede or weaken the efforts of the Party and Government toward a further democratization of our life, toward a better fulfillment of our tasks, toward development of the economy and national culture, toward a further rapid improvement in the workers' living conditions.

The Polish working class and all the workers of the country express decisive indignation over the insolent imperialist attack in Poznan. Mass meetings and open Party gatherings are taking place in enterprises of Warsaw, Lodz, Lublin, Silesia, the Baltic coast area, and other regions of the country at which the workers are holding up to shame the organizers and inspirers of the provocation against the people.

Such a mass meeting took place at the Warsaw Dimitrov Plant. Worker Hauser stated: "Imperialist provocateurs tried to cast a shadow on our achievements. They wanted to destroy the peaceful life of the Polish people. Our people paid too dearly for the victories achieved under a people's democratic system. We demand severe punishment for the organizers of the provocation." The participants of the meeting adopted a resolution expressing profound indignation over the imperialist agents' provocation.

The workers of the Warsaw Automobile Plant state in a resolution adopted at a meeting: "We will not permit a split in the unity of the working class and its Party in the struggle for further democratization of our lives."

The collective of the Kedzierzyn Nitrate Fertilizer Combine adopted a resolution which states: "We will not permit the forces which detest whatever is our weal and our hope to try to destroy all the fruits of the constant labor of our workers and engineers, dedicated to the prosperity of our people's motherland."

Expressing the opinion of all the workers of the country, the newspaper *Trybuna Ludu* writes: "We will defend our greatest blessing, Poland, which we raised by the tremendous labor of all the people from the abyss of military destruction, against the hostile plans of native and foreign reaction. We will incapacitate the criminal hand which is trying to strike a blow for which all the people must pay. But, so that this hand will not be able to strike a blow against Poland, vigilance, common sense, and action must be mobilized. The Party, the working class, and the public must be consciously opposed to the provocateurs."

Trybuna Ludu states: "No provocation will succeed. The Party, Government, and the entire country will not leave the path upon which we have embarked. We will not reduce but, on the contrary, will increase efforts to improve our economy, to increase industrial and agricultural production. This is the only way to improve each person's life, the only path to strength and prosperity in People's Poland."

The newspaper *Zycie Warszawy* writes: "Today we all recognize how much we need peace and solidarity, unity of action under the leadership of the Polish United Workers Party, and vigilance against enemy intrigues."

In an official statement on the Poznan events, the Polish United Workers Party Central Committee expressed assurance that every attempt to incite disorders and demonstrations against the people's rule would be duly rebuffed by all workers and Polish citizens.

All Polish people unanimously support this conviction. The workers and employees of enterprises and institutions are sending letters to the Party Central Committee stating their desire to rally further around the Polish United Workers Party and the people's government and their readiness to defend with all their might the achievements of the people's democratic system.

5. YUGOSLAV REACTION: "THE EVENTS IN POZNAN," *Borba,* JULY 1, 1956

WARSAW, JUNE 30—The message of the Polish Prime Minister to the Poznan citizens has thrown more light on the early history and causes of the tragic clashes in this city the day before yesterday in which 38 people lost their lives and 270 were wounded.

The Polish Prime Minister considers that he should not conceal the fact that discontent existed in the Poznan factories which was caused by certain irregularities with regard to the remuneration of the workers. Today's Warsaw papers say that the representatives of the Government received a delegation of thirty representatives of Poznan enterprises and evaluated their demands positively. The official communiqué issued today states that the objective motives of the Poznan demonstrations should be sought in the workers' discontent caused by the unsettled wage scale and social problems as well as by the unsatisfactory living conditions. But this is not a complete explanation of the bloody clashes into which these demonstrations developed because it is also obvious even to the most superficial observer that a considerable majority of the workers are lending support to tendencies which aim at a democratization of public life and the improvement of economic conditions, and because they see in them prospects for the bettering of their own living conditions.

The first announcement of the Polish Press Agency already said what can now be found in the Polish Prime Minister's statement, that the prime initiator and instrument of these types of disorders have been actions provoked, premeditated, and prepared in advance. If one bears in mind that these disorders took place in Poznan at the very time of the great International Fair, that they coincided with the visit of the U. N. Secretary General to Poland, and that they occurred at the time when the process of democratization of public life was in full swing, when it was expected that the Plenum of the CC of the Polish United Workers Party was going to initiate a settlement of the most serious problems of economic policy, and when Poland was striving to assert herself as an active factor on the international political stage—it is impossible not to have the impression that the economic difficulties of the workers have served as a weapon in the hands of antisocial forces.

One comes logically to the conclusion that the true meaning of the Poznan disorders must be sought in the attempt of reactionary forces to compromise the process of domestic development in Poland which, after long years of Stalinist deformation, is now following the path of democratization and concern for the people's everyday needs.

It remains to be seen who were the organizers and instigators of this action, prepared well beforehand, according to the assertions of the Polish Government representatives, and what were their immediate aims. Detailed explanations about the course of the tragic events in Poznan are also essential, explanations that would tell why so many people lost their lives and how an armed clash could have come about between the organs of the state and the demonstrators.

But one should undoubtedly welcome the Polish Prime Minister's statement that the bloody events in Poznan "will not prevent or diminish" the efforts of the Polish United Workers Party and of the Government, efforts which are aimed in the direction of further democratization and development of the economy and improvement of the living conditions of the working people, and his words that the leadership of the country is also prepared in the future to accept "healthy and patriotic criticism" of mistakes and irregularities which are standing in the way of socialist development. Really nothing would be less justified than an eventual attempt to proclaim the very democratization of social development as the culprit for the unfortunate events in Poznan, because in this way one would brand as the murderer that factor which alone has the possibility of playing the role of physician.

6. YUGOSLAV REACTION: "THE WORLD TODAY: POZNAN EPILOGUE," *Borba,* JULY 6, 1956

AFTER THE DRAMATIC events last Thursday, Poznan continues to lead a normal life. The state of emergency has been abolished, the workers have returned to their work, regular traffic has been restored, the trade fair has closed without much excitement but nevertheless with good commercial results. It is of particular importance that Poland remains loyal to democratization. This is quite a different epilogue from the one expected by the provokers of the bloody disorders and organized provocations against the present efforts of Poland, and therewith against the vital interests of the Poznan and Polish workers. The working people of Poland are resolutely supporting the process of democratization because this process serves their vital interests. However, we find as enemies of this positive aspiration all those who must, of necessity, suffer defeat as a result of its further penetration. The fact that this or that group of enemies is more tenacious and ruthless—this does not change at all their joint counterrevolutionary and antidemocratic position. The Polish leadership was able to discriminate between the hostile saboteurs and Poznan workers, just as an objective observer must make a distinction between the economic difficulties of the country and provocation made with the intent of trying to take advantage of the serious economic situation and dissatisfaction because of that situation. Economic difficulties are the result of an erroneous course in the past which had to have its effect both on the living conditions and material position of the Polish people. The Poznan provocation, however, represents resistance to a positive orientation which will gradually but surely bring improvement in all fields of life, remove elements of dissatisfaction, and in so doing also eliminate the possibility for political machinations of the enemies of such an orientation.

Therefore the attitude of the Polish leadership that they will continue, without hesitation and slowing down, the process of democratization seems to us to be doubly useful and important. On the one hand, this attitude reflects the firm conviction that Poland has no other way if she wants to develop as a democratic and socialist country. On the other hand, it confirms the determination to have done with the past and with everything that has made that past harmful to Poland and her people.

(*Signed*) D. Trailovic

Meanwhile, Polish authorities arrested 323 persons in connection with the riots. About half of these were later released, and the Government prepared indictments against 154. (See Chapter IV, Document 2.) At the same time the Government offered a tax rebate to the Poznan workers, payable in three monthly installments beginning in July.

CHAPTER III

THE PARTY TAKES STOCK: SEVENTH PLENARY SESSION OF THE CENTRAL COMMITTEE OF THE POLISH UNITED WORKERS PARTY, JULY 18-28, 1956

ON JULY 18, the Central Committee of the PUWP convened for its seventh plenary session. The session extended until July 28. It coincided with the presence in Poland of a Soviet delegation headed by N. A. Bulganin and Georgi K. Zhukov who came on July 20 for the celebration of the twelfth anniversary of Poland's liberation from Nazi occupation, and stayed until July 28.

In the course of their visit, the Soviet leaders made two important pronouncements, one on problems connected with the current phase of development toward socialism, another on the finality of Poland's western frontiers.

Speaking at the Palace of Culture and Art, on July 21,[1] Bulganin said among other things:

> The enemy is aware that the countries of socialism are strong by virtue of their unity, brotherly solidarity, and unselfish assistance to one another. For this reason the enemy will stop at nothing to liquidate or at least weaken the camp of socialism which is growing more solidly united every day.
>
> The enemy would want to estrange us from one another so that he may then deal with the Socialist countries one by one. No matter how much the enemies of socialism may try, however, their plans for provocation will burst like so many soap bubbles.
>
> . . . We know it for a fact that elements hostile to our cause have used the press of socialist countries to sow their poisonous seeds. Some leaders of these press organs have given way to inimical influence and have forgotten that the Party press must, first of all, faithfully and consistently fight for the realization of Marxist-Leninist ideas and must be a fighting propagandist in that struggle which is conducted for the cause of socialist construction.

---

[1] See *Trybuna Ludu,* July 22, 1956, also *Pravda,* July 22, 1956.

We Marxist-Leninists held and hold that every country contributes something new to the historic exercise of building socialism, that in the interest of building socialism, the many-sided growth of socialist democratism is indispensable.

But we cannot idly bypass attempts that are aimed at weakening the international ties of the socialist camp under the slogan of so-called national peculiarities. We cannot pass by in silence attempts which aim at undermining the power of the people's democratic state under the guise of "spreading democracy." No matter how well intentioned the people who are given to such experiments may be subjectively, they are in essence opposed to the best interests of their nation and are acting harmfully with respect to the sacred cause of socialism and democracy.

. . . On the basis of the experience of the CPSU we can state that the Party press is a powerful and effective weapon in the hands of Communist and Workers Parties. If the press bases itself on a correct, Marxist principle, it can certainly play its honored role as collective propagandist and collective organizer of the masses, in the struggle for the realization of the ideas in question.

. . . The recent events at Poznan, provoked by enemy agents, serve as additional proof that the international reaction has still not abandoned its delirious dreams of restoring capitalism in the socialist countries. We cannot forget this for a second. To be easygoing under these conditions would be an unforgivable sin.

Having delivered himself of this admonition, Bulganin together with Zhukov assured the Polish people that their western frontiers were unalterable.

1. DECLARATION BY N. A. BULGANIN AND G. K. ZHUKOV ON THE WESTERN BORDERS OF POLAND, JULY 25, 1956[2]

FRIENDS, CITIZENS OF SILESIA!

We bring you brotherly greetings from the Soviet Union.

We are happy that justice triumphed and Silesia returned to your native Poland.

No one will ever be able to disturb this act of justice.

---

[2] *Trybuna Ludu,* July 26, 1956.

The western frontiers and Silesia are now forever Polish.

The guarantee of this will be the friendship of the peoples of our socialist camp, the friendship of the Polish and Soviet peoples.

Long live People's Poland!

July 25, 1956   N. Bulganin

G. Zhukov

While Bulganin and Zhukov toured the country, the Central Committee of the PUWP elected three new members (Edward Gierek, Roman Nowak, and Adam Rapacki) and two new alternate members (Stefan Jedrychowski and Eugeniusz Stawinski) to the Politburo, acknowledged the resignation of Jakub Berman, heard a report by its First Secretary, Edward Ochab,[3] and adopted a resolution which mapped out future policy in some detail.

2. Resolution Adopted by the Central Committee of the Polish United Workers Party at Its Seventh Plenary Session, July 18-28, 1956[4]

I

THE DECISIONS OF THE Third Plenum of the Central Committee and particularly Party discussion since the 20th Congress of the CPSU have opened a new era in the life of the Party and in the development of the political situation at home.

Our Party has submitted to just criticism the ideological and political distortions of the past resulting from the deviations from the Leninist principles of Party and state life—the cult of personality, restrictions of democracy, and violations of the rule of law. The Party has undertaken to put right the errors and distortions.

Expressing the most profound desire of the working class and of the people's masses, our Party has proclaimed and initiated a course aiming at the deepening of the democratization

[3] See *Trybuna Ludu,* July 20, 1956.

[4] *Trybuna Ludu,* July 31, 1956.

of the country and the implementation of a program for improving more speedily than hitherto the living standards of the working masses, particularly the working class.

This new course of the Party and the people's power leads to the strengthening of the bonds linking the Party and the people's power with the masses.

Adopting the new course and implementing it with all consistency as the only right course, the Party must bear in mind that in a class society, with a still considerable influence of bourgeois and petit-bourgeois ideology, the process of democratization will not only strengthen socialist tendencies, but will also activize the bourgeois elements. The bourgeois elements are attempting to exploit this process for the organization of their forces and for an intensified influence upon the working masses. The prerequisite for the proper development of the process of socialist democratization is to make these attempts to enliven bourgeois tendencies impossible, as well as to consolidate the leading role of the Marxist-Leninist Party.

Directing the process of democratization, the Party should at the same time introduce socialist consciousness not only into the ranks of the working class, but also into the ranks of its allies, overcoming gradually but consistently anarchistic, petit-bourgeois tendencies and utopian opinions detached from the concrete setup of political forces.

Inadequate consideration by the Party of these factors pertaining to the present setup of the class forces has had a negative effect on the development of the political situation.

The Central Committee plenum contends that the tragic events in Poznan, which caused a deep shock throughout the Party and throughout the working class and the nation, cast a new light upon the political and social situation of the country.

It is a fact that demagogues and hostile rabble-rousing elements succeeded in exploiting the particuar dissatisfactions of the ZISPO workers and of the workers of several other enterprises, caused by procrastination in dealing with their serious grievances and justified demands, thus bringing about strikes and street demonstrations.

It is a fact that this situation was exploited by underground, counterrevolutionary groups, drawing their inspiration from alien sources hostile to Poland, so as to carry out a criminal provocation and armed actions against the people's power at the very time of the International Fair, in order to give an international importance to the events and in order to undermine Poland's position.

It is a fact that this bloody provocation aimed against the people's state has brought home to the workers who went into the streets the true goals of the provocateurs. It found no support on the part of the working class in Poznan; it remained isolated in the country and met with the condemnation of public opinion.

The Poznan events cannot be treated in isolation from the situation in the country. They set for the Party the task of carrying out a profound evaluation of the sources and causes lying at its foundation.

It is necessary to point to new factors which have become apparent in the political situation of the country.

In the first place, the process of democratization, of enforcing the Leninist norms in Party life, and of making good the bureaucratic distortions initiated by the Party is being carried out in a situation in which a feeling of disappointment has accumulated, particularly among the workers and the working intelligentsia, as a result of unfulfilled hopes for a genuine improvement in the living standards in the course of the implementation of the Six-Year Plan.

Dissatisfaction in many workers' centers is being accentuated by prolonged and frequently soulless dealing with the just demands and grievances of the working man. This leads to the upsetting of proper relations between the different sections of the working class and the Party and the people's power; it gives birth to feelings of mistrust and disappointment which are exploited by disrupting elements, to whom sense of responsibility for the interests of the toiling masses and the people's state is alien.

The Party leadership underestimated and did not draw the attention of the Party organizations in time to the fact that the development of socialist democracy, under the complex political situation and difficult economic situation, called for a particularly solicitous and operative approach to the just demands of the workers—demands which it was possible to meet—and, at the same time, for determined resistance by Party organizations against demagogic demands and disrupting actions.

In the second place, the immensely animated, fertile, and on the whole correct discussion in our Party and in the entire community since the 20th Congress of the CPSU which has taken the right direction has had a particularly sharp and painful course. It took place directly after a painful loss to the Party and to the community, namely the death of Comrade Bierut.

The shock which occurred in the Party under the influence of the truth about the serious mistakes committed by Stalin and about the distortions of the Party and social life connected with the cult of personality in our country has been deepened by the revelation of the provocation that had as its victim the CPP and its leaders.

In the course of the discussion, propaganda and the press have made a substantial contribution to the process of democratization and have justly criticized the distortions of the past and the unfavorable phenomena of our life.

At the same time, however, clear symptoms of one-sidedness have occurred—the overstressing of the subjective and underestimation of the objective causes of our difficulties. Some papers have passed over in silence and have even frequently denied the historic achievements of the nation attained under the leadership of the Party. On many occasions there has been an inadequate sense of responsibility for the genuine character of the information and little concern for the reality and factualness of the demands put forward. The press and propaganda failed to oppose with adequate vigor false views and anti-Party attacks.

In a situation in which many old and deeply rooted views and conceptions obviously had to be revised, symptoms of ideological disarmament, as well as of political disorientation and demobilization, among a part of the Party *aktiv* and among Party members have become manifest.

The great intensification of public criticism of diverse errors and distortions in various sectors of the country's life and economy were not accompanied to an adequate degree by practical measures, primarily in the economic field, which would consistently aim at correcting distortions, at speedier dealing with grievances, and at overcoming the difficulties mounting along the road of socialist building. The Party Central Committee failed to submit with the necessary speed a well developed and constructive program for overcoming the existing difficulties.

At the same time, there were many cases in which Party activists and Party bodies, particularly in the provinces, frequently showed inability and sometimes even dislike of implementing in practice the Leninist norms of Party and social life. This led to their detachment from the working masses.

Against this background, the symptoms of the growing impatience among the masses have become particularly accentuated.

In the third place, after the Third Central Committee Plenum essential changes for the better occurred in the activities of the security services.

However, the delays in the decision concerning the rehabilitation of persons unjustly charged and sentenced in the past and concerning the liquidation of results of distortions in the security apparatus extended the period of the sharp criticism of that apparatus. This caused symptoms of demobilization in the organs appointed for the defense of the people's power and of public order.

The criticism of the false thesis on the inevitable sharpening of the class struggle parallel to the development of socialist building, which was in the right direction, has been understood in many Party branches in a simplified manner. An equally false thesis saying that the class struggle has already died down in our country, or alleging it was impossible to sharpen it in a determined internal or international situation, also began to spread.

This led to a weakening of revolutionary vigilance in the Party and in the organs of the people's state, to disregard for the strength of the enemy, who despite the narrowing of his social base and despite the destruction of the reactionary underground, retained the ability to act and to organize actions hostile to the people's power.

All these factors characterizing our present political situation manifested themselves in an intensified form during the Poznan events.

The events in Poznan resounded with a loud echo throughout the country, causing, on one side, an increase of vigilance and readiness for mobilization in our Party of all those who were conscious, and on the other side, an activation of the reactionary underground, of the hidden forces of the class enemy, and of the foreign agencies at home.

Fully aware of the responsibility for the further development of the country, the Party should rally its forces in the battle for strengthening the bonds with the masses, for a speedier improvement of living standards, and for a further democratization of the life of the Party and of the country against the background of the action program contained in the decisions of the Seventh Plenum of the Central Committee.

The Party should carry out with all vigor a transformation of the methods and style of its work and of the work done by all the organs of power that will guarantee unflinching implementation of that program.

II

The Party should become aware and bring home to the entire community the true economic situation of Poland, the nature of our difficulties, and the realistic possibilities and means of improvement and further economic development of the country.

As a result of the selfless work of the millions-strong masses during the period of the Six-Year Plan, important tasks outlined by the Party and Government have been carried out and powerful foundations have been laid for the industrialization and socialist transformation of Poland. The regained territories have been rehabilitated; the capital has been rebuilt; an appreciable production and defense potential has been created in our country; the ranks of the working class have doubled; the social structure and the setup of class forces in the country have altered.

In the realization of the Six-Year Plan a great part was played by the assistance of the USSR and cooperation with the people's democracies. Poland has become an important link in the world socialist system. These are undeniable historical achievements accompanied by profound cultural transformations and by progress in many fields of life—achievements which provide powerful testimony to the superiority of socialism over capitalism.

However, the implementation of these tasks, particularly in the first phase of the implementation of the Six-Year Plan—before the Second Party Congress—have absorbed too many resources and means of our economy at the expense of the neglect of other tasks of the Six-Year Plan, and in particular, of the considerable stepping up of the living standards of masses as laid down in the plan. The violent increase of employment and expansion of many social amenities were accompanied by an only negligible increase of real wages, while the situation of a part of the workers did not improve, and with regard to some groups, even deteriorated.

In the course of the implementation of the Six-Year Plan several disproportions occurred in our national economy. They have made it impossible to achieve an increase in living standards of the nation envisaged by the plan.

A serious disproportion arose between the pace of the development of industry and the pace of the development of agriculture, the base for the food supply of the population and the raw material base for light industry. This disproportion resulted from the underestimation of the production needs of agriculture, from the weakening of the incentives for the material interests of peasants, both individual farmers and members of cooperatives, owing to the distortion of the principles of the worker-peasant alliance and owing to the violation of the rule of law in the relation between the state and the peasants. The making good of these distortions after the Second Party Congress and the concentration of efforts upon the stepping up of agricultural production, despite the fact that they have already brought about tangible results, could not eliminate this excessive disproportion.

A considerable disproportion occurred between the insufficiently developed raw material base and between the needs of the processing and building industries. This is the main cause of the tension in the plans for the supply of raw materials and other materials and of the lack or inadequacy of reserves, as well as difficulties in cooperation resulting from the above, lack of rhythmical implementation of plans, idleness of machinery, failure to exploit production capacity in many enterprises, and so forth, all of which have very painful effects.

A considerable disproportion occurred between the excessive size and costs of capital investments—as a matter of fact, frequently widely scattered investments which were not always fully justified economically—and the possibilities of the national economy. This has caused an excessive proportion of investments in the national revenue, the freezing of important resources in investments which realize returns slowly, and at the same time, neglect of the modernization and exploitation of the production potential of the old enterprises.

The burden of investments and of defense expenditure was considerably increased during the years 1951-53, during the period of growing international tension in connection with the war in Korea, when the necessity arose for a speedy expansion of the defense industry. This entailed costly investments and the mobilization of skilled cadres, frequently at the expense of the development of civilian industry.

As a result of the wrong policy toward craftsmen and the particularly faulty fiscal and supply policy, a completely unjustified and detrimental restriction of the output of crafts and of small industry has occurred, as well as a hampering of the development of servicing points.   This has rendered difficult the increase of mass consumption goods, the widening of their range, and a better meeting of the demands of the population.

In the course of the implementation of the Six-Year Plan, an excessive centralization of the planning and administration of economy has taken place, as well as an excessive growth of the state apparatus and of the administrative and economic apparatus and the bureaucratization of the methods of the leadership.   These phenomena have hampered the initiative of the masses and of the economic workers directly in charge of the enterprises, have caused waste and have retarded technical progress and economic expansion in general.

All the above-mentioned disproportions and distortions in economic life have become particularly painful at present. The difficulties are increased by the reduction of coal exports caused by the necessity of meeting demands at home and of reducing the excessive tension of work in coal mining.   This necessitates a certain reduction of imports.

The entire Party should become aware that the difficulties existing at present which restrict an appreciable improvement of the standard of living of the working masses are of a temporary nature.

Contrary to the Six-Year Plan in which the fundamental achievement was the great step made along the road leading to the industrialization of the country accompanied, however, by an inadequate increase of the living standards, the new Five-Year Plan should, with the support of the production potential already created, yield such an increase of industrial and agricultural production as would enable the achievement of a considerably speedier growth of the living standards of the masses.

The fundamental premises of the Five-Year Plan should be:

a) the stepping up of the real wages of workers and employees by 30 percent, with the proviso that the wages of the lower paid workers would increase above this average, and the stepping up of the average income per capita of rural population by 30 percent.

b) the improvement of housing conditions of the urban population through the building of houses, amounting to 1.2 million rooms during the 5-year period.

These tasks are difficult but fully realistic, provided we are able to exploit and rationally develop the production capacity created during the Six-Year Plan and to set in motion the great reserves existing both in agriculture and in industry.

The guarantee of the realistic character of these tasks is:

First: The fact that several large investments from the period of the Six-Year Plan will only now and in the next few years be in full production, and it will be possible to achieve further increase of production with considerably smaller financial and material outlays.

The genuine increase of industrial production for the requirements of the national economy and of the population should also be attained through turning part of the defense industry over to civilian purposes.

Second: The fact that we possess large cadres of skilled workers, technicians, and engineers who have been trained during the past period, and that the influx of unskilled labor into industry and the cost of their training can be considerably lower under the Five-Year Plan than during the Six-Year Plan.

Third: The fact that in agriculture, owing to the liquidation of several distortions since the Second Congress and owing to the greater assistance of the state and effective working of the incentives bringing about material interest, a production increase is taking place, particularly with regard to stockbreeding. The consistent implementation and deepening of this policy can insure a further considerable increase of vegetable and livestock production.

The implementation of the program for the improvement of the living standards of the working masses, the principal premise of the Five-Year Plan, calls for a consistant and bold change of the methods and directions of our economic policy.

1—The indispensable condition for setting in motion the internal reserves of our national economy is the execution of profound changes in the existing system of management.

The general direction of these changes spells the deepening and widening of the democratic traits of our system, *liquidation of excessive centralization of planning and management, and further widening of the prerogatives of socialist enterprises,* creating foundations for wide social initiative and economic control on the part of the working masses.

The decisions on the widening of the prerogatives of the directors of enterprises, the reduction of the number of centrally established and controlled indices and tasks, should be regarded as first steps in this direction.

A revision of many regulations pertaining to the national economy should be carried out. They should be made more uniform and their number should be reduced. The economic administration should be simplified and the clerical apparatus should be steadily reduced, while those dismissed should have alternative employment secured.

The decentralization of the system of management of the national economy calls for a further widening of the prerogatives of the people's councils, both provincial and district, as well as municipal and parish councils, with regard to direct management of affairs connected with agriculture, small industry, commerce, transport, municipal economy and housing, building, education and vocational training, culture, and health protection.

At the same time, the powers of the excessively developed apparatus of the provincial people's councils should be restricted and some of these powers should be transferred to the district and municipal councils.

The district and municipal authorities should become centers directly managing the local economy and administration.

The number of ministries and central boards should be reduced. The organization of supplies and cooperation should be streamlined, among other ways, through the provision of the possibility of direct contacts between enterprises, suppliers, and recipients. Changes should be carried out in the organization of foreign trade which would insure the participation of enterprises, producers, and recipients in the conclusion of transactions. Proper economic incentives should be created, as well as conditions for the material interest of the staff in the expansion of production for export.

In connection with these changes the cadres of experts, large numbers of whom are at present detached from production and occupied in purely administrative work, should be transferred directly to industrial enterprises, which frequently feel the shortage of highly skilled employees.

The appreciable reduction of the administrative apparatus, possible only by changing the system and method of managing the socialist economy, should be carried out with all vigor and determination, despite the resistance of conservative and bureaucratic elements. However, this change must be made in a planned and thought-out manner, for this calls for a transitory period, during which conditions must be created for purposeful employment of the dismissed officials and employees, for their training for new jobs, in industry, building, transport, in the municipal economy, in commerce, and diverse servicing enterprises.

2—The fundamental condition for the exploitation of the reserve existing in the socialist enterprises is *the raising of the direct material interest of the staff in the economic results of the enterprise.*

The policy of wages and economic incentives should serve the creation of fundamental conditions for raising the living standards of the working masses, in the form of increased productivity, technical progress, and steady reduction of production costs. That is why one should combine relatively speedier rising of the wages of the lower paid workers with an encouragement of foremen and technical personnel, particularly engineer-mechanics and engineer-technologists, to raise their professional skill. It is of immense importance to simplify the system of wage calculations which will make possible their control by the workers.

The liquidation of excessive centralization of management and the reduction of the administrative apparatus must be accompanied by the widest possible introduction of the principle of strict economic accounting and profitability of enterprises and the release of economic incentives encouraging the staff and the managing personnel not only to implement the quantitative indices of the plan, but also to step up the quality of output, to widen the range of goods, to combat squandering, and to reduce production costs in order to assure technical progress and an increase in productivity. It is necessary to strengthen the importance of the plant fund through the increase of allocations from profits made by the enterprise. The plant fund should be earmarked for additional emoluments for the staff and for the improvement of housing conditions, for new buildings and repairs.

3—One of the decisive conditions for the improvement of the work of industry is the *streamlining of the management of materials and the systematic improvement of supplies of materials and the systematic improvement of supplies to enterprises and inter-enterprise cooperation.*

The production plans of all branches of production must be based on a realistic assessment of the possibility of supplies of raw material and semi-products, fuel, and ancillary materials. In addition to the just struggle against excessive accumulation of reserves of raw materials and semi-products, tools, and so on, it is necessary to aim at insuring for all enterprises such allocations of reserves of materials, fuels, and semi-products as would make possible a rhythmical implementation of plans, the observance of technological requirements, and the most rational exploitation of existing production capacity.

In order to insure rhythmical production it is necessary to introduce a proper system of cooperation and specialization in production, in particular in the machine industry, and to apply material incentives favoring a discipline in deliveries.

4—*The strictest possible discipline is indispensable, both in financial and real investments.*

Investments should be concentrated on projects which are in the process of building and on projects which allow rapid achievement of maximum economic returns, combating all symptoms of squandering, squandering at the planning stage, construction of projects according to the requirements of modern technology, taking fully into consideration the indispensable hygienic and labor-safety equipment.

It is necessary to undertake with determination every initiative for the achievement of the volume of production envisaged by the plan without additional investment, or even with its reduction.

5—It is necessary to expand and deepen considerably economic research and to insure the practical exploitation of the results of that research and the participation of scientists and economists in planning current and long-term economic policy. Particularly urgent is the determination of methods for examining the effectiveness of the investment policy and production for export.

6—In regard to agriculture and relations with the peasantry, *it is necessary to continue with all consistency the policy outlined by the Second Congress and by the Fifth Plenum of the Central Committee,* the correctness of which is being confirmed by clear symptoms of increasing agricultural production. The bonds between town and country must also be strengthened and simple forms of cooperation and consolidation of producer cooperatives must be developed.

A 25 percent increase in agricultural production, called for in the Five-Year Plan, can be achieved only if increased machinery, credit, and investment assistance is accompanied by increasing incentives of material interest, both in regard to individually farming peasants and to the producer cooperatives, through the development of free market purchases, contracting, and so on.

It is necessary to consider as possible and useful the abolishing of compulsory deliveries of milk as of January 1, 1957. As a result, the interest of peasants and producer cooperatives in stockbreeding should be raised.

Abolishing compulsory milk deliveries will yield appreciable additional benefits to the countryside. It should contribute to the full and timely implementation of compulsory deliveries of grain, livestock, and potatoes, the general amount of which will remain unaltered in accordance with the decisions of the Fifth Plenum.

In order to create favorable conditions for a further increase of grain production and in order to streamline the distribution of fertilizers, it is necessary to link the allocation of fertilizers to peasants from the so-called free market pool with the compulsory deliveries of cereals according to fixed regional norms.

At the same time it is necessary to take into consideration the necessity of insuring the required quantity of fertilizers for pastures and so on.

Of no less importance for the exploitation of the reserves in agricultural production is the extending of consistent investment assistance to agriculture through an improved supply of machines and tools and through the increase of the range of services by the State Machine Stations.

The neglect of the needs of rural building can be felt more and more acutely and this has an adverse effect both on agricultural production, particularly with regard to stockbreeding, and on the housing conditions of the rural population, which induce a flight of the population from country to city. In this connection it is necessary to adopt measures that would insure not only an appreciable increase in the allotment of building materials for the countryside, with a range which would take into consideration its requirements, but also a guarantee that these materials will be used as planned.

It is necessary to aim at the creation of economic conditions which will counteract the excessive exodus of people from agriculture.

The Party, aiming at a further expansion and strengthening of producer cooperatives, should implement with all consistency the decisions of the Fifth Plenum of the Central Committee ordering increased state assistance to the producer cooperatives and the expansion of material incentives so as to interest the cooperators in raising collective production, taking into consideration to the widest possible extent the demands put forward by the Second Congress of producer cooperatives.

Implementing with all vigor the program for the assistance to small and middle-holding peasants, embraced in the decisions of the Fifth Plenum, the Central Committee considers as imperative the consistent rectification of errors committed toward the richer farms owned by middle-holding peasants, who, to the detriment to the cause of the worker-peasant alliance, have been frequently termed kulaks. It is imperative as well to remove the errors and distortions with regard to kulak farms.

It is necessary to eliminate altogether the practice of mechanical and superficial assessment of the size of the farm and the designation of richer farms as kulak farms. The only yardstick justifying the designation of a farm as a kulak farm is permanent exploitation of other people's labor in the form of systematic hire of labor and in the form of permanent usury, renting of land, speculation, repayment in labor, and so on.

The policy toward kulak farms should be flexible and varied, so that the practice of restricting should not lead to the cutting down of their production as was the case in some regions of the country.

While combating with determination the resistance of the hostile part of the kulaks against duties toward the state and their propaganda against the producer cooperatives, it is also necessary to make it possible for kulak farms to survive. An end must also be put to the practice, incompatible with the law of People's Poland, of hampering genuine division of farms among children who are setting up families.

It is also necessary to bring an end to the practice of making it difficult for certain kulaks to reduce their weakened farms provided the possibility exists for a partial taking over of these farms. It is necessary to consider it permissible to accept loyal kulaks into the consolidated producer cooperatives, provided that the village consents. The kulak farms which have the necessary conditions for normal production, for farming the entire land, and for the development of stockbreeding should have an opportunity to benefit from the advantages of contracting and should qualify, on certain determined conditions, for the assistance of the State Machine Stations, the purchase of fertilizers, and for obtaining credits, with a simultaneous restriction by the state of their exploitation and profiteering tendencies.

7—Considerable reserves for the growth of production and services for the needs of the population and, at the same time, for increase in employment, *exist in the expansion of small industry, work cooperatives, crafts, and cottage industry*. One should apply here, particularly with regard to crafts, an economic policy that would remove the errors with regard to supplies, taxes, and credits, and also the erroneous, centralized, and bureaucratic system of management, and open to the small state, cooperative, and crafts producers wide opportunities for expansion.

It is necessary to subordinate to the maximum possible degree the small industrial state enterprises to the district and municipal people's councils and to transfer to them supervision over work cooperatives. The apparatus of the higher organs of the small industry and of the work cooperatives must be radically curtailed and their prerogatives restricted to planning, supervision over the conditions for expansion, and to technical assistance and instructions. In the work cooperatives it is necessary to step up appreciably the role of self-government.

The organization of small state and cooperative enterprises demands a reduction of the administrative apparatus and a maximum simplification, so as to insure to these enterprises the greatest possible degree of independence in adaptation to the requirements of the local markets and to the possibilities of obtaining local supplies. The activities of the enterprises of small industry and of the work cooperatives should aim at basing themselves on the principles of full profitability, and the fixing of prices should be simplified to the maximum. The prerequisite for the expansion of the production of the small producers is improvement of the supplies of raw materials from local sources, as well as of machines and tools.

State assistance and protection should be extended to individual craftsmen, toward whom important errors have been committed during the past period. It is necessary to bring an end to the false practice of treating the craftsmen as the representatives of a stratum alien to socialism.

On the contrary, the crafts should be treated as an important supplement of the socialist state and cooperative industry, mainly in the field of services and production for the needs of the population.

It is necessary to recognize as inadvisable the existence of auxiliary cooperatives as the exclusive intermediary between state enterprises and private handicraft. On the other hand, it is necessary to support the voluntary association of artisans for the purpose of facilitating supplies and sales. At the same time, it is necessary to combat abuse, bribery, and speculation practiced under the pretext of promoting the sound initiative of artisans.

Workshops employing up to four assistants as well as a suitable number of apprentices, depending on the trade, should be treated as handicraft workshops.

The taxation policy should be based on simple principles preventing arbitrariness on the part of financial departments, and the extent of taxation should be diminished. It is necessary to increase the supplies of materials and raw materials for handicrafts, widen credit assistance, increase loans for setting up workshops and servicing establishments, and allot premises for them, as well as enable them to purchase machines and tools in socialist enterprises.

Craftsmen should have the right to sell their products freely either directly to retail state, cooperative, and private shops, or on the spot in their own workshops. Socialist enterprises—

industrial and trading—should be permitted to place orders with craftsmen without previous refusal to execute these orders by local small-scale socialized production establishments, provided, however, that the prices, quality, or the delivery date are more advantageous than those offered by small-scale socialized establishments.

Constant implementation of the listed changes in the direction and methods of the economic policy of the country, combined with increasingly broader initiative and devoted efforts of the working class, peasants, and intelligentsia, should guarantee the execution of the basic tasks of the Five-Year Plan.

An improvement in the living conditions of the working class is already being attained, within our economic possibilities, and will be systematically implemented in the coming years as well.

In order to achieve this, the Central Committee considers it necessary to undertake, among other things, the following steps:

a) To continue to implement the plan, announced by the Party and Government, of raising and regulating wages and salaries, above all, of the relatively lowest paid groups of workers. The total sum originally providing for 5 billion zlotys annually, this year should be raised to 7 billion zlotys. The regulation of wages should be carefully prepared by the organs of economic administration and trade unions so as to prevent disadvantageous changes in the earnings of any group of workers.

b) To recognize as inadmissible the revision of the work norms applied so far in establishments if this revision will cause a drop in earnings. The principle must be introduced that individual changes in norms in the enterprise may be carried out only in conjunction with essential changes in the technological process and the organization of production, in agreement with the appropriate trade union bodies.

All general changes of norms in the various branches of the economy must be carried out only in conjunction with an appropriate change of rates, so that earnings do not suffer. Decisions in this matter can be adopted by the ministries only in agreement with the executives of the trade unions.

c) To insure the implementation of the commitments stemming from collective agreements and other legal acts—coal allowances, payment in kind, protective clothing, and so forth.

d) To examine in the near future the decisions and regulations concerning working conditions and wages from the point of view of their compatibility with existing labor and wage legislation, as well as to make up for all possible injustices done to working people.

e) To achieve a radical improvement of industrial safety and hygiene conditions, sanitary and hygiene installations, and the quality of special clothing and equipment for personal protection.

f) To base the observance and strengthening of socialist work discipline on the worker's consciousness and educational measures provided for in labor regulations, adapted to the conditions in every branch of the national economy. In connection with this, recognize that the time is ripe for PUWP deputies to present a motion in the Sejm of the Polish People's Republic to abolish the law on socialist labor discipline.

g) In order to put an end to the abnormal working conditions in the coal industry, it is necessary to insure a sufficient number of new recruits and reduce the number of planned working Sundays from 23 in 1956 to 12 in 1957, and to abolish them completely in 1958. This will create the necessary premises for an improvement of the situation in coal mining.

At a time when the coal balance sheet, both for home requirements and export, is extremely tight, the normalization of working conditions in coal mining must be accompanied by full mobilization of the efforts of the workers, engineers, and technicians to achieve an improvement of the organization of work in coal mining, as well as to promote the coal-saving campaign throughout the entire national economy.

h) While pursuing a policy of diversifying and widening the range of commodities produced, it is necessary to combat with determination the tendencies of withdrawing less expensive articles while a demand for them exists. Supervision over the organs called upon to fix and control prices should be intensified.

i) As the reorganization of the administrative apparatus progresses, vacated premises should be utilized to improve the housing conditions of the working people.

j) To raise as of January 1, 1957, the family allowances for families of lower paid workers with many children to support.

k) To introduce a strict regime of economies in the field of expenditures on state representation, office equipment, propaganda purposes, and so forth.

As a result of these steps, this year some 3.6 million persons employed in various fields of the national economy will receive higher wages, which will amount annually to over 7 billion zlotys. Of this sum old-age and other pensioners will receive some 800 million zlotys.

Further pay raises must be strictly coordinated with the volume of goods and services which can be assigned to meet the needs of the population. Purchasing power not covered by supplies on the market will not contribute to raising the standard of living but, on the contrary, will become a source of economic difficulties, a shortage of goods, and, consequently, of profiteering.

The Party organizations must widely and patiently explain to the masses the present economic situation, the sources of our difficulties, and the roads and prospects for constant improvement mapped out in the Five-Year Plan.

The strengthening of labor discipline, mobilization of the personnel to work as efficiently as possible, prevention of all wastage and disorganization in production, concern for a rapid, effective, and wise settlement of the grievances of manual and intellectual workers—these are the key tasks facing at present all Party organizations in the struggle for the plan, the struggle on whose success depends to a decisive degree the improvement of the living standards of the working people.

All disturbances in the normal functioning of establishments undermine the fulfillment of our economic plans, become the source of considerable losses, and turn against the interests of the working class and of the people's state.

III

The Central Committee declares that the trend toward the democratization of the life of the country, the liquidation of the consequences and the remnants of the cult of personality, the consolidation of the socialist rule of law should continue to be realized most consistently as the only way of consolidating the ties of the Party and the people's power with the masses and drawing the million-strong masses of the nation into actual participation in governing the state and constructing a new socialist life.

All attempts to hamper the process of democratization as a result of the Poznan events would be erroneous and politically harmful. Quite to the contrary, the situation in the country proves that orientation toward overcoming bureaucratic distortions is still not being realized with sufficient consistency, particularly in such a decisive field as relations in socialist work establishments between the administration, the trade unions, and the workers' personnel.

The indispensable and invigorating process of democratization in our country cannot be carried out spontaneously without taking into account that it is taking place in a country in which socialism is only being built, in which class contradictions, the influence of bourgeois, reactionary, and nationalistic ideology, fed and exploited by the class enemy and foreign imperialist agents, exist and are at work. This means that the struggle of the Party for democratization and the elimination of bureaucratic distortions should be conducted—while broadening the field of activity and independent initiative of the working class and of all the popular masses and not hampering sound and creative criticism based on socialist principles—in a manner that will not leave any room for the activity of backward, hostile, and antisocialist forces, that will combat in a determined manner alien views hostile to Marxism-Leninism, as well as all attempts at undermining the people's power and the gains of the working masses.

The necessity of democratizing the life of the country does not arise from urgent political needs, but is linked with the fundamental objective requirements of the development of socialist construction and of the people's democratic state.

The very fact of the conquest of power by the working class under the leadership of its Party and of carrying out fundamental revolutionary reforms constitutes a tremendous leap in the direction of true democracy, for it cuts the roots of exploitation and oppression of the popular masses. But it does not automatically solve the problem of relations between the Party, the state, and the popular masses.

Experience shows that from the moment the people's power becomes consolidated, the Party faces the danger of bureaucratic distortions, which express themselves in a tendency to restrict democracy and to apply mainly administrative methods of government, transgressing the principle of collective leadership. This inescapably leads to isolation of Party and state cadres from the masses and to grave political errors.

In the early stages of Soviet power, Lenin many times pointed to the danger of bureaucratic distortion. Lenin said, "The continuation of the struggle against bureaucracy is unconditionally and absolutely necessary for the victory of further socialist construction." Lenin pointed out that "it is possible to fight against bureaucracy to the end, to complete victory, only when the whole population takes part in governing the state."

Our Party and the people's power did not succeed in avoiding serious bureaucratic distortions. Over a period of a number of years there was an increasing centralization of power, of administration and planning, which nullified the extension of the rights both of local organs of authority and of all institutions of popular representation. Responsibility before the higher organs of the state and economic apparatus did not go together with responsibility before the millions-strong masses of working people.

The excessively overgrown administrative apparatus to a considerable degree replaced the constitutional authority of the people's councils, restricted the influence of social organizations and of cooperative self-government, thus often concealing the democratic and popular character of our state.

The struggle against bureaucracy separating the people's power from the masses constitutes one of the most important tasks of the Party in the work aimed at developing socialist democracy.

The Party should, step by step and in an intransigent manner, pave the way for the process of democratization, looking for proper solutions on the basis of the present alignment of class and political forces, as well as on the basis of the requirements of successive stages of socialist construction.

The Central Committee considers it necessary to take the following steps in order to combat bureaucracy effectively and to further socialist democracy:

1—Broadening Workers' Democracy in Work Establishments. The Party should combat methods of bureaucratic management in work establishments, methods which lead to the distortion of the correct principle of one-man leadership, to manifestations of arbitrariness on the part of the administration, to keeping personnel away from problems pertaining to the management of the works, to numerous manifestations of callousness toward the grievances and needs of the workers, and to restricting the influence and proper role of the trade unions as a representative of the workers.

One should unflinchingly observe the principle of one-man leadership, which guarantees efficient management of the economy of an enterprise. At the same time, the Party organizations should use their right to control the activity of economic administration more effectively, broadening the influence of the Party organization taken as a whole on the activity of the establishment, developing in all Party members a sense of responsibility for the management of the establishment, and increasing the activity and initiative of all personnel.

Together with broadening the rights of the directors of socialist enterprises, one should broaden the competence and the rights of the works councils with regard to the administration, and develop effective forms for direct participation of the workers in examining all matters pertaining to the implementation of plans, the expansion of the establishment, and the working and living conditions of the working staff.

The works councils should have the right: to participate in the solution of all matters connected with the material situation of the personnel and the working conditions, and above all in the solution of all matters pertaining to wages and norms, bonuses, working time, special clothing, leaves, hiring and firing, work discipline, the allocation of apartments and their repair, social and cultural facilities, and so forth; to participate in working out the plan of the establishment within the limits provided for the establishment's management; to participate in decisions pertaining to the utilization of the works funds; and to control and see to it that the collective work contracts and the collective agreement are implemented.

The administration and the works council should regularly consult the opinion of the workers in all essential matters concerning the establishment, as well as make reports to the workers concerning their activity, the implementation of the collective work agreement and of state plans.

Broadening the rights of the works councils, while fully preserving the principle of one-man leadership in socialist enterprises, entails the possibility of differences of opinion between the works council and the administration of the establishment, particularly with regard to matters pertaining to the defense of the interests of the workers and observance by the administration of labor regulations. The solution of these differences belongs to the higher organs of economic administration and to the trade unions.

The Party organizations and the directors of work establishments should exert much greater efforts than before to draw engineers and technicians more actively into plant affairs and to utilize their qualifications, experience, and devotion to work.

The increased rights of the management of establishments and of works councils call for increased activeness by Party organizations, which should watch over the development of workers' democracy and the means of political work, insure the correct linking of the interests of the state with those of the personnel, oppose particularist tendencies and impulsiveness, and contribute a maximum of socialist consciousness to the everyday life of the establishment.

The practice of branch collective agreements defining the conditions of wages and work of the workers and employees in the basic branches of the national economy should be restored.

The development of worker's democracy in the establishments is of decisive importance for the improvement of the situation of the workers and for the elimination of their grievances, for the enhancement of the feeling among them that they are the masters of the establishment, of responsibility for production, labor discipline, and exemplary order in the establishment.

2—Broadening of the Autonomy and Rights of the People's Councils. The Party should combat the distortion of the legislative role of the people's councils on all levels, as well as the bureaucratic practice of substituting the executive organs and administrative apparatus for the councils. The Party should overcome improper methods in directing the councils, consisting in the fact that the Party organs or the Party apparatus make detailed decisions pertaining to matters within the jurisdiction of the councils and thus restrict the independence and initiative of the councils.

The liquidation of excessive centralization of authority and a considerable broadening of the rights of the councils in the economic field, and therefore a necessary increase in the size of the local budget and the linking of this budget with the budget of a greater number of socialist enterprises, will create real foundations for enlivening the activity of the councils. This enlivenment will be achieved provided there is a considerable broadening of the actual control of the councils over the presidia, of the factual and not formal responsibility of the executive organs before the councils. This requires not only that the councils should hold regular sessions, but also that the councilors should have access to all fields of the council's activity, that the commissions of the councils, which are organs of social control over the work of the presidium, and of enterprises and institutions subordinated to them in villages, towns, and districts, should operate regularly.

Conditions should be created for independent financial management of the councils by raising their own sources of revenue without additional burdens on the population.

Particular attention should be paid to establishing close links between the councils and the personnel of work establishments, to increasing the participation of worker councilors, particularly those who work in big establishments.

Enlivening the activity of councils on all levels will be of decisive importance for the democratization of relations in the countryside, as well as for the establishment of closer links between the working peasants and the organs of people's power.

3—Enhancement of the Role of the Sejm and the Improvement of the Work of the Government and of the Ministries. Enhancing the role of the Sejm and safeguarding the full implementation of its constitutional tasks must be an integral part of the democratization of the political life of the country.

To insure that the Sejm fulfills its functions as the supreme legislative body and an organ controlling the activity of all other state organs, it is indispensable to subject the activity of the Government to a more effective control by the Sejm, to restrict the practice of issuing decree laws and to submit more often than hitherto draft laws to the Sejm for consideration, to improve the work of the Sejm committees, to convene plenary sessions more often than hitherto, as well as to make information concerning the activity of state organs more accessible to the deputies.

In order to increase the responsibility of the deputies and councilors to the electors it is necessary to draw up legal regulations on the procedure of recalling representatives in the Sejm and in the people's councils, in accordance with the provisions of the Constitution.

Work should be continued on improving the efficiency of the Government.

The range of problems requiring the decision of the Council of Ministers should be limited to basic problems with a simultaneous extension of the powers, independence, and responsibility of ministers.

4—Full Observance of Socialist Legality. The problem of the consolidation of socialist legality constitutes an integral part of the entire process of the democratization of the country. The Third Plenum of the Central Committee of our Party has already emphatically condemned infringements and breaches of the principles of legality, showing their sources in infringements of the Leninist standards of Party and social life, infringements of the principles of collective leadership, lack of control by the Party and the Government over security organs, and the concomitant excessive expansion of the functions and scope of activity of these organs.

After the Third Plenum substantial changes in the activity of the security organs, the prosecutor's offices, and the courts were put into effect. After the 20th Congress of the CPSU this process deepened still more.

The Party endeavored to overcome the delays in the implementation of the decisions of the Third Plenum concerning the observance of legality and effected correct changes in the methods and direction of activity of the organs of the administration of justice.

The Central Committee approves of the decisions of the Politburo insuring rehabilitation to those unjustly imprisoned, redress of wrongs, as well as punishment of those responsible for brutal infringement of legality and employment of inadmissible methods during investigations.

The problem of full observance and strengthening of legality should be the subject of the constant concern of the entire Party and of all organs of the people's power. Party organizations should show an uncompromising attitude with regard to any manifestation of abuse of power, with regard to injustice and wrongs suffered by citizens; they should combat with all determination infringements of law and stand guard over the equality of citizens before the law, as well as over their equal responsibility for any breaches of the law of the Polish People's Republic.

Of special importance for the consolidation of the confidence of the peasants toward the People's Government and for the strengthening of the worker-peasant alliance is the determined combating of any manifestation of the infringement of legality in economic, administrative, public order, and other problems, manifestations shocking the correct sense of justice of the working peasants.

The strict observance of labor legislation in work establishments should be insured, as well as the putting into effect of the decisions of the arbitration commissions and of the provisions of collective agreements.

Safeguarding of the strict observance of legality cannot by any means be interpreted as a suspension of the struggle against the enemy who is active and ready to take desperate steps, or as a justification of the lack of revolutionary vigilance toward the reactionary underground and foreign agents.

The observance of socialist legality means at the same time both the observance of the rights of the citizens by organs of the state power and the observance of the laws of People's Poland and of public order by the citizens.

The Central Committee deems the following as indispensable:

a) the further strengthening of prosecuting organs and the extension of their effective supervision over the investigation work of the citizens' militia and public security organs;

b) the consolidation of the independence of the courts and their protection against any interference from outside in their pronouncement of verdicts, the raising of the professional and political qualifications of judges, as well as improving the efficiency of the courts;

c) the improvement of the activity and enhancement of the vigilance and militancy of the security organs in the struggle against forces hostile to the people's state and against foreign diversion.

Party organs should render special political assistance to the organs of public security and citizens' militia, and determinedly fight attempts at charging the security organs with responsibility for offences committed by certain former members of the personnel of these organs. It is necessary to strengthen among the broad masses of the community the prestige of and confidence toward the security organs—selfless guardians of the gains of the revolution and of democracy.

5—Development of Criticism from Below and Openness of Political Life. The development of free, bold, and matter-of-fact criticism, criticism based on a socialist viewpoint, at meetings and in the columns of the press is an indispensable prerequisite of the democratization of the country's life, the most effective means of combating deficiencies, errors, and bureaucratic distortions. After the 20th Congress of the CPSU the big scope of discussion and of criticism of our deficiencies and neglects brought to the surface a great wealth of initiative and creative thought on the part of the working people. Party organizations, while supporting the development of creative criticism, first of all criticism from below, should oppose any attempts at stifling criticism, persecuting for criticism, and disregarding criticism. But one should not lose sight of the fact that alien and hostile elements often attempt to take advantage of the freedom of criticism in order to slander the achievements of People's Poland and to attack the policy of our Party.

An indispensable condition of democratization is the openness of political life, making available to the community information on the activity of the Government and of the Sejm, the public explanation of the policy of the Party and the people's power, of its motives and results.

In connection with this, one should markedly restrict the scope of state and economic secrets, bringing it down to the really indispensable minimum, and make it a duty for the organs of people's power to inform the population about their activities.

The democratization of state and social life is a process which should be accompanied by the concern of the Party for increasing the resourcefulness and efficiency of the functioning of the organs of people's power and their administrative apparatus, for increasing their authority.

The Party should help the masses in promoting thousands of socially experienced leaders, devoted to the cause of socialism and characterized by a high sense of responsibility.

IV

The Central Committee notes that the trend toward the democratization of the country's life and the elimination of bureaucratic distortions, which is indispensable for the realization of the economic programs mapped out by the Party and for the further construction of socialism, for the consolidation of the people's power and the effective combating of hostile activity, requires changes in the Party's work.

There can be no democratization of the country's life without a further democratization of the Party, which is the leading force of our people's state. This is a precondition of the correct development of the whole process of democratization and of the leading role of the Party in this process. Without the consistent application of Leninist principles of Party life, without the strengthening of conscious discipline based on the active participation of all Party members in the shaping of policy, the Party cannot strengthen its links with the masses. This is an indispensable condition for convincing the masses of the correctness of the policy of the Party, for the mobilization of the masses to overcome the difficulties which are facing the country.

The Party can fill the function of the vanguard of the working class and of the leading force of the people's state only if its policy is being shaped in an unbreakable union with the working class, the masses. In the meantime, petrification and bureaucratic distortions are still deeply rooted in the work of many Party organs and organizations, undermining their links with the masses.

1—In the present situation, the task of the Party organs to transfer the center of gravity of their work to political activity among the masses, to the direction of the activity of the basic Party organizations which are in daily contact with the masses, is becoming one of their most important duties. This problem today confronts the town and factory organizations with particular sharpness. In a number of work establishments great sensitivity, and even impatience, prevails among the workers. This is caused by numerous grievances as well as by the fact that workers' suggestions on possible solutions are often met by procrastination and callousness on the part of economic organs.

On the other hand, there are many illusions as to our present economic possibilities, illusions often fed by irresponsible voices in the press.

In this situation, Party organizations should be aware of everything in the minds of the masses, of their desires, demands, motions, and critical voices; they should be at the head of the progressive strivings of the masses; they should examine the difficult problems put forth by the masses; they should search for correct solutions of these problems, in accordance with the policy of the Party; they should fight at the head of the masses for the improvement of the situation in their locality, for the elimination of grievances and shortcomings, for the implementation of the tasks mapped out by the Party.

In expressing the progressive, revolutionary, and creative aspirations of the masses, and heading the fight to carry them out, the Party organizations should oppose unjust and unrealistic demands and demagogic slogans, and explain to the masses the present political and economic situation of the country, gain the active support of the masses for the initiative of the Party and Government, aimed at overcoming difficulties and improving their living conditions.

Cohesion of the basic Party organizations, their united action, is today more than ever indispensable for the implementation of these responsible tasks, for their effective influence on the factory personnel.

Rallying around themselves the broad masses and stimulating the activeness of these masses, the Party organizations should mobilize them to be vigilant against the instigations of hostile elements, rouse them to frustrate determinedly any steps infringing on the interests of the working class, the interests of the nation, and of the people's state.

A precondition for the implementation of these tasks is the intensified and direct assistance to Party organizations, especially in big work establishments, on the part of Party and state leaders.

2—Already the Third Plenum of the Central Committee stated that considerable shortcomings in the activity of all Party organs and organizations consist in wrong methods of work, which lead to the weakening of intra-Party life, as well as to distortions in relations between the Party organizations and the masses.

After the Third Plenum, despite certain changes for the better—considerable development of criticism from below, the restoration to a considerable degree of the principle of collective work in the Party bodies, increased independence of many Party links—no decisive turn was attained either in intra-Party work or in relations between the Party and the masses.

The slow changes in the methods of Party work and the tendencies toward a return to old practices have deep ideolog-- ical causes.

The past errors in the methods of Party work stemmed, among other things, from oversimplified and incorrect views of the leading role of the Party, which accumulated over many years.

Our Party, as the vanguard of the working class, the leading class wielding power in alliance with the working peasantry, constitutes the leading political force of the people's state. This .means that the Party should map out the direction, draw up the guiding lines of activity of the organs of state power, supervise their activity, and exercise control over them with the active participation of the masses.

In the past, however, the Party bodies not infrequently took to direct management and administration, thus duplicating the organs of state power and economic administration, restricting their independence and responsibility.

Instead of being the center of political inspiration and control for all organs of authority and social organizations, as well as concentrating their main efforts on political activity among the masses and on shaping the consciousness of these masses in accordance with the aims and tasks being put forward by the Party, the Party bodies concerned themselves mainly with administrative activity, and considered in the most minute details each step of the organs of state authorities, a fact which unavoidably led to paper obstruction and bureaucratization of the style of work, as well as to an excessive overgrowth of the Party apparatus.

Hence the excessive role of this apparatus and the diminishing of the role of elected Party bodies. The Party apparatus gradually took over the main burden of Party work, whereas the members of the Party bodies often abstained from tackling decisive problems and were regarded as "nonstaff instructors" and "nonstaff activists." The Central Committee notes that the Party must proceed to introduce gradually new methods of work in Party bodies and organizations; gradual introduction of these methods is necessary because this is linked up with overcoming old habits which do not recede at once but only as new methods, acquired by way of practical experience, are mastered.

The correct orientation of the work of Party bodies and organizations toward the solution of key problems of essential political, economic, and cultural importance, which are occupying the minds of the broad sections of workers, peasants, and of the intelligentsia, must be accompanied by a systematic and radical improvement in the methods of Party work. This will create an atmosphere conducive to drawing wide sections of the Party activists and the whole membership of the Party into the discussion of all problems of the policy of the country on the basis of equal rights in an atmosphere of real and not formal collective leadership, conducive to development of criticism from below.

In cadre work, which constitutes one of the most important factors in political leadership by the Party, the practice of detailed interference in personnel matters should be radically discarded by the Party bodies and apparatus, the practice which restricts the responsibility of the managers of state, economic, and social organs for cadres and, consequently, for their whole work.

The nomination of personnel by Party committees should be substantially restricted to apply only to top leading posts.

As far as leading posts filled by elections are concerned, the Party committees can recommend candidates, strictly observing, however, the opinion of the electors, their democratic rights, and the principles of legality.

The Party committees should watch over the correct direction of general cadre policy in state and economic organs, as well as in social institutions in their respective areas. Overcoming bureaucratic methods of Party work and the consistent democratization of the life of the Party will exert a decisive influence on the activity of state and economic organs, as well as on social organizations, trade unions, the ZMP [Polish Youth Union], the ZSCH [Peasant Self-Help Union], and so forth, the activity of which should be directed by the Party along political lines. It should be an especially important task of all Party organizations to extend assistance to the ZMP organizations, with a view to improving the forms of their work among the youth, enriching their ideological substance, developing their political initiative, and intensifying their concern for the living conditions of young people in town and country.

3—The proper role should be restored to the Party bodies in their plenary composition. Plenary meetings of the committees at all levels must not only be held regularly but must also change their character. From bodies often merely approving motions prepared by the executives, these committees should fully turn into bodies drawing up, in accordance with the line of the Party, concrete tasks for their own Party organizations and adopting decisions on the whole of the activity of the respective organizations which elected them.

An end should be put to the wrong practice of concentrating all powers of the Party bodies in the hands of the executives, which only from time to time, at their own discretion, submit proposals to the plenary meetings of the Party bodies for approval.

In order to restore to the Party bodies their proper role it is necessary that:

a) The members of the Party bodies, as political leaders, should maintain links with the Party organizations and non-Party centers in order to get to know personally the problems preoccupying people, the real views and worries of the workers, peasants, and the intelligentsia, to assist Party organizations in the solution of problems facing them. This firm principle in the work of the members of Party bodies acquires special significance at the present moment.

b) The members of the Party bodies should be versed in all problems of the policy of the Party on the national and local scale, and not only called to take part in the solution of problems concerning their own sector of work.

c) The executives should be required to submit reports on their whole activity at regular plenary meetings.

4—The reshaping of Party work requires overcoming a number of distortions in the work and functioning of the Party apparatus.

The employees of the Party apparatus—in their majority devoted Party activists, often having long-standing experience in political struggle and activity—cannot be treated as merely efficient executors of concrete organizational, narrow, functional tasks, duplicating state and economic functions. This distortion had particularly adverse effects on the education of the employees of the political apparatus, who in these conditions did not acquire proper theoretical and professional knowledge, did not develop the indispensable political independence and orientation corresponding to the growing tasks of the Party.

The Central Committee instructs the Secretariat to carry out a critical analysis of the structure of the Party apparatus with a view to abolishing unnecessary links, with a view to merging sections and sectors.

. The main task of the Party apparatus is to provide assistance to lower level Party organizations, to control the execution of the Party's resolutions and decisions, as well as to prepare material for evaluation and decision by the Party.

An important task of the Party apparatus is to follow the political and professional development, the methods, type, and results of the work of the local cadres, to prepare material for evaluation of the local cadre situation and policy, to assist, by their observations and remarks, the Party organizations and heads of the various sections of state, economic, and social work. The Party apparatus should carry out these functions in constant and direct contact with the masses, giving the highest consideration to their opinion, criticism, and initiative, fighting with persistency and with the deep sense of responsibility of a Party worker to see to it that the voice of the masses reaches the various bodies and leadership, that the opinion of the masses is given full consideration, that legitimate demands and initiatives are implemented as quickly as possible, that problems stemming from the life of the masses are solved, that the questions and doubts of the working people are given a rapid and correct answer, and the attempts of enemies to become active are properly rejected.

The employees of the Party apparatus should be kept informed about the entire activity of a given body, take part in the evaluation of the various sectors of local life, take part in conferences at which they should express their views as being coresponsible for the work of the Party bodies.

The Party apparatus should be recruited from among people of high political qualifications and moral attributes.

The Central Committee recommends to the Secretariat to strengthen district, large establishment, and municipal committees with qualified and experienced employees of the Central Committee and the *wojewodztwo* [regional] committees. The leading Party activists should—to a considerably greater degree than hitherto—be recruited from among local activists, trained by the given Party organization.

5—The task of strengthening the leading role of the Party is closely bound up with the necessity of effecting a change in the Party's attitude, as well as in the attitude of the Party bodies, toward social organizations.

The mass social organizations—the trade unions, the ZMP, the ZSCH—have not escaped serious bureaucratic ailments and are not playing to the full their proper role as organizations educating the masses in the spirit of socialism, representing the workers, peasants, and young people, and drawing millions of people into governing the country.

The independence of social organizations has often been fettered by commandeering, by breaches of their internal democracy, and by the replacement of their bodies by Party bodies.

Social organizations cannot play the role of transmission belts of the Party to the masses in a one-sided manner; they should at the same time give expression to the democratic aspirations of the masses, inform the Party of the moods, problems and needs of the various sections of the community, stimulate creative criticism and social initiative.

The Party should put an end to the harmful practice of commandeering social organizations and exercise its leading, ideological, and political influence through Party members democratically elected to the organs guiding the activity of these organizations. A rise in the independence of these organizations will help to enhance the prestige and confidence they enjoy among the masses.

6—In the past period, when the leading role of our Party in the National Front was consolidated, our cooperation with the United Peasant Party and the Democratic Party developed on the whole successfully.

The allied political parties have their own democratic and radical traditions. The Peasant Party has considerable influence among a section of the peasants, and the Democratic Party among artisans and part of the intelligentsia.

Within the National Front there are and will continue to be broad possibilities for the allied political parties and groups, especially in the Sejm and in people's councils, to conduct independent activity and develop their own initiative, on the basis of the leading role of the working class and its Party, which is recognized by them, as well as of the common goal in the struggle for democratization, for peace, for the construction of socialism.

Millions of believers, and among them progressive Catholic groups, have made their great contribution to the cause of building socialism in our country.

This proves that differences in world outlook are no obstacle in rallying all the patriotic forces within the National Front.

The National Front is developing in the course of the common struggle to implement the program of the National Front against all the centrifugal and reactionary tendencies weakening the unity of the nation.

7—The Party is of the opinion that the criterion for evaluating a citizen should be his present attitude and work. Unjustified and incorrect are the prejudice and signs of distrust shown to former members of the Peasant Battalions who were active during the [German] occupation. Furthermore, it is necessary to combat firmly all forms of discrimination against former members of the Home Army[5] as well as former soldiers of the Polish military formations in the West who are conscientiously working for the good of People's Poland.

8—The Party is firmly opposed to all manifestations of nationalism and national chauvinism, combats all manifestations of discrimination against citizens belonging to national minorities, favors respect for the full equality of the rights of citizens, regardless of nationality, for insuring them conditions for unhampered development of education and culture in their mother tongue and for their full participation in the economic, social, and political life of the country.

---

[5] Polish underground army which staged the uprising against the Germans in Warsaw in the summer of 1944.

9—The democratization of the Party's internal life must develop on the basis of the ideological and organizational unity of the Party ranks. The unity and cohesion of the Party grows in strength only when all its members feel themselves to be the cocreators of its policy, coresponsible for its activity. That is why it is necessary to insure to Party members freedom of sincere expression, unfettered ideological discussion, and exchange of views permeated with concern for the Party's affairs. This exchange of views must be accompanied by conscious and absolute discipline in the execution of adopted decisions.

The clash of opinions at Party meetings does not signify that the Party will agree to the propounding, within its own ranks, of views incompatible with the teachings of Marxism-Leninism and with the general line of the Party. Statements and discussions in the Party press should take place on the basis of the ideology of Marxism-Leninism and should be in accord with the Party's general line.

The Party press and organizations have the duty of waging an ideological struggle against views incompatible with the ideology of Marxism-Leninism and with the general line of the Party; in cases when Party members propounding harmful and anti-Party views refuse to give them up, organizational measures should be employed against them. Freedom of criticism in discussion must not be abused for purposes incompatible with the principles of the Party.

The Party cannot agree with the view that combating alien and openly mistaken views, or views that are hostile, in the press and at meetings can harm discussion and stifle criticism. Combating hostile views harming the cause of socialism is absolutely necessary in order to maintain the unity of the Party, to isolate the class enemy, to consolidate the leading role of the Party.

10—The Party must create conditions which favor, in all respects, the unhampered development of scientific and artistic activity serving the interests of socialist building.

While furthering the Marxist-Leninist world outlook among scientific and cultural workers, the Party should consistently oppose all doctrine-mongering, dogmatism, and restriction of the freedom of scientific discussion, as well as the fettering of artistic work corresponding to the ideals of socialist humanism.

The entire Party should realize that the full implementation of Leninist principles is a matter requiring a long time, *a long struggle* against conservative tendencies, against ossification and routine, that it is a matter of persistently overcoming old habits, a matter of amassing new experience, and of confronting it with the requirements of life.

Our Party's program of activity stems from the needs and aspirations of the working class and the Polish people; it stems from the ideas stimulating the entire international working class movement, which after the 20th Congress of the CPSU has entered a new period of development.

The decisions of the 20th Congress, opening up new prospects before the working class movement throughout the world for a struggle against the menace of war which, in view of the emergence and consolidation of the world socialist system, has ceased to be inevitable, decisions opening up before the working class movement new prospects and ways of struggle for socialism, have become a mighty stimulus for the work and struggle of our Party, for all the Communist and Workers Parties throughout the world, strengthening the international ties of solidarity and the militant forces of the working class.

It is the historic merit of the CPSU that by undertaking a bold and determined struggle against deviations from Leninist principles—against the cult of personality and its consequences —it has stimulated all the fraternal Communists and Workers Parties to carry out a critical evaluation and analysis of their own activity, to break with dogmatism, to apply Marxism-Leninism creatively in the search for ways, peculiar to each country, leading to the triumph of socialism.

Our Party, loyal to the ideology of Marxism-Leninism, profiting from the historic experience of the CPSU and other fraternal parties, and expressing, as fully as possible, the national interests of Poland, is solving the tasks of socialist building in accordance with the conditions and needs of our country.

Our Party, being aware that the struggle to advance the interests of the working class, the struggle for peace and for the consolidation of independence, is the cause of the entire international proletariat, is striving to tighten the bonds of solidarity and cooperation with the CPSU and all fraternal parties, seeing in it an infallible guarantee of confounding the designs of imperialism and reaction, a guarantee of the consolidation of peace and the victory of socialism.

CHAPTER IV

FROM THE SEVENTH TO THE EIGHTH PLENARY SESSION OF THE CENTRAL COMMITTEE OF THE POLISH UNITED WORKERS PARTY (JULY 28-OCTOBER 19, 1956): THE REINSTATEMENT OF WLADYSLAW GOMULKA AND THE POZNAN TRIALS

Immediately after the conclusion of the Central Committee's plenary session and acting on instructions from it, the Politburo initiated talks with Wladyslaw Gomulka and reinstated him as a member of the Party.

1. COMMUNIQUÉ ON THE REINSTATEMENT OF WLADYSLAW GOMULKA AS A MEMBER OF THE PUWP, AUGUST 4, 1956[1]

THE SEVENTH PLENUM of the PUWP Central Committee resolved to annul the resolution of the Third Plenum of the PUWP Central Committee of November, 1949, in the part concerning the unfounded and wrongful accusations of tolerance with regard to enemy agents formulated against comrades Wladyslaw Gomulka, Marian Spychalski, and Zenon Kliszko.[2]

After the Seventh Plenum, representatives of the Politburo of the PUWP Central Committee had a talk with Comrade Wladyslaw Gomulka during which, among other things, the fundamental problems of the Seventh Plenum of the PUWP Central Committee were discussed.

The Politburo, having heard a report on the course of this talk, decided to restore to Comrade Wladyslaw Gomulka his rights as a Party member.

---

[1] *Trybuna Ludu,* August 5, 1956.

[2] On August 5, Kliszko was appointed Under Secretary of State in the Ministry of Justice.

After the seventh plenary session of the CC of the PUWP, mass organizations, the trade unions, the union of youth, and the National Front displayed lively political activity.

The central body of the National Front met at Warsaw on August 13. At the conclusion of a two-day meeting it turned to the people with an appeal:[3]

Citizens! People's Poland has entered a new period of development. We are now facing new tasks aimed at increasing the prosperity, strength, and sovereignty of our Fatherland. This calls for the unification of all of the nation's forces in a joint, sensible and selfless action. . . .

Citizens! On the basis of the achievements of the last twelve years, overcoming the mistakes and distortions alien to our system, we shall speed the improvement of the living standard of all citizens of Poland, deepen the democratization of social life, and in this manner build socialism, the system of social justice.

These aims are contained in the program put before the nation by the PUWP. . . .

Citizens! This program can be implemented only through the joint efforts of the whole nation. The National Front in its activities so far has not properly fulfilled its tasks. The habits of bureaucratic administration, political formalism, and lack of confidence in the people which have been manifest in the political life of our country have stunted the development of the National Front as well.

Today we possess incomparably better conditions for action. We have a concrete program. Let the National Front become a living center of discussion and conflicting views and an earnest search for the best method of work. . . .

Let the National Front become a basis of support for the people's councils, the author of every good initiative, a center of social control, and the spokesman for public opinion.

Citizens! In December, 1956, the Polish Nation, united on the basis of the National Front program, will go to the polls to elect a new Sejm, the supreme organ of the people's authority. The new Sejm will face particularly important legislative and control work, designed to implement our political and economic

---

[3] *Trybuna Ludu,* August 15, 1956.

tasks. The National Front should do everything in its power to elect leaders who enjoy the confidence of the electors, who will be united with the masses of the people, and who know their needs and aspirations. . . .

An editorial on the National Front session in *Trybuna Ludu* (August 18, 1956) noted that "in the present situation it has become clearer than ever before that socialism cannot be built by the hands and brains of the Party members alone. The purposeful and conscious cooperation of millions of hands and minds is required."

On August 18 the central board of the ZMP (Polish Youth Union) held its third plenary session. The resolution adopted by the ZMP, said, among other things,[4] that

as a result of distortions in the international working class movement which were brought to light by the 20th Congress of the CPSU and as a result of distortions in the Party, state, and generally speaking the social life of our country, a serious ideological and moral crisis arose in a large part of the younger generation. . . .

A serious crisis also arose in the life and activity of the ZMP. . . . In the course of the last few years [it] was gradually losing its revolutionary character and did not adequately fill its role as the guiding force of the younger generation. . . .

As a result of sectarianism, dogmatism, and clichés on the one hand and a lack of understanding of the character of the masses on the other hand, the "jellylike" quality of the organization and the insignificance of its ideological and political character became ever more evident. . . . The bonds of the ZMP with the masses of youth were considerably impaired as well as the confidence of youth in the ZMP as its leader. . . . Our Union can fulfill its role as the leader of the youth and exert its influence only as an independent organization expressing its attitudes in its activities. This independence cannot come to the ZMP as a windfall. It must be achieved by efforts.

The struggle for new features of the ZMP is not an easy one and cannot be a short one, for the distortions of the past have thrust their roots deeply into the organism of the Union. This struggle requires the stubborn overcoming of bad habits and

---

[4] *Trybuna Ludu*, August 24, 1956.

conservatism among a considerable part of the activists, the reeducation of all leaders, reduction of the size of the apparatus, the restoration to this apparatus of its normal role in the organization, and the replacement of people not able to master the new tasks. . . .

The Central Board states that to release the social activeness of the Polish youth it is indispensable to overcome the formal attitude prevailing in the ZMP toward the traditions of the youth movement, the sectarian attitude toward the traditions of the "Wici" movement, and to a larger extent than in the past, to take advantage in educational work of all progressive traditions of the youth. . . .

The new forces of democratization growing in the ZMP should be developed and supported by the whole organization. Our Union must become a militant ideological organization, a vanguard of the youth struggle for socialism, for human relations really worthy of man. . . .

Our Union must become an organization whose every cell will be a center of bold, free thought, a center where the new man is shaped, freeing himself from obscurantism and religious prejudices—not a servile loyalist, not a hypocritical prattler, but a noble-hearted man, sensitive to human suffering and problems, an uncompromising revolutionary. . . .

The ZMP Central Board also resolved to hold an extraordinary Congress in February, 1957.

On August 18, the eighth plenary session of the Central Council of Trade Unions opened. The resolution adopted by it stressed the need for greater democracy "within the unions in the election of new officers" and called on the Central Council of the unions to "review and abolish all decisions which stifle the independence and democracy of trade unions."

It associated itself with the economic goals outlined in the July resolution of the Central Committee of the PUWP, and demanded in particular that an existing government decree on work norms be revised, that the competence of labor mediation committees be enlarged by granting them rights to settle all disputes that might arise including disputes on wages and work norms, and that a trade union inspection system be set up with real powers to enforce the proper implementation of labor laws in factories.

In addition the trade unions drew up a draft decree on the rights of works councils for submission to the Sejm.[5]

On August 24 the legislative committee of the Sejm met and for the first time failed to endorse a decree which the Council of State had passed. The committee recommended that the decree dealing with civic documents and registrars should be submitted to the Sejm for approval with appropriate amendments.

Between August 25 and September 2 a delegation of the Central Committee of the PUWP visited in Yugoslavia.[6]

On September 5, a new session of the Sejm opened. One of its tasks was to draft a new electoral law. The deliberations were accompanied by increasingly bolder demands to enable the Sejm "effectively to discharge its functions of legislation and review."[7]

On September 11 a Polish delegation headed by Edward Ochab (and including Franciszek Jozwiak-Witold, Oskar Lange, and Mieczyslaw Marzec) left to attend the Eighth Congress of the Chinese Communist Party.

On September 21, the Warsaw board of the Polish Youth Union met and passed three resolutions: one supporting a resolution of the Association of Polish Journalists asking for a new press act and a clear definition of the scope of the authority of the Central Office for Control of the Press another protesting against the omission of ZMP representatives from committees studying the release of office space for living quarters and a third advancing a demand for placing in the public domain the contents of talks between Politburo representatives and Gomulka prior to his reinstatement in the Party.

On the same day, the Prosecutor General of Poland reviewed the status of preparations for trials in connection with the Poznan riots of June.

---

[5] See *Glos Pracy*, organ of the central Council of Trade Unions, August 24, 1956.

[6] See *Trybuna Ludu*, September 3, 1956.

[7] See *Trybuna Ludu*, September 8, 1956. See also Julian Hochfeld, "Control and Responsibility" *Zycie Warsawy*, September 23, 1956, and an editorial under the title "Problems of the Sejm" in *Trybuna Ludu*, September 24, 1956.

2. Interview with the Prosecutor General of Poland, Marian Rybicki, on the Poznan Trials, September 21, 1956[8]

I WOULD LIKE TO STATE at the outset, said the Prosecutor General, that the investigations conducted by the public security organs under the supervision of the Prosecutor's Office since the first days following the Poznan incidents, despite the persistent information spread by certain Western radio stations, did not concern those who took part in the strike and the workers' demonstration that were held in Poznan on June 28, 1956. The analysis and the appraisal of the character and reasons of the entire Poznan incidents were made by the Seventh Plenum of the CC of the PUWP. Proper conclusions had been drawn from this evaluation. They are, and will be, realized by state authorities. On the basis of this analysis and evaluation, which find full corroboration in the material collected by the Prosecutor's Office, the scope of the investigation of the matters connected with the Poznan incidents has been limited to the prosecution of tangible violations committed during those events, namely, murders, violent attacks on institutions and state offices, on soldiers of the Polish Army, and on the functionaries of the state apparatus, attacks on the militia stations and posts, combined with the seizure of arms, robbery, breaking into premises and pilfering of state and private property.

The materials of the investigation had indicated that during the course of the Poznan incidents antisocial and criminal elements were especially active, and organized themselves into groups displaying exceptionally intense hostility toward the organs of authority.

Question: What is at the present time the number of arrested persons who are being investigated, or against whom the acts of indictment have been filed?

Answer: The number of persons detained and placed in custody as a preventive measure amounted, in the middle of

---

[8] *Trybuna Ludu,* September 22, 1956.

July, to 323 persons, but has been considerably reduced in the course of the investigations. At the present time, 154 persons are under arrest. The investigation in the case of some of these persons has already been concluded, and the *wojewodztwo* [province] Prosecutor's Office in Poznan has referred 58 cases, together with the acts of indictment, to the *wojewodztwo* Court in Poznan.

Question: What violations are covered by the first indictments and who are the accused?

Answer: The first indictment refers to three persons: Jozef Foltynowicz, Kazimierz Zurek, and Jerzy Sroka, who took part in the bestial murder of Corporal Zygmunt Izdebny, a functionary of public security, on June 28, in the area of the central railroad depot. The murderers beat and massacred Corporal Izdebny in an exceptionally cruel manner, shouting at the same time provocative and inciting cries that he murdered a woman and two children. This, of course, was not true, since Corporal Izdebny, who had arrived that day in Poznan from Marlewo, where he lived permanently, was on his way, unarmed, from the station to work where he was to take over the guard duties at the Public Security Office. The culprits, together with other attackers, three times prevented an ambulance from giving medical assistance to Izdebny, who was badly beaten. As a consequence of this bestial beating, Izdebny died shortly after arrival at the hospital. The accused are further characterized by the fact that immediately after committing this bestial murder, they broke into a railway vending stand and plundered its merchandise.

The second indictment covers ten individuals, who are accused of carrying out attacks on the Military Training Station of the Higher Agricultural School, on the prison, as well as on the militia stations, in order to obtain arms, and also of utilizing these arms to carry out violent attacks on the *wojewodztwo* Public Security Office, militia posts, and, in addition, of robbing shops and apartments.

Among the accused, there are notorious adventurers and hooligans, with court sentences and with frequent records in the

offices of the militia.   Thus, for example, Janusz Kulas had been
up on court charges of hooliganism and theft on three previous
occasions, Wladyslaw Kaczkowski had been sentenced twice for
theft and forgery of documents, Zbigniew Blaszyk had served
two prison terms for participating in fights.

The third indictment against Zenon Urbanek and others
covers a nine-man group of criminals, who are accused of robbing the prison of arms and of using those arms against the
functionaries of the Public Security, who were in the office
building at Kochanowski Street.   As a result of shots fired by
the accused several persons among innocent bystanders had been
killed or wounded.   In addition, some of the accused engaged
in petty theft during the incidents.

The other indictments before the *wojewodztwo* Court in
Poznan have a similar character.   In addition to these acts, the
City Prosecutor's Office in Poznan brought two indictments to
the District Court for the city of Poznan, which embraced exclusively perpetrators of thefts.   The initiators of these thefts were
prisoners who escaped on June 28 of this year from the prison
at the Mlynska Street, namely: Feliks Gralewski, who has a
previous record of seven convictions, Bogdan Krugielko, who
has three previous convictions, and Sylwester Bubolec, who has
been convicted five times before—all of them for common
crimes, robberies, and theft.

In accordance with the prevailing schedules envisaged by
the code of the criminal procedure, we should anticipate that
the first court trials will begin at the end of September.[9]

---

[9] The trials of two groups of accused, Urbanek and his accomplices
and Foltynowicz and his accomplices, opened in Poznan on September 7.

Urbanek and his associates were sentenced on October 12.   The
maximum sentence was six years of imprisonment and one of the accused
got a suspended jail term.

On October 22, after the eighth plenary session of the Central
Committee of the PUWP (see Chapter V), the sentencing of Kulas and
his group, whose trial ended on October 18, was postponed until
November 6 and a group of other prisoners were released.

On October 23 a review of all indictments as well as the release
of all persons who were not charged with murder or robbery was

Meanwhile, preparations for convoking a new plenary session of the Central Committee of the PUWP were in progress.

On October 10, the resignation of Hilary Minc, chief architect of Poland's six-year economic plan, from his post in the Politburo was announced. The reason: ill health.

On October 15 the Politburo met again.

3. COMMUNIQUÉ OF THE POLITBURO OF THE CENTRAL COMMITTEE OF THE POLISH UNITED WORKERS PARTY ON CALLING A NEW PLENARY SESSION, OCTOBER 15, 1956[10]

THE POLITBURO OF THE Central Committee of the PUWP held a meeting today. It was devoted to preparations for the eighth plenary session of the Central Committee of the PUWP which will be convened *on Friday, October 19.* [Italics in *Trybuna Ludu.*]

Comrade Wladyslaw Gomulka took part in the meeting.

---

ordered. A total of 94 persons, including some of the accomplices of Kulas and Urbanek, were immediately freed.

The only group remaining in prison was that of Foltynowicz. Subsequently, a retrial of that group, to open on December 11, was also ordered.

[10] *Trybuna Ludu,* October 16, 1956.

CHAPTER V

NATIONAL COMMUNISM TRIUMPHANT: FROM THE EIGHTH PLENARY SESSION OF THE CENTRAL COMMITTEE OF THE POLISH UNITED WORKERS PARTY (OCTOBER 19-21, 1956) TO THE CONCLUSION OF POLISH SOVIET TALKS IN MOSCOW (NOVEMBER 18, 1956)

At 10 A.M. on October 19 the Central Committee of the PUWP met. The first order of business was the cooptation of Wladyslaw Gomulka, Marian Spychalski, Ignacy Loga-Sowinski, and Zenon Kliszko to the Central Committee.

Later in the day a Soviet delegation arrived at Warsaw.

1. COMMUNIQUÉ ON TALKS BETWEEN PARTY DELEGATIONS OF THE SOVIET UNION AND POLAND, OCTOBER 20, 1956[1]

ON OCTOBER 19, A DELEGATION of the Central Committee of the CPSU arrived in Warsaw to discuss with the Politburo of the Central Committee of the PUWP current problems of interest for the two parties.

The CPSU Central Committee delegation comprised N. S. Khrushchev, chairman of the delegation, and L. M. Kaganovich, A. I. Mikoyan, and V. M. Molotov, members of the Presidium of the CPSU Central Committee. On the Polish side, the following members of the Politburo of the PUWP Central Committee took part in the debates: J. Cyrankiewicz, W. Dworakowski, E. Gierek, F. Jozwiak-Witold, R. Nowak, Z. Nowak, E. Ochab, A. Rapacki, K. Rokossowski, R. Zambrowski, and A. Zawadzki—as well as candidate members of the Politburo of the PUWP Central Committee H. Chelchowski, S. Jedrychowski, and E. Stawinski.

---

[1] *Trybuna Ludu,* October 20, 1956.

Comrade W. Gomulka took part in the debates.

The debates were held in an atmosphere of Party-like and friendly sincerity. It was agreed that a delegation of the Politburo of the PUWP Central Committee would go to Moscow in the nearest future to discuss with the Presidium of the CPSU Central Committee problems of further strengthening the political and economic cooperation between the Polish People's Republic and the Soviet Union, and of further consolidating the fraternal friendship and coexistence of the PUWP and the CPSU.[2]

In the early morning hours of October 20, 1956, the Soviet delegation departed from Warsaw. At 11 A.M. the Central Committee of the PUWP resumed its session.

2. ADDRESS BY WLADYSLAW GOMULKA BEFORE THE CENTRAL COMMITTEE OF THE POLISH UNITED WORKERS PARTY, OCTOBER 20, 1956[3]

WHEN I ADDRESSED the November Plenum of the Central Committee of the Polish United Workers Party seven years ago, I thought that it was my last speech to the members of the Central Committee. Although only seven years have elapsed since that time, or eight years since the August Plenum, where an abrupt change occurred in the Party's policy, these years constitute a closed historic period. I am deeply convinced that that period has gone into the irrevocable past. There has been much evil in those years. The legacy that that period left the Party, the working class, and the nation is more than alarming in certain spheres of life.

Two and one-half months ago, the Seventh Plenum of the Central Committee appraised the positive and negative aspects of the past period and outlined guiding principles of action for the future. Despite my desire I could not be present at that Plenum. Many of you referred also to me at that Plenum and

---

[2] See Document 11 in this chapter.

[3] *Trybuna Ludu,* October 21, 1956, also *Nowe Drogi,* No. 10, 1956, pp. 21-46.

considered the possibility and need of my return to Party work. This was made dependent on my views on the resolutions adopted at that Plenum. Therefore, I consider it my duty to tell you my attitude toward these resolutions, what my views are on the present situation, and what in my opinion should be the shape of the future.

I have certain reservations as regards the resolutions of the Seventh Plenum. These reservations concern the appraisal of the past, as well as the Party's policy in the field of agriculture. Apart from this, I consider these resolutions to be correct and treat them as a correct line of action. They will demand closer definition and supplementing in the course of their implementation. Certain problems of importance for the present day have been left out from these resolutions. Some of them can be solved today since they have become ripe, and with others it is necessary to wait until they ripen in our minds and suitable conditions arise. The most important thing is not the fact that resolutions have been adopted and have been agreed upon but that these resolutions should be put into practice.

My reservations to the Seventh Plenum resolutions, as concerns the evaluation of the past, cover economic and political problems. The reservations concern both the merits of the evaluation, as well as the responsibility of people for errors and distortions made—a responsibility stemming from this evaluation.

ON THE RESULTS OF THE SIX-YEAR PLAN

The Seventh Plenum resolutions refer to the achievements attained and errors committed in the course of the Six-Year Plan (1950-55). The resolutions cite the extensive expansion at that time of the productive capacity of our industry, especially of heavy industry, as the most important result of the Six-Year Plan outweighing all others. I am far from belittling any of the achievements of our country. All of us, just as the entire nation, rejoice at the increase and growth of the production of our industry. I have no grounds to doubt the given indices of increase of industrial production. I accept them as true. There are, however, certain "buts" which force me to make a reappraisal of the evaluation of our economic achievements during the past Six-Year Plan.

Let us examine the achievements of the Six-Year Plan in coal mining. In 1949, that is in the last year of the Three-Year Plan, coal production amounted to over 74 million tons. In 1955, that is in the last year of the Six-Year Plan, the corresponding figure was 94.5 million tons. These figures indicate that coal output went up by over 20 million tons, and this could really be considered a considerable achievement if this rise meant an increase in the mining industry's productive capacity. But statistical data reveal that in 1955 the miners worked 92,634,000 hours overtime and this constitutes 15.5 percent of the total number of hours worked in this time. Calculated in terms of coal this amounts to 14.6 million tons of coal extracted outside normal working hours.

Let us go further and see what labor productivity was like in mining at that time. In 1949, coal output per working day per worker throughout the industry amounted to 1,328 kilograms [2,921.6 pounds]. In 1955, it dropped to 1,163 kilograms [2,556.4 pounds], that is by 12.4 percent. If we compare coal output per worker employed underground, this drop amounts to 7.7 percent per working day. In relation to 1938, which for various reasons cannot be taken as a basis of comparison, but illustrates the present state of the coal mines, output per working day per person employed in the mining industry dropped in 1955 by 36 percent.

It emerges from the data quoted that coal mining not only has no achievements to its credit in the Six-Year Plan but even fell below the level of the year 1949.

The economic policy in relation to the mining industry was marked by unpardonable thoughtlessness. The system of work on Sundays was introduced, and this could not but ruin the health and strength of the miners, and at the same time made it difficult to maintain colliery installations in proper working order. The practice was also introduced of employing soldiers and prisoners in some of the collieries. Mining personnel has not been stabilized and changes every year in a vast percentage. This policy could not but undermine the coal extraction plan; it could not but lead to the present state of the collieries.

Comrades, here is a second example. At the cost of tremendous investments, we built an automobile factory in Zeran. New industrial establishments have come into being, establishments which produce at disproportionately high production costs only limited numbers of automobiles of an old type which consume plenty of fuel, automobiles which today hardly anyone produces in the world. Can the construction of an industrial establishment of this kind be called a contribution to the productive capacity of our industry? What kind of benefits can the national economy draw from this?

Generally speaking, after the conclusion of the Six-Year Plan, which according to its premises was meant to raise high the standard of living of the working class and of the entire nation, we are faced today, in the first year of the Five-Year Plan, with immense economic difficulties which are growing from day to day. We contracted important investment credits for the expansion of industry, and when the time came for the payment of the first installment we found ourselves in the situation of an insolvent bankrupt. We had to ask our creditors for a moratorium. Those in charge of our national economy obviously were unable to grasp the simple fact that credits have to be husbanded in such a way, that is, invested, so that they can be repaid to the creditors within the time limits laid down by means of the production achieved with the aid of those credits.

In the meantime a considerable part of these credits in the shape of machines and installations has so far found no application in production and will not find any such application for long years to come, and part of it must be considered irretrievably lost. Machines or equipment which have been ordered for projects long ago deleted from our economic plans continue to arrive to this day. The results of the Six-Year Plan, our present position, and our chances for the future are clearly shown by the adverse balance of payments in our foreign dealings.

The balance of payments in the Five-Year Plan shows a considerable deficit despite the moratorium granted us and the postponement to the next Five-Year Plan of the payment of one-half of the sums due to be paid during the current Five-Year Plan. In this situation the reality of the Five-Year Plan, which has been worked out, is greatly impaired.

We know the danger of the lack of a sufficient number of marketable goods on the domestic market in relation to the amount of money in circulation.

Do the resolutions of the Seventh Plenum speak of all that? They do not. Of course, the fact that the resolutions give a milder appraisal of the past is not of the greatest importance. What is essential is that a precise economic analysis is indispensable for a correct working out of the plans for the future. Such facts, as have been cited, can in no way be passed over in silence. For it should be said clearly that the whole nation— and in the first place the working class—has to pay for a bad economic policy. The Central Committee of the Party has failed to draw, at least, the necessary Party consequences with regard to the people who bear the responsibility for this state of affairs.

NEGATIVE BALANCE SHEET OF AGRICULTURAL POLICY

In the agricultural sector of the national economy, whose definition at the Seventh Plenum has aroused reservations in my mind, we also find phenomena on which every responsible man should reflect profoundly, and from which he should draw the necessary conclusions.

Beginning in 1949, that is in the course of the past six years, the Party began the campaign for the collectivization of agricultural production. During that period, some 10,000 cooperative farms were set up, affiliating some 6 percent of peasant farmsteads. Today, after 6 years of experience, it is not amiss to have a closer look at the economic consequences of the Party's agricultural policy for the past period.

In our conditions, just as in the conditions of every country which does not have at its disposal a surplus of land, rural policy should be characterized by a sustained effort to intensify agricultural production. Poland can nourish its population from its own resources only through increasing yields, through increasing agricultural production per hectare of land. Everybody is agreed on that, at least in words. In practice, however, methods yielding different results are applied.

Let us see what is the value of the over-all product, calculated in constant prices per hectare of land in all sectors of our agricultural economy, that is, in individual economy, on cooperative farms, and on state farms under the Ministry of State Farms.

All data quoted pertain to 1955. There was 78.8 percent of farm land in the possession of individual farmsteads. Income-dividing cooperatives held 8.6 percent, and the state farms 12.6 percent of the total area of farm land owned by these three types of farms. The over-all product as produced by these farms, taken as 100, is divided as follows: individual, 83.9 percent; cooperative farms, including cottage allotments, 7.7 percent; and state farms, including auxiliary holdings of agricultural workers, 8.4 per cent.

When estimating the value of over-all production per one hectare of arable land we arrive at the following picture (in terms of constant prices): individual farms, 621.1 zlotys; cooperative farms, 517.3 zlotys; and state farms, 393.7 zlotys. Thus, the difference between individual and cooperative farms amounts to 16.7 per cent, while in comparison with state farms, individual farm production was higher by 37.2 per cent.

In comparing the obligations of individual and cooperative farms from the point of view of quota deliveries for the state and of land tax, we find that these obligations, when estimated per hectare, are smaller in the case of cooperative than of individual farms, particularly with regard to land tax. The difference in these obligations to the advantage of the cooperative farms constitutes an actual state grant for cooperative farms.

Another item is represented by the additional payments for services given by the State Machine Stations to cooperative farms. The total of these additional payments in 1952-55 amounts to about 1,700,000,000 zlotys. It is difficult to establish what part of that amount comes under the heading of additional payments for services rendered to the cooperatives, as the State Machine Stations also worked for other institutions. Besides, payments will continue to grow, as the payment due from cooperatives for the services of the State Machine Stations has lately been reduced.

So this is another form of state subsidy from the treasury for the producers cooperatives. But it is not the last either.

It follows from the annual reports of cooperative farms for the year 1955 that in fixing the workday wage the principle was adopted that it was necessary to establish a certain minimum income as a workday wage regardless of the economic results of the given cooperative farm. The average workday wage on all cooperative farms in the country is about 25 zlotys, the produce-making part of the workday wage being estimated at free market prices. Differences between various cooperative farms with regard to the scale of the workday wage are not great, particularly with regard to the part of the wage paid in kind.

Since not all cooperative farms were able to pay the accepted workday wage minimum—for the results of their production prevented them from doing so—a comparatively simple solution was found: payments, or part payments, arising from other obligations of the cooperative farms with regard to the state and due in 1955 were delayed and transferred to the following years. The financial means which should have been used for these payments were allocated to the workday wage fund. On the national scale this sum amounts to over 500 million zlotys. In this way the distributable income in some cooperative farms was artificially increased, which made it possible to raise the workday wage by some 27 percent.

Irrespective of these forms of state assistance, the cooperative farms received additional important credits from the state.

Long- and medium-term obligations of the cooperative farms on December 31, 1955, amounted to over 1,600,000,000 zlotys, and their short-term obligations to over 900,000,000 zlotys.

It can be added that the cooperative farms availed themselves of preferential treatment also in the purchase of artificial fertilizers. In the economic year 1954-55 artificial fertilizers, in terms of the pure contents, were used to the amount of 58.6 kilograms per hectare of arable land. In individual farmsteads, only 28.1 kilograms per hectare were used in that period.

This, in brief outline, is the economic picture of cooperative farms. It is a sad picture. Despite great outlays, they had smaller results and greater production costs. I do not mention the political aspect of the problem.

It is for the above reasons that I have reservations as to the resolutions of the Seventh Plenum as they concern the agricultural policy of the Party, mapped out at the Fifth Plenum of the Central Committee.

In examining our economic reality we find in it also other features giving cause for profound concern.

The practice in implementing the Six-Year Plan was that on certain selected sectors a maximum of investment outlays were concentrated, without taking into consideration other fields of economic life. And yet, the national economy constitutes an integral whole. It is impossible to favor excessively certain branches of the economy at the expense of others, for the loss of proper proportions brings harm to the economy as a whole.

Particular concern must be aroused by the housing problem in the countryside. Whereas in towns and settlements, where the housing situation is also very difficult, a great effort is being put into new housing, home repairs and maintenance, in the countryside matters are simply alarming.

During the period of the Six-Year Plan, about 370,000 rooms were built in the countryside, of which some 260,000 were built individually with the owner's means, and some 110,000 were constructed under the socialized building scheme.

In 1950, we had over 2,690,000 houses in the countryside with over 7,500,000 rooms. On the assumption that the average life of a building—considering postwar conditions—is 50 years, we should build 150,000 rooms in the countryside every year in order to maintain the number of rooms existing in 1950. This amounts to about 900,000 rooms for the Six-Year Plan, while only some 370,000 were built. It must be concluded that during the Six-Year Plan about 600,000 rooms fell in ruin or are now in a state of ruin. The real state of affairs may even be worse still, as the repair and maintenance of houses could not be properly effected in that period on account of a lack of building materials. Especially in Poland's western and northern parts, the shortage of residential rooms is growing fast. The housing plight is systematically mounting there from year to year.

In a planned economy and with a sound husbanding of resources you can temporarily restrict requirements in one branch of the economy and transfer the funds thus saved to speedier development in another sphere. The planning should be such as to fill in quickly, after a certain time, the gaps in the formerly restricted sector. This ought to be made easier by the increased resources and production potential brought about in the sector formerly privileged with regard to investments.

The result of our former practice of planning and management is that we did not implement in the scheduled time the envisaged tasks on the privileged sector, that we froze and wasted tremendous means there, and that we did not create conditions for eliminating the economic gaps in those sectors which were consciously restricted before. Thus, for instance, we are aware of the needs of residental building. We are aware that we ought not to limit for another day the conditions for the development of rural building. We have mapped out the growth of urban building and at the same time we are faced with tremendous difficulties in meeting these requirements, seeing that we failed to set up the necessary production base in building materials.

A chain is only as strong as its weakest link. We want to give—and we must give—quickly to the countryside. Yet we are unable to do so without detriment especially to industrial building. Nobody is going to work miracles here.

The position is not much better in the field of public services, health resorts, or sanatoriums. I have no close knowledge of these branches of the national economy. Sewerage, water mains, urban transport, roads, building, all that goes to make up the communal economy and health resorts, is bound to spring ever widening leaks if something is not done in time. And for this you again need funds and materials.

I wish to stress once more: I am far from belittling the achievements of the Six-Year Plan. But the appraisal of these achievements must be based on the actual situation, that is, we should view these achievements from the economic position which was our starting point for the Five-Year Plan. And this start is accompanied by very great difficulties.

All of us are faced with the problem how to solve these difficulties, what to do and where to begin in order to overcome all the difficulties and to march forward along a road which would be ever less rough. Much will have to be changed in our former practice in order to reach this goal.

THE LESSONS OF POZNAN

The key to the solution of these great difficulties is in the hands of the working class. Everything, both present-day and future prospects, depends on its attitude. And the attitude of the working class depends on the policy of the Party, as mapped out by its leadership; it depends on the skill in governing the state on the part of the Government and all the supreme organs of the state.

The working class recently gave a painful lesson to the Party leadership and the Government. When seizing the weapon of strike and going out to demonstrate in the streets on the black Thursday last June, the Poznan workers shouted in a powerful voice: Enough! This cannot go on any longer! Turn back from the false road.[4]

The working class has never resorted to strikes as a weapon of struggle for its rights in a thoughtless manner. Particularly now, in People's Poland, which is governed in its name and in the name of all working people, this step was not taken thoughtlessly by the working class. It is obvious that the measure was exceeded, and one can never exceed the measure with impunity.

The Poznan workers did not protest against People's Poland, against socialism when they went out into the streets of the city. They protested against the evil which was widespread in our social system and which was painfully felt also by them, against the distortions of the fundamental principles of socialism, which is their idea.

The working class has associated all its hopes for a better life with the idea of socialism. It has fought for socialism from the first days of its conscious life. And when the course of history made it possible for its representatives to assume the reins of government in Poland, the working class devoted all its enthusiasm and all its forces to the implementation of the idea of socialism.

The working class is our class, our unflinching strength. The working class is ourselves. Without it, that is, without the confidence of the working class, each of us could not in fact represent anything more than his own person.

The clumsy attempt to present the painful Poznan tragedy as the work of imperialist agents and provocateurs was very naive politically. Agents and provocateurs can be and act anywhere, but never and nowhere can they determine the attitude of the working class.

If agents and provocateurs were able to inspire the working class to action, the enemies of People's Poland, the enemies of socialism would have a much easier task and could easily attain their goals. But the point is that this is not so.

There was a time in Poland when forces hostile to socialism, often directed by foreign centers serving non-Polish interests,

---

[4] See Chapter II, Documents 1-3.

had a really widespread underground organization. There was a time when the People's Government in Poland was attacked with arms and defended itself with arms, when hundreds and thousands of our Party members, soldiers, and civil servants were killed. This was a time of severity whose traces have not until this day completely disappeared from human hearts and feelings. This was in the first years of the construction of People's Poland. But in those days, so difficult for the People's Government, no agents and no underground organization, in spite of favorable conditions, succeeded or were able to make a breach in the ranks of the working class, to penetrate politically any section of the working class. For the working class could not be the leading and most progressive section of the nation if the reactionary forces were able to find support in its ranks. Agents, provocateurs, or reactionaries never have been the inspiration of the working class, they are not and never will be.

The causes of the Poznan tragedy and of the profound dissatisfaction of the entire working class are to be found in ourselves, in the leadership of the Party, in the Government. The inflammable materials had been accumulating for years. The Six-Year Plan, advertised in the past with great energy as a new stage of the high growth of the living standards, disappointed the hopes of the broad working masses. The juggling with figures which showed a 27 percent rise in real wages during the Six-Year Plan proved a failure. It only exasperated the people even more and it was necessary to withdraw from the position taken by poor statisticians.

The 20th Congress of the CPSU stimulated a turn in the political life of the country. An animating, sound current went through the Party masses, the working class, the entire society. People began to straighten their backs. The silent, enslaved minds began to shake off the poison of mendacity, falsehood, and hypocrisy. The stiff clichés previously predominant on Party platforms and at public meetings as well as in the press began to give place to creative, living words.

Sometimes a false note was perhaps heard, but it was not this note that gave the general direction. There came a powerful wave of criticism of the past—the criticism of violence, distortions, and errors by which no sphere of life had been unaffected. Everywhere, above all at Party and general meetings in work establishments, the demand was voiced for an explanation of the causes of evil and for appropriate measures to be taken with regard to the people bearing the main responsibility for the distortions in economic and political life. Above all, the working people wanted to know all the truth, without any embellishments and omissions. They waited for the truth. They awaited answers to tens of questions which they put publicly in petitions.

In the situation which arose following the 20th Congress, when it was necessary to act quickly and consistently, to draw conclusions from the past, to go to the masses with all frankness and to tell them the whole truth about the economic situation—the causes and sources of distortions in political life—the Party leadership failed to work out quickly a line of concrete action. The fact that the Seventh Plenum was several times delayed is one proof of it.

Among the charges which were raised against me in the past was that my attitude in different matters stemmed from an alleged lack of faith in the working class. This is not true. I have never lost faith in the wisdom, common sense, selflessness, and revolutionary attitude of the working class. In these values of the working class I believe also today. I am convinced that the Poznan workers would not have gone on strike, that they would not have demonstrated in the streets, that no men would have been found among them who even resorted to arms, that our fraternal, workers' blood would not have been shed there had the Party, that is the leadership of the Party, presented the whole truth to them. It was necessary to recognize without any delays the just claims of the workers; it was necessary to say what can be done today and what cannot be done; it was necessary to tell them the truth about the past and the present. There is no escaping from truth. If you cover it up, it will rise as an awful specter, frightening, alarming, and madly raging.

The leadership of the Party was frightened of it. Some were afraid of responsibility for the results of their policy; others felt more strongly linked with their comfortable posts than with the working class in whose behalf they occupied these posts; and still others—and these were the most numerous —feared that the working class would be unable to understand the most profound essence of the truth it demanded from its representatives, that it would not interpret properly, as it should be interpreted, the causes and sources of the errors, distortions, and provocations which had taken place. The weakening of faith in the working class became widely apparent in the central and provincial Party apparatus.

WE MUST TELL THE WORKING CLASS THE WHOLE TRUTH

Governing the country requires that the working class and the working masses should give the credit of confidence to their representatives who hold the reins of government in the state. This is the moral basis of exercising power in the name of the working masses. The credit of confidence can be continuously renewed only on the condition that obligations toward those giving the credit are fulfilled. The loss of the credit of confidence of the working class means the loss of the moral basis of power.

It is possible to govern the country even in such conditions. But then this will be bad government, for it must be based on bureaucracy, on infringing the rule of law, on violence. The essence of the dictatorship of the proletariat, as the broadest democracy for the working class and the working masses, becomes in such conditions deprived of its meaning.

The working class could have withdrawn its credit of confidence from certain people. This is normal. And it is also normal that such people should leave their posts. To change all the bad features of our life, to change the state in which our economy is at present, it is not enough to replace this or that person. This is even easy. To remove from our political and economic life all the bad things which are hampering its development and which have been accumulating for years, it is necessary to change a great deal in our system of People's Government, in the system of the organization of our industry, in the methods of work of the state and Party apparatus. It is necessary, in short, to replace all bad parts of our model of socialism, to replace them with better spare parts, to improve this model by means of the best existing patterns and to introduce into it our own, still more perfect designs. And this is much more difficult. This requires both time and work. It requires courage coupled with wisdom. The leading principles of these changes are partly contained in the resolutions of the Seventh Plenum, they are partly discussed today by us, and will be more than once discussed by us in the future.

What is it that today limits our possibilities in this field? First of all, the impatience of the working class, stemming largely from its living standards. And these are closely connected with our economic situation. Not even the greatest wizard can pour water out of an empty jug.

Many work establishments do not work normally and do not fully exploit their production capacity. The cause is to be found in the difficulties in supplying them sufficiently with materials and raw materials. And these we must import, or else we must expand our own supply base. The former is closely connected with our exports, the latter requires both time and means. For the time being the position is that in many work establishments the productive capacity and the labor power of the workers employed there are not fully utilized by us. It is no secret to anyone that administrative staffs in some factories are in excess of what is required.

I have already mentioned that we are threatened by shortages in commodity supply on the home market; that is, the total rise in earnings is not accompanied by the same amount of commodities. And even should we change the entire Government and the entire Party leadership nothing will change on the market for the better and it could only change for the worse if we fail to produce the missing amount of goods. There are only two alternatives to remedy the movement of prices: either increase the quantity of goods to equal the purchasing capacity of the population, or adjust the purchasing capacity of the population to the quantity of goods.

In these circumstances we must tell the working class the painful truth. We cannot afford at the present moment any considerable increase of wages, for the string has already been stretched so tight that it can break. Every further increase of wages is indissolubly linked with the stepping up of production and with the reduction of unit costs. This is by no means pleasant, either for us or, especially, for the working class.

I am not in a position to say anything definite as to when it will be possible to find further means to raise the living standards of the working class. But this depends first of all on two factors; first, on the improvement in the management of industry and the whole national economy and, secondly, on the workers themselves, that is, on the increase of labor productivity and the reduction of production costs.

ECONOMIC ADMINISTRATION AND MATERIAL INCENTIVES

The question of the change in the management of industry is profoundly structural in character. What matters here precisely is to improve our model of socialism. The problem of workers' self-government currently discussed by the workers in work establishments and by various Party and state organs boils down to what I was saying about production and living standards. To put the whole economic machinery upon new tracks without having thoroughly tested the efficiency of the functioning of the new mechanism which we want to create is a dangerous thing. Every new mechanism must undergo tests, for, as a rule, it has various defects and shortcomings. No work establishment can put on the market a new machine without building and testing the prototype of this machine. One should greet with great appreciation the initiative of the working class concerning the improvement of industrial management, concerning the participation of workers in the management of their work establishment. This proves the great and justified faith of the working class in socialism. The leading economic, political, and state organs must work intensively in order to help the workers' initiative so that wherever it is possible, a generalization of proposed forms should be made. But one should make haste slowly in so far as broad-scale practice is concerned.

The best conditions for experimenting in this field are to be found in the entire raw materials industry and in those work establishments which themselves both begin and complete the whole production process, and also those factories which do not encounter supply difficulties while cooperating with other factories. Experiments in these work establishments should be started without delay.

In my opinion one should carry out exhaustive research and decide whether, for example, in the coal mining industry one can apply greater material incentives strictly linked with an increase in the extraction of coal. The form of this interest could roughly look as follows:

Each mine has its periodic plan of coal extraction, worked out while taking into account the concrete conditions in the given mine and based on present work productivity. The planned tasks of various mines should not be lower than the actual coal extraction in the previous year, provided there are no essential changes in work conditions. Such a plan should be worked out by the management of the mines with the participation of representatives of the workers' personnel.

Once there is such a starting point, that is a periodic plan, for instance a yearly plan, one should create for the workers material incentives stemming from the overfulfillment of the plan. These incentives would consist in that every ton of coal extracted above the plan should be suitably divided between the workers of the given mine and the state as the mine's administrator.

A fixed percentage of all coal production in excess of the plan might be earmarked for the collective and suitably distributed between the various categories of mine workers. The distribution of the coal should be decided upon by the workers themselves. The coal produced in excess of the plan which is destined for distribution among the collective of the mines would be credited to every worker who is entitled to a coal bonus in kind, that is, everyone so entitled would decide on the way it is to be used. It may be assumed, for instance, that some of the workers would like to sell their coal bonus abroad and obtain certain goods in exchange. In this case, they ought to be enabled to settle this speedily and to obtain the desired goods at prices without customs duties with merely the cost incurred in the purchase, transport, and delivery of those goods. Again, some workers may want to acquire, in lieu of the coal bonus, building material for erecting a cottage. Such an initiative should in fact be welcomed and a convenient ratio established for the exchange of the coal allowance for building materials.

The way in which everyone entitled to the coal allowance would use it for his needs would depend entirely on himself. There would not be any major trouble over this. What it all boils down to is whether there are real chances for creating material incentives. The miners could be guaranteed that this system would extend to the end of the Five-Year Plan.

Should labor productivity, with the assistance of such a system, be brought to the level of 1949, there would be a grant to workers, in the form of a coal allowance, of a certain percentage of the coal extracted above the planned figures, amounting for example to an average of 15 tons of coal annually per miner. This would constitute—calculating the coal at its export price—some 300 dollars, that is, a sum worthy of the interest of each worker.

I think that when examining the various aspects of material incentives or ways of raising the living standard by increasing output, the form which I have outlined generally is worthy of close inspection by the miners, by their trade union, and by the management of the collieries. In any case, it is worth while to try out such a system in several coal pits for some length of time. If it passes the test, then it should be given wide application in mining.

This example, which fits the mining industry best, illustrates the fundamental thought which must pervade the idea of workers' self-government and cooperation in the management of a given work establishment. To produce more and cheaper and better: This is the road which leads to the rise of the standards of living of the working class and of the whole nation. It is on such a foundation that workers' self-government must rest. In this resides the source of all sorts of material incentives capable of application in the present economic situation.

In the concrete conditions of a given work establishment only one of these three elements—more, cheaper, and better—may suffice to increase the earnings of personnel.

One thing is universal and must apply everywhere: What is involved is a lowering of overhead. If it is not possible in some establishments to produce more or if the quality of output is not good, it is probably possible to produce more cheaply. A reduction in overhead can be achieved through economies and a full exploitation of raw materials and materials, through technical perfection, through a good organization of labor, the liquidation of staff surpluses, full employment of labor, and so forth.

Workers' self-government, aiming at lowering the costs of production, cannot remain indifferent to the problem of excessive numbers of personnel. The employment of two people where one can do the job is truly comparable to inviting two people to dinner on which only one can satisfy his appetite. It is the duty of the administration of work establishments and of the central leadership of industry to insure to workers full supplies indispensable for the normal running of production, that means, full utilization of the labor power of every worker employed in the work establishment. This must be the main, basic line. But if insurmountable difficulties arise somewhere, and when such a situation lasts months and even years, it is necessary to establish the surplus of manpower existing in a given work establishment in order to employ the people superfluous there according to their qualifications, possibly in other places. The manpower superfluous in the main process of production can also be employed in auxiliary, side-line production which can be organized in favorable conditions.

A separate, and still more acute, problem is the liquidation of the so-called administration overgrowths. We have been talking and writing about it for years and the issue has not moved a step forward in our country. I even doubt whether we realize how vast this overgrowth is, at today's system of management of industry, of the entire economic life, and at today's administrative system of the state apparatus.

It is impossible to find a way to avoid solving the problem connected with the liquidation of administrative overgrowth. The longer we put it off, the sooner the economic situation might grip us at the throat and compel us to immediate cuts, which could previously have been staggered. Then it will be difficult to prepare men for work in different trades.

The endeavors to base our economic life on better foundations than hitherto—to produce more, cheaper, and better—cannot be confined to the problem of workers' self-government, for this is only a fragment of reconstruction, which is an organizational and political whole.

While solving the problem of lowering production costs, both the workers' self-governments and the works administration must, above all, know their real production costs. This is of utmost importance for the whole of economic life. The difficulties in fixing and consequently, in a certain sense, in lowering production costs are inherent in the prices being fixed by the state for goods produced by work establishments under its control.

This matter is very complicated. It is a big question by itself. Its essence is the wrong opinion that in conditions of socialist production the law of value does not operate. Hence, in goods turnover between state enterprises prices are fixed in an arbitrary manner, even below production costs.

Such an economic policy is wrong. Every product or article represents a certain defined value, a certain quantity of social labor expended in its production. The more labor it contains the more expensive it is. To find out how much has in fact been expended, or saved, in the production processes, one must know the actual cost of every single element of production, such as raw materials, machinery, electric power, labor power, and so forth. An arbitrary fixing of prices does not allow us to find this out with any precision. One would have to save above all on those products which are the most expensive, on which the most of productive power has been spent. One cannot save very much on that which is less expensive, although even that is always desirable.

In short, the price system existing so far in our state economy should be changed and prices should be adjusted to value. Such a change would eliminate numerous anomalies in our economic life. But, what is most important, it would make it possible for every work establishment to ascertain the real costs of its production.

In our socialist economic system, every production cost should be based on real business accountancy, not on a fictitious one as has often been the case so far. Our socialized economy, while observing all the needs of central planning, should take into account the need of autonomy of socialist enterprises. Things should not be so that all producing establishments in the country constitute some sort of single enterprise run by the state, which arbitrarily manages it.

The change of prices in goods turnover between state enterprises, that is, the achievement of a state of affairs in which it is possible in every enterprise to fix the real production costs, will improve our present pattern of socialism. The implementation of this object is complicated on account of the prices of consumer goods. No disturbances likely to affect the index of the real value of wages must be permitted here.

The acute dearth of building materials can be partly remedied by means of private production or through cooperative production by peasants' associations. The chief bottleneck to private initiative in the production of building materials is the supply of coal and also of cement. But this is not the only difficulty. We are also aware of difficulties of an administrative nature. The elimination of the latter and the creation of the most favorable conditions for whoever is willing and able to develop the production of building materials, particularly tiles, roof tiles, and lime, should be evident in the policy of Party and Government.

The line of development of the handicrafts mapped out by the Seventh Plenum must be implemented in practice. Here, too, the most difficult problem for the State is to ensure the flow of material supplies. There are, however, also other causes hampering the development of handicrafts. The taxation policy, that is the so-called extra tax assessments, is most important among these causes. I am of the opinion that if we maintain the system of extra tax assessments we shall never create suitable conditions for the development of handicrafts. With the aid of extra tax assessments one can always ruin any workshop. One should derive a reasonable manner of taxation, enabling the artisan to work without apprehension, which means that one should liquidate the system of extra tax assessments as harmful.

The problem of premises for artisans' workshops is a thorny one, but not everywhere. In Poland's western and northern territories there are wrecked premises which, given appropriate repair, could serve for the establishment of a workshop. The expenses incurred by the craftsman in the rehabilitation of such premises should be credited entirely to taxes, that is, such a workshop should be exempted from taxes for an appropriate period. The decision in such matters ought to be left to people's councils. Altogether a policy of broad privileges for productive private initiative in town and countryside should be applied in these territories.

DIFFERENT FORMS OF COMMUNAL PRODUCTION; THAT IS OUR ROAD TO SOCIALISM IN THE COUNTRYSIDE

Agricultural policy also calls for certain corrections. With regard to cooperative farms, the basically sound cooperative farms should be assisted in the form of repayable investment credits, and all sorts of state grants should be abolished. The cooperatives which have poor chances of development and which bring only economic losses should not be granted credits. One should rather submit to the members of such cooperatives the problems of the dissolution of the cooperatives. In such a case the problem of the repayment of state credits granted in the past to cooperatives, that is, to the members of cooperatives, arises. I am of the opinion that just as it is not permissible to grant credits lightheadedly, it is not permissible either to give up state money granted in the form of credits.

I see prospects for the development of the cooperative farm movement only under the following conditions:

1—The joining of cooperative farms is voluntary. This means that not only threats or psychological compulsion but economic compulsion as well are excluded. Tax assessments and the establishment of the size of quota deliveries could also be an instrument of compulsion.

2—The members of the cooperatives govern themselves. The cooperative is nothing but a self-governing agricultural production enterprise. The board is elected by the free will of the members. The management of the resources of the cooperative should also be according to the will of the members.

3—The cooperatives have the right of acquiring for their own means or, under given conditions, for state credits, any machines they need for agricultural production or for auxiliary work establishments existing at the cooperatives.

The State Machine Stations should be based on the principles of full profitability, as repair workshops. They may possess a certain number of big agricultural machines, reserved for bringing assistance to cooperatives and individual farmsteads.

4—The state grants to the cooperatives indispensable credit assistance for investment purposes, gives them priority during the conclusion of contract purchase agreements for the delivery of the most profitable agricultural raw materials, guarantees to them priority in the delivery of artificial fertilizers, and supplies other similar forms of assistance.

If as a result of the abolition of various forms of grants the development of the cooperative farms is perhaps slowed down, we shall not lose anything as a result, either economically or politically. We can only gain, both at present and in the future. The abolition of grants removes the unhealthy, uneconomic, impermanent foundation, which is constantly threatening to collapse, on which producers' cooperation has been based. Instead of dispersing strength and resources on the building of new cooperatives, which base their existence on grants given by the state, we should concentrate our efforts on raising the level of economy of the already constituted cooperatives. The numerical growth of cooperation should be fostered primarily through the expansion of cooperatives in the rural communes where they have already been set up.

If the effects achieved so far in the campaign we set up for cooperative farms in the countryside are what they are today, then the causes of this state of affairs should not be sought in the idea of cooperation itself, which is a good one, correct, and just, but which has been distorted as a result of bad policy, bad methods, and by people incapable of sound economic thinking.

Cooperative farming in the countryside will be effective when the deeply human sense of the community of all working people is widely stimulated among the peasants. The broadest expression of this community, which could be termed solidarity, is common labor on a common task, which, in the case of the peasants, is the soil. Common labor contributes most to the fostering of people's social consciousness, arousing the understanding that man does not live for himself alone, but others as well. The moral precept that a man cannot be like a wolf to another man becomes most profound and achieves its highest beauty only among people voluntarily associated in common labor.

If we regard the working class as the leading, most progressive part of the nation, it is not because somebody has happened upon such a term, or that it is a propaganda slogan serving narrow Party political ends. The leading place of the working class is determined, among other things, by its community of production, which has been shaping and is shaping the worker as an individual with the highest social consciousness and therefore as the most progressive.

If we say that the countryside needs cooperative farming, since it is a higher socialist form of production, it is not because someone has thought out such doctrinaire principles divorced from life but because we want to awaken among the working peasants a sense of the profoundly social production community. We want to abolish all forms of exploitation of man by man; we want the peasants' toilsome labor to be eased by machines as far as possible; we want to turn out the greatest possible total product with the least possible expenditure of labor per person affiliated to the peasant production community in order to raise the yields and harvests per hectare to the highest possible level. Then, our peasants and workers, the entire nation will live better. The social role of the peasantry will then be changing. Associated in various forms of producers' communities, the working peasants will become just such champions of social progress as the workers toiling jointly in their factories.

This great social idea of transforming the production relations in the countryside requires not only state assistance in its implementation. It also requires great propaganda and explanatory work to popularize the importance of cooperative farming. In order to build cooperative farms we need creative and progressive thinking, which is the monopoly of no party and of no single man. In the field of raising cooperative farming to a higher level, in the search and application of the best forms of cooperation, there is a vast field of competition between our Party and the Peasant Party, as well as between all those in favor of strengthening the socialist system, the system of social justice. Why should not, for instance, the Catholic progressive movement compete with us in the search for forms, and their realization, of cooperative farming? It is a poor idea to maintain that only Communists can build socialism, only people holding materialist social views.

The road to setting up a vast network of cooperative farms in Poland's countryside is a long one. A quantitative development of producer cooperation cannot be planned because, on the basis of voluntary entry in a cooperative, this would amount to planning the growth in human consciousness, and that cannot be planned. The consciousness of the masses is shaped by their experience in life. It is shaped by facts. There are not a few facts in our present state of cooperative farming which repel the peasant masses from the cooperative farms. Such facts must be liquidated.

The practice in the past years was such that all forms of collective work employed for a long time by the peasants were thoughtlessly destroyed. Their machines, which were their common property, were taken away from them. This practice proceeded from the premise that socialism can be built on the basis of the poverty and decline of peasant holdings. Dogmatic minds were incapable of grasping that under the people's democratic system all forms of cooperation led to socialism in the countryside, that these forms help to raise the sense of the production community, that they raise both the output and the standard of living of the population, and that socialism can best develop precisely on the basis of the prosperity of the working peasant. There is nothing more correct than to develop such voluntary forms of peasant associations. Their emergence ought to be facilitated *inter alia* through the liquidation of the Rural Machine Stations and the transfer of the machines held by them to peasants' associations on terms of full repayment under conditions favorable for them.

Diverse forms of the production community is our Polish road to socialism in the countryside. These forms will shape our model of socialism. Its structural features are already being changed by us through our decision to change the tasks of the State Machine Stations and by telling the cooperative farms that they can purchase their own machines needed in production. The more applications there are from cooperatives for the purchase of such machines the faster this matter will be implemented.

The same applies to parish machinery centers. They will be abolished when the peasants form associations and apply for the purchase of their machinery.

Another page of the defeat of the thoughtless agricultural policy in the past period is the economic ruin of a great number of peasant farms listed in the category of kulak holdings. Equally thoughtless is the idea still heard today that the positive effect of the agricultural policy pursued in the past is the surrender of the ruined kulak to the people's power. This kind of surrender could have been achieved at any time and there was no need for the years of the policy of so-called restricting the kulak, which in reality was not a policy of restricting exploitation but a policy of ruining the kulak's farm. After all, even today it would be possible to achieve the wholesale surrender of all remaining prosperous peasant farms not yet ruined. There is nothing easier than to achieve such a surrender, such a cheap, or rather costly, victory, bearing in mind how much we are paying for the import of grain.

The improved agricultural policy is beginning to bear the first fruits. These are felt first of all by the countryside, where incomes have increased this year by several billion zlotys. In the long run, one should see a further, more essential change of agricultural policy. When this change will occur depends on the economic situation. I have in mind the abolition of quota deliveries, which cannot be a system and an economic feature in our system. Quota deliveries are a phenomenon rather characteristic of war conditions. It should not be assumed that this form of deliveries of the countryside for the state is some unchangeable feature of the building of socialism.

The prospect of abolishing quota deliveries does not free anyone from current duties toward the state. Quota deliveries are a form of taxation paid in kind. Taxes must be paid everywhere in the world, not only in our country. Until a fully just rate of these taxes is established—in the first place by a proper classification of every farm, something which is being done, although too slowly—the tax in the form of compulsory deliveries must be paid in accordance with the previous norms, slightly adjusted for the benefit of the peasants in certain localities. This matter has been neglected lately to a certain extent both by the peasants and the people's councils.

The Government must and will combat every abuse whatsoever and every breach of the law, and must show concern and will show concern that no citizen, that no peasant, is wronged by the authorities; but on the other hand the Government must expect the citizens to discharge their duties toward the state. Quota deliveries are still today one of the forms of state taxation, and this taxation must be paid in full. This we must make clear and explicit to ourselves, the peasants, and the people's councils.

I believe that it is necessary to revise, in favor of the peasants, the terms on which fallow land, especially in the western and northern territories, are transferred to the peasants for rehabilitation. In these territories, a protracted period of exemption from tax ought to be applied for bringing fallow land under the plow and a long period of usufruct of such land should be established in the guise of free lease. What matters is that every usufructuary should be interested in an optimal cultivation of that land and not just in short-term exploitation.

As concerns the state farms, I see, first and foremost, the need to transform thoroughly their organizational structure as well as to reform thoroughly the system of remunerating agricultural workers and employees. The administration of state farms ought to be simplified as far as possible. All attention and skilled personnel must be concentrated where this is most important, that is in the economy, and remuneration for work must be made dependent on the total production of every farm, after fixing a definite starting point for the value of production.

On state farms the idea of workers' self-government must be fully applied. Perhaps more than anywhere else there exists here the necessity of highly skilled management at the top of each farm.

There are considerable possibilities in our country of raising agricultural production by the three types of farms. These possibilities depend, first, on a correct and long-term agricultural policy; second, on deliveries of appropriate agricultural machines to each type of farm by industry—and, first of all, of artificial fertilizers—and third, on raising the qualifications of each peasant. And it is on this that we must concentrate our main attention if we want to catch up with such countries as Czechoslovakia, and especially Germany, in so important a field of the national economy as agriculture.

OUR RELATIONS WITH THE CPSU AND THE USSR

I shall now pass to another group of problems which preoccupy our whole Party and our whole nation to no smaller a degree than economic problems. I have in mind, above all, such problems as the democratization of our life, as well as the development of inter-Party and interstate relations with our great fraternal neighbor—the CPSU and the Soviet Union.

How did it happen that our Party, which advanced, and did so sincerely, to the fore of its aspirations the watchword of the people's power, whose aim it is to implement the most humanitarian idea of socialism, that this Party of ours, staying at the helm of people's power in Poland, permitted the many distortions which took place in the recent past? We shall look for a long time yet for a full answer to this question. It is contained in the problem of the roads leading to the construction of socialism, as well as to the shaping of the model of socialism.

The best description of the social content inherent in the idea of socialism is contained in the definition that socialism is a social system which abolishes the exploitation and oppression of man by man. But this means no more, for instance, than the statement that an aircraft is a machine that can rise into the air and fly. Similarly, as the construction of an aircraft is preceded by the evolution of design based on various features facilitating the rising of the machine into the air, the construction of socialism must be preceded by the scientific theory of socialism. This theory was created by the first classics of Marxism.

They never imagined their theory to be complete. On the contrary, they always maintained that theory must be always alive, must develop on the basis of practical experience and must always be enriched. Even a theory of socialism evolved in the best possible way at any given time in any given conditions cannot embrace all the details of life which is richer than theory.

What is immutable in socialism can be reduced to the abolition of the exploitation of man by man. The roads of achieving this goal can be and are different. They are determined by various circumstances of time and place. The model of socialism can also vary. It can be such as that created in the Soviet Union; it can be shaped in a manner as we see it in Yugoslavia; it can be different still.

Only by way of the experience and achievements of various countries building socialism can the best model of socialism under given conditions arise.

The Soviet Union was the first state in the world where a socialist revolution took place. Lenin and the Bolshevik Party undertook for the first time in history the gigantic task of transforming the theory of socialism into a material, a social, reality.

In the face of tremendous difficulties which accompanied the reshaping of the system of tsarist Russia, backward from every point of view, into a socialist system, during the period when the Party was directed by Stalin, the practice was begun of liquidating in an increasingly ruthless manner the normal clash of views concerning problems brought forth by life which occurred within the Party while Lenin was alive.

The place occupied in the Party by intra-Party discussion was taken—as this discussion was gradually being eliminated—by the cult of personality. The mapping out of the Russian road to socialism passed gradually from the hands of the Central Committee into the hands of an ever smaller group of people, and finally became the monopoly of Stalin. This monopoly also encompassed the theory of scientific socialism.

The cult of personality is a specific system of exercising power, a specific road of advancing in the direction of socialism, while applying methods contrary to socialist humanism, to the socialist conception of the freedom of man, to the socialist conception of legality.

After World War II the Soviet Union ceased to be the only country building socialism. People's China and a number of people's democracies, including Poland, which entered the road of socialist construction, appeared in the world arena. The Workers Parties of these countries, and thus our Party too, were confronted by problems which previously did not exist in practical form. To these problems belong such questions as the road to socialism in conditions proper for each country, which to a certain degree influences the shaping of the model of socialism, as well as the question of the mutual Party and state relations between the parties and governments of the countries of the socialist camp.

The mutual relations between the parties and states of the socialist camp do not and should not give any cause for any complications. This is one of the main features of socialism. These relations should be shaped on the principles of international working class solidarity, should be based on mutual confidence and equality of rights; on granting assistance to each other; on mutual friendly criticism, if such should become necessary; and on a rational solution, arising from the spirit of friendship and from the spirit of socialism, of all controversial matters. Within the framework of such relations each country should have full independence, and the rights of each nation to a sovereign government in an independent country should be fully and mutually respected. This is how it should be and— I would say—this is how it is beginning to be.

In the past it was unfortunately not always like this in the relations between us and our great and friendly neighbor, the Soviet Union.

Stalin, as the leader of the Party and of the Soviet Union, formally recognized that all the principles enumerated above should characterize the relations between the countries of the camp of socialism. Not only did he recognize them, but he himself proclaimed them. In fact, however, these principles could not fit within the framework of what makes up the cult of personality.

ON THE CULT OF PERSONALITY

The cult of personality cannot be confined solely to the person of Stalin. The cult of personality is a certain system which prevailed in the Soviet Union and which was grafted to probably all Communist Parties, as well as to a number of countries of the socialist camp, including Poland.

The essence of this system consisted in the fact that an individual, hierarchic ladder of cults was created. Each such cult comprised a given area in which it functioned. In the block of socialist states it was Stalin who stood at the top of this hierarchic ladder of cults. All those who stood on lower rungs of the ladder bowed their heads before him. Those who bowed their heads were not only the other leaders of the Communist Party of the Soviet Union and the leaders of the Soviet Union, but also the leaders of Communist and Workers Parties of the countries of the socialist camp. The latter, that is the First Secretaries of the Central Committees of the Parties of the various countries who sat on the second rung of the ladder of the cult of personality, in turn donned the robes of infallibility and wisdom. But their cult radiated only on the territory of the countries where they stood at the top of the national cult ladder. This cult could be called only a reflected brilliance, a borrowed light. It shone as the moon does. Nonetheless it was all powerful in the sphere of its action. Thus in each country there was a ladder of cults from top to bottom.

The bearer of the cult of personality was omniscient, knew how to do everything, solved everything, directed everything, and decided everything within the sphere of his action. He was the most intelligent man, regardless of his personal knowledge, capacity, or other personal qualities.

It was not so bad when a reasonable and modest man was dressed in the robes of the cult. Such a man usually did not feel well in this attire.   One can say that he was ashamed of it and did not want to wear it, although he could not completely take it off.

No leader of a Party organization could work normally, even when he worked collectively with the whole leading body, for in such a system, that is in the political system of the cult of personality, there were no conditions for such work.

But it was worse, and even completely bad, when the honors of power, and thus the right to the cult, were seized by a mediocre man, an obtuse executive, or a rotten climber.   Such people buried socialism thoughtlessly and with precision.

Under the system of the cult of personality, the Party as a whole could act independently only within the framework of subordination to the chief cult.   If someone attempted to transgress these limits, he was threatened with excommunication by his comrades.   If the matter concerned a whole Party, it was excommunicated by the remaining Communist Parties.

Under such conditions, could the mutual Party and state relations of the Parties and countries of people's democracy on the one hand, and the Communist Party of the Soviet Union and the Soviet Union on the other hand, be shaped on principles of equality?   Clearly not.   It was prevented by the system of the cult of personality, a system organized with precision, crushing every independent socialist thought.

The system of the cult of personality molded human minds and shaped the manner of thinking of Party activists and Party members.   Some believed and were convinced that the only infallible interpreter of Marxist science and the only man to develop and enrich it correctly, who pointed out the only right road to socialism, was Stalin.   Everything, then, at variance with his ideas and indications had to be harmful, was bound to entail a deviation from Marxism-Leninism, to be heresy. Others who had doubts were convinced that every attempt at publicly professing their sentiments would not only change nothing but would result in awkward consequences to themselves.   Still others did not care for anything except the road leading them to a comfortable desk or safeguarding such a desk.

It would be a great error and confusion of notions if some-one attempted to say that the cult of personality and the author-ity of an individual are one and the same. The difference between one notion and the other resides in the fact that the cult of personality deforms and distorts the idea of socialism, discourages working people from socialism, while the authority of hundreds and thousands of Party leaders and of the people's power greatly favors the development of socialist construction, and is simply indispensable in directing the Party and the state. This authority, however, cannot be imparted to people, it can-not be pinned on the breast, as a medal or a decoration. It should be won, it should be worked for with reason and modesty. Our Party and the people's power in Poland will be all the stronger, the more people there are with authority, that is, such leaders and activists who enjoy the confidence of the working class and of all the working people. This is why we say one should combat with all the necessary energy the cult of personality or its remnants, and fight with all one's strength in order to gain authority.

I should not like to dwell longer on the sad pages of the past, in which the system of the cult of personality reigned in our country. That system violated the democratic principles and the rule of law. Under that system, the characters and con-sciences of men were broken, people were trampled underfoot and their honor was besmirched. Slandering, falsehood, and lies, even provocations, served as instruments in the exercise of authority.

In Poland, too, tragic events occurred when innocent people were sent to their death. Many others were imprisoned, often for many years, although innocent, including Communists. Many people were submitted to bestial tortures. Terror and demoralization were spread. On the soil of the cult of per-sonality, phenomena arose which violated and even nullified the most profound meaning of the people's power.

We have put an end to this system, or we are putting an end to it once and for all. Great appreciation should be expressed to the 20th Congress of the CPSU which so greatly helped us in the liquidation of this system.

Although the system of the cult of personality was born in the Soviet Union, this does not mean that all the evil which happened in Poland could be put on Stalin, on the CPSU, or the Soviet Union. We also had our own, domestic variety of Beriaism. Beriaism and all its general and individual varieties constituted the component parts of the system of the cult of personality. Beriaism is a page full of provocation, blood, prisons, and the sufferings of innocent people.

There are matters in the activity of the Polish variety of Beriaism which require more thorough investigation and clarification. It is not a matter of presenting for payment a bill for one's personal wrongs. Such an idea of personal accounts is entirely alien to me. These matters were too important to be paid in petty personal coinage. But there are matters which for Party reasons and for reasons of principle demand clarification.

The Party must consider its good reputation. It must be clean. And if anybody consciously besmirched its good name he can have no place in its ranks.

I shall put my idea in a concrete form: The leadership of the Party should set up a commission to inquire whether in the cases of people who are now being rehabilitated and who were arrested in the past on the instructions or with the agreement of the Politburo or part of the Politburo, there were no instances of deliberate provocation, or deliberate charging of people with deeds which they had not committed and which are subject to the penal provisions of our Penal Code.

Clarification of this matter is essential and it should be elucidated by a commission composed of completely impartial people. The findings of the commission of inquiry should finally bring to an end the internal Party chapter connected with the activity of the Polish brand of Beriaism.

NO ONE WILL BE ALLOWED TO EXPLOIT THE PROCESS
OF DEMOCRATIZATION AGAINST THE STATE

All of what we call today distortions and deformations in our life in the past period could not but have profoundly shaken the entire Party, the entire working class, the entire nation. Various currents have swept the country, but the most powerful is the slogan calling for the democratization of our life, the demand to put an end to the system which we call the cult of personality. It must be said that the Party leadership has not always been quick enough to take its place together with the Party at the head of this sound movement and to guide it. And if the Party leadership could not keep pace with this movement, then it is understandable that neither could Party organizations.

There even arose confusion, which is exceptionally harmful for the course of the democratization itself. All the opponents of socialism, all the enemies of People's Poland cannot but take advantage of this situation. The greater activity shown by the elements which have nothing in common with the aspirations of the working class and the nation to democratize the whole of our life has also caused certain waverings among some comrades in the Party leadership and in the provinces as to the methods of democratization and its essence. That is why it is necessary firmly to tell ourselves, the Party, the working class and the entire nation:

The road of democratization is the only road leading to the construction of the best model of socialism in our conditions. We shall not deviate from this road and we shall defend ourselves with all our might not to be pushed off this road. And we shall not allow anyone to use the process of democratization to undermine socialism. Our Party is taking its place at the head of the process of democratization and only the Party, acting in conjunction with the other parties of the National Front, can guide this process in a way that will truly lead to the democratization of relations in all the spheres of our life, to the strengthening of the foundations of our system, and not to their weakening.

The Party and all the people who saw the evil that existed in the past and who sincerely desire to remove all that is left of the past evil in our life today in order to strengthen the foundations of our system should give a determined rebuff to all persuasions and all voices which strive to weaken our friendship with the Soviet Union.

If in the past not everything in the relations between our Party and the CPSU and between Poland and the Soviet Union shaped up in the manner it should have in our view, then today this belongs to the irrevocable past. If in one or another field of our life there still are problems which require settlement, then this should be done in a friendly and calm manner, for such conduct should characterize the relations between the parties and states of the socialist camp. And if there is anyone who thinks that it is possible to kindle anti-Soviet moods in Poland, then he is deeply mistaken. We shall not allow harm to the vital interests of the Polish state and the cause of building socialism in Poland.

The system of the cult of personality and all the harm that it caused belongs to the irrevocable past. Polish-Soviet relations based on the principles of equality and independence will create among the Polish people such a profound feeling of friendship for the Soviet Union that no attempt to sow distrust of the Soviet Union will find a response among the people of Poland. Such relations are guarded first of all by our Party and together with it by the entire nation.

THE PARTY MUST BE UNITED AND CONSOLIDATED

In order that the Party should be able efficiently to fulfill its tasks and head the process of democratization, it must above all be united and of one mind and must fully apply the principles of democratic centralism in its ranks and in its life. It must strictly observe in its practical work all the principles of the thesis on the Leninist standards of Party life. These principles were propounded also in the past but often found very little expression in practice. In the forefront of these principles

one should place the problem of the election of Party authorities, the openness of Party life, the right to maintain one's
own views while observing the principle that majority decisions
are binding on all Party members.

The last principle is of special importance at the present
time. The Party's unity of action must be implemented on this
basis. The numerous tasks facing the Party at present can be
implemented successfully only with the common effort of the
million-and-a-half-strong membership of the Party pulling in
the same direction. And this direction has been outlined by
the Seventh Plenum. The present plenum should provide a
closer definition of the general outlines presented by the Seventh
Plenum.

It will be necessary to change a great deal in the practical
work of our Party and in the methods of its activity. In this
connection such matters as a clear demarcation between the
jurisdiction of the Party apparatus and state apparatus with
the maintenance of the leading role of the Party, are in the
forefront. The demarcation must be such as to make everybody responsible for his own work. Otherwise nobody is
responsible and the interests of the Party and the state suffer.
The principle that the Party and the Party apparatus do not
govern but guide, that the task of governing belongs to the
state and its apparatus must be expressed in the concrete substance of work and its practice and not only in words as is
still widely done today. This problem demands detailed investigation, and this must be one of the next tasks to be tackled by
the Party leadership.

It has become a widespread practice in the work of the
Party to take away the more active worker from factories and
put him to work in the Party or state apparatus. This practice
has done much harm. Thus the Party apparatus became inflated
and was either bureaucratized in the conditions of the existing
system of work or took on other unhealthy forms, while the
important political and productive cells were being deprived of
the best members of the Party.

The Party will be living the life of the working class, most intensely, will be in a position to shape in the best possible manner its consciousness, when the vast majority of conscious and active leaders are working shoulder to shoulder with the workers in the work establishments.

It is also necessary to insure adequate control by Party bodies over the Party apparatus, beginning first of all with the central apparatus. There is no doubt that these matters will be dealt with by the next Party congress.

Also the work of the Government needs improving. The Politburo has already adopted the first resolutions in this field. The composition of the Government must conform to the real needs of the country through suitable reorganization of its work.

All targets which we propose to ourselves require calm reflection, and time. Even if the best conceptions of a new organization of our industry and the best forms of democratizing our life are applied, nothing can be done overnight.

One cannot fail to see that recently there has set in a certain amount of confusion also among the organs of state power called upon to guard public order. Various kinds of hooligan outbursts have become more evident which do not often meet with a proper reaction on the part of the citizens' militia. One must make it clear to ourselves and to all whom it may concern: the people's power will punish every abuse in its apparatus, but will combat and must combat with the same determination all breaches of public order and of the peace of the citizens. The citizens' militia must always be respected and supported by the public when it intervenes to protect public order. One must not tolerate any form of insult to the uniform of the guardian of public order by hooligans, who must be severely punished for violating the law.

THE SEJM MUST BECOME THE SUPREME ORGAN OF STATE POWER

Among the many ailments of the past period was also the fact that the Sejm did not fulfill its constitutional task in state life. We are now facing elections to the new Sejm which ought to occupy in our political and state life the place assigned to it by the Constitution.   The elevation of the role of the Sejm to that of the supreme organ of state power will probably be of the greatest importance in our democratization program.

The foremost task of the Sejm is to exercise the highest legislative and controlling power.   Conditions should be created which are indispensable to enable the Sejm to fulfill this task. This includes both political conditions which are created by the process of democratization of our life and legal conditions which would guarantee to the Sejm its constitutional powers.

The question arises: What does our Party want to guarantee to the Sejm in the way of legal norms?

I think that in the forefront is the problem of Sejm sessions which up to now have been taking place too rarely.   Of special importance in the legislative work of the Sejm is the introduction of such a procedure of the work of the Sejm committees which would enable them to concentrate in their minds the drafting of legal acts.

It follows from this postulate that part of the deputies should fulfill their duties on a professional basis, that is to say that they should be relieved from gainful employment for the period they exercise the functions of Sejm deputies.

The issuing of decrees by the Council of State should be restricted to urgent problems and, at the same time, the Sejm should be guaranteed the right to annul or amend those decrees.

The Sejm should exercise large-scale control over the work of the Government and of the state organs.   To insure this, the introduction of certain changes in the Constitution is indispensable.   In my opinion, Sejm control over the executive organs of state power should be exercised by an institution subordinated directly to the Sejm and not to the Government, as has been the case up to now.   The Supreme Chamber of State Control, subordinated to the Sejm, should be restored.

I also hold that the Sejm should have the right to exercise control over our trade agreements with other states.   As a matter of fact, taking into account the interests of the state, those agreements contain nothing that would call for the control of a small group of people. Information given to public opinion by the Government and the Sejm on our trade agreements will automatically stop various absurd rumors concerning our foreign trade.

The Sejm should also have the right to endorse all our treaties with other countries, concluded by the Government and ratified by the Council of State.

The Sejm is also called upon to evaluate the work of the Government, and it comes within the Sejm's terms of reference to draw conclusions with regard to those persons who fail in the proper discharge of their duties.

This is how in broad outline I would see the Sejm in its role of legislator and controller of the state administration. A sensible definition of the powers of the Sejm and even extension of these powers beyond the limits envisaged in the Constitution, accompanied by a sensible definition of the tasks of the Party toward the state apparatus, do not lead to a collision between the Sejm and the political substance contained in the thesis on the guiding role of the Party.

The elections will be carried out on the basis of the new electoral law which allows the people to elect and not only to vote. This is a very important change. Grouped within the National Front the parties and the social organizations are putting forward one common election program. But any program is implemented not only by the parties but also by people acting on behalf of those parties. Those candidates who enjoy the greatest confidence will be elected. It is clear that those who do not enjoy the confidence of broad sections of electors will not be elected to the future Sejm.

Of importance is not only the problem of what powers the Sejm will have. The role it will play in the life of the state and of the nation, in the process of democratization in our country, will depend to a no lesser degree on the people who will be elected to the Sejm. We can instruct our Party that it should put forward as candidates the best comrades, those people who are most strongly associated with the working class and with the entire nation.

We can only recommend to our allies in the National Front that they should put forward as their own candidates to the Sejm people who will care for the jointly elaborated election program not only in words but also in their hearts and minds.

What the present Plenum adopts will be carried by us, comrades, to the Party, to the working class, and to the nation with our heads raised, for we shall be bringing them truth. And truth shown to the nation without disguise will give us strength, will restore to the People's Government and to our Party the full confidence of the working masses. This confidence is indispensable for the implementation of our plans.

Postulating the principle of the freedom of criticism in all its forms, including criticism in the press, we have the right to demand that each criticism should be creative and just, that it should help to overcome the difficulties of the present period instead of increasing them or sometimes even treating demagogically certain phenomena and problems.

We have the right to demand from our youth, especially from university students, that they should keep their ardor in the search for roads leading to the improvement of our present reality, within the framework of the decisions which will be adopted by the present Plenum. One can always forgive young people many things. But life forgives no one, even youth, for thoughtless acts.

We can but rejoice at the ardor of our young comrades. For it is they who are to take over from us the posts in the Party and in the state apparatus. But we are fully justified in demanding from them that they should join their enthusiasm and ardor to the wisdom of the Party. Our Party should say clearly to the young people: march in the vanguard of this great and momentous process of democratizaion but always look up to your leadership, to the leadership of all People's Poland—to the Party of the working class, to the Polish United Workers Party.

On October 21, 1956, the Central Committee of the PUWP concluded its eighth plenary session. It elected a new leadership[5] and adopted a resolution.

The new leadership included Wladyslaw Gomulka as First Secretary. The other eight members of the Politburo were Jozef Cyrankiewicz, Stefan Jedrychowski, Ignacy Loga-Sowinski, Jerzy Morawski, Edward Ochab, Adam Rapacki, Roman Zambrowski, and Aleksander Zawadzki. The newly elected secretariat of the Party included, in addition to Gomulka, Jerzy Albrecht, Edward Gierek, Witold Jarosinski, Edward Ochab, Wladyslaw Matwin, and Roman Zambrowski.

3. RESOLUTION ADOPTED BY THE CENTRAL COMMITTEE OF THE POLISH UNITED WORKERS PARTY AT ITS EIGHTH PLENARY SESSION, OCTOBER 19-21, 1956[6]

THE CENTRAL COMMITTEE of the PUWP, approving the political line laid down in the speech of Comrade Gomulka-Wieslaw, has adopted the following resolution:

I

1—The Central Committee notes that at the present moment the decisive task for the further progress of Poland toward socialism is the strengthening of the leading role of our Party as the guiding political and ideological force of the working class, of the Polish nation, and of the people's state.

The Party will fulfill its leading role only when, with elan and without hesitation, it will carry out the correct policy outlined by the Seventh Plenum of the Central Committee, a policy directed at the systematic improvement of the living conditions of the working people of town and country, of profound socialist democratization.

(A major obstacle to the consistent implementation of the decisions of the Seventh Plenum was the lack of unanimity and

---

[5] *Trybuna Ludu,* October 22, 1956.

[6] *Trybuna Ludu,* October 25, 1956; also *Nowe Drogi,* No. 10, 1956, pp. 3-13.

consistency in the Politburo of the Central Committe in solving the concrete problems of the process of socialist democratization in the life of the Party and the country. In this situation the work of the Central Committee was in many cases paralyzed. This weakened the leading role of the Party in view of the rapidly growing political activity of the masses.)[7]

The Party must assume the leadership of the working class and all the leading socialist forces of the nation in the process of overcoming the vestiges, mistakes, and distortions of the past period in order to complete this process irrespective of inevitable temporary difficulties and hesitations and in spite of the maneuvers of the reactionary forces.

The Party must resolutely overcome within its own ranks conservatism and timidity, fear of the new, clinging to outworn doctrines and models, attempts at retreat and return to old methods of direction, and government burdened with Stalinist and native distortions.

Only under these conditions will we be able to overcome the attitudes of disorientation and defensiveness and mobilize and close the Party ranks. Only under these conditions will we be able to give the right direction to the quest of the people who sometimes blunder but who are passionately devoted to the cause of socialism.

Only under these conditions will we be able to overcome the false liberal bourgeois tendencies among the hesitant elements, particularly in certain circles of the intelligentsia.

Only under these conditions will we be able to isolate and overpower the forces of reaction which are intensifying their activity in an attempt to aggravate the class struggle, and are trying to exploit the democratization of the political life of the

---

[7] The basic points of the resolution were reprinted in *Pravda* on October 28, 1956. While *Pravda* made clear that it was printing only the "basic points," it indicated an omission in only one place. For the rest, the *Pravda* version showed no breaks in the continuity of the text. The passages in parentheses in the translation appearing here are those which were *omitted* in *Pravda*.

country against socialism, and hereby against democracy, and to drive a wedge between Poland and the Soviet Union.

In its struggle against conservative forces, against attempts at turning back, at hampering the development of intra-Party democracy, at stifling criticism, at abusing legality, at defending bureaucratism, Little Caesarism, and at reintroducing discrepancies between words and deeds, the Party will rally and guide all the live forces of socialism.

The Party must put itself at the head of the movement of the advanced plant crews seeking to improve methods of economic administration and to increase the direct participation of workers in the management of socialist enterprises and in the government of the country. [It must put itself] at the head of the peasants' drive to develop self-government, to extend democratism and the delegation of the powers of the people's councils, and to increase agricultural output. [It must put itself] at the head of the socialist intellectual movement of unexampled vitality which is now spreading among the intelligentsia.

The Party will help the ZMP [Polish Youth Union] and the youth in their ardent efforts to participate as widely as possible in the political life of the country, in the ideological and organizational searchings which will make it possible to link more closely the progressive portion of youth with the Party and to strengthen its influence on the entire young generation. In the struggle for socialist democratization the Party will establish closer links of cooperation with the allied parties—the United Peasant Party and the Democratic Party—thus strengthening the political core of the National Front.

2—The Party will not consent to the purely formal and declaratory treatment of Party decisions and will not permit comrades who desist from active and resolute implementation [of these decisions] to remain in responsible positions.

The Party must guarantee the indispensable and hitherto improperly observed conditions of intra-Party democracy: the open character of Party life, and above all, continuous informa-

tion of Party members about the policies of the leading Party
organs on current issues of Party policy; the Party must respond
to the problems and postulates put forward by members of the
Party and Party organs must systematically submit reports to
the Party members who have elected them.

The Party will pay particular attention to insuring in all its
organizations from top to bottom conditions for the free election of Party organs in accordance with the principles of the
Party Statute; unfettered nomination and discussion of candidates for Party posts; secret election not only of Party committees but also of executive bureaus and secretaries, including
the Politburo and the Secretariat of the Central Committee.

(In order to insure the proper selection of employees for
the Party apparatus and increase their responsibility to Party
organs, it is imperative to adopt the principle of electing
responsible employees of the Party apparatus at plenary sessions
of Party organs. In accordance with the decisions of the
Seventh Plenum the Party must speed up work on the simplification of the structure and on the change of style of work of
the Party apparatus and insure such disposition and use of
Party cadres which would strengthen the activity of the basic
Party organizations in plants and institutions, particularly in
the large factories.)

Unity and cohesion in the Party's ranks are the basis of
the Party's power, the indispensable conditions for its effective
work. Freedom of discussion and exchange of ideas among
Party members on the subject of Party policy must be accompanied by stern, ruthless discipline in the implementation of
Party tasks once decisions have been taken. The Party will
not tolerate attempts at weakening Party discipline or failure
to implement the decisions and tasks set by the Party.

Unity in the Party's activity is possible only on the basis
of the ideological unity of Communists, on the basis of the
principles of creative Marxism-Leninism. The unity of Party
work must be strengthened through bold ideological and practical revision of the mistakes and distortions of the past period,

through basic criticism from the Leninist point of view, from the point of view of programmatic principles of the Party, of opinions that are not in conformity with the Party line.

The ideological unity of the Party and the cohesion of its ranks does not mean that there is no place for difference of opinions among Party members with regard to the decisions of Party organs. The Party adheres to the Leninist view that within the framework of the Party program there are permissible and inevitable differences of opinion among Party members on many problems of the day-to-day activity of the Party. Members of the Party holding such divergent views may uphold them, submit them to the organization to which they belong or to a superior Party organ, but they cannot appeal to opinion outside the Party against the position taken by the Party. In practical activity they must unconditionally carry out the Party's decisions.

(The Party maintains that Party organs cannot use disciplinary means to compel members of the Party to renounce their divergent views.) There is, however, no place in the Party for people whose opinions are contrary to the programmatic principles of the Party or whose practical activity is opposed to those principles.

The Party condemns opinions and methods which introduce into the ranks of the Party artificial lines of division according to racial origins, and manifestations of discrimination against any groups of the population because of their origin, which tend to foster anti-Semitism and other nationalistic trends which are alien to the Party ideology and demoralize the Party cadres. The Party cadre policy must be guided exclusively by considerations of principle such as political qualifications and professional qualifications of the comrades; their opinions, ideological maturity, and moral attitude; their links with the masses, and devotion in the struggle for the cause of the working class and the working people.

The Party will combat all attempts to pit the working class against the intelligentsia, either by minimizing the leading rule of the working class, or by minimizing the importance of the intelligentsia in building the new system and in developing the national economy and culture. The vacillations which appear among some elements of the intelligentsia cannot serve as a pretext for discrediting the progressive intellectual movement among the intelligentsia, which is becoming ever closer associated with the working class.

In the present period of the renaissance of Leninist principles in the workers' movement, of the profound revitalization of revolutionary thought, and of the intensification of the struggle against alien influences and distortions in theory and practice, it is imperative to concentrate the forces of the Party on the ideological front in order to formulate the Party's attitude on current ideological problems, to guide the intellectual movement in the country, and to counter symptoms of disorientation as well as hostile ideology.

3—The Party is of the opinion that the principle of responsibility of Party and state leaders in the fulfillment of the duties and functions entrusted to them must be fully restored as one of the basic principles of socialist democratism. This principle, though formally recognized, has been abused in practice during the past period. People who were compromised in their activities through indolence or serious errors, who cannot correct them, cannot remain in responsible positions.

(While emphasizing this attitude most forcefully the Party opposes attempts at discrediting before public opinion honest leaders who are devoted to socialism, and who form the overwhelming majority of the Party and state apparatus, on the sole ground that in this or that period, while realizing the tasks entrusted to them with the best of intentions, they committed errors or were not able to oppose a policy that is correctly recognized today as mistaken and burdened with distortions.)

The Party will resolutely combat manifestations of self-aggrandizement and counter the isolation of Party and state leaders from the masses.

4—The Party welcomes the manifold initiative of the workers aimed at a true and direct participation by the working masses in the administration of socialist enterprises.

The experiences of the last months and, more particularly, the variegated initiative of the workers show that the decisions adopted on this subject by the Seventh Plenum endeavoring to broaden the workers' democracy merely by extending the rights of workers' councils are inadequate and no longer correspond to the strivings of the most active part of the working class. It is imperative to establish workers' self-government as an organ of workers' participation in the management of enterprises. ([This organ] should, within the limits of established rights of the enterprise, decide jointly with the director on such basic problems as the setting of the production plan and evaluation of its fulfillment, expansion of plant, technical progress, organization of work and output, matters of output norms, wage rates and premia, distribution of the plant fund, and so forth.)

The basic idea which should guide the workers' self-government participating in the management of plants should be: to produce more, cheaper, better. This is the way to higher living standards for the working class and the entire nation.

(The statute of the self-government must safeguard the interests of both the enterprise and its personnel, as well as the interests of the national economy as a whole, and the proper linkage of central planning with far-reaching autonomy of the enterprise.

Workers' self-government should have the right to participate directly in the appointment and dismissal of the director of the enterprise. The introduction of self-government does not violate the operational principle of one-man management of the enterprise within the framework of the directives of the plan and the appropriate decisions of the self-government. The broad rights of self-government must cause not a weakening but a strengthening of the authority of the director.)

Workers' self-government should be at first introduced into enterprises which are best prepared for it. (The experiences of these enterprises should then be extended by suitable legal enactments.)

5—The Party will strive to create political as well as legal conditions to enable the Sejm, the supreme organ of authority of the people's democratic state, to exercise fully its basic constitutional functions. Legislative work must be centered in the Sejm. The Sejm must fully use its constitutional powers of broad control of the work of the Government. (For that purpose, the Supreme Chamber of Control should be set up as an organ of the Sejm. In connection with approval of basic state documents, line budget and annual national economic plans, and with ratification of major international agreements, the members of the Sejm must be given an opportunity to examine thoroughly the entire complex of the problems involved. The Sejm must have an opportunity to express its view on all essential proposals of the government. Only in exceptional cases should matters coming within the competence of the legislative chamber be decided on by a decree of the Council of State, and the Sejm, through its committees, should be steadily and currently informed about the work of the Government.

The Central Committee favors that some of the members of the future Sejm should be permanently freed from professional work so as to be able to devote themselves fully to their work as deputies. Steps should be taken to hold Sejm sessions more frequently and to devote the recesses between the sessions to systematic work on the part of Sejm subcommittees. Under such conditions the parliament will become an effective instrument of public control over the activities of the Government and the state administration.)

The Party enters the electoral campaign as a member of the National Front, conscious of its responsibility for further strengthening the people's democratic state and safeguarding the socialist development of the country. The Sejm elections will be carried out under conditions of an extraordinary upsurge of political activity, in a situation in which new millions of people have been drawn into active participation in the social and political life of the country through the process of democratization.

The main front of this electoral struggle will run between the forces of socialism, rallied under the leadership of our Party, and the forces of reaction which will undoubtedly attempt to exploit difficulties in the political situation of the country as well as economic difficulties to take action against our Party, to weaken the cohesion of the National Front, and which will try to exploit for hostile, antisocialist agitation the sentiments of embitterment and the still persisting mistrust among some of the working people. Freedom in our country can only serve the working people—the creators of a new socialist system. For the enemies of socialism and of the rule of the working people there can be no freedom.

(The elections will be conducted on such principles as to let the voters have their say and decide not only on the electoral program, as has been the case hitherto, but also choose between candidates, and to determine *by whom* and *how* this program will be realized in the Sejm. At the same time the Party must oppose all attempts at pitting one candidate against the other because of their affiliation to this or that party associated in the National Front.)

The National Front program in the present Sejm elections, a program to which the basic contribution has been made by the Seventh and the Eighth Plenums, forms a directive for the work of the Party both in and out of the Sejm, as the leader of the masses in the cities and the countryside. It is a program for which the Party bears responsibility before the working class and the people.

II

1—As a result of the resolutions of the Seventh Plenum concerning the more rapid improvement of the material welfare of the working masses of town and country, a further adjustment and increase of the wages of the basic groups of workers and employees was carried out. This resulted from the beginning of 1956 in an increase of the earnings of more than 4 million working people, that is, 58.9 percent of the total number of workers and employees. In addition, 514,000 persons have become eligible for higher pensions. As a result the total income of workers and employees has risen by more than 9.5 billion zlotys annually; for those who were affected by the increase in wages, this means an increase of their monthly average earning by 177 zlotys.

At the same time, as a result of the increase in the production and supply of a number of farm products, particularly meat, and as a result of an increase in state purchase prices, the money income of the rural population has markedly increased. The sums obtained from the sale of farm products to the state increased by 7.5 billion zlotys in comparison with 1955.

(In order to improve the fuel supply for the population, more than 1.2 million tons of coal were earmarked to improve coal supplies for the population of town and country during the current year, at the expense of the reduction in the quantity of coal set aside for export. The improvement in the coal supply available to the population depends on the full implementation of the plan for the extraction of coal by the mining industry and of the plan for the transport of coal by rail.)

Owing to the favorable results achieved in agriculture and to the assistance of the USSR and Czechoslovakia, the quantity of goods placed on the market has been increased, particularly of some industrial articles and of meat.

The above-mentioned measures by the Party and the Government brought about a further improvement in the situation of the working masses, but at the same time the danger has arisen of a gap between the increased purchasing power of the population and the quantity of goods on the market. (Consequently, the raise next year can as a rule include wage adjustments only in the mining industry and [can affect] only very small groups in other branches of the economy.)

A further increase in wages without a corresponding additional quantity of goods on the market would inevitably disturb the equilibrium of the market, rapidly exhaust the stocks of goods available, raise prices, lower the value of money, and unleash speculation, that is, it would turn against the interests of the working people and jeopardize the improvement so far achieved. A further increase in the real wages of the working class and in the incomes of the rural population can be effected only by increasing production, providing new means which would allow us to balance the growing purchasing power of the population and to satisfy to a higher degree the needs of the working people. (Depending on the economic results of the enterprises in 1957, the deduction earmarked for the plant fund will be increased. This will broaden the possibility of raising the incomes of workers and employees.

The Party calls on all workers and employees to remember that their justified aspirations to improve their own material situation depend upon the actual possibilities of our national economy whose equilibrium and prosperity determine in the final analysis the living conditions of each working family.) In this situation the Party should firmly resist any demagogy calling for pressure upon the Government and the economic organs in order to achieve greater raises which would exceed the economic possibilities of the state.

(The Party and the Government have undertaken steps aimed at gradually refunding sums arising from cases of violation of the provisions of collective agreements and of labor legislation regulations in past years. The right and justified claims arising from this situation should be settled in a planned manner—in the course of two to three years, depending on their amount and the economic resources of the country.)

2—While the implementation of economic plans in industry and agriculture is on the whole favorable, there are danger points in some important sectors of the national economy, such as coal extraction, the production of metallurgical coke, the engineering industry, the industry of building materials and the building trade, small-scale industry, and cooperatives. It is imperative to undertake with all the necessary firmness preventive measures to overcome the difficulties, above all in the field of supplying the population with goods and extending the services to a degree corresponding to the increased purchasing power, and also in the field of supplying industry with raw materials, and in the implementation of the plan of residential construction.

(In order to achieve this the Central Committee recommends:

[a] After a thorough analysis of the purposefulness and effectiveness of planned investments, to carry out further restrictions in the investment plan for the year 1957, above all by reducing construction work in industry. The building materials thus saved should be earmarked for sale to the rural population and for improving the supplies for residential construction.

[b] To utilize more broadly the potential of the special [i.e., defense] engineering and chemical industry for civilian production, particularly for production of consumer goods.

[c] In order to increase the output of mass consumption goods it is necessary to promote the output of by-products and to abolish all restrictions in this field—provided the tasks of the state plan for basic production is implemented—and also to exclude the by-products from the state plan, to grant complete freedom in the field of prices and sales of by-products, and to earmark the profits derived from this production for the plant fund of the enterprises.

[d] To undertake without delay measures aiming at an increase in the production of building materials beyond the current plan of the industry of building materials; with this aim in view, to facilitate the production of bricks, slag concrete, and so forth, as well as of substitute materials in metallurgical works, power stations, and other work establishments by utilizing waste and scrap materials. This production should be developed as a production of by-products and above all should serve the individual needs of their own workers and employees, and should be made available for sale to the local population as well. It is necessary to put into operation small building

material plants which are now idle, within the framework of local industry, either by transferring them to work cooperatives or to housing construction cooperatives, to peasants' associations, or through leasing them to private persons. All surpluses of buildings materials beyond the needs of socialized construction should be earmarked to increase the supplies for the countryside as well as for individual construction.

[e] To raise the prices on some articles so far sold at shockingly low prices and causing waste or requiring subsidies from the state budget such as sawn timber, lime, bricks, roofing tiles, newspapers, tickets to rural movies.

[f] Gradually to introduce in state-owned cooperative small-scale industry complete freedom of sales and the principle of fixing prices in accordance with market conditions, gradually to broaden the scope of local industry, transferring to the people's councils the small and medium plants which are producing consumer goods from local raw materials. It is imperative, while carrying out the recommendation of the Seventh Plenum concerning the development of handicrafts, to create conditions enabling artisans to establish sales centers for their own products.

[g] To facilitate the development of small private enterprises in those fields of production in which they can contribute to an increase in the quantity and variety of goods without drawing upon the raw material resources of the state and cooperative industry. This applies in particular to local quarries, lime pits, brick kilns, the extraction of peat, agricultural and food processing, small catering establishments, and so forth. In towns and townships with an insufficient network of socialized trade it is necessary to facilitate the opening of private shops and stands.

[h] To expand the system of vocational training of youth on the job while reducing at the same time the scale of vocational training of lower grades in the branches of the economy where there is no shortage of manpower.)

3—The situation in the countryside places before the Party the need to solve a number of urgent problems and to execute with great consistency the tasks previously undertaken. The results of agricultural production are, generally speaking, favorable. (The grain harvests are higher than the average harvests in the past years, but somewhat smaller than in 1955. On the other hand, the harvests of root crops, mainly potatoes, are better than last year. Fodder reserves have increased recently, thus making possible the further development of animal breeding and the reduction of grain imports to a certain degree. The pig and cattle population is rising.) At the same time a number of unfavorable phenomena are appearing in relations between town and country as well as in the sphere of the socialist transformation of agriculture.

First, during the present intensive campaign of purchasing agricultural produce an increasing weakening of the implementation of the quota deliveries of grain, meat, and especially milk can be observed.

The Party is in favor of developing the peasants' material interest in higher agricultural production and will strive step by step to base relations between town and country on commodity exchange.

(As a result of the rise of agricultural production and the stabilization of the level of quota deliveries, there has been taking place since 1954 an increase of the share of contractual and free market purchases in the total volume of purchased agricultural produce. A reduction of quota deliveries will depend on the rate at which agricultural production and the state food reserves will increase.)

The maintenance of quota deliveries is at present and for a considerable time will remain an economic necessity, since without them we should not be in a position to secure food supplies to the working class and urban population, maintain the value of the zloty, or guarantee a correct distribution of the national income between the population of town and country. Hence the necessity to break all attempts aiming at undermining quota deliveries and to mobilize the entire countryside for the discharge of its duties toward the people's state. (This task assumes special importance in the present economic situation of the country.)

Second, in the work on the socialist transformation of the countryside the Party's attention in the immediate future should be concentrated on strengthening cooperative farms which possess conditions for sound development. (More particularly, they should be given assistance which would make possible a steady rise in their output as well as in their share in the total marketable output and secure on this basis an increase in the income of members of the cooperative farms. This assistance should apply to capital outlays, mechanization of production processes, agronomical guidance, priority in contract purchases and in supplies of artificial fertilizer. The cooperative farms must be free from interference by state and Party organs in their internal affairs. The cooperatives must have complete autonomy in matters of organization of production, remuneration for work, disposal of property, distribution of income, construction, relations with other enterprises, and so forth. Cooperatives must be given the opportunity of purchasing agricultural machines and implements, tractors and cars out of their own means as well as on credit.)

While continuing the effort to strengthen the cooperatives, it is necessary at the same time to make possible the dissolution of cooperatives which have no conditions for further development and which discredit cooperative farming. (All attempts to maintain their existence by means of free economic assistance by the state should be recognized as harmful. Initiative in this matter should be taken over by the National Council of Cooperative Farms, the people's councils, and Party authorities.)

The Party, by conducting simultaneously a policy of furthering the development of production of individual peasant farmsteads, stresses its repeatedly expressed standpoint that cooperative farming in the countryside is necessary because it liquidates all form of exploitation of man by man, imbues peasants with the feeling of deep social community and community of work, eases the difficult and toilsome work of the peasants through the use of machines, and opens up the possibilities of achieving big crops from every hectare of land. The peasants, the workers, and the whole nation will then be living better. Communal production by the peasants is a great and difficult task of our program without the implementation of which the full triumph of socialism in our country is inconceivable.

Third, experience shows that the present forms of supply of machine services to agriculture, especially to cooperative farms, fail to give the expected results, are expensive and inefficient. The investment outlays and the costs of the State Machine Stations [POM] and the Rural Machine Stations [GOM] are out of proportion with the economic results achieved.

It is therefore deemed advisable:

(a) To liquidate gradually the Rural Machine Stations as state centers and to sell the machines and equipment of the Rural Machine Stations to peasant teams and machine partnerships or to cooperative farms, which should be provided for this purpose with the indispensable credits if necessary. (Until the teams and machine partnerships are organized it is necessary to reduce subsidies for the Rural Machine Stations at cost level.)

(b) To preserve and strengthen the State Machine Stations situated in areas of high development of cooperative farming and possessing the indispensable material and technical basis. These centers should become profitable in view of the sufficient acreage of the cooperative farms serviced by them and of the adequate set of machines in their possession. (Their services to the cooperative farms should be payable exclusively in cash— not in kind.) The State Machine Stations situated in areas of low development of cooperative farming where material and technical conditions as well as large distances separating them from cooperative farms make the work of the State Machine Stations unprofitable and highly expensive should be reorganized to serve as repair bases for cooperative and peasant machines and as centers for rental of combines and other heavy machines.

Fourth, in order to create propitious conditions for the further struggle to raise agricultural production it is necessary at present to secure with all energy the implementation of the resolutions of the Seventh Plenum regarding liquidation of the distortions in the policy toward the more well-to-do section of the middle peasantry and toward kulak farmsteads, [distortions] which frequently led not to the restriction of exploitation but to the restriction of agricultural production on those farmsteads.

(Fifth, in order to strengthen the sense of ownership of the peasants it is necessary to abolish restrictions on the sale of land and on the right to inherit land, including land allotted to peasants under the agrarian reform, and under the settlement scheme in the recovered territories.)

III

The struggle for democratization, for socialist construction, and for the consolidation of the leading role of the Party is most closely linked with the participation of People's Poland in the camp of socialist states, in the international movement of the forces of socialism and progress, fighting for abatement of international tension and for peaceful coexistence. Our Party inseparably links the interests of People's Poland with the unshakable principle of the Polish-Soviet alliance, with the interests of the entire socialist camp.

The resolutions of the 20th Congress of the CPSU which have had an important influence on transformations in the international working class movement, as well as the intellectual movement which they set off and which is vigorously developing in the Communist and Workers Parties, enables us today better to understand and remove the sources of the distortions and errors of the past period, not only within the various countries of our camp, but also in relations among the Parties.

As a result of these transformations, conditions have been created for shaping the relations between the Parties in our camp on foundations fully consistent with the spirit of Leninism.

In the implementation of the tasks of socialist construction the Party avails itself of the experience of the first socialist country, the USSR, and of other countries striving toward the same aims as ourselves, but it considers incorrect the methods of mechanically copying and taking over the models and forms applied in other countries. The Party will search for ways and solutions stemming from the specific conditions of our country and our historical development, in accordance with the interests of the Polish working class and the Polish nation. The Party is of the opinion that ways of socialist development can be different in various countries and various historical conditions, and that this abundance of forms of socialist development adds to its strength on the international scale.

The bonds linking the socialist countries arise from a community of aspirations and from a common aim—the building of socialism and Communism. These bonds not only exclude, but, on the contrary, they imply the full sovereignty and independence of each country and nation in a choice of ways and means to build a new, superior system which are most appropriate and which best suit its historical conditions.

The relations among Parties and states should be shaped by the principles of international working class solidarity. They should be based on mutual trust and equality of rights, on mutual assistance, on mutual friendly criticism whenever necessary, on reasonable settling of all controversial matters in the spirit of friendship and socialism. Within the framework of such relations each country should possess full independence and sovereignty, and the right of each nation to sovereign government in an independent country should be fully and mutually respected.

The Party determinedly combats all attempts undertaken by the reactionaries in the country and in the international arena to undermine the unity of the countries of the socialist camp and to weaken the Polish-Soviet alliance. At the present moment the Party must oppose any manifestations of anti-Soviet propaganda, it must firmly combat attempts to incite nationalistic and anti-Soviet feelings.

Polish-Soviet relations based on principles of equality and independence will give birth in the Polish nation to a feeling of friendship for the Soviet Union which will be so profound that no attempt to sow mistrust of the USSR will find a response in our country.

Unity and close cooperation of socialist states constitute the most durable foundation of our policy, of the consolidation of independence and peaceful development toward socialism, and at the same time they serve the interests of the universal struggle of the nations for peace, progress, and socialism.

The course of events in Poland understandably evoked reaction in the Soviet Union and in the people's democracies.

The Soviet Union did not follow up the Polish events with an immediate policy statement. The declaration of the Soviet Government concerning relations with the East European people's democracies, issued on October 30, 1956, may be construed as the official answer to the turn of events in Poland and to the first phase of the Hungarian revolt.[8]

In the meantime, except for the consultation between Soviet and Polish Communist leaders in Warsaw and a highly critical article in *Pravda* on October 20, 1956, under the title "Antisocialist Pronouncements in the Polish Press",[9] comment by Soviet sources consisted of extensive reporting on the developments in Poland.

The *Pravda* article of October 20 asserted:

Statements which preach rejection of the socialist path have been appearing in the Polish newspapers more and more frequently of late. This may seem strange, but it is a fact: The press, which is called upon to serve as a sharp, effective weapon in the struggle to strengthen the people's democratic system, day after day publishes articles which shake the very foundations of this system, sow disbelief in the building of a new life, and poison the souls of readers with the imported venom of an ideology alien to the working people.

---

[8] See Part Four, Chapter I, Document 1.

[9] A full translation of the article appears in *The Current Digest of the Soviet Press*, VIII, No. 40 (November 14, 1956) 12-13.

Until recently the authors of such pronouncements disguised themselves by claiming that they were exposing the consequences of the "cult of personality" and advocating restoration of the Leninist norms of Party life.

But now these phrases, which, incidentally, sounded blasphemous from the lips of slanderers who had been given the opportunity to use the pages of the Polish press to the detriment of the Polish United Workers Party and the people's state, have also been cast aside. Throwing off their masks, these people are publicly renouncing Lenin and Marx.

One does not have to go far for examples. A certain Z. Florczak declared war on Marx publicly today with an article in *Nowa Kultura,* organ of the Polish Writers' Union, an article significantly entitled "Discussion with the West."

With loose-tongued abandon this author urges that "we put an end to the jargon (?!) which the Communist camp has developed to talk to the masses." What "jargon" is referred to? Z. Florczak states without any embarrassment: "We must put an end to the slogans 'Workers of the World, Unite!,' 'reaction,' and 'the building of socialism,' since these slogans were the slogans of battles, the slogans of the armed stage of the revolution. The slogan 'Workers of the World, Unite!' cannot mean anything now."

Thus, this unruly boy who calls himself a writer proposes with unbounded cynicism that we bury a slogan which is sacred to every proletarian, a slogan with which the best people of the international working class have lived, fought, and died for a century, winning victory after victory and now building and establishing a new society. . . .

One could (though with great difficulty!) try to explain the appearance of this filthy concoction by an ignorant writer in the organ of the Polish Writers' Union as some sort of incomprehensible oversight by its editors. But the fact is that such articles have been appearing in certain Warsaw newspapers more and more frequently of late and, whether the leaders of the ideological front in Poland wish it or not, such articles constitute a widespread campaign which is shaking the very foundations of the people's democratic system.

Not to mention the fact that anti-Soviet pronouncements are also resounding in this hoarse choir of slanderers. For 39 years our people have grown accustomed to hearing slander from the bourgeois camp, and it does not frighten them, but the fact that a slanderous campaign is now being conducted openly in the press of a people's democracy linked to the Soviet Union by a treaty of alliance and friendship naturally grieves the Soviet people. The fact that this campaign, as shown by recent pronouncements in the Polish press, is aimed primarily and chiefly at undermining socialism in Poland itself is also alarming.

Today, for example, the newspaper *Zycie Warszawy* carried a long article by Jerzy Putrament entitled "The Crux of the Matter," which directly ties in with the sermons of the new overthrower of Marxism, Florczak. . . .

What does this revisionist propose? Abolish the "dictatorship of the State Planning Commission" and as he puts it, eliminate the "omnipotence of the chief administrations." What then does he propose in place of the system that has developed in people's Poland and that has been tested by life itself? He puts forth four "slogans": "Openness in state life, decentralization, democratization, and sovereignty." Well, and what about what the Polish people have fought and are fighting for so selflessly and successfully—socialism? This word stuck in the author's throat; he did not even mention it. What is more, his entire article is essentially an attempt to provide some basis for the rejection of socialism.

Other similarly outspoken pronouncements openly directed at undermining the socialist achievements of the Polish people could be mentioned.

This antisocialist campaign launched in some Polish newspapers and constituting open flirting with bourgeois elements is evoking justifiable dissatisfaction and indignation among honest patriots and the broad masses of the working people of the Polish People's Republic. They are demanding that the rampant revisionists and capitulators who are using the Polish press for their own filthy purposes be curbed.

Putrament, one of the writers mentioned in the article, replied for himself in *Zycie Warszawy* on October 21, 1956, while in *Trybuna Ludu* (October 21, 1956) Zofia Artymowska answered in more general terms:

I understand that the correspondent of *Pravda* has the right to engage in a discussion with Florczak's article and even with an article of Jerzy Putrament (which, however, in my opinion is difficult to criticize.)

But [there is] the question of how one discusses things. The phrases repeated in the entire article such as "unruly boy," "slanderer," "ignorant scribe," "revisionist," and so forth sound strange indeed.

It is with bitterness, great bitterness, that we recall the time when, just as the *Pravda* correspondent, we used similar expressions, not in relation to the enemies of our ideology but in relation to comrades who held different views on certain matters. By using quotations torn from their context, we imputed to them counterrevolution and restoration of capitalism. . . .

In the communiqué, issued on October 19, on the talks between the delegation of the CC of the CPSU and the leadership of our Party, reference is made to a Party atmosphere and friendly sincerity. But the *Pravda* correspondent, writing his article that very day, unfortunately used language in which neither frank, nor Party-like, nor friendly discussions were conducted. I do not believe that by acting in such a manner he acted in accordance with the spirit of this communiqué; I do not believe that he rendered a service [to the cause] of deepening the friendship with our nation.

The methods of discussion constitute an important, indeed a very important, problem. . . .

One regrets to state that [the *Pravda*] article, both as regards its contents and title, contains a series of harmful and even simply untrue formulations.

A few words about the title, or more exactly about the sense of the article, of which the title, one has to admit, is a faithful representation.

"Antisocialist statements in the pages of the Polish press" concern not only Zbigniew Florczak or Jerzy Putrament. For, if "antisocialist statements which contain a hint of repudiation of the road to socialism" are appearing, in the opinion of the correspondent, "ever more often," and the press "publishes daily articles undermining the foundation of that system," and there resounds in Poland "a hoarse chorus of slanders," then this is evidently a phenomenon of some importance. Thus the author generalizes [on the basis] of his two examples, of which one is half untrue and the other totally at variance with the truth.

And this is again a method which, it would seem, should not play any role in serious factual discussions: a method of false generalizations which give a distorted picture. It has to be said that these false generalizations were received in our country with astonishment.

One could ask why should the Soviet comrades, reading *Pravda* every day, get the incorrect impression that Jerzy Putrament, who is not only a member of the Central Committee of our Party but has fought all his life for socialism and is fighting for it with equal ardor in the article in question, "cannot swallow the word socialism"?

Why should the Soviet comrades reading *Pravda* be of the opinion that the great turning point taking place in the international working class movement after the 20th Congress, which constitutes not only in words but also in deeds a return to Marx, to Lenin, to the Leninist standards of Party life, to intra-Party democracy, and to the true, wide rule of the people, is "a defection from socialism"? After all, the distortions, the errors, and even the crimes exposed by the 20th Congress constituted a danger to the cause of socialism, but the process, which is taking place today in our country, is a process of great regeneration, a process from which the forces of socialism will emerge more powerful than ever before.

Here I would like to devote a few words to the problem of Polish-Soviet friendship. This friendship constitutes the cornerstone of our policy. It is not a matter of this or that expediency but of internationalism, which the Polish Communists and the progressive people in Poland guarded as the apple of their eye in the most difficult times of heavy trials. . . .

If today Polish comrades criticize certain aspects of Polish-Soviet cooperation in past years, this does not mean that they oppose the friendship and the alliance between our nations. It means that the errors which they want to correct harmed this friendship. . . .

Do we not see the tremendous efforts, the tremendous work of transformation of the Soviet land done by the hands of the millions of workers and peasants, who are as close to us as brothers?

Are there, nevertheless, evident in Poland anti-Soviet sentiments? Undoubtedly—and the duty of each Communist is to counteract them. The best weapon against anti-Soviet nationalism is today exactly the realization of the principles outlined by the 20th Congress. If, however, someone classifies the criticism of all methods, condemned at that Congress as anti-Soviet statements, he is at best deceiving himself. He is not contributing . . . to the elimination of the imprint of Stalinist practices from relations among fraternal nations, and, therefore, is not contributing to the deepening of friendship. . . .

The sentiments of the Hungarian Journalists' Association, the editorial board of *Szabad Nep,* and the central board of the Petofi Circle of the Hungarian Union of Working Youth were expressed in laudatory telegram on October 22, while *Borba,* the central press organ of the Yugoslav League of Communists, conmmented on Polish developments on October 23.

4. Yugoslav Comment: "The Plenum of the Polish Party," *Borba,* October 23, 1956

THE EIGHTH PLENUM CONCLUDED its work by adopting resolutions on the further democratization of life in Poland and by electing a new leadership. As reported, the new members elected to the Politburo are Cyrankiewicz, Gomulka, Jedrychowski, Sowinski, Morawski, Ochab, Rapacki, Zambrowski and Zawadski. Wladislaw Gomulka has been unanimously elected First Secretary of the Central Committee. With such decisions one phase in the development of the Polish workers' movement has been successfully terminated, its unity has been strengthened, and because of this socialism in Poland has also been strengthened and new possibilites have been created for its further deepening and advance.

The unanimity which was powerfully manifested on the occasion of the election of the new Politburo of the Party and the First Secretary of the Central Committee is clear proof that the Polish workers' movement has succeeded in achieving unity on healthy, constructive foundations. And that very unity is a guarantee that the edifice of socialism in Poland stands today on firm and healthy foundations.

The plenum of the Central Committee adopted a clear political line which aims at rectifying the mistakes committed in the past, especially those relating to socialist democracy. The socialist forces in Poland have succeeded in tiding themselves over this difficult crisis, one which this great European country has experienced for a number of years, and which obstructed a speedier and more comprehensive socialist development.

In the whole of the internal fermentation in Poland, the attitude toward socialist democracy occupied the central place from the outset. It was perfectly clear that the fate of socialism in Poland would in fact depend on the answer to the question of how the further democratization of Polish life will take place. The decisions of the plenum of the Central Committee of the Polish Party reveal that this major question of the workers' movement has today been settled in a positive and constructive way, for as stressed by Comrade Gomulka, democratization is the only possible path for the socialist construction of Poland.

It is undeniable that Poland has already, and especially in the course of this year and last year, taken significant steps forward along the lines of democratization of internal life. Now after a number of decisions of historic significance have been unanimously adopted these efforts will yield ever more marked results.

The fact that the Polish working class as well as the over-whelming majority of the Polish working people were actively engaged in the preparations for the plenum indicates that they were profoundly aware that important issues of socialist development in Poland were at stake. And this very broad and decisive engaging of the forces of the Polish working masses was the decisive factor which enabled the Polish Party to pass such important and positive decisions quite easily.

Various reactionary remnants of the old political life of Poland, who had hoped that they would be able to exploit the democratization of the country for their own antisocialist purposes, were badly deceived. The Eighth Plenum of the Central Committee has shown that the Polish workers' movement has succeeded in creating firm unity on a healthy basis. And precisely such unity on the basis of a clear orientation toward socialist democracy is the best guarantee that socialism in Poland will develop successfully by means of those democratic forms which correspond to its needs.

Socialism in Poland has now acquired new opportunities for developing in both depth and breadth. There was never such unity between the Polish working class and its leadership as has now been manifested, and never were the aspirations of the Polish working people so clearly expressed and formulated as they are during these days.

The decisions of the Eighth Plenum, which indisputably mean the strengthening of socialism in Poland, can only be positively reflected in Polish-Soviet cooperation and in the relations between Poland and the other socialist countries. Any progress in the building of socialism in one country at the same time represents a contribution to the deepening of friendly cooperation among socialist countries on a basis of equality. It is certain that the greater the achievements of socialist countries, the better and more perfect will be mutual cooperation between socialist countries.

The Polish Plenum is of great significance, not only for socialism in Poland, but also for socialist forces all over the world, and of great significance for the whole of the international labor movement. It has once again been confirmed that the paths and forms of socialist development in individual countries differ of necessity, and that the richness of these forms only accelerates the rate of socialist development in the world. The Plenum of the Central Committee of the Polish United Workers Party has also, in this sense, undoubtedly made a significant contribution to the treasury of international socialism.

The strengthening of socialism in Poland will be positively reflected in international relations generally, for every strengthening of genuine socialist relations means at the same time a new contribution to the policy of active, peace-loving coexistence, to the development of international cooperation and the stabilization of world peace.

In Poland the decisions of the eighth plenary session of Central Committee of the PUWP were followed by an upsurge of popular sentiment. Some public demonstrations were marked by minor incidents of hooliganism (e.g., Warsaw) while others took on an anti-Soviet character and threatened to get out of hand (e.g., Wroclaw), although the authorities managed to keep them within bounds.

In the meantime, the new leadership of the PUWP, especially Wladyslaw Gomulka, proceeded to define the position of the Party and Government on general domestic and foreign policy issues in a number of public statements.

5. LETTER FROM THE FIRST SECRETARY OF THE POLISH UNITED WORKERS PARTY, GOMULKA, TO THE WORKERS AND YOUTH, OCTOBER 23, 1956 [10]

DEAR COMRADES, WORKERS and Youth! On behalf of the PUWP Central Committee I thank you for the words of solidarity and recognition with which you have welcomed the results of the Eighth Plenum of our Party's Central Committee.

The solidarity, support, and trust of the working class is the most important issue for us, the indispensable condition enabling us, as the Party leadership, to carry out the difficult duties imposed on us by the necessity to lead the country out of the present economic and political difficulties along the path of a successful march to socialism.

At the Eighth Plenum of the Central Committee we told all the bitter truth about the economic situation of the country. The Party considers that the principal task at the present moment is to overcome difficulties in our economic construction, to create conditions in which the working class will be able

---

[10] *Trybuna Ludu,* October 24, 1956.

better to exploit the production forces of socialist industry for increasing production. For it is only increase in the output of our industry and agriculture, only increase in the volume of goods indispensable to meet the requirements of the populations, which can bring about an improvement of the living conditions of the broadest masses.

At the Eighth Plenum of the Central Committee we told the entire Party, the working class, and the nation that only by marching along the path of democratization and eradicating all the evil from the past period can we succeed in building the best model of socialism, a model which will conform with the needs of our nation. A decisive part on that road must be played by widening the workers' democracy, by increasing the direct participation of workers in the management of enterprises, by increasing the part played by the working masses in governing all sectors of the country's life.

We shall not deviate from this road of democratization, and we shall not allow ourselves to be driven away from it. Nor shall we allow anyone to exploit the democratization of the country's life against socialism.

At the Eighth Plenum we told the entire Party and the nation that by building socialism in Poland we shall strengthen the relations of friendship and brotherhood between Poland and all the countries of socialism, and in particular with our great neighbor the Soviet Union. We shall develop these relations on principles of international workers' solidarity, on the basis of mutual trust and equality of rights, on the basis of mutual assistance.

Within the framework of such relations every country ought to have complete sovereignty and independence, and the rights of every nation to a sovereign government in an independent country ought to be fully and mutually respected.

That's how it should be and that's how it is going to be.

That is why our Party urges all those who want to remove all the evil vestiges of the past to resist with determination all the temptations and all the voices designed to weaken our friendship with the Soviet Union, to resist with determination all attempts at provocation, which could only damage the work of democratization of People's Poland.

We can assure you that we are doing everything possible— and that we have already achieved positive results—to remove everything that could still be exploited for undermining our good neighborly relations with the Soviet Union.

Comrades!

We are entering a new era of Poland's development. This is not an easy period, for it is impossible to remove within a day or two the evil inheritance of the past and surmount numerous difficulties which bestrew our path.

Only a just and bold policy of the Party, enjoying the support of the working class and of the broadest people's masses, only hard and honest work of the nation, aiming at the achievement of results in our economy, only the union of all progressive and socialist forces in the National Front, can lead us to the goal.

Comrades!

I salute you from the bottom of my heart and express the conviction that the working people, together with the entire Polish working class, will march under the leadership of the Party along the new road to socialism.

Warsaw, October 23, 1956

6. EDITORIAL: "CLEAN STREAM AND DIRTY FOAM," *Trybuna Ludu,* OCTOBER 24, 1956[11]

IN THESE EXCITING AND UNUSUAL days the working class has spoken up loudly. This class rules the nation, not by someone's leave or decree, but on the strength of social realities. In these exciting and unusual days the leading role of the Party was clearly and tangibly reasserted; the Party united as never before with the class which gave it birth, with the masses of the peasantry, with students, with the progressive intelligentsia,

---

[11] Reprinted in *Pravda,* October 25, 1956.

with the Polish People's army. The Party is united with the nation.

Listening, with deep emotion, to the awakened and at the same time wise voice of our working class, our people, our Army, we sense the strength of that bond.

That voice backs the new leadership of the Party elected in agreement with the will of the people. It is for reforming that which was bad, for further democratization, for strengthening the alliance and friendship with the Soviet Union and all the nations of the great socialist family based on the Leninist cornerstone of full equality and mutual respect for the sovereignty and independence of each nation.

Love for the homeland and for the cause of socialism have burst forth with a high flame in Poland. The political maturity and the discipline of the working class arouse admiration. In the case of every great mass movement, certain circles develop symptoms of irresponsibility and lightheadedness that diverge from the great current of healing [reform]. It would therefore be naive to think that the forces which have been attempting to poison this great, renovating, and clean current with the venom of anti-Soviet demagogy have capitulated.

Reactionary troublemakers, utilizing the understandable disturbances in society, are trying to ride the wave of the quickening movement of reform. They attempt to sow anti-Soviet feelings. The majority of those who—as was the case in Wroclaw—let themselves be temporarily infected with nationalistic demagogy, surely do not know what motivates these native and foreign reactionary troublemakers. Their designs are directed against both the most vital national interests of Poland and the cause of socialism in Poland. However, the spell of the enemy's propaganda is short-lived.

Evidently these gentlemen disdain the political wisdom and the historical memory of the Polish working class and of the entire nation.

Can anyone be found who has forgotten the blood shed by the Soviet Union in its common fight with us against German fascism which brought extermination to the Polish nation?

Can anyone be found who has forgotten that the brother-hood of Soviet-Polish arms won us the return of the oldest Polish lands?   And that the Polish-Soviet alliance is an iron shield which guards Poland and Europe from the rebirth of German militarism which already today openly extends its hand for atomic weapons?

We will n⸱ᵗ be lectured to about independence by Chancellor Adenauer, who, in these days so full of hope and trust for us, could not hold back from loudly demanding once more the revision of the Oder-Neisse frontier.   We will not be lectured to about independence and "correct" relations with the Soviet Union by gentlemen who recruit Waffen-SS officers for the German army.

Our Party, our working class, our nation want to strengthen the alliance and the friendship with the Soviet Union, and that is exactly why they want to cleanse that friendship of all that weakened its strength.   That is why we want to strengthen that alliance by adhering to the principle of equality and the mutual recognition of independence.

In these days of truth the Party through Comrade Gomulka and the resolution of the Eighth Plenum stated in full voice and with a sense both of national honor and of unbreachable proletarian internationalism that the relations between Poland and the Soviet Union, between the Polish United Workers Party and the Communist Party of the Soviet Union, should be socialist, equal, and brotherly.

"If in the past not everything between our Party and the CPSU and between Poland and the USSR has been as it should have been, then today it is all a matter of the irretrievable past," said Comrade Gomulka at the Plenum.

Even within a family, misunderstandings and baseless suspicions occasionally arise.   All the more so between states. But between socialist countries misunderstanding can be, should be, and will be removed.   We are aware in these critical moments that beneath the official façade displayed up to now, there is still concealed in Poland a not inconsiderable number of anti-Soviet piques and resentments.   These piques and resentments were nourished and incited by everything that amounted to half-truth or even falsity, everything that was a vestige of the past period, against which the 20th Congress of the CPSU opened its struggle. This was connected with a lack of appreciation for the sovereignty, equality, and independence of socialist Poland.

We desire friendship between the USSR and Poland. We want a living, complete, and therefore unfailing friendship, unfailing because it is based on the Leninist norms of equality and on a clear awareness of the Polish nation. We now have all the conditions for freeing once and for all the relations between Poland and the USSR and Polish-Soviet friendship from everything which could have hitherto harmed those relations and that friendship to the joy of the enemies of socialism and peace. Irresponsibility and, in particular, the work of reactionary forces will be countered by the militant revolutionary vigilance and the political sagacity of the Polish working class, the Polish working people, and Polish youth. The Polish working class defending the program which it so vigorously formulated in the last few days will frustrate all attempts against this program.

"And should anybody think that it would be possible in Poland to stir up anti-Soviet sentiments, then they are greatly mistaken. We shall not permit any harm to the vital interests of the Polish state and the cause of building socialism in Poland."

These words of Comrade Gomulka show all of us, Party and non-Party, young and old, what should be done during these days of the great process of healing.

7. ADDRESS BY THE FIRST SECRETARY OF THE POLISH UNITED WORKERS PARTY, GOMULKA, BEFORE A CITIZENS' RALLY AT WARSAW, OCTOBER 24, 1956[12]

COMRADES! CITIZENS! Working People of the Capital!

I greet you in the name of the Central Committee of the

---

[12] *Trybuna Ludu,* October 25, 1956.

Polish United Workers Party which at its last plenary session turned over the helm of the Party to a new leadership.

A great deal of evil, injustice, and many painful disappointments have accumulated in the life of Poland during the past years. The ideas of socialism, imbued with the spirit of the freedom of man and respect for the rights of a citizen, have been greatly distorted in practice. The words were not borne out by reality. The heavy toil of the working class and of the entire nation did not yield the expected fruits.

I deeply believe that these years belong to an irrevocable past.

The Eighth Plenum of the CC of our Party executed a historic turn. It created a new period in our work, a new period in the history of socialist construction in Poland, in the history of the nation.

The leadership of the Party has told the working class and the entire nation the whole truth, the unvarnished truth, leaving nothing unsaid about our economic and political situation, about difficulties which will have to be overcome in order to march forward and to achieve a lasting improvement in the life of the workers in Poland.

The leadership of the Party does not want and will not give empty promises to the nation. We turn with full confidence to our class, the working class, to the intelligentsia, to the peasants.

We are telling them: We have powerful forces of production built by the effort of the working people during the past years, but these are not fully utilized. We have considerable resources in our national economy, in thousands of factories and mines, in industry and agriculture, which are still being squandered, to no small degree, due to wastefulness and poor management.

We have numerous ranks of the working class, of working men who love their profession, who mastered new techniques, whose labor productivity, however, is still low; we have real opportunities of increasing agricultural production, production of food, and raw materials for industry, but they are still tied up by the errors of agricultural policy of the past years.

Workers and employees of all sectors of national economy! Help the Party and the Government in the great work of improving the socialist economy of People's Poland!

Develop the economic initiative of your crews, search, together with us, for the best forms of participation of the working class in the management of enterprises. Raise labor productivity, combat waste, and lower the cost of production. Take advantage of all opportunities of increasing industrial and agricultural output in order best to fulfill the growing needs of the masses.

The Party is telling the unvarnished truth to the working class.

The increase in the earnings of millions of people during the past months will be a lasting one only when the increased purchasing power of the population is balanced by an increased volume of goods on the market. At the present we cannot afford further wage increases because the string has already become so tight that it threatens to break.

Further wage raises will be possible only if there is increase of goods of mass consumption and if there is a decrease in production costs. To produce more, better, and more cheaply is the only road leading to a higher standard of living of the working class and of the entire nation.

Comrades! The Eighth Plenum, by selecting a new leadership, has declared a determined struggle against all that hindered and strangled the socialist democratization of life in the country until now.

The Party will demand of its workers full responsibility for carrying out the tasks entrusted to them. (Persons who compromised themselves because of their inefficiency or serious mistakes cannot remain in responsible posts. [*Ovation.*]

Only by following consistently the path of democratization and uprooting all the evil of the past period, shall we achieve the creation of the best model of socialism corresponding to the needs of our nation. [*Applause.*]

A decisive role on this road must be played, above all, by a broadening of our workers' democracy, by increasing the direct participation of working crews in the management of enterprises, by increased participation of the working masses of the city and the countryside in the government of the people's state.) [13]

We will not permit anyone to take advantage of the cause of regeneration and of the peoples' freedom for purposes alien to socialism.

The Eighth Plenum of the CC, outlining our own roads to socialism which stem from the needs of the Polish working class and of the Polish nation, reaffirmed with utmost strength the unshakable bond linking People's Poland with all socialist states, and has especially emphasized alliance with the Soviet Union.

The mutual relations between the parties and states of the socialist camp, welded together by an identity of aims and interests, should not cause any misunderstandings. Of this consists one of the main features of socialism. These relations should develop on the basis of the international solidarity of the workers, of mutual trust and complete equality of rights, of granting mutual aid, of mutual and friendly criticism, should there be a need for it, on reasonable solution of all controversial problems, a solution stemming from a spirit of friendship and from a spirit of socialism.

Within a framework of such relations every country should have full independence and sovereignty, and each nation's right to sovereign government in an independent country should be fully and mutually respected.

Independent nations and sovereign states, which are building a system of social justice, a socialist system, and which are cemented from within by a strong and unbreakable will of achieving this purpose in a manner most suitable to each country, must act together and in unity in the world arena in order to strengthen, by mutual effort and determined attitude, the invincible ideas of peace—ideas which embrace all mankind—and the striving for peaceful coexistence of all nations of the world.

The Soviet Union, the oldest country of socialist construction in the world and the most powerful socialist state, consti-

---

[13] The speech was reprinted in *Pravda,* on October 25, 1956. Parentheses in the translation indicate passages omitted by *Pravda.*

tutes the backbone of such an alliance of all socialist states.

We see our place in the world camp of socialism, and we understand our fraternal, friendly relations with the Soviet Union in this light.

We deeply believe that the friendship between Poland and the Soviet Union, based on Leninist principles, will be a truly fraternal friendship, stemming from the heart of the nation, and not only from the official policy of the Party and the Government. [*Prolonged ovation.*]

I can assure you that these principles are finding an ever fuller understanding, and that these principles are shared not only by our Party, but by the Communist Party of the Soviet Union as well.

(Our last meeting with the delegation of the CPSU allowed the Soviet comrades to orient themselves better in the political situation in Poland.

Recently, we received assurances from the First Secretary of the CC of the CPSU, Comrade Khrushchev, to the effect that he does not see any obstacles to the development of our mutual Party and state relations on the basis of the principles outlined by the Eighth Plenum of the CC of our Party. [*Prolonged ovation.*]

All concrete matters pertaining to our internal affairs will be solved in accordance with the estimate of the Party and the Government. The question whether we need Soviet specialists and military advisers, and for how long we need their aid, will depend on our decision alone. [*Prolonged ovation.*]

At the same time, we received assurance from Comrade Khrushchev that within two days Soviet troops in Polish territory will return to their locations, in which they are stationed on the basis of international treaties, within the framework of the Warsaw Pact.[14] [*Ovation.*])

---

[14] Multilateral Mutual Defense Treaty, concluded between the Soviet Union and the East European people's democracies on May 14, 1955, in Warsaw. The Treaty calls for a joint military command under Soviet Marshal Ivan S. Konev.

This is closely connected with the presence of the Soviet troops in the German Democratic Republic. As long as there exist bases of the [North] Atlantic Pact in Western Germany, as long as the new Wehrmacht is rearming there and is fomenting chauvinism and revisionism aimed against our frontiers, the presence of the Soviet Army in Germany will correspond to our highest state interest. It also is in accord with the interest of the toiling masses of the GDR, against whom the arming and the threats of the militaristic and revanchist circles of Western Germany are also directed.

(In these circumstances, we should reject, with even greater decisiveness, all attempts at anti-Soviet agitation undertaken by the reactionary and anti-popular forces, and all maneuvers of the international reaction which desire to weaken the alliance between our fraternal nations.

Comrades! The Eighth Plenum of the CC of our Party has received a warm welcome from the working class and the widest masses of the people. At thousands of meetings throughout the entire country, workers, the intelligentsia, students, soldiers, and all the toiling people had expressed their approval and support, and their trust in the new leadership.

Nothing is more important for us, for the Party, for its leadership, than this trust and support. There is nothing more important for the nation, for the realization of its desires and aspirations, than unity between the Party and of the people, a unity stronger than ever before.

In the name of the Central Committee, I am expressing warmest thanks to the workers of many industrial enterprises who, in a noble upsurge, expressed their readiness to work overtime, and even to float a state loan, although there is no need for it at the present moment, and for voluntary deductions from their earnings in order to help the people's authority and the new leadership of the Party. I thank the students of the Polish universities who demonstrated in these days so much enthusiasm for and trust in the Party. I thank the soldiers and officers of the Polish Army who demonstrated their loyalty to the Party and to the Government and their support for the results of the Eighth Plenum.

The nation can completely trust its army and the command of the army [*ovation*], which, in our country, as everywhere in the world, is completely and entirely subordinated to the government of its country. [*Applause.*])

Comrades! The tremendous wave of the political activity of the masses brought about by the Eighth Plenum here and there has encountered forces hostile to socialism, opposed to the Polish-Soviet alliance, inimical to the people's authority, forces which would like to distort, hinder, and retard socialist democratization.

Comrades! Let us not allow reactionary troublemakers and various hooligans to obstruct our way. Let them keep away from the pure current of the struggle of socialist and patriotic forces of the nation! Drive away the provocateurs and reactionary loud mouths! The state authority will not tolerate for a moment any action directed against the Polish state interests and against our state system.

Comrades! Time is pressing. The Party must embark on the solution of daily, difficult problems of our economy and state life. How can you help the Party and the Government today? Above all, every one of you should stand at your workbench, at your post, and demonstrate your loyalty and devotion to our cause by intensified work or study.

Today we turn to the working people of Warsaw and of the entire country with an appeal: enough meetings and demonstrations! Time has come to embark on daily work—full of faith and consciousness that the Party united with the working class and with the nation will lead Poland on the new road to socialism.

Long live the unbreakable bond of the Party with the working class and with the entire toiling people!

Long live socialism!

Long live People's Poland! [*Ovation.*]

Throughout this period the Polish press continued to devote attention to the developments in Hungary. On October 28 *Trybuna*

Ludu printed an editorial on the "Hungarian Tragedy"; the following day it reproduced an appeal by the leadership of the PUWP to the Hungarian Communists.[15]

On October 30 the Soviet Government issued a declaration on relations with the people's democratic countries. The declaration was featured in *Trybuna Ludu* on October 31.[16]

Polish reaction to the Soviet declaration was recorded in an editorial in *Trybuna Ludu.*

8. EDITORIAL: "THE SOVIET DECLARATION AND THE POLISH *Raison d'Etat," Trybuna Ludu,* NOVEMBER 1, 1956

THE PUBLICATION IN YESTERDAY'S newspapers of the Soviet Government's declaration doubtlessly constitutes a very important international event. The announcement of the removal of distortions and errors which accumulated in the mutual relations between the Soviet Union and the people's democracies during the Stalinist period constitutes another important step toward strengthening relations between socialist countries. This declaration was met with special interest and satisfaction by public opinion in Poland, a country vitally interested both in the alliance with the Soviet Union and in basing this alliance and friendship on the foundation of full equality of partners and sovereignty of countries participating in it; that is, on the basis of the principles so forcefully put forth by our last Eighth Plenum.

Nobody in Poland forgets that we regained freedom after World War II thanks to the Soviet Union. Likewise, nobody in Poland forgets that from the very beginning the Soviet Union has displayed a clear and consistent attitude in the matter of our regained territories and the western frontier. So far the Soviet Union is the only power among the states occupying Germany which has shown such an attitude, the only power which guarantees, both by diplomacy and force of arms, the integrity of our territory.

---

[15] See Hungary, Chapter VII, Documents 2 and 3.
[16] See Part Four, Chapter I, Document 1.

This should be kept in mind, especially now, when, after the Soviet announcement, the matter of the revision of treaties whereby army units are stationed in the territory of other states has become imminent. Soviet units find themselves in Poland primarily on the strength of the Potsdam and the Warsaw Treaties. Their main task is the protection of the communication lines leading from the USSR to the GDR and as a rear guard. The continued stay of Soviet troops in the GDR results from the as yet legally unsettled German question and the division of the country. It is clear that as long as American, British, and French bases exist, as long as troops of the Western powers are stationed there, the presence of Soviet troops in the GDR is also necessary and justified. Naturally, a completely different situation would result if *all* foreign troops were withdrawn from Germany. Unfortunately, proposals of this nature, repeatedly submitted by the USSR and Poland, have been consistently rejected by the Western powers.

Thus the problem facing us and Poland is not easy. How are we to reconcile the common striving of the people and the Government for full sovereignty with the accepted necessity of the communication lines of Soviet troops defending not only the vital interests of the Soviet Union but also the vital interests of the Polish People's Republic, the Polish *raison d'état?* It is not an easy problem, and we know that the leadership of our Party and Government devotes much attention to this question now, on the eve of the announced Polish-Soviet talks.[17]

One can firmly believe that on our part we shall aim at a solution of the problem wherein the authority of our Government shall be exercised fully over the entire territory of our country, and no movements of troops connected with communications to the GDR will be carried out without the knowledge and consent of our Government. Such are—we repeat—the general line and the assumptions of the proposals which are now being discussed and whose goal is a harmonious fusion of demands arising from our geographic and political position

---

[17] See Document 11 in this chapter.

with demands arising from the right of a nation to full sovereignty.

We are fully convinced that other, still unsettled questions between our two countries, and among them also economic matters, will be solved in the same spirit. And as far as Soviet advisers are concerned, that matter, as we know from Comrade Gomulka's announcement at the Warsaw meeting on October 24,[18] is wholly within the competence of the Polish Government on the strength of an agreement with the Soviet Government. The new army appointments are the best proof that this problem is being solved in accordance with the letter and the law of friendly mutual relations, based on full equality, which we are creating between our country and our Soviet ally and neighbor.[19]

Putting aside, however, the Polish aspect of the Soviet declaration, it must be said that its significance reaches far beyond our country. Whereas the 20th Congress of the CPSU made an evaluation of negative phenomena connected with the Stalinist period and unveiled sometimes tragic consequences of the old practices, this declaration of the Soviet Government aims at eliminating all that still remained from the old and prevented socialist countries from developing a sincere and deep friendship. Without doubt, the declaration has also drawn conclusions from the tragic Hungarian lesson, where the summon-

---

[18] See the preceding document.

[19] Some of the more important dismissals made in the Polish military command during the ten days succeeding the Eighth Plenum included General Witaszewski as head of the Political Administration of the Army, General Turkiel, Commander of the Air Force, Generals Benski and Andrejewski, Colonel Karliner, and others. The Minister of National Defense, Konstanty Rokossowski, went on leave and was later, on November 13, relieved of his post.

The new appointments included Marian Spychalski, as Deputy Minister of National Defense (later Minister) and chief of the Political Administration of the Army, General Frey-Bielecki as chief of the Air Force, General Kuropieska as commander of the Warsaw military district, Colonel Fonkowicz as chief of the cadre section of the Ministry of National Defense, and others.

ing of Soviet troops for aid by the Gero-Hegedus group has weighed on the development of events.

At the moment when Anglo-French forces are engaged in open military aggression against Egypt—without even having the formal excuse of having been called by someone for aid—the Soviet declaration must have undoubtedly evoked wide acclaim in world public opinion. It will show all those who tried to utilize the events of the last days in order to equate capitalism and socialism that there is no such similarity and cannot be because imperialism is aggressive and rapacious by nature, whereas in the socialist world the committed errors and deviations—no matter how tragic—are being eliminated. In the great moral conflict which divides the contemporary world, the Soviet declaration will undoubtedly strengthen the partisans of democracy, peace, and equality of nations, big and small. Undoubtedly it will also weaken the partisans of a "strong arm" policy, aggression, and armed intervention in the internal affairs of other states.

Here in our country, the Soviet declaration will be, without doubt, favorably greeted by the overwhelming majority of the nation which, during the recent events, could so excellently combine a decisively patriotic attitude with calmness, discipline and a sense of Polish *raison d'état*.

We are reminded of this in connection with irresponsible actions, occurring here and there, in which it is forgotten that the presence of Soviet units in Poland—of course, in mutually defined bases and quantities—is closely bound up with our national security, especially as the problems of Germany, disarmament, and collective security are still unsettled. If we want to learn anything from the recent events, two conclusions are probably most important: first, that we have at present a leadership which, thanks to its attitude, commands sufficient prestige at home and abroad to settle all outstanding problems; and secondly, that we have recently gained recognition in the world as a nation which succeeded in adding to the glorious tradition of romantic outbursts a considerable amount of political realism and level-headed soberness, together with a patriotic spirit. The interests of the nation, socialism, and peace demand that we confirm this opinion every day in all its aspects by a sober and balanced appraisal of historical facts and by confidence in the leadership which acts on the basis of collaboration and alliance between the socialist countries, and which aims at insuring peace and security founded on the full sovereignty of our people's state.

On November 2, 1956, in the wake of Hungary's unilateral abrogation of the Warsaw Pact,[20] the Central Committee of the PUWP turned to the Polish people with an appeal.

9. Appeal by the Central Committee of the Polish United Workers Party to the Working Class and the Polish Nation, November 2, 1956[21]

Comrades, citizens! The Polish people are following the tragic course of events in Hungary with tremendous tension. From the bottom of our hearts we have always been on the side of the Hungarian workers and of all those who fought together with them for socialist democratization, against the forces wanting at any price to maintain in Hungary the old manner of governing, hated by the people.

When, as a result of a tangle of errors, armed clashes occurred, the former leadership of the Hungarian Workers Party, instead of entering immediately and consistently on the road of solutions in conformity with the interests of socialism, with the will of the working class and the majority of the nation, called for the assistance of Soviet troops. The consequences of this decision were tragic. Fratricidal fighting engulfed Budapest.

Recently Hungarian events entered a new and dangerous phase. Reactionary elements are ever more clearly gaining the upper hand. The foundations of the socialist system are

---

[20] See Hungary, Chapter VIII, Document 13.
[21] *Trybuna Ludu*, November 2, 1956.

threatened. Chaos and anarchy are spreading throughout the entire country. Reactionary bands are committing lynchings and are bestially murdering Communists.

The Polish working class and our whole nation are following this development of events with the greatest concern. The forces of reaction pushing Hungary to disaster meet with decided condemnation in Poland.

Our Party trusts that the working class and working masses of Hungary will succeed in uniting and repelling the attacks of the reaction. We are of the opinion that the problem of the defense and maintenance of the People's power and of the gains of socialism in Hungary can be solved by the forces of the Hungarian people, headed by the working class, and not by intervention from without.

This opinion is dictated to us by the program and ideological principles of our Party. Comrades, citizens! The course of events in Poland has been and is different.

The historic turn effected at the Eighth Plenum of the PUWP Central Committee has put before our Party and nation a new program which the new leadership of the Party is implementing and will continue to implement with the active participation of the working class and of the whole nation.

The unity, calm, and composure displayed by the Polish people during the crucial days of the Eighth Plenum enabled us to shape relations between the Soviet Union and Poland, both on the Party and state level, on the principles of sovereignty, equal rights, and friendship. This significant fact creates the foundations for strengthening the forces of socialism, for strengthening the Polish-Soviet alliance.

On the basis of the Potsdam Agreement, units of Soviet troops are stationed in Poland. Their task is to guard communication lines between the Soviet Union and the GDR [German Democratic Republic]. Until a peace treaty is concluded with Germany, or until an agreement is reached between the Four Powers on the withdrawal of all occupation troops from the whole of Germany, the stay of these Soviet units will be necessary. It is necessary and indispensable not only from the point of view of the security of the Soviet Union but also to a still greater degree from the point of view of our own security and the inviolability of our frontiers against the schemes of German militarism. It is known that the Soviet Union is so far the only one of the Four Powers which has recognized and guaranteed our western frontiers.[22]

The location and numerical strength, as well as all movements of Soviet units in Poland, will be settled in agreement with the Polish Government and with its consent. In these conditions, the stay of Soviet troops on our territory will in no way infringe upon our sovereignty, will in no way restrict our right to exercise our authority in our own country in accordance with our own views.

Here and there demands for the withdrawal of Soviet army units from Poland are being voiced. The Party leadership stresses most emphatically that such demands in the present international situation are contrary to the most vital interests of the nation and the Polish *raison d'état*.

Comrades and citizens! In the past few days international tension has increased. The grave situation in Hungary and the Anglo-French aggression against Egypt are creating serious danger.

At such a time, it is of particular importance to preserve complete calm, to strengthen the coherence of the Party and the unity of the Polish people. In a situation when reactionary elements are attempting to raise their voices, putting forth provocative slogans directed against the Polish-Soviet alliance, when here and there thoughtless and irresponsible acts are being committed, the working class and all enlightened citizens should firmly rebuff them in the name of the independence of our country and of the gains of socialism.

This is not a time for demonstrations and meetings. Calm, discipline, feeling of responsibility, consolidation around the leadership of the Party and the people's authorities for the

---

[22] See Chapter III, Document 1.

realization of our correct policy in this difficult and crucial period—these are the main demands of the moment.

Stand a vigilant guard over the achievements of the Eighth Plenum, approved by the Party and the whole nation.

This is demanded by the interests of socialism in Poland. This is demanded by the Polish *raison d'état*.

10. ADDRESS BY THE FIRST SECRETARY OF THE POLISH UNITED WORKERS PARTY, GOMULKA, BEFORE A NATIONAL CONFERENCE OF PARTY ACTIVISTS, WARSAW, NOVEMBER 4, 1956[23]

COMRADES! IN THE POSTWAR work of our Party, two periods can be clearly recognized. The first period, which began in 1944, was brought to a violent close at the plenary session of the Central Committee of the PUWP held in August, 1948. The second period, which then started, slowly began to come to an end in 1955. At first the end of this period was very vacillating and indecisive. The powerful impetus for the practical development of this process was the 20th Congress of the CPSU and, in particular, the speech by the First Secretary of the CPSU, Comrade Khruschev, at the closed session of the 20th Congress.[24] Of considerable importance to the growth of this process was the rehabilitation of the Communist Party of Poland, which in 1937 was falsely and slanderously accused and dissolved by the Comintern.[25] These external factors were, however, nothing more than an incentive which contributed to the speedy setting in motion and great activation of the large store of internal forces which were increasingly pressing for the ending of this second period in the life of the Party and in the life of the whole Polish people.

The tragic Poznan events and the Seventh Plenum of the Central Committee of our Party can be called milestones along

[23] *Trybuna Ludu,* November 5, 1956.

[24] See *The Anti-Stalin Campaign and International Communism,* pp. 1-89.

[25] See Chapter I, Document 1.

the road leading to the final liquidation of this second period in the life of our Party.

All the great turning points in the life of the nation and events of historical significance are always marked by a date on the calendar. It seems that it will be correct to point to the Eighth Plenum of the PUWP Central Committee as the date marking the opening of a new, third, period in the postwar life of the Party and of the people. The previous period belongs to the irrevocable past.

The Party must direct the process of democratization.

The eighth plenary session of the Central Committee of our Party outlined roughly the new program—the program of changes which are to cover nearly all spheres of the life of our nation. The substance of the intended changes, expressed in the most general and broadest terms, amounts to the democratization of our life in the spirit of the basic principles of socialism, that is, in the spirit of social justice and the rule of the people.

All the changes, those completed and those planned, aim at strengthening the basis of the people's authority, the socialist social order which, after the removal of various distortions which are contrary to its real essence, is the best social system for the working class and for the broadest strata of the working people in towns and villages.

The democratization of our life, the democratization which is aimed at strengthening the people's authority by means of wide and direct participation of the working classes and all the strata of the working people in the administration of the socialist state, can be put into effect correctly, that is, in accordance with the best interpreted interests of the working people, only when the process of democratization is directed by the Party of the working class. We are such a Party.

The Party of the working class in Poland is the Polish United Workers Party. The principle that the process of democratization is directed by the Party of the working class, in whose ranks the most conscious peasants and the most progressive strata of the working intelligentsia are also united, is an unequivocal canon. Infringement of this principle must inevitably lead to distortion of the process of democratization and to revival and activation of backward trends represented by reactionary and capitalist elements hostile to the rule of the people.

All the leading organs of the Party and all the members of the Party must realize this fully. They must act in such a way —not in words alone but in their practical everyday work—as to stand at the head and guide the process of the changes which are being carried out or are intended in our life, the process of socialist democratization.

In order that our Party may be able to meet fully the tasks which are placed before it in the new period, the tasks which were put forward at the Eighth Plenum, that it should raise its activities to the level of a fully authorized and actual guide of the process of democratization of our life, it must, first of all, achieve changes in its internal life. It must begin democratization within itself, that is, apply in its life to the full extent the principles of democratic centralism. It must apply in practice all that is meant by Leninist norms on Party life. This is the main link which we must grasp today in order to direct correctly the whole wide process of democratization.

The problem is reduced to this: All Party authorities, all organs, Party leadership from top to bottom, should be democratically elected. Only then will they have the full confidence of the Party masses, which is an imperative condition for raising the activity of the whole Party to the level demanded by the tasks of the present period of great changes.

Since the Eighth Plenum a wave of personnel changes of Party leadership at all levels of all Party organizations has been spreading throughout the country. The changes carried out and the demands of the Party masses for further personnel changes in the various Party organizations and authorities result from different sources. Some are healthy, and these should be exploited; others are unhealthy, and these should be buried.

It is a healthy source if, as a result, men with old, fossilized views and conservative tendencies are removed from Party organizations, men who are immunized against the problems which are thoroughly animating the working classes and the whole nation.   Such men are not only not needed as Party authorities but their participation in the leading organs of the Party can only be harmful.

Unhealthy personnel changes in the leading Party organizations are those which concern men devoted to the working classes and able to forge into deeds the decisions of the Eighth Plenum.

The sources of these changes stem both from the mistakes which these comrades made in the past, often not of their own volition, for they only carried out the orders of higher Party authorities in good faith.   They also stem from a certain disorientation and confusion which became apparent among many Party members and in many Party organizations as a result of the situation created after the Seventh Plenum and during the preparations and the gathering for the debates of the Eighth Plenum of our Party.

Not one of us can deny that members of the Party, as well as non-Party men, had not a few reasons for complaints against a great many of our comrades holding various leading posts in Party organizations and authorities.

In the former system of ruling, the system which we call the cult of personality, even the best men sometimes went wrong. They were led astray by the conditions in which they worked. In these conditions even the best and the most courageous were unable to speak in a clear voice of the working class and people's masses.   I doubt whether it would be possible to find Party activists and workers holding various responsible posts who could not be accused of doing something wrong when their past work is evaluated at this time.

That is why the criticism by Party masses, by the working class, and by the nation which is today addressed to a number of our good comrades is justified.   The whole Party now has to pay for the mistakes of the past, for the system which is called Stalinism.

But it is wrong, though often unavoidable, to remove from Party organs men only because in the past they did not carry out their duties as it is expected of them today.

Party leaders and activists do not suddenly appear from nowhere. They must be educated for a long time. A good enlightened cadre of Party leaders is a great and valuable treasure of the working class. The central leadership of the Party will always defend good, honest Party leaders who are wholeheartedly devoted to the working class and the nation. Party members have the full right to elect to Party authorities and to organizations comrades whom they trust most, who, according to their opinion, will do their duty best. At the same time the Party leadership has the right and duty to tell the Party masses the following:

Ponder deeply any changes in the leadership of your Party organization. Do not underestimate the value of the most active Party members who, despite their mistakes and shortcomings, constitute your cadres and spring from your own ranks. Introduce changes in one direction only—change men and Party authorities for the better.

A different category of accusations against some comrades, accusations causing disorientation and confusion among many members, belongs to matters in connection with the changes effected by the Seventh Plenum and at the Eighth Plenum of the Central Committee of our Party. Among these are just and unjust accusations. They must be properly classified so that Party members and all Party organizations will have a clear opinion of the true state of affairs.

We have already mentioned that the Eighth Plenum opened a new period in the activities of the Party and the life of the whole nation. Besides, we do not even have to talk about it, it is seen and felt by every man in Poland. The turning point of our policy effected by the Eighth Plenum was not and could not have been produced by a single individual. Nor was the period of approach to that turning point confined to the days immediately preceding the Eighth Plenum. The idea of the necessity of that turning point ripened slowly in the minds of the central leadership and in a measure among the local Party activists. The consciousness of activists striving to put our Party on a new path had been shaped in accordance with the will of the Party masses, the working class, and the whole nation.

In conditions in which the remnants of the old system were still in power, at times when the frankness of Party life was still restricted beyond the limit defined by the exigencies of the interests of the state, when a free exchange of opinion and discussion of Party policy were restricted by the very ways of thinking of the Party activists, in these conditions—which have passed—the Party could not be properly informed of what was happening at the leadership level.

Among Party members, there were only rumors—which even today are obscure to many of them—that two political currents had emerged in the Party leadership and that there were two groups. One of these groups came to be called the Natolin group and the other the Pulawy group.[26] This resulted in confusion and disorientation among the Party ranks. Before and after the Eighth Plenum people began to include individuals in one group or the other. This matter must also be cleared up.

The necessity of a change in Party policy was gradually growing in the minds of the central Party leaders, and without doubt in the minds of almost all members of the Central Committee and also leading Party activists. This is perfectly normal and explicable. On the contrary, it would be more difficult to understand if there had been no doubts. When such matters as those facing the Eighth Plenum are being considered there can be no immediate unanimity among all Party members nor among men bearing the supreme responsibility for the policy of the Party.

---

[26] The Natolin group was identified as favoring closer alignment with the Soviet Union and less democratization in Poland.

What was the essence of the basic political differences among the Party leadership before the Eighth Plenum? To reply to this question one cannot, unfortunately, use any political documents dating back to the period before the Eighth Plenum. The two political streams which existed in the former leadership of the Party, and in part of the Party *aktiv,* did not show themselves in the past clearly on the surface of life. They furrowed channels for themselves beneath the surface.

One of those streams was revealed fully only at the Eighth Plenum, while the second showed itself only partially at the plenum. It is our task to see that the under-the-surface current should disappear completely.

The political differences in the leadership of the Party, that is, in the Politburo during the period before the Eighth Plenum of the Central Committee of the Party, can be reduced to two basic problems: (1) the conceptions of Poland's sovereignty and (2) the conception of what should be included in what we call the democratization of our life within the framework of the socialist system.

Some members of the Central Committee of the Party feared that settling our Party and state relations with the CPSU and the Soviet Union on the principles adopted by the Eighth Plenum would bring unfavorable consequences. While not questioning the need for carrying out certain changes, they were in favor of preserving the previous state of affairs. This was the main line of division in the leadership of the Party.

The differences in the understanding of the context of the democratization of our life were not clear. All the same, they did exist in the leadership of the Party. Irrespective of these basic political differences, there were other problems of appointments to leading Party and state posts and the question of approaching this problem from the national point of view.

Some comrades approached this problem in a very simplified way which could be taken for anti-Semitism. In addition to that, before the Eighth Plenum, many comrades, irrespective of what views they held on problems discussed earlier, differed among themselves on the problem of my return to active Party life. It was, in this case, a problem not only of my person but of the right evaluation of all phenomena which in the past had been described as right-wing, nationalist deviation from the Party line.

We can therefore say, comrades, that irrespective of the main line of differences within the Party, there existed in the Party leadership and the *aktiv* various other lines of division, which linked some men otherwise divided by the main line of differences. It is obvious that such a state of affairs paralyzed the work of the Party leadership, which in turn must have caused disorientation within the Party, together with all its attending causes. This disorientation was deepened even further by the arrival in Warsaw of the delegation of the Presidium of the CPSU on the day of the opening of the plenary session of the Central Committee of our Party, as well as by the movement of Soviet military units stationed in Poland's western territories on orders by the Soviet Command. In the atmosphere and situation thus created not only the masses of Party members but also the great majority of the main Party *aktiv* must have been lost, and the local branches must have been even more lost.

I am recalling this because now there are often cases of raising accusations against some comrades for the so-called passivity which they displayed during the debates of the Eighth Plenum. Some are even of the opinion that the undecided attitude these men displayed at that time disqualifies them from holding any posts in Party organs and authorities. Such accusations could be considered correct only against men who were in the know of the situation and the events which accompanied the debates of the Eighth Plenum. But they are without justification with regard to comrades who, while having the best intentions, did not at that time show the desired initiative as a result of lack of knowledge of the situation and the resulting disorientation.

Today, after the Eighth Plenum, digging out the past line of division can harm a number of people. The terms Natolin group and Pulawy group should be crossed out and eliminated from our language.

Members of the Party and Party activists should not be judged on the basis of their past views but on the basis of their present work. (*Ovation.*) The only yardstick determining the political attitude of comrades is their attitude toward the decisions adopted at the Eighth Plenum—their attitude not merely as expressed in their declarations, but their actual attitude proved and checked in their everyday practical work.

The Party must be and will be monolithic from top to bottom, on the basis of putting into life the tasks mapped out by the Eighth Plenum. (*Ovation.*) Unjust and unjustified, as well as harmful, are all the attempts to divide the Party leadership into old and new people. The leadership of the Party is monolithic. It stands on the basis of the decisions of the Eighth Plenum, and all the voices aiming at its division should be considered harmful. (*Ovation.*)

Comrades, the development of the situation after the Eighth Plenum calls for swift action. Mature yet swift decisions are necessary, decisions which would enable all the Party organizations and organs to place themselves at the head of the powerful movement of political activity and initiative of the masses, cleanse it, in the course of the struggle, of nationalist and hostile elements, and direct it for the purpose of a correct and effective implementation of the policy of the Party. For these reasons it is necessary for us, with a feeling of full responsibility, to draw prudently and yet swiftly all the political and organizational conclusions from the situation which has arisen both inside the Party and in the country.

One of the tasks leading in this direction is the organization of elections of new Party authorities at all levels. The need for holding report-election meetings and Party conferences in the present period follows not only from the fact that the time limits envisaged in the statute have elapsed and that the postponement of the elections to the Sejm will enable us to make proper preparations for the elections inside the Party, but also from the real fact that the process of the change in Party authorities, in the provincial committees, the district committees, and some Party organizations has already begun. This movement is a healthy one, and on the whole follows a correct course.

Here and there, however, the movement bears marks of spontaneity, and the task in point is to contain it within the framework of the statute.

The elections of Party organs cannot, however, be treated as a task of purely organizational nature. In every situation, and particularly in the situation in which we now find ourselves, Party elections amount to an important and responsible political task aimed at strengthening the unity of the Party, its militant character, and the strength of its political influence and guidance of the masses.

In order to achieve that goal, comrades who understand the political line of the Party and enjoy confidence and prestige among members of the Party and non-Party people, comrades who are permeated with a profound sense of responsibility to the masses for personal attitude and activities, as well as for the activities of the whole Party, should be elected to Party organs at all levels.

How are the elections to be held in order that such comrades may be elected to the Party organs, that irresponsible bigmouths and demagogues, people who do not understand the policy of the Party, should be prevented from being elected to Party posts?

An indispensable and principal condition is to present to all the Party organizations a broad explanation of the policy of the Party, to remove by means of basic Party discussion doubts and erroneous views. On the basis of our experience and of the course of events in the world, Party organizations must be politically and ideologically armed and made capable of resisting all the provocative attempts at exploiting the processes which are taking place in our country for anti-Soviet action or for other hostile action against the people's rule and the interests of the nation. The explanation of the policy of the Party on the basis of transformations taking place in our Party and in the whole international workers' movement must proceed parallel to the critical assessment of the previous activities of every Party organization, of the retiring authorities, and parallel to the outlining of concrete ways and means of implementing the decisions of the Eighth Plenum.

Fervent and thorough criticism of the mistakes in our past and the activities of individual comrades must be primarily animated by one aim—the consolidation of the power and unity of the Party. One must with the greatest possible force oppose tendencies to abuse Party criticism for personal scheming and revenge and, first of all, as happens here and there, for high-handed political lynching of Party activists.

One must give all help and loyalty to all those comrades who, admittedly slowly and with internal resistance, are honestly and with conviction accepting the new Party line. At the same time, one must at present remove from influence on Party organs those comrades who are as yet unable to understand that the fight carried on by our Party for the democratization and sovereignty of our country consolidates the construction of socialism, that this fight is by no means weakening but on the contrary strengthening the mutual friendship between our Party and the CPSU.

One must with full deliberation liquidate the still surviving practice in many Party organizations of distorting the principles of internal Party democracy. This finds its expression in, among other things, attempts to rig discussions and elections and in imposing candidates for executive posts. The growing wave of political activity within the Party is already disposing of many of these bad habits.

At the elections of Party officials at all levels, the Central Committee's instruction of May, 1954, is binding. We propose to add to it the following changes and amplifications intended to deepen the democratic character of elections:

1. The number of delegates at a conference in an enterprise should be from 50 to 200; at a district, city, or section

conference from 100 to 300; and at provincial conference more than 400. The maximum number of delegates we shall leave for the Provincial Committee to decide.

2. Party Committees are obligated to ensure the participation of all delegates by informing them, as well as all the Party organizations, in ample time about the date, place, and the agenda of the conference. To this end the Party press should also be used.

3. While holding to the principle that comrades devoted to the Party, enjoying confidence and authority, as well as having experience in Party work, should be elected to positions of Party authority, those comrades can also be elected who have held Party positions for a shorter time than was stipulated in the Central Committee's instructions.

4. When nominating and discussing candidates for Party offices we should observe the following principles:

At a report-election meeting all present Party members and candidates have the right to nominate; the right of the presidium of the meeting to present a list of candidates, as stipulated in the Central Committee's instructions, should not be observed; at Party conferences, on all levels, the provisional list of candidates for offices should be determined by the council of delegates' representatives called by the conference. The council of representatives meets under the leadership of a chairman whom it elects. The right of all delegates at the conference to nominate other candidates and to supplement the list proposed by the council should be fully guaranteed so that the number of proposed candidates should be considerably larger, even twice as large, as the number to be elected.

5. All nominated comrades, regardless of objections raised against them during the discussion, should be placed on the list of candidates. The meeting or the conference will express its attitude toward those candidates whose names met with objections, not by a voice vote, as we had hitherto done, but by election, that is by secret ballot.

6. The election of secretaries of the executive committees of departmental and basic Party organizations and of secretaries

and members of the executive committees of the Party on all levels should be held by secret ballot at plenary meetings of these committees.

7. Observing, according to the Central Committee instruction, the principle that reports be prepared collectively by the retiring officers, the right of these officers at a Party meeting or conference to voice a critical appraisal of the work of the Party leadership should not be limited in any way. The right of all members of Party bodies to voice their separate opinion on various matters at Party meetings or conferences should also be guaranteed.

Certainly, the cited changes do not fully take care of what we would like to say in connection with the elections of Party officials.

Further details will be sent to Party organizations in the near future.

In practice, hitherto, the meaning of the tasks and the work of the Party apparatus were defined by a warped understanding of the Party's leading role. The leading role of the Party was identified with direct leadership and intervention by the Party apparatus in the daily work of the state's apparatus and social organizations. Party bodies constituted a peculiar, centralized "super-government." This found a clear expression in the composition of the executives, which included almost exclusively directors of key sectors in the state apparatus and social organizations; for example, chairmen of district people's councils, chiefs of security offices, militia commanders, ZMP chairmen, and trade unionists. They were elected because of the positions they held, regardless of their personal work or value to the Party.

This make-up of the executive, which puts in its hands the power to steer directly the life of the whole area, led in practice to the identification of the Party with the apparatus of the people's rule. It favored the replacement, or at least the duplication, of the work of the state apparatus and social organizations, and did not create conditions for exchange of thought and the confrontation of opinions of the leading Party workers. The proper functioning of the Party organization requires a composition of the executive that includes comrades close to the masses, known and valued by the masses regardless of their professional position—comrades controlled by and acting for the whole organization. With such principles the tasks, the composition, and the structure of the Party apparatus will look different. A numerically smaller Party apparatus, composed of workers who enjoy authority and regard among Party members and non-Party people, is necessary so that Party authorities can have direct connections with the lowest Party organizations, Party members, and non-Party people in order to mobilize them politically. This apparatus is needed to put the Party program into operation and, at the same time, to communicate to the Party authorities the moods, the opinions, the initiative, and the wishes of the masses. The Party apparatus cannot directly intervene in the work of the state and social apparatus; it cannot, as in the past, act before society as the "appointed defender" of each regulation promulgated by a ministry, central administration or director without regard to what the Party and non-Party masses think about these regulations. It should inform the Party authorities about these opinions and aid Party organizations in correctly grasping these moods and opinions.

The system of Party work which prevailed among us during previous years led to an excessive growth of the Party apparatus, even though generous and devoted Party members were chosen for the apparatus—members who at times were taken from places where they enjoyed authority and recognition and where they even had better material conditions. Incorrect direction of the Party apparatus had the result that considerable numbers of selfless and exceptional comrades taken into the apparatus lost contact with their environment and came to execute orders, fell into routine, and did not develop as political workers.

This system of Party work on the one hand slowed up the development of the Party, and on the other hand harmed many valuable and devoted Party workers.

The Party leadership intends to change radically the system of Party work. This is to be done by the process of the widest and direct inclusion of the working masses in administration and by rendering independent all the links of our political, social, and economic life which is now taking place.

When new elections of Party authorities are being carried out, one must at the same time liquidate errors and distortions committed in the past with regard to a certain part of former PPS [Polish Socialist Party] leaders. There are a certain number of former PPS activists who consistently fought for the unity of the Polish workers movement and yet were removed from Party activities by a sectarian cadre administration. Such a state of affairs is not profitable for the Party and does unreasonable harm to those people. There is a group of former PPS leaders who before unification had some doubts and showed an insufficiently consistent attitude in the matter of the unity of the workers' movement.

Today, some of these people are Party members and have no opportunity of taking an active part in Party work. Some of them are outside the Party. There are also leaders who have been excluded from the Party. Eight years have elapsed since the unification of the workers' movement. In that time the situation has changed, as have the people's ideas. Today we must return to these problems and give everybody who agrees with the present Party line a chance to join actively in our Party and state life. We must also make good the harms done to comrades of the former PPS who were accused and groundlessly thrown into prison. We must settle our accounts with the past in a just manner and make good any harm done to men and the Party.

There are a number of indications that the majority of former PPS leaders who were removed from political life have received the decisions of the Eighth Plenum with great satisfaction and have thus doubtlessly expressed the opinions of a definite section of the people's masses. We must, therefore, without delay make it possible for these comrades to return to active Party life, and make full use of their vocational skills and political experience. (*Applause.*)

The Politburo has set up a commission consisting of comrades Loga-Sowinski, Baranowski, Jablonski, Motyka, Zaborski, and Werblan for a speedy consideration and settlement of the problem of former PPS members of basic importance.

Similar commissions must immediately begin working in provinces, towns, and, if necessary, even in districts.

In all justified cases one must ensure that proper use is made of old leaders of the workers' movement both from the CPP [Polish Communist Party] and the PPS who were unjustly removed from political life. (*Applause.*)

While not excluding the possibility of coopting former PPS men who accept the decisions of the Eighth Plenum into the Party committees, or even into the executive bodies of Party organs, we must, first of all, create conditions enabling them to stand for Party offices. Let members of the United Party, that is, former PPS and former PWP [Polish Workers Party] elect men to the leading posts of their Party such comrades whom they give their fullest confidence. The decisions of the Eighth Plenum apply equally to all of them. When electing men to Party posts, the most important problem is the election of men who would best implement these decisions.

Party elections should be carried out as soon as possible because the whole Party should have officers democratically elected, enjoying the deep confidence of all, or at least of the great majority, of Party membership.

A Party possessing such officers would never be isolated from the working class and the whole nation, as has happened in the past.

The election of Party officers is aimed at strengthening the leading role of the Party and linking it more closely with the working class and all the working people.

In these elections, no doubt, a certain number of good comrades and valuable activists will be dropped from Party posts. We must take that into account. It is also certain that a number of men of not only low but actually weak leadership values will be appointed. We must remember that too.

The first, that is, the good, conscious comrades, should always face the leadership of the Party boldly and tell them the truth, both about their previous work and about the tasks facing Party organizations and the newly elected leadership. One can and one should own up to all of one's mistakes, but at the same time every Party activist has the right and the duty to tell Party members how work should be done to implement the decisions of the Eighth Plenum, so that the great process of transformations in the life of the Party and in the life of the nation should go correctly, that is, should strengthen the foundations of the people's rule in Poland.

It is only on this road that the nonelected, valuable Party activists can in a short time obtain the confidence of the Party masses.

On the other hand, men of little value who will find themselves in Party posts will be very quickly unmasked by their electors and, no doubt, will in a short time be replaced by better comrades.

Changes which are taking place in the life of the Party will cause a decrease in the Party apparatus. Some comrades may become uneasy because of this, for they have to face the problem of finding different jobs. This matter should be solved primarily by giving some the opportunity for work in production and by training others for new professions. Central Party authorities should take special care of the latter. Local Party authorities should assure a return of Party members who have a profession to various establishments.

Our Party attaches decisive importance to basic Party organizations in production centers. Because on them depends primarily how the worker's self-government will work, how the intended great change in the administration and direction of factories will be carried out. That is why we need the greatest possible number of comrades, experienced in political work and devoted to the cause of socialism, in production centers. There they will grow into real workers and leaders of the working class. The Party apparatus is an inescapable necessity. But the place of the overwhelming part of the most conscious Party members and the field for their Party action is primarily in factories. Then, the Party will have the best and the closest ties with the working class and nothing can be more important for the Party and for the efficient realization of its plans than a deep bond with the working class and the working masses. (*Ovation.*)

The work of the whole Party, and particularly of its leadership, is at present made easier by the principles of nonsecrecy of Party and state life which is now being implemented on a constantly wider scale. The leadership of the Party and the Government now speaks publicly about matters which in the past were passed over in silence. Internal information within the Party is still far from good, but this too should be improved soon. The pressure of work connected with the implementation, or preparations for the implementation, of the directives outlined by the Eighth Plenum, as well as the events in the international arena, tend to delay improvements in the dissemination of information within the Party.

The leadership of the Party gives first priority in political work to the problem of consolidating in the consciousness of the whole nation the importance of friendship between Poland and the Soviet Union. The newly formulated foundations on which we want to base the good and friendly relations with our Eastern neighbor, as well as the brotherly relations between our Party and the CPSU, are meeting with the full understanding of the leaders of the Party of the Soviet state. That is why we must oppose the work of the rabble-rousing, provocative elements which oppose Polish-Soviet friendship all the more firmly. With the political opponents of socialism we can—and we should—discuss things. But the conscious, and even the unaware men who harm the interests of the Polish state and the Polish nation, men to whom words of truth do not penetrate, must be ruthlessly driven away. (*Long ovation.*) This is an important task of Party organizations as well as of state authorities and organs called upon to guard the public order and fight the enemies of the Polish state.

In this connection, I should like to say a few words on the subject of our security organs.

We intend to reorganize the work of the public security apparatus in the immediate future. The sphere of competence of the public security organs will be narrowed and limited to fighting espionage, terror, and other hostile action aimed against the rule of the people and the interests of the state. The public security apparatus will be subordinated to the Ministry for Internal Affairs. The Committee for Public Security will thus be liquidated.

The security organs have recently been subjected to a flood of criticism and attacks. It must be said that this was not without reason. The distortions which occurred in the whole of our life were particularly pronounced in the work of the security organs. This was openly admitted and stated by the Party when it cast away from itself and the nation the old system of ruling. The people who were guiltiest were either dismissed from the security apparatus or arrested. The Party commission formed at the Eighth Plenum will examine and pronounce whether there are still people guilty of serious crimes in the central apparatus of the security organs. It will also put forward the necessary proposals if such are needed.

We thus see that the leadership of the Party and the Government are drawing all conclusions in order to liquidate completely the evil which, in the past, prevailed in those organs.

At the same time we must not forget that the overwhelming majority of those who worked and are working in the security organs are honest and devoted people who are bound to the people's rule for life and death. Many of these people gave their lives in the first years after the liberation in the fight against the armed reactionary underground movement. This must never be forgotten. (*Applause.*) Neither must we extend the guilt for the distortions and crimes which occurred in the security organs to the whole security apparatus and all its employees.

The security apparatus has been and is going through a process of profound reeducation.

The value of the security organs and the fact that the security service employees come from the ranks of the working classes and that they are closely bound to the Party and the nation was proved by their attitude during the critical days of the Eighth Plenum. (*Ovation.*)

The public security employees have proved that, together with the whole Party and all the progressive forces in our country, they stand unflinchingly on guard over the interests of the nation, that they wholeheartedly support changes in our life, and that they are ready to prevent any attempts aimed against the political line mapped out by the leadership of the Party.

The organs of security have undergone a great process of renovation and have understood their tasks in the service of the nation and in the service of the working people.

The vigilant and devoted work of the security organs is today particularly necessary because the forces of international reaction sponsoring all anti-Polish revisionist trends are intensifying their espionage and diversionist-propaganda activities. In this situation, the organs which protect internal order and the security of the country must be shown special solicitude and given assistance in their difficult and responsible work.

Comrades, among the economic tasks which require special attention and increased effort in the Party organization, particularly among members of the Party working in the state apparatus, the problem of compulsory deliveries to the state comes to the fore. In this field, serious neglect and arrears have occurred. These must be swiftly liquidated. Party organizations, and particularly those which work in the countryside, should exploit all opportunities in order to carry out the speediest implementation of compulsory deliveries. At the same time, both the central and the provincial press should devote special attention to this question.

The most important problem facing the Party at present is the development of the election campaign preceding the Sejm elections. Our party will go into the elections with a program of action outlined at the Eighth Plenum.

Our Party candidates will appear on the joint lists of candidates put forward by National Front committees. On these lists, side by side with activists from our Party, will be representatives of the United Peasant Party and the Democratic Party, as well as representatives of Catholic groups and non-Party activists.

Because the number of candidates appearing on the lists will be larger than the number of seats in each constituency, it is very important to choose the right candidates from our Party. The most popular activists, men who have strong and deep links with the working class and the people's masses, should be chosen as candidates, men who during the recent time were able to strengthen their links with the nation and who will guarantee that they will properly discharge the duties of a Sejm deputy.

The way in which candidates will be chosen has not yet been decided. This calls for an agreement with other parties and groups which are members of the National Front. But all this should not prevent us from putting forward names of candidates and obtaining Party and non-Party opinion about the value of each candidate.

Our Party is of the opinion that candidates should be chosen in an understanding between all parties and groups taking part in a particular constituency, and that such candidates should be tested and the opinion of the voters taken into consideration, primarily at meetings in places of employment, in peasant centers, and in centers of the working intelligentsia.

As a result of such campaign there is the possibility that new candidates will be put forward. Therefore the need for selection between the candidates will arise. The final choosing of the prescribed number of candidates for each election district should take place at an authoritative, democratically convened meeting of the National Front for the constituency.

At such a meeting representatives of members or representatives of district committees of the National Front should be present, as well as representatives of larger enterprises, peasant organizations, and centers of the intelligentsia, chosen at their own meetings. There the final decisions will be taken as to which of the candidates will be put on the election list.

Party organizations and leadership should cooperate in the election campaign with all parties and groups of the National Front, and particularly with the United Peasant Party, which, apart from our Party, is the second most important political force in the country, able to unite the widest peasant masses around the National Front program and around the decisions of the Eighth Plenum of our Party.

Comrades, the situation in our country is influenced, not to a small degree, by events in the international arena, and first of all, by the imperialist warlike action of Britain, France, and Israel against Egypt. Britain and France, continuing the policy of colonialism, are kindling war in the Near East. This policy is being condemned by all the nations of the world and is also condemned by the Polish nation. Our Party, in a manifesto to the whole nation, has also expressed its views on the events taking place in Hungary. The implementation of our aims as outlined at the Eighth Plenum and on the development of our international situation will depend on ourselves and on how closely the whole nation will follow the directions of the leadership of the Party and the Government.

We often hear the demands that the leadership of the Party and the Government should tell the working class and the whole nation the truth. We say the truth today too, we must closely and ruthlessly carry out the directives of the Party and the People's Government so that Poland should never find herself in the situation in which Hungary found herself. (*Long ovation.*)

At the present difficult time the best guarantee of internal peace consists in a strong, united, and active Party. (*Ovation.*)

Of all tasks facing us the most important one is the consolidation and activation of the 1.5 million Party members. This depends not only on a proper policy pursued by the Party leadership but in the first place on you, the leaders of Party organizations, and on thousands of local Party activists.

Every Pole who loves his country and feels responsible for the security of his nation understands the significance of the present historic moment. But there are citizens and comrades hotheaded enough not to be guided by reason but only by feelings and reflexes. There are also irresponsible people, there are adventurers who can only shout but not think.

It is the sacred duty of the Polish working class, the duty of patriotic Polish youth, of the whole enlightened community to oppose with determination any irresponsible and dangerous excesses. (*Applause.*)

In the name of the good of our country, for peace of our homes, we shall not tolerate any disturbances or rabble-rousing. The seriousness of the situation demands that, as in the October days, we show with determination our unity of decision; that in this difficult period we gather around the new leadership of the Party and Government, support its bold and well-considered policy and its action, aiming at the consolidation of socialist democracy and Polish sovereignty. (*Ovation.*)

Comrades, let us work calmly at our respective places of work. Let us fulfill our duties to the Party, the working class, the whole nation, and our people's state as best we can. This is our patriotic and socialist duty, the command of the hour. (*Long, stormy applause.*)

11. COMMUNIQUÉ ON TALKS HELD BETWEEN PARTY AND GOVERNMENT DELEGATIONS OF THE SOVIET UNION AND THE POLISH PEOPLE'S REPUBLIC, MOSCOW, NOVEMBER 18, 1956[27]

TALKS BETWEEN THE Delegation of the Central Committee of the CPSU and the Government of the Soviet Union and the Dele-

---

[27] *Pravda,* November 19, 1956.

gation of the Central Committee of the Polish United Workers Party and the Government of the Polish People's Republic were held in Moscow from November 15 to November 18, 1956.

The Soviet side was represented in the talks by N. S. Khrushchev, First Secretary of the Central Committee of the CPSU (head of the Delegation); members of the Presidium of the Central Committee of the CPSU: K. Y. Voroshilov, President of the Presidium of the Supreme Soviet of the USSR; N. A. Bulganin, Chairman of the USSR Council of Ministers; A. I. Mikoyan and M. Z. Saburov, First Vice Chairman of the USSR Council of Ministers.

The Polish side was represented in the talks by Wladyslaw Gomulka, First Secretary of the Central Committee of the Polish United Workers Party (head of the Delegation); members of the Political Bureau of the Central Committee of the Polish United Workers Party: Aleksander Zawadzki, Chairman of the Council of State of the Polish People's Republic; Jozef Cyrankiewicz, Chairman of the Council of Ministers of the Polish People's Republic; Stefan Jedrychowski, Chairman of the State Economic Planning Commission.

Present at the talks were also: from the Soviet side—Marshal of the Soviet Union G. K. Zhukov, alternate member of the Presidium of the Central Committee of the CPSU, Minister of Defense of the USSR; B. P. Beshchev, A. G. Zverev, and I. G. Kabanov, Ministers of the USSR; K. I. Koval, Head of the Chief Department of Economic Relations; N. S. Patolichev, Deputy Foreign Minister of the USSR; P. K. Ponomarenko, USSR Ambassador to the PPR; Army General A. I. Antonov; G. I. Tunkin, Head of the Treaties and Law Department of the USSR Foreign Ministry; from the Polish side—Eugeniusz Szyr, member of the Central Committee of the PUWP; Witold Trampszynski, Deputy Finance Minister of the PPR; Ambassador Maria Wierna, Director-General of the Foreign Ministry of the PPR; and Henryk Kotlicki, Director-General of the Finance Ministry of the PPR.

I

The talks and meetings which took place
of sincerity, friendship, mutual understandi
enabled the delegations to carry out a fru
opinions on the development and strengtheni
relations as well as on the most impor
problems.

The talks and exchanges of opinion that
the delegations showed a mutual desire
between the Communist Party of the Sovi
Polish United Workers Party and between
basis of Lenin's principles of equality amon
showed the similarity of views of the So
Polish People's Republic in the estimati
national problems.,

Both delegations consider that the aggre
states are trying to disrupt the certain relaxa
tension that has been achieved in recent ye
of this policy is the attack by Britain, Fr
Egypt, which only recently freed itself from
ism and is striving to consolidate its fre
independence.

Both delegations declare that the aggr
can in no way be justified. They condem
entailed great loss of life and much da
unusable the Suez Canal, so important fo
ping, including Soviet and Polish shipping
time made the situation in the Near Eas
world more acute.

Both delegations declare that the state
the war should, in accordance with the rele
United Nations, withdraw their forces fro

The Soviet Union and Poland will g
to Egypt's just claims.

Both delegations consider the situatio
a great country as the Chinese People's

fault of the imperialist circles of certain countries, is still deprived of her lawful place in the United Nations, a situation which hinders the solution of many important international problems.

The Soviet Union and Poland will do everything possible in order to bring about the restoration of the legitimate rights of the Chinese People's Republic in the United Nations organization, seeing in this one of the most important conditions for transforming the United Nations into an effective international instrument for maintaining universal peace.

Both delegations consider that, in the present aggravated situation, all states and in the first place the great powers should make every effort to reach agreement on the reduction of armed forces and armaments, on the banning of atom and hydrogen weapons and the liquidation of military bases on foreign soil.

The substantial reduction of the armed forces of the United States, Britain, France, and the USSR in Germany and the banning of atomic and hydrogen weapon tests could be an important step in promoting and easing international tension and creating an atmosphere of trust between states.

Agreement on the problem of disarmament would undoubtedly promote the creation of the necessary conditions for the settlement of the most important international problems, including the German problem and the problem of collective European security, in which not only the Soviet Union and Poland, but all the European peoples are interested.

Both delegations declare that the Soviet Union and Poland will make every effort to achieve success in the settlement of the disarmament problem, in the interests of the peoples and universal peace.

The delegations exchanged views on the question of the events in Hungary. Both delegations express their confidence that the Hungarian working class and the whole Hungarian nation will discover enough power in themselves to defend the achievements of the people's democratic system. Both sides will give support to the Revolutionary Worker Peasant Gov-

ernment whose program, proclaiming the renunciation of the
harmful errors of the policy of the former Rakosi Government,
is directed toward the development of socialist democracy and
the consolidation of fraternal cooperation with the other socialist countries on the basis of full equality and regard for state
sovereignty.   The delegations are of the opinion that some
decisions adopted by the United Nations with regard to Hungary
do not aim at helping the Hungarian people but at diverting
the attention of the peoples from the aggression against Egypt.

II

In the course of friendly talks both delegations examined
and discussed in detail all aspects of the relations between the
Soviet and Polish states, as they developed up to the present.
Both parties are of the opinion that the declaration of the
Soviet Government of October 30, 1956, on the "Principles
of Development and Further Strengthening of Friendship and
Cooperation between the Soviet Union and Other Socialist
States" is of great importance for the development and strengthening of friendship between socialist countries.   Both parties
are of the opinion that the principles laid down in this declaration conform to the decisions adopted on this question by the
eighth plenary session of the Central Committee of the Polish
United Workers Party and to the policy of the Polish Government. During the talks both parties devoted particular attention
to the further development and strengthening of the friendship
between the peoples of the Soviet Union and the Polish People's
Republic and expressed confidence that the indestructible union
and fraternal friendship between the USSR and the PPR will
widen and consolidate, developing on the basis of complete
equality, respect for territorial integrity, national independence
and sovereignty, and of noninterference in internal affairs. The
Soviet-Polish alliance, in which both the Soviet and Polish
peoples are equally interested, is a reliable guarantee of their
security.   This alliance is a most important factor for the
strengthening of the independence of the Polish People's Repub-

lic and the inviolability of her frontier on the Oder and Neisse, the frontier of peace.

The parties express profound confidence that the consistent realization of the above-mentioned principles of cooperation between the Soviet Union and the Polish People's Republic will contribute to the further strengthening of the alliance between the two states, to the strengthening of the unity of the socialist camp and peace in Europe.

III

During the talks questions of economic relations between the Soviet Union and Poland in the light of the Soviet Government declaration on the "Principles of Development and Further Strengthening of Friendship and Cooperation between the Soviet Union and Other Socialist States" were examined in detail.

Both sides have declared their determination to develop and strengthen economic cooperation between the two countries on the basis of equal rights, mutual benefit and fraternal mutual help.

In the course of the negotiations the existence of certain outstanding financial accounts for previous years between the sides was determined.

Both sides, on the basis of mutual interests, agreed to regard as settled as of November 1, 1956, the Polish debts arising out of the use of credits granted by the Soviet Government to Poland in payment of the full value of coal delivered by Poland to the Soviet Union in 1946-53 on the basis of the agreement of August 16, 1945. Agreement was also reached on the settlement of financial accounts in connection with railroad transport and noncommercial payments, etc.

The Soviet Government is ready to deliver to the Polish People's Republic 1,400,000 tons of grain in 1957. The above grain deliveries will be made on credit.

The Soviet Government has also agreed to grant to the Polish People's Republic long-term credits to the amount of 700,000,000 rubles for the payment of commodities delivered by the Soviet Union to Poland in accordance with a mutually agreed list.

IV

Both sides discussed problems connected with the temporary stationing of Soviet troops in Polish territory.

The parties declare that until now agreed decisions have not been reached which could provide European states with sufficient guarantees against the rebirth of German militarism.

The constant objections by revanchist forces to the correct and existing frontiers between European states and, in the first place, to the established and existing western frontier of Poland also constitute a material reason hampering the normalization of relations in Europe.

Both sides reached the conclusion that this state of affairs, as well as the existing international situation, continue to make the temporary presence of Soviet troops in Poland's territory necessary.

This is also connected with the necessity of the presence of Soviet troops in Germany on the basis of international treaties and agreements.

It was settled that both sides would, in accordance with the development of the international situation, consult on problems connected with the stay of Soviet military units in Polish territory, their number, and their composition.

At the same time both sides accept the following principles determining the status of these units in Polish territory:

The temporary presence of Soviet troops in Poland can in no way affect the sovereignty of the Polish state and cannot lead to their interference in the internal affairs of the Polish People's Republic.

The disposition and number of Soviet troops is to be determined by special agreements between both sides.

The movement of Soviet military units outside their stations requires the agreement of the Government of the Polish People's Republic or other competent Polish authorities.

The Soviet military units located in the territory of the Polish People's Republic and their personnel, together with their families, are obligated to respect and adhere to the provisions of Polish law. The limits of Polish and Soviet jurisdiction with regard to the personnel of Soviet military units in Poland will be settled by special agreement.

The times, routes and orders of transit of Soviet troops across Polish territory are to be settled by definite agreements between both sides.

Appropriate agreements determining the legal status of Soviet troops during the time of their temporary stay in Polish territory will be concluded in the near future.

v

Guided by the desire for the further consolidation of Polish-Soviet friendship, the delegations have agreed on the principles along which the Soviet authorities concerned will promote the further repatriation of Poles having families in Poland and the return to Poland of persons who for reasons beyond their control could not make use of their right to repatriation on the basis of the Soviet-Polish agreements of 1945.

The Soviet delegation has stated that a proposal is to be submitted to the Presidium of the Supreme Soviet on the early release and repatriation or the handing over of persons in captivity to the Polish authorities. The sides have agreed that a meeting of representatives of competent bodies of both sides will take place in the near future to agree on the times and methods of repatriation.

During the negotiations it was noted that cultural cooperation between the USSR and the Polish People's Republic has developed successfully in recent years. An agreement on cultural cooperation between the Soviet Union and Poland providing for further comprehensive development of Soviet-Polish ties in the domain of science, culture, and the arts was signed in Warsaw on June 30, 1956.

Close cultural cooperation between the Soviet Union and Poland will again in future contribute effectively to the consolidation of sincere fraternal friendship between the Soviet and Polish peoples.

Both sides will exert all efforts to inform their peoples comprehensively of the measures which are being taken in political, economic, and other spheres of the life of the Soviet Union and the Polish People's Republic and the mutual achievements in socialist construction as a means of further intensifying Soviet-Polish friendship and mutual understanding.

The delegation of the Central Committee of the Communist Party of the Soviet Union and the Soviet Government and the delegation of the Polish United Workers Party and the Polish Government express their firm conviction that the broad and frank exchange of views which took place in the course of the talks will contribute to the further development of friendly relations between the Soviet Union and the Polish People's Republic and between the two Parties, to the benefit of the peoples of the two countries, and that it will further the interests of strengthening peace and security throughout the world.

PART THREE: *Hungary*

CHAPTER I

ASSESSING THE LESSONS OF THE 20th CONGRESS OF THE CPSU

One of the developments of the 20th Congress of the CPSU relating specifically to Hungary was the posthumous rehabilitation of Bela Kun, leader of the first Hungarian Communist revolution in 1919 and a prominent figure in the international Communist movement.[1] The restoration of Kun to the ranks of "honored fighters" of the Communist movement was significant because he had been one of the victims of Stalinist purges in the 1930's (when he disappeared without a trace), and because of his rivalry with Matyas Rakosi, First Secretary of the Hungarian Workers Party. Kun's demise coincided with Rakosi's rise to leadership in the Hungarian Communist movement.

Shortly after the conclusion of the 20th Congress, the Central Committee of the Hungarian Workers Party (HWP) met to hear the report of Matyas Rakosi, its First Secretary and leader of the Hungarian delegation to Moscow, on the decisions and lessons of the Congress. The resolution adopted by the Central Committee marked the beginning of Hungary's own campaign against the "cult of personality."

1. Resolution Adopted by the Central Committee of the Hungarian Workers Party, March 12-13, 1956[2]

ON THE BASIS of the recommendation of the Politburo, the Central Committee of the Hungarian Workers Party has discussed the report of the delegation to the 20th Congress of the CPSU.

The Central Committee is in full agreement with the assessment presented by the 20th Congress on the present international situation and the internal situation of the Soviet Union,

---

[1] See E. Varga, "The Seventieth Anniversary of the Birth of Bela Kun," *Pravda*, February 21, 1956.

[2] *Szabad Nep*, central organ of the HWP, March 15, 1956.

and it approves the conclusions drawn therefrom. The extremely rapid development of the Soviet Union in all spheres of economic, political, and cultural life, its foreign and internal policy, based on Lenin's teachings and reflecting the wisdom of the Party, have gained new allies in the international arena, opening up new possibilities for peaceful cooperation and competition between countries of differing economic and social systems, between the socialist and capitalist world system, and also for the creation of a lasting peace. The findings of the Congress on the possibility of averting war and on the various forms of transition to socialism are suited to increase and strengthen the international unity of the working class, the rallying of the masses, and the huge camp of the friends of peace, democracy, and socialism.

The Central Committee is filled with sincere joy at the great economic successes of the Soviet Union and the magnificent objectives of the Sixth Five-Year Plan which provide tangible proof that within a comparatively short period in history the Soviet Union will surpass the most highly developed capitalist countries as regards per capita output. It is with joy that the Central Committee welcomes the continued rise in the material and cultural well-being of the Soviet people, the raising of real wages and incomes, the reduction in working hours, the general introduction of compulsory secondary school education by 1960, and all other measures envisaged by the plan.

The Central Committee is in profound agreement that the source of these successes lies in the restoration of the Leninist norms of Party life, the elimination of the cult of personality, and the creation of collective leadership which are suitable to develop freely the unlimited creative strength of the Party and of the entire Soviet people in all spheres of economic, political, and cultural life.

On the basis of all this, the Central Committee entrusts the Politburo to work out without delay, with the active participation of the members of the Central Committee, of the Party organizations, Party members, workers and their organizations, as well as the state organs, those measures which are applicable, in conformity with the resolutions of the 20th Congress of the CPSU, to the specific conditions of Hungary, and also entrusts the Politburo to insure the enforcement of these measures. The Central Committee finds that the political line of our Party, worked out by the Third Congress of the Hungarian Workers Party, has proved to be correct.[3] Further, while priority must be given to heavy industry, agriculture must be developed first of all and higher crop yields and the socialist reorganization of agriculture must be insured. The consumer goods industry must be developed, the speedy raising of the technological level of industry insured, comparative backwardness eliminated, and we must continue to increase industrial and agricultural production and to raise the well-being of the people by increased productivity.

A tenacious and systematic struggle must be pursued in the Party so that collective leadership shall become a reality to the fullest extent on all levels. Democracy within the Party must be further developed and, relying on the achievements that have already been attained, socialist legality must be strengthened even more. Under the leadership of the Party and the working class, the Patriotic People's Front movement must be expanded.[4] It must be filled with political content so that it shall be capable of mobilizing the whole of our country's working population in the defense of peace and for the building-up of a socialist Hungary. The 20th Congress has given fresh impetus to the enforcement of the fine policy which was laid down at the Third Congress of the Hungarian Workers Party

---

[3] The Third Congress of the HWP was held in Budapest from May 24-30, 1954.

[4] Attempts at reviving the Patriotic People's Front (the Hungarian version of "national" fronts which exist in all people's democratic countries) and transforming it into an operating organization had been made sporadically throughout the period of the "New Course," under the premiership of Imre Nagy, between July, 1953, and March, 1955. The removal of Nagy as Premier in April, 1955, and the restoration of a more hardened political and economic rule under Rakosi halted the attempts.

and which was freed from right-wing distortions by the resolution adopted by the Central Committee in March, 1955.[5]

All Party organs and Party organizations, from the Central Committee down to the basic organizations, must do away with formal bureaucratic Party work. The direct implementation of practical tasks, the organization and direction of implementation, and the deepening of relations with the working masses must constitute the core of the Party's work.

Ideological, scientific, cultural, and propaganda work must take into consideration to the largest extent the findings and principles of the 20th Congress of the CPSU. The Central Committee definitely asserts that backwardness in ideological work can be eliminated only if we do not brook ideological inertia, trends toward rigidity in Marxism-Leninism, and dogmatism. Enlightenment work must be linked in the closest possible manner with life and the practical aspects of socialist construction.

Propaganda and agitation work must be altered in such a way as to enable it, in addition to popularizing the policy of the Party, directly to promote the solution of the economic tasks facing the country by spreading correct working methods, progressive experiences, and fresh knowledge.

The Central Committee entrusts the Politburo with the task that, when drafting the directives for the Second Five-Year Plan, it shall make use of all the lessons that have to be concluded from the 20th Congress of the CPSU on the development of the Hungarian people's economy and of the Hungarian people's democracy in general.

The Central Committee calls on the Party committees and basic organizations, all members of our Party, profoundly to study and analyze the material of the 20th Congress and to

---

[5] The reference is to a meeting of the Central Committee at which the "New Course" in Hungary was terminated. Nagy was deposed as Premier a month later, and Rakosi staged a comeback as the most powerful Communist in Hungary. These events followed hard on the heels of the removal of Malenkov as Soviet Premier. Several months later, in November, 1955, Nagy was expelled from the HWP.

make use of the advice designed to improve Party work. The study and implementation of the resolutions of the 20th Congress of the CPSU in practical work is suited to give fresh impetus to ideological, cultural, and practical work. It means great help in the implementation of the momentous resolutions of the Third Congress of the Hungarian Workers Party and of last year's resolutions of the Central Committee,[6] in the fulfillment of the tasks lying ahead of us and in the building of socialism in Hungary.

The Central Committee of the Hungarian Workers Party

---

[6] The most significant of these resolutions adopted on March 4, 1955, condemned the policy of Imre Nagy, reemphasized the primacy of heavy industry over consumer goods production, and resumed agricultural collectivization which had been all but suspended during the previous two years. (*Szabad Nep,* March 9, 1955.)

CHAPTER II

ANTI-STALINISM IN LOW GEAR
MARCH-JUNE, 1956

The ensuing four months—until another meeting of the Central Committee on July 18—witnessed skirmishing of increasing intensity between Rakosi, Hungary's foremost practitioner of "Stalinism," and a large portion of the intellectual community together with spokesmen for the youth.

Shortly after the Central Committee's March meeting, Rakosi announced the rehabilitation of Laszlo Rajk, the leading Communist victim of Stalinist purges in Hungary, who had been condemned to death as a "traitor and Titoist deviationist" in 1949. The charges on which he had been tried were now revealed to have been based on "provocative accusations leveled by Gabor Peter," the former Communist police chief.[1] At the same time it was announced that several of Rajk's codefendants, who had been sentenced to long prison terms, as well as a number of imprisoned Social Democrats would be released. (*Szabad Nep,* March 29, 1956.)

Meanwhile, the Hungarian writers opened a new round in their struggle for greater creative freedom. Earlier encounters which came to a head at a meeting of the Writer's Union on November 10, 1955, prompted the Party to adopt a resolution condemning "right-wing opportunism" which under the present conditions was manifesting itself "most openly and in a most organized manner in the literary sphere." The resolution, printed in *Irodalmi Ujsag,* the journal of the Writers' Union, on December 10, 1955, also stated that "Certain writers—including Party members—have forgotten to serve the public and have become the spokesmen of the declining classes and the most backward strata. . . . There were some writers (Tibor Dery, Zoltan Zelk, Tamas Aczel, and others) who rejected the Central Committee's resolution of March, 1955, or acknowledged it only seemingly. . . .

---

[1] Lt. Gen. Gabor Peter was sentenced to life imprisonment in March, 1954.

The Party's competent organs must examine the cases of those writers who have opposed the Central Committee's resolution of March and attempted to organize an opposition faction within the Party."

These threats of reprisal, reinforced by virtue of being reprinted in *Pravda* on the following day (December 11, 1955), succeeded for a time in dampening the expression of criticism, although none of the accused writers went so far as to indulge in self-accusing self-criticism. Nor were the threats followed by actual reprisals.

Now, emboldened by the 20th Congress of the CPSU, the writers struck back with renewed vigor. Their campaign of demands for greater freedom and criticism of the regime reached a climax at a meeting held on March 30, 1956, for the purpose of electing a new secretary general of the Writers' Union. On this occasion pro-regime spokesmen clashed violently with a number of writers, some of whom, like Sandor Lukacsy, denounced Rakosi so strongly that they were expelled from the Party. (*Szabad Nep*, April 13, 1956.) The meeting itself was adjourned until April 3 when the writers proceeded to defeat Csabai, the Party's candidate for the post of secretary general of the Union. The vote against him was reportedly 100 to 3. In his stead, Geza Kepes, a poet and former member of the National Peasant Party, was chosen by a vote of 103 to 2.

Echoes of this struggle resounded throughout the Party press and in *Irodalmi Ujsag*. Supporting the Party, Professor Istvan Soter pled for "partisan [or "party-minded"] literature," but even he advocated a somewhat "looser" interpretation of partisanship. (*Irodalmi Ujsag*, March 31, 1956.) Others, like Peter Kuczka, took a stronger stand against partisanship in literature. "What is the writer's duty," he asked, "when he discovers or thinks he has discovered, contradictions between . . . theory and practice? Does he have the right, and is it his duty, to mention this . . . to propose ways of solution? . . . Can principles of laws be laid down without knowledge and analysis of facts? Is it conceivable that we can come to correct conclusions without debates?" (*Irodalmi Ujsag*, April 7, 1956.) In the same issue of *Irodalmi Ujsag* a young writer, Tibor Tardos, in an article entitled "Independent Communist Thinking," bemoaned the destruction of creative individuality and the escape from reality into the abstract:

I broke away . . . from real newspapers and radios which could have fed me with living news. I weaned myself away from universal science. . . . Gradually, I began to forget that there are films in the world in which people come and go naturally, in which there are real streets, real persons, in which good is not always rewarded and bad is not always punished. I gave up the habit of real conversations. I visited factories and country schoolyards, and whenever I heard complaints, I found an explanation; I said it was an exception, an exaggeration; in fact, sometimes I even thought: it was the voice of the enemy. And the time came when suddenly we even discarded respect for human life . . . sacrificing it to faith. And we, who not long ago, in our youth, had sworn by the tremendous power of thought, stood here with crystal-clear hearts but empty heads, like dried out amphorae in a museum. And the amphorae nodded consent to everything.

A strong attack against the regime was penned by Gyula Hay under the title of "The Triumph of Human Dignity" (*Irodalmi Ujsag*, May 5, 1956), in which he said among other things:

A new spirit, a new tone, a new style must appear in all aspects of life. This is no easy matter. We know the terrifying consequences of all forms of the cult of personality: the wrong and harmful resolutions passed without opposition, thoughtless servility, the establishment of smaller or larger associations of yes-men, the persecution of criticism, the whitewashing of liars . . . the crushing of [human] rights and law, illegalities demanding sacrifice, or—to remain in the field of literature—the disruption of literary work by the adoption of administrative measures and by elevating dogmatism, scholasticism, and the stupid bureaucratic mentality to the status of aesthetic ideals. . . .

The fact that a few events at the end of last year had a paralyzing and harmful effect on literature did not surprise any thinking writer. There were quite a few who openly prophesied [earlier] what the effect of the mistakes in literary policy [would be]. . . . [Until the 20th Congress] no heed was paid to the opinion of these experts, who are the best in literature and the most progressive in politics. . . . The cult of personality poisoned our whole literature. Perhaps there wasn't a single person among us who, for a time at least, did not confuse enthusiasm for the

great cause with rapturous enthusiasm for individual persons.
. . . The time has come for us to be converted to the truth, the
over-all, unconditional, profound truth which serves the people
and the Party.   May Socialist realism come [at last]!   Let us
put an end to pseudo-Socialist apologetics!

Again and again, we are told that our literary policy abolished
the cult of personality as far back as June, 1953, and that it was
only subsequent rightist distortions that prevented complete
improvement.   Well, in the case of literature, it would be rather
hard to accept this explanation. . . . We know that in the field
of literature the June resolutions were [suppressed].   June never
really became effective and the slightest literary expression of
the June spirit evoked administrative countermeasures.   What
kind of rightist distortions were they that called forth this
literary policy?   Were they perhaps the eight or ten quotations
from poems that are being repeated over and over again whenever administrative interference is mentioned and which, in our
present, cleaner atmosphere, appear anything but rightist?

While demanding greater freedom, the writers also expressed
their despair with respect to the past and present.   Testimony of
the fears of writers and poets can be found in a poem by Zoltan
Zelk, one of the leaders of the opposition to Rakosi.   (*Irodalmi
Ujsag,* May 5, 1956.)

> I am not worthy of praise
> Believe me, my friend, it chills my bones
> When you praise my courage.
>
> I am not a tiger; I am a human being
> My worn heart is a nest of fears,
> Believe me: I am scared.   I am scared.
>
> I am a human being, I live like a human being
> How can I be brave?
> I fear only that I may be worthless,
> Of this I am more afraid than of death.

In the face of mounting opposition Rakosi sought to define the
limits of permissible criticism.   Writing in *Pravda* (May 2)[2] on

---

[2] The article was reprinted in *Szabad Nep* on May 3, 1956.

the "Living Embodiment of Lenin's Ideas," he said among other things:

The cult of personality spread unfortunately to most of the people's democratic countries, including Hungary, and caused a whole series of such manifestations as the narrowing of internal Party democracy and the infringement of socialist legality. It is, therefore, impossible to rate the immense value of the work of the CPSU during recent years and, following its example, work done by the Communists of the people's democracies in the interest of implementing Lenin's principles. . . .

It must be noted, however, that enemies of socialism trying to use in their own interests our every step are seeking grounds for their subversive activities. This can also be seen with us in Hungary. The enemy raises much ado, speculating on mistakes exposed by us, striving to evoke distrust in our ranks.

The results of the 20th Party Congress are incontrovertible. Enemy attempts to raise confusion in our ranks fail as they dash themselves against the unity of the Communist ranks. Where they try to exploit internal Party democracy in the interest of spreading rotten, hostile views, their feeble attempts must be liquidated. . . . At the same time care must be taken with every means available to support criticism and self-criticism as a healthy, creative manifestation of internal Party democracy. The principle of internal Party democracy must be strengthened, and the development of the initiative and creative powers of the masses must be insured. At present hostile elements in some places are trying to belittle in the eyes of the masses the role and significance of Party leadership. The Communists, however, know well how important it is to defend and protect the prestige of Party leadership built on the basis of collectivity.

On May 18, speaking before the Party *aktiv* of the Budapest organization of the HWP,[3] Rakosi, while admitting past mistakes and promising improvements, stated that the "Party had not accomplished its absolutely necessary ideological and political educational mission" among the writers:

Following June, 1953, when we [*sic*] self-critically exposed our mistakes, a portion [of the writers] . . . began to find only faults, and to belittle the accomplishments of socialist construc-

---

[3] *Magyar Nemzet,* organ of the Patriotic People's Front, May 19, 1956.

tion. The rightist views which asserted themselves in various quarters in our political life began to gain ground among the writers as well. Some of them began to deny the partisan character of literature, and the need for the directing role of the Party. Under the slogan of free criticism they often took a stand in opposition to the Party's ideological and organizational unity.

Speaking of the class struggle, Rakosi echoed the notion then prevailing throughout the Communist camp that Stalin had unnecessarily exaggerated the sharpening nature of class struggle as socialism was being successfully introduced. Nevertheless, Rakosi reminded his listeners that in Hungary "we defeated the old ruling classes only recently and they still actively nurture the hope of restoration, of getting back in the saddle. We must realize that these strata are relatively numerous among us and their spirit is supported by the nearness of the West, hostile newspaper and radio propaganda, and even often by direct financial support. Under these circumstances the class struggle, although in a less obvious, more complex, more covert form, naturally continues in our country, as indeed we have witnessed precisely during the weeks following the 20th Congress."

The voices of criticism were not stilled. On June 2, Sandor Fekete assailed Hungary's cultural isolation and demanded broader exchanges with the West, as well as the circulation of Western books and motion pictures. At the same time Tibor Tardos demanded freedom to travel and quoted from Adam Wazyk's famed "Poem for Adults"[4] to underline his displeasure at distortions of the truth. (*Irodalmi Ujsag,* June 2, 1956.) Criticism increased toward the end of June at another meeting of the Writers' Union (June 27) and a tumultuous public meeting of the Petofi Circle[5] (the last before the summer recess) which was attended by a crowd of 6,000 people. To this Rakosi responded with a resolution (issued on behalf of the Central Committee) condemning the writers and Imre Nagy and admonishing even the Party's central organ, *Szabad Nep,* for the role it played in abetting erroneous views.

---

[4] See Poland, Chapter I, Document 2.

[5] A debating society formed in March, 1956, within DISZ, the Communist youth organization in Hungary.

1. RESOLUTION ADOPTED BY THE CENTRAL COMMITTEE OF THE HUNGARIAN WORKERS PARTY, JUNE 30, 1956[6]

AS A RESULT of the historic 20th Congress of the CPSU and on the basis of the resolution of the Central Committee of the Hungarian Workers Party of March 12 and 13, 1956,[7] Party democracy, democratism in state and social life, and socialist legality have been strengthened in our country. The Party has scored notable initial successes in the struggle against sectarianism and the remnants of the cult of personality. The Leninist principle of collective leadership is asserting itself more and more in Party work. The constructive criticism and the sound and creative debates and suggestions of the workers, working peasants, and intellectuals are lending a new impetus to the building of socialism.

We must particularly welcome the fruitful debates developing in Party organizations. At these debates many correct and sound proposals aimed at improving our achievements and correcting past mistakes have emerged.

This healthy development, however, is threatened in certain places by a demagogic attitude directed against the Party and People's Democracy. Party organizations and Communists in many places have opposed such endeavors. Yet, in certain cases, members of our Party have neglected their duty, mainly because they believed that by a firm stand against the wrong attitudes they would give the impression of stifling criticism. Gaining courage from the patience of the Party and the Communists, anti-Party elements have launched an increasingly strengthening attack against the policy and leadership of our Party and against our people's democratic system.

The Petofi Circle of the DISZ [the Union of Working Youth] has become one of the focal points of these attacks. The evening debates of this circle had a sound tendency at the beginning. Lately, however, certain elements opposing the

---

[6] *Szabad Nep,* July 1, 1956.
[7] See Chapter I, Document 1.

policy of our Party have increasingly tried to exploit these evening debates for spreading their anti-Party views, to mislead public opinion, particularly the younger elements of the public, and to recruit followers among wavering elements.

Certain speakers at the latest debates of the Petofi Circle (Dery and Tardos)[8] have gone so far as to deny the leading role of the Party and the working class, and advocated bourgeois and counterrevolutionary views. Together with a few other speakers, in a one-sided and demagogic manner, they exaggerated the mistakes committed in the course of building the Party and People's Democracy and kept dead silence—nay denied—the revolutionary achievements of the Party and the people. They slandered Party and state officials whose work has become identified with the great successes of the Hungarian People's Democracy. Taking into consideration the extreme popularity of the 20th Congress [of the CPSU] and of Leninist principles, these speakers gave the appearance of standing on the platform of the 20th Congress and of Marxism-Leninism in order to conceal, in this way, their anti-Party and anti-people's democratic views. In so doing they misled honest workers including even Party members, who failed immediately to recognize that they were facing a malignant anti-Party movement.

It is characteristic of the antidemocratic attitude of the latest evening debates of the Petofi Circle that organized groups, in a scandalous manner, disturbed the speeches of comrades representing the views of the Party and the remarks made by honest Communists who attended the evening in large numbers.

The open opposition against the Party and People's Democracy is mainly organized by a certain group which has formed around Imre Nagy.

The press failed to take a stand against the anti-Party views. Certain newspapers and periodicals, on the other hand,

---

[8] Tibor Dery and Tibor Tardos were consequently expelled from the Party. They were reinstated in September, 1956.

have published misleading and unprincipled laudatory reports and occasionally even gave space to articles with provocative content. The erroneous article in the June 24 issue of *Szabad Nep* has caused confusion in several places among Party members. This article failed to oppose hostile demagogic views and exaggerated certain sound traits of the debates of the Petofi Circle.

The Central Committee of the Hungarian Workers Party decisively condemns the anti-Party manifestations which took place in the Petofi Circle. Our Party and the entire working nation expect that an end be put to anti-Party and anti-people's democratic symptoms.

In the spirit of the 20th Congress, the Party has passed a number of important decisions during the past few months and is preparing further measures to remedy mistakes and speed up our progress. No amount of demagogy whatever can prevent our Party from continuing its march along the road of socialist democratism. Our Party will unflinchingly continue to develop the democratism of state and social life, in order to insure constructive discussion and Party-like criticism, firmly to insure the Leninist norms of Party life by fighting against any manifestation of the cult of personality, dogmatism, and sectarianism, and for the further consolidation of socialist legality.

The Central Committee calls on Communists, on all Party members, and on every follower of our People's Democracy to champion everywhere the policy of the Party and Government. Let them defend, above all with enlightenment-work and persuasion, the cause of the Party, the working class, and of socialism and let them popularize the aims of the Party. Let them most energetically oppose anti-Party and antipopular demagogic manifestations wherever they encounter them and regardless of who propagates them.

Let Party members and Party organizations vigilantly watch over the unity of the Party and strengthen Party discipline. Let them bear in mind that he who wishes to disrupt the unity of the Party, he who wishes to drive a wedge between the Central Committee and the Party membership, the Party or state functionaries and the people, is playing into the hands of the enemies of the working people. The Central Committee calls on Party members and on non-Party workers to increase revolutionary vigilance because, as a result of anti-Party and demagogic views, the danger of hostile troublemaking has increased.

The Poznan provocation[9] is a warning to every Hungarian worker and every honest patriot firmly to oppose attempts at troublemaking and to help the unfettered development of those forces which, on the basis of Marxism-Leninism and in the spirit of the 20th Congress, lead our People's Democracy to new successes.

The Central Committee of the Hungarian Workers Party is convinced that members of our Party, workers, peasants, and intellectuals, and every follower of the People's Democracy will unite under the leadership of the Party and on the side of the Government, for the further development of our people's democratic achievements and for the building of socialism.

The Central Committee of the Hungarian Workers Party

Szabad Nep responded to the resolution with an apology.

2. EDITORIAL: "IN DEFENSE OF DEMOCRACY AND THE PARTY LINE," *Szabad Nep*, JULY 3, 1956

THE DECISION of the Central Committee which appeared on Sunday rejects the ruinous opportunist views and attempts at disrupting the unity of the Party which had gained ground recently. After the events of the past few days the *majority* of the Party *aktiv* expected the Central Committee to define its attitude.

After the 20th Congress of the CPSU profound changes were set in motion in Hungary. Collective leadership is assert-

---

[9] See Poland, Chapter II, Documents 1-3.

ing itself more and more in the Party, and Communist criticism and self-criticism are coming into full play in Party organizations, factories, villages, and offices. Workers criticize the faults of Party work and the shortcomings of the state and economic administration ever more boldly, and submit clever and competent proposals to remedy them. Our Party and Government have rehabilitated our comrades who were condemned unjustly, granted a large-scale amnesty to others who were sentenced for political crimes, and have taken firm measures to enforce socialist legality. Acting on the proposal of the Central Committee, the Government has already taken various steps to eliminate bureaucratic limitations from our administration; the field of competence and economic independence of managers and local councils has been widened.

Those fruitful debates which dealt with various political, ideological, and economic questions in the light of the 20th Congress were also levers of our growing and steadily developing democracy. The debates were particularly fruitful about the directives of our Second Five-Year Plan. Hundreds of thousands of workers, working peasants, and intellectuals took part in these debates, most of which were very useful and instructive in that they widened the political horizon of the participants. Many valuable proposals and criticisms were made which are well worth taking into consideration. All this proves that Party democracy and the democratic character of our entire public life are developing ever more vigorously under the guidance of our Party's Central Committee. The Central Committee wants to speed up this trend of development in the future.

However—as the resolution of the Central Committee which appeared two days ago points out—the healthy democratic development which began after the 20th Congress is threatened by the fact that opportunists, demagogic views, and even ideas hostile to the Party and People's Democracy have gained ground in many places, first of all in the debates of the Petofi Circle of the DISZ, in some weeklies and periodicals, for instance in certain numbers of the *Irodalmi Ujsag* [Literary Journal] and the *Beke es Szabadsag* [Peace and Freedom], and also in certain meetings arranged by some Party and mass organizations.

Journalism was hardly mentioned at the latest debate of the Petofi Circle, although it was convened to discuss problems relating to the press and information. Instead, many opportunist, harmful, and even hostile views were expressed on that occasion. Some called for a new revolution, for a new "ides of March,"[10] and for "structural changes." But what kind of "new revolution" can we talk about? We already had a socialist revolution in our country, and the most progressive social class, the workers, in alliance with the working peasantry and every toiler, are in power. We are, therefore, justified in pointing out that in the language of socialism a new revolution of this kind is called a counterrevolution. Our working class and working people are well aware of this.

Tibor Dery used the debate for launching an open and brutal attack on Party unity. He attacked the leaders of the Party and the Party's activists. He said that liberation would start only now. But our liberation took place in 1945. Such statements, therefore, disparage and reject all that has been created and achieved by our people in the course of almost twelve years of freedom. Tibor Dery appealed to his audience to disseminate his anti-Party views all over the country. This is an open appeal for anti-Party actions which has nothing to do with ideological debates or with democracy. Dery's speech was received with profound indignation by, and aroused stormy protests from, the Communists who attended the debate.

Certain speeches delivered during the latest debates, the cheers and expressions of approval with which they were received, and even statements in *Irodalmi Ujsag* have clearly expressed disparagement of the leading role of the working class and the Party. Those who allege that the working

---

[10] The reference is to March 15, 1848, an important date in the revolutionary struggles of Hungarians for emancipation.

class is not active, does not participate in politics, and does not understand the significance of the 20th Congress of the CPSU defile the working class. Those who express such ideas by word of mouth or in writing do not know the truth or wish to mislead others. The Hungarian working class led the struggle for a revolutionary change even during the Horthy fascism under the leadership of the Party. It is the leading force of our socialist constructive efforts today. Its political conduct is infinitely better than the policy of those who attack the Party and our People's Democratic system. The working class fights, and will continue to fight, boldly against everything that might endanger our achievements or the application of the lessons of the 20th Congress in our country.

It cannot be considered accidental that these opportunist, harmful, and anti-Party views were voiced by those who still maintain a close and systematic contact with Imre Nagy, who has been expelled from the Party because of his anti-Marxist views, hostile to the Party and People's Democracy, and his factionalist activities.

Unfortunately, these brutal, anti-Party views were not always met by the rebuff they deserved. This could happen because these debates—especially the recent debates arranged by the Petofi Circle—were attended not only by honest people who loved the Party dearly and who wanted to help and to further socialist construction—although a number of them have been misled by demagogy—but because the debates increasingly became rallying points for individuals opposed to the Party and to the ideas of socialism, including persons who have been expelled from the Party and bourgeois elements. These people turned the debates into scenes of attacks against People's Democracy. They shouted down and disturbed the speeches which presented the correct Party attitude, but they enthusiastically applauded every attack on the Party and People's Democracy. They were not disturbed by the presence at these debates of representatives of the imperialist press who eagerly seized the opportunity to write of the slanders told about our political system.

All these events outraged honest and loyal Communists and non-Party citizens, workers and intellectuals alike. They justly expected the Central Committee to reply and to inform public opinion.

We are convinced that the overwhelming majority of the Party membership, workers, working peasants, and intellectuals, will receive with satisfaction the Central Committee's resolution, published last Sunday, which rejects and condemns the attack which is developing against the Party and People's Democracy and reminds the Party, the working class, and the working masses to be on guard. We must be on our guard. We have been reminded of this duty not only by the debates, hostile to the Party, which took place in the Petofi Circle, but also by the imperialist provocation at Poznan.[11]

The Central Committee's resolution is an appeal to every supporter of People's Democracy: do not allow the demagogues to mislead you. Only with the Party and guided by the Party can you successfully struggle for the assertion of the ideas of the 20th Congress and for the development of socialist democracy.

The Central Committee of our Party is struggling to introduce the spirit of the 20th Congress of the CPSU in the Party and in the whole country more quickly. It fights resolutely against the remnants of the cult of personality, against sectarianism, against hardened and ossified views and dogmatism. It intends to struggle with even greater determination for the all-round development of socialist democracy. But to achieve this, it is necessary that Communists should fight—above all with political weapons and conviction—for the purity of Marxism-Leninism and for the policy of the Party. They should watch over the unity of the Party, they should prevent the driving of a wedge between the Party and its leaders, they should rally behind the Central Committee in serried ranks.

---

[11] See Poland, Chapter II, Document 1.

It is the duty of the press to lend adequate support to this endeavor, to arm Communists and all supporters of our regime with ideological weapons, and to struggle for the purity of ideological and political life. Lately, the press has failed to take a sufficiently strong stand against incorrect views. It did not condemn the anti-Party atmosphere at certain debates. It was not by accident that many of our comrades have sharply criticized a *Szabad Nep* article, published under the title "The Daylight of the Spirit," which gave a false appraisal of the debates in the Petofi Circle.

Our Party does not reject everything which was said at these debates or was printed in the press. It does not condemn those who took part in the debates. This is made evident by the [Central Committee] resolution.

We must state as an established fact that these debates were actively attended by a very large number of Party and non-Party members, honest people, loyal to the Party, who love our regime. Many correct speeches were delivered during the debates, and many correct articles and workers' letters appeared in the press. Many of these criticized, and justly, the mistakes committed in the past and at present.

The Party and its Central Committee paid due attention to the correct critical remarks made about their policy and work by Party and non-Party members who are loyal to the Party and our democratic system, who wanted to help the Party to correct mistakes, to work out new and important ideological and political problems. Of course, many important and correct measures have already been taken and it is an unhealthy sign that these were not mentioned during the debates. Indeed, many mistakes were criticized at the debates whose correction has been in progress for a long time. Correct critical remarks, however, must be dealt with. The Central Committee and the Government will work out appropriate measures with a view to continuing the democratization of our public life and to enlivening our ideological and economic work.

Erroneous views were also uttered in the course of the various debates which were simply due to lack of experience or lack of information. In such cases the mistake can be corrected by explaining the correct, Marxist and Party-like point of view. One of the most important tasks of these debates is to clarify incorrect views and to develop correct ones.

The resolution of the Central Committee is not directed against these incorrect views; what it rejects are the opportunist views hostile to the Party. We must wage an energetic ideological and political struggle against opportunism, all the more so since it can easily become a weapon in the hands of the class enemy. *The Central Committee and the Party want democracy, a socialist democracy where there is no room for the enemies of the people, and where views are clarified in Party-like debates. What we need are debates which help us solve our problems, strengthen the unity of the Party, consolidate the ties between the Party and masses, solve important ideological questions, and promote the work of the Party and our productive efforts.* [Italics in *Szabad Nep*.]

The Central Committee of our Party is resolved to proceed steadily on the road defined by the 20th Congress. It raises high the banner of socialism. All those who have placed their faith and confidence in the ideas of the 20th Congress, and who want to struggle and to work with the people and for the people, must rally under this banner.

On July 15, *Szabad Nep* returned to the theme of intellectual freedom. Under the title "Freedom of Criticism and Demagogy," the paper analyzed the speeches made by Tibor Dery and Tibor Tardos at the June 27 meeting of the Petofi Circle. The speeches were found to be at variance with "Leninist principles" of Party unity. Dery "made personal attacks on several members of the Party leadership and slandered leaders of Hungarian literary life." Tardos's speech in turn "could be interpreted as an appeal for factionalism." For all this the paper could not bring itself to brand the two writers as "deliberate enemies of our regime and counterrevolutionaries."

CHAPTER III

THE RESIGNATION OF MATYAS RAKOSI
JULY, 1956

On July 18 the Central Committee of the HWP convened to effect important personal changes in its leadership and map future policy. The meeting was attended by A. I. Mikoyan, Member of the Presidium of the CPSU and Deputy Premier of the Soviet Government.[1]

1. RESOLUTIONS ADOPTED BY THE CENTRAL COMMITTEE OF THE HUNGARIAN WORKERS PARTY, JULY 18, 1956

ON RELIEVING MATYAS RAKOSI OF HIS POST[2]

THE CENTRAL COMMITTEE, establishing Matyas Rakosi's merits in the Hungarian and international labor movement, in the struggle for the better future of the Hungarian people and for a socialist Hungary, concurs with what is contained in Comrade Rakosi's letter[3] and relieves him, at his own request, of his membership in the Politburo and of the post of First Secretary of the Central Committee.[4]

---

[1] Mikoyan's presence in Budapest was not revealed until July 21 when the Central Committee session terminated, and he was seen off at the airport by a delegation of leading Hungarian Communists. The announcement noted that "he had talks with the leaders of the Government and Party." Mikoyan's itinerary took him from Budapest to Yugoslavia—where he had a two-day visit with Marshal Tito—Bulgaria, and Rumania before returning to Moscow.

[2] *Szabad Nep,* July 19, 1956.

[3] See Document 2 in this chapter.

[4] Although the resolution as well as Rakosi's letter maintained that he resigned at his own request for reasons of health, it was later revealed that the circumstances of his resignation were at variance with these claims. "Up to now it was perhaps correct not to speak of it," wrote Zoltan Horvath in an article under the title "Irrevocably Forward" (*Nepszava,* October 14, 1956), "but it would be wrong to keep silent

ON THE ELECTION OF THE FIRST SECRETARY OF
THE CENTRAL COMMITTEE

The Central Committee has unanimously elected Comrade Erno Gero[5] as First Secretary of the Central Committee.

ON ROUNDING OUT THE CENTRAL COMMITTEE

The Central Committee, in accordance with its rights established in article 20 of the organizational statute, has coopted as regular members Tivadar Matusek and Erno Molnar, candidate members of the Central Committee, as well as comrades Laszlo Foldes, Jeno Hazai, Imre Horvath, Janos Kadar, Gyula Kallai,[6] Gyorgy Marosan, and Imre Mezo. The Central Committee has coopted as candidate members comrades Jeno Fock, Jozsef Hajdu, Janos Horvath, Janos Kukucska, Karoly Nemeth, and Erno Rudas.

ON ROUNDING OUT THE POLITBURO

The Central Committee has elected as members of the Politburo comrades Janos Kadar, Karoly Kiss, Gyorgy Marosan,

---

forever about the fact that on July 18, 1956, Matyas Rakosi did not resign from the post of First Secretary to the Hungarian Workers Party, but was called upon by the supreme body of the Party to give up his post. And this was not made necessary for reasons of health but because of his complicity in all the acts for which Mihaly Farkas and certain former officers of the state security force will have to answer before the competent courts.

"One has to make it clear without ambiguity that a past record of almost half a century in the service of the workers' movement and 16 years in prison are not enough to provide safe conduct for the crimes which led to the staining of the cause of the People's Democracy and socialism and to disgracing our work of building socialism. We would be misleading our workers if we did not tell them openly that at this moment Rakosi is far away from our country and that our Party and our people do not wish that it should be otherwise."

[5] Gero, like Rakosi, had spent many years in Moscow and was his close associate.

[6] Some of the newly appointed Central Committee members served jail terms under Rakosi's regime. Of those who were being reinstated in high office, Kadar and Kallai rose to particular prominence. Kadar was elected secretary of the Central Committee while Kallai headed the cultural section of the Central Committee's secretariat.

and Jozsef Revai. At the same time it has elected comrade Janos Kadar secretary of the Central Committee. The Central Committee has elected comrades Sandor Gaspar and Sandor Ronai candidate members of the Politburo.

2. Letter of Resignation of Matyas Rakosi[7]

HONORABLE CENTRAL COMMITTEE! I request the Central Committee to relieve me of the post of First Secretary of the Central Committee and of my membership in the Politburo. One of the reasons for my request is that I am in my 65th year and that my illness with which I have now been suffering for 2 years with growingly aggravated effect hinders me from discharging the work devolving upon the First Secretary of the Central Committee. Furthermore, the mistakes I have committed in the field of the cult of personality and socialist legality make it difficult for the Party leadership to concentrate our Party's attention to the fullest extent upon the tasks lying ahead of us. By asking to be relieved of my post I desire to serve the great cause of our Party, our working people, and of socialism.

(*Signed*)   Matyas Rakosi

3. Oral Statement by Matyas Rakosi Concerning His Resignation[8]

HONORABLE CENTRAL COMMITTEE! May I add a few supplementary remarks to my request. As regards my condition of health, I have been suffering hypertension for the past 2 years, my blood pressure is rising, and a few days ago the physicians sent to the Politburo a report from which I would like to quote one sentence: "We do not in any way consider Comrade Rakosi's present condition as satisfactory and consequently we ask for the most urgent intervention so as to prevent a deterioration of his condition."

---

[7] *Szabad Nep,* July 19, 1956.
[8] *Ibid.*

My comrades frequently mentioned in the past two years that I do not visit the factories as often as I used to in the past. They were right, the only thing they did not know is that this was due to the deterioration of my health. My state of health began to tell on the quality and amount of work I was able to perform, a fact that is bound to cause harm to the Party in such an important post. So much about the state of my health.

As regards the mistakes that I committed in the field of the "cult of personality" and the violation of socialist legality, I admitted them at the meetings of the Central Committee in June, 1953, and I have made the same admission repeatedly ever since. I have also exercised self-criticism publicly.

After the 20th Congress of the CPSU and Comrade Khrushchev's speech[9] it became clear to me that the weight and effect of these mistakes were greater than I had thought and that the harm done to our Party through these mistakes was much more serious than I had previously believed.

These mistakes have made our Party's work more difficult, they diminished the strength of attractiveness of the Party and of the People's Democracy, they hindered the development of the Leninist norms of Party life, of collective leadership, of constructive criticism, and self-criticism, of democratism in Party and state life, and of the initiative and creative power of the wide masses of the working class.

Finally, these mistakes offered an extremely wide opportunity for attack to the enemy. In their totality, the mistakes that I committed in the most important post of Party work have caused serious harm to our socialist development as a whole.

It was up to me to take the lead in the repairing of these mistakes. If rehabilitation has at times proceeded sluggishly and with intermittent breaks, if a certain relapse was noticed last year in the liquidation of the cult of personality, if criticism

---

[9] See *The Anti-Stalin Campaign and International Communism*, pp. 1-89.

and self-criticism together with collective leadership have developed at a slow pace, if sectarian and dogmatic views have not been combated resolutely enough—then for all this, undoubtedly, serious responsibility weighs upon me, having occupied the post of First Secretary of the Party.

Honorable Central Committee! It is more than four decades since I became an active fighter in the socialist movement. I was present when our Party made its first tentative steps. I took part in the fights of the Hungarian commune and in the struggle against the terror of the Horthy regime. After the long years of imprisonment I was allowed to see the liberation of our country by the powerful Soviet Union and I was allowed to be there, in the first ranks, when Hungarian Communists succeeded, amidst strenuous and hard fights, in carrying to triumph the great cause of socialism in our country. I am certain that our Party, relying on our working people, will now again advance united and in the spirit of the 20th Congress, by overcoming all difficulties and all enemies, and by gaining strength in the battles, along the road of democratism and socialist construction toward a happier future.

Following Rakosi's resignation, his successor, Erno Gero, delivered the Politburo's report to the Central Committee. In part Gero's speech was a diatribe against disturbing influences in the Party and the enemies of the people's democratic regime:[10]

The changed international situation compels American imperialism and the other imperialist circles to change their tactics, but they do not give up the struggle, they simply continue it by other means and methods. They seek to disrupt the unity of the socialist camp. They try to exploit the fact that with the liquidation of the cult of personality which had been built up around Stalin and with the development of socialist, proletarian democracy, elements who flourished under the old antipopular regimes are once again beginning to stir in the People's Democracies. They try to mobilize these elements by exploiting

---

[10] *Szabad Nep,* July 19, 1956. Substantial portions of Gero's speech were reproduced in *Pravda,* July 20, 1956.

the opportunities provided by democracy, in behalf of their reactionary, imperialist interests.

The imperialists do everything in their power to create trouble in the People's Democracies by relying on these internal reactionary elements, to try to loosen the relations between the USSR and the People's Democracies, and to attempt to weaken the socialist camp. When we say that with the recession of the threat of a direct war the ideological and political struggle becomes more acute, then we must add to this forms of struggle which are very far from ideological in character, namely, the smuggling of spies, diversionists, and provocateurs into the People's Democracies and the Soviet Union and the regular provocative incursions of military planes[11] and the gangster attack committed against the peaceful passengers of one of our civil airplanes a few days ago[12], etc. Furthermore, we have to bear in mind such forms as for instance the bloody provocation of Poznan. It would be a grave mistake not to draw a lesson from the Poznan provocation as regards our situation and our tasks. As a matter of fact, the enemy openly mentions—more than one imperialist paper and radio station did mention—that the enemy aims at having "Hungarian Poznans." Hungry pigs dream of acorns! . . .

Touch wood, no Poznan has occurred in Hungary, although one imperialist radio station boastfully described the Petofi Circle events [of June 27] as a "little Poznan." There were sound features in the Petofi Circle and several of the motions made there should be taken to heart, as was clearly stated in the June 30 resolution of the Central Committee. The Petofi Circle included many honest people, loyal to the Party and to our People's Democracy, among them not a few Communists, who

---

[11] The reference is to alleged violations of airspace over the satellites and the Soviet Union by U. S. military planes which the governments of the USSR, Poland, Czechoslovakia, and Hungary officially protested against in the summer of 1956.

[12] The reference is to the flight of a group of Hungarians who on July 13, 1956, "kidnaped" the captain and crew of a passenger plane in midair and at gunpoint forced them to land in Germany. Crew and passengers who expressed a preference for returning to Hungary were permitted to do so. The airplane was returned on July 27, 1956.

cherish the Party, are unquestionably loyal to socialism, are good Hungarian patriots as well as adherents of proletarian internationalism. At the same time, however, it must also be said that in and around the Petofi Circle a second political center began to form, which challenged the nation's only real, political center, the Central Committee of the Hungarian Workers Party. It is beyond doubt that this [challenge] had an organized character.

In part, however, Gero took a defensive stand for the lack of genuine improvement in conditions since the 20th Congress of the CPSU.

Before and after the 20th Congress the policy of our Party was essentially correct. The main line of our Party corresponded to the building of socialism and the interests of our people and country. After the 20th Congress, at the meeting of the Central Committee held last March[13] there was no possibility for the Central Committee itself to elaborate in detail the tasks that had to be performed in the spirit of the 20th Congress and with due regard to the specific conditions prevailing in Hungary. Perhaps it would have been more advisable to hold the meeting of the Central Committee 1 or 2 days later and to pass, at the meeting itself, resolutions that would have embodied concrete tasks. In the circumstances the Central Committee was only able to give the Politburo general instructions and directives on how to work out the plans. The Politburo actually began to perform the task.

In our opinion, the line of the Politburo was correct after the 20th Congress. Yet for some time there was a certain wavering and procrastination in the enforcement and implementation of the correct political conception and political attitude. This was due partly to the fact that Comrade Matyas Rakosi, First Secretary of the Central Committee, was unable, though striving to do so, fully to reorganize his own work and the work of the Secretariat of the Politburo and of the Central Committee to conform with the new requirements. One must bear in mind that the Secretariat of the Central Committee is mainly responsible for the enforcement of the resolutions of the Politburo and Central Committee.

---

[13] See Chapter I, Document 1.

A certain part was also played in this state of affairs by the grave mistakes committed in the field of the cult of personality and legality, mainly before July, 1953. The liquidation of these mistakes was begun in 1953, later got bogged down, started again with renewed ardor, and is now nearing completion.

Finally, the uncertainty was also partly caused by the fact that for various reasons the Politburo did not feel that it could rely on the unanimous support of the Central Committee. They felt that no unanimous views were held within the Central Committee as regards relations to the Politburo or to its individual members, and that on the other hand there was no full unanimity among the members of the Central Committee as regards the policy of the Party. In this respect the onus must mainly rest with the Politburo for failing to show enough resolve and courage in eliminating the retarding factors; in combating assiduously the ideological-political errors of the past. . . .

Although there were debates in Party organizations, the membership became more active, and the work of the Party improved, the most important questions touching on the fate of the country were not discussed in the first place within the Party, under the direction of the Central Committee, the Politburo, and the leading organs of the Party. In addition, it must be noted—though this is by no means of decisive importance—that the central leadership of DISZ, or more accurately its executive committee, erred when it permitted guidance of the Petofi Circle to slip from its hands. It was a serious mistake to permit the direction of *Szabad Nep* and of the press in general to slip out of our hands, and we did not guide our broadcasting properly, which, naturally caused no small confusion among our cadres, activists, members, and honest workers who cling to the Party and support our People's Democracy.

The Party's future policy was elaborated in a resolution adopted at the close of its three-day session.

4. With Party Unity for a Socialist Democracy
Resolution Adopted by the Central Committee of the Hungarian Workers Party, July 18-21, 1956[14]

THE 20th CONGRESS OF THE Communist Party of the Soviet Union has had an exceptionally great impact on the whole political, economic, cultural, and social life of our country.

Our Party, the working class, and the working people received with joy and enthusiasm the historic statements of the 20th Congress about the consolidation of peace, the continued progress of socialism, and the possibility of establishing unity in the workers' movement. The Leninist statements about the active and peaceful coexistence of countries with different social systems, about the various roads leading to socialism, and the bold conclusion about the possibility of avoiding war and safeguarding peace have made a deep impression on the Hungarian working people. The working people's attention has been arrested particularly by the Sixth Five-Year Plan which aims to raise the level of Soviet economy in all fields and to insure the material, cultural, and social progress of the Soviet people.

The Central Committee, expressing the opinion of the entire Hungarian working people, establishes with gratification the fact that international tension has relaxed to a certain extent, and that there is a possibility of liquidating the so-called cold war.

The Central Committee states as a fact that the bold step taken by the Communist Party of the Soviet Union to disclose and to eliminate completely the harmful consequences of the cult of personality has lifted a heavy burden weighing on the international labor movement, and will lead to the further flourishing of the international labor movement. This also bears evidence to the fact that the Central Committee of the CPSU was and is guided by the Leninist spirit which continues to develop the ideas of the great Lenin and applies Marxism-Leninism to our age in a creative way.

[14] *Szabad Nep,* July 23, 1956.

The Central Committee points out that certain imperialist and internal reactionary circles which are increasing their clandestine activities want to distract attention from the historic resolutions adopted by the 20th Congress in the interest of the peace of the Soviet people and all peoples and the victorious progress of socialism, and endeavor to turn the attention of the public to those negative phenomena which were apparent in the work of Stalin in order to disturb the unity of the international Communist and workers' movement and to confine to narrow limits the decisive impact on the peoples of the ideas of the 20th Congress.

The Central Committee is in full agreement with the analysis contained in the June 30, 1956,[15] resolution of the CPSU Central Committee on the emergence and spreading of the cult of personality, and establishes as a fact that the cult of personality does not spring from the essential characteristics of the socialist system. On the contrary, it is alien to the socialist system. Socialism, as a genuinely democratic and popular regime, eliminates the cult of personality and its harmful consequences—wherever it has arisen—and further develops socialist democracy.

The Central Committee regards unity among the countries of the socialist world system, and the strengthening of international solidarity among socialist countries and all the communist and socialist parties of the world, as the main guarantee of safeguarding world peace and the people's socialist progress.

I. PRINCIPAL MEASURES TAKEN BY THE PARTY AND
THE GOVERNMENT IN RECENT MONTHS

The Central Committee in recent months has decided on its guiding line for future policy, relying on the resolutions passed by the Third Congress of the HWP, before that by the June, 1953, and other important sessions, as well as on the rich experiences of the building of socialism in Hungary and

---

[15] See *The Anti-Stalin Campaign and International Communism*, pp. 275-306.

on the lessons which can be drawn from the 20th Congress of the CPSU.

The Party's objective has been to put the economic problems of socialist construction into the forefront of its work, to organize the struggle for the fulfillment of production plans in industry, agriculture, and the other fields of economic life, and further to increase output and cut prime costs. The Party will exert continued efforts to raise the living standard of the workers, and first of all of the working class, to increase the productive security of the working peasantry, and to improve the social and cultural circumstances of the working people.

The Party and Government have taken steps to eliminate bureaucracy and exaggerated centralism, which have hampered our economic progress, and have begun initial preparatory work for a radical improvement of economic management. The Party has begun the great work of the continued democratization of our state life, and is firmly continuing to proceed along the path of consolidating socialist legality.

As regards international relations, the Party consistently pursues a policy aimed at deepening cooperation with socialist countries and promoting active and peaceful coexistence among countries with different social systems.

1. The joint efforts of the Party, the Government, and the workers to fulfill and overfulfill production plans were, in general, successful. Industry considerably overfulfilled the production plans laid down for the first half of 1956, in spite of the fact that a number of unfavorable factors had an adverse effect on production.

In the first half of 1956 the output of socialist industry exceeded by 6.8 percent the output of the corresponding period in 1955, and labor productivity was 4.9 percent higher than in the same period last year. This shows that the favorable development which began in industry in 1955 continues. In agriculture—as far as can be established today—a fair average crop can be expected.

There was progress also in the field of export trade which is so important from the point of view of the people's economy. In this first half of the year the balance of our foreign trade was active; this means that if we increase our efforts our foreign debts will decrease by the end of the year.

In spite of this promising development, there are still considerable difficulties in our people's economy, especially as regards the raw material supplies to the factories (e.g., difficulties in fuel supply).

2. On the basis of the results achieved in production, and acting on the initiative of the Party and the trade unions, the Government has fixed the minimum basic wage payable to time-rate workers at 650 forints. In consequence, 170,000 workers received wage increases. In several economic branches the Government has effected a wage settlement which, coupled with wage increases, has made the wage system more just and realistic, and has introduced a premium bonus system which insures an increased material interest in production. On May 1 the Government cut the prices of 6,500 commodities by 10 to 40 percent. This has meant for the workers the saving of some 900 million forints a year. The Government has cut the working time of those workers who are employed in jobs harmful to their health from 48 hours to from 36 to 42 hours a week.

As a result of the Party's solicitude and the measures taken by the Government, the supply of food and industrial consumer articles has improved during the past few months. Providing town populations with meat supplies, which has been a difficult problem for some years past, has been significantly improved, and this is true to a large extent also in the countryside.

In the first half of 1956 retail trade showed an increase of about 8 percent, to a value of 1.6 billion forints higher than in the corresponding period of 1955. In spite of the improving trend of commodity supplies, trade has not yet been able to meet demand completely in many articles.

3. The measures elaborated and carried out by the Government, on the initiative of the Party, with a view to improving economic management have been aimed primarily at liquidating the conspicuous absurdities of exaggerated centralism. These measures have had, generally speaking, a favorable influence, but the resolutions about rationalization and the merger of some counties, county districts, and administrative areas have created uncertainty in several places in Government and economic administration. Important measures have been taken in the past few months, or are being elaborated, regarding the simplification of the technical and financial administration of capital investments, the introduction of commercial methods in the raw material economy, granting greater independence to enterprises and banks regarding financial economy, insuring an elaboration of plans with greater care, and reducing the number of plan-preparations. It is particularly important that plans in agriculture impose fewer limitations on the producers than hitherto. Public discussions on the Second Five-Year Plan took place with the participation of the largest number of workers; 22 great enterprises have already independently prepared their Second Five-Year Plan. All these changes exercise an influence in the direction of further decentralization and democratization of the economic system, and the correct utilization of material incentives.

4. The Party has initiated several measures to increase the independence and to consolidate the material basis of local councils. Thus the local councils' sphere of economy has been enlarged and their financial and budgetary rights have been increased. The first steps have been taken to insure greater democracy in the work of the Presidential Council and the National Assembly and to improve the work of parliamentarians.

Steps have been taken to consolidate legality and, especially, to eliminate those infringements of law which affected large segments of the workers. On the initiative of the Party, the Government has settled certain problems relating to labor law.   Settlement of the case of those working peasants listed as kulaks is of special importance in the villages.

The elimination of the consequences of grave violations of law, committed in the past in certain political criminal cases, has begun during the past few months and is nearing completion, and the entire process will be completed in a short time. Innocent people, revolutionaries, Communists, veteran fighters of the labor movement, and our comrades who were condemned prior to 1953 on the basis of trumped-up charges and as a result of illegal procedures have come back to our ranks.   We are again struggling alongside them to build socialism.   The return to Party life and to work by the unjustly condemned comrades has strengthened the confidence of the Communists, of the working people, in the Party.

Altogether, 474 cases were reviewed in the course of the rehabilitation procedure.   The great majority of these have already been rehabilitated.   The judicial rehabilitation, the settlement of Party and trade union membership, the material compensation of, and assignment of functions to our formerly jailed Party members has been almost completed.   In this respect, however, we have additional tasks ahead.   Among those Party members who won merits in the past and were wrongly arrested are Ferenc Donath, Zoltan Horvath, Janos Kadar, Gyula Kallai, Gyorgy Marosan,[16] Gyorgy Palffy, Laszlo Rajk, Pal Schiffer, Tibor Szonyi,[17] and Imre Vajda, former members of the Central Committee; Geza Losonczy and Istvan Szirmai, former candidate members of the Central Committee; and others who have been rehabilitated.   Their expulsion from the Party has been annulled, and some of them have again been elected members of the Central Committee.   Arpad Szakasits has been judicially rehabilitated, and the investigation into the problem of his Party membership is in progress.[18]

---

[16] See Document 1 in this chapter.

[17] See Chapter V.

[18] Szakasits is a former Social Democratic leader, President of Hungary from 1948 to 1950, when he was arrested.

Measures have been taken to remedy the wrongs suffered by the members of the rehabilitated comrades' families.

5. The normalization of state relations between Yugoslavia and Hungary was the most important event in our foreign policy during the past month. The sincere desire of both parties to reach an agreement has made a solution of disputed economic questions possible. Hungary has strengthened ties with the other socialist countries. During the last session of CMEA (the Council of Mutual Economic Assistance) in Berlin,[19] socialist countries coordinated their long-term economic development plans in many respects. We have successfully developed our trade contracts with a number of capitalist countries. The Government has abolished the technical frontier barrier, which has evoked favorable reaction from the world's progressive public opinion.

6. The social activity of the working class and the working masses has increased significantly during the past few months. Hundreds of thousands took part in discussions dealing with the plan. The interest of the workers has increased in the affairs of the enterprises, public life, and international events. Political life has become very lively during the past few months. Since 1953 the Party has waged a struggle against the cult of personality, for establishing collective leadership, and for asserting Leninist principles in Party life. Our development has become livelier. The struggle for the complete elimination of the harmful consequences of the cult of personality in the life of the state and Party have gained in intensity. Party democracy and bold Communist criticism have been developed, fruitful discussions gained in momentum.

Since the 20th Congress our Party, state, social, and economic organizations and our public life as a whole have been imbued to an increasing extent with the spirit of a healthy and developing democracy.

---

[19] May 18-25, 1956.

II. THE TASKS AHEAD

The Central Committee notes that on the basis of results achieved during the past few years and the past few months and by eliminating mistakes, further measures must be taken in the next few months to extend socialist democracy and to tighten Party and state discipline in accordance with the principles of democratic centralism.

1. Our Tasks in the Fields of Industry and Agriculture. In the course of building socialism one must concentrate on the mastering of economic tasks. Therefore the greatest attention must be focused on the tasks of the Second Five-Year Plan. During the Second Five-Year Plan, we must continue to develop socialist industrialization on the basis of a substantial development of techniques so that the production of socialist industry in 1960 will be 47 to 50 percent higher than in 1955. In determining the principal proportions of industrial development the starting point must be the fact that the basis of the development of the entire national economy and of technical progress is heavy industry. Accordingly, in industry the manufacturing of the means of production will be increased by 58 to 60 percent and that of consumer goods by 38 to 40 percent.

The increase in production of socialist industry during the Second Five-Year Plan will make it possible for industry, as the leading branch of the national economy, to meet domestic demand as well as export requirements to a greater extent. In the interest of increasing industrial production—relying on technical development and close cooperation with the socialist countries—we must insure substantially greater utilization than hitherto of existing industrial equipment, the gradual replacement of obsolete machines by new ones, the smooth supply of raw materials, the even rhythm of production, and, as a result of all these, a steadily rising productivity.

In agriculture, through the further development of socialist large-scale cultivation and by increasing the production of the individual farmers, a steady increase in production is the main task.   Between 1955-1960 total production should be about 27 percent higher than during the previous Five-Year Plan.   It is necessary to demonstrate *the superiority of agricultural producer cooperatives in a convincing manner by their economic and cultural prosperity,* so that as a result of this, the majority of the peasantry adopt the road of socialist large-scale farming. The Central Committee *is firmly resolved to consolidate and strengthen agricultural producer cooperatives and to implement the policy of socialist transformation of agriculture.*   This is emphasized the more since recently the development of views hostile to the producer cooperatives has shown renewed momentum.   The Party, relying on local councils and other mass organizations, must carry out a continuous and constant work of enlightenment among the peasantry in the interest of showing the justification of the producer cooperatives.   Besides emphasizing the advantages of the agricultural producer cooperatives we must assist, more than hitherto and without any restriction, in the formation of the lower-type agricultural producer cooperative groups and their gradual progress along the road of cooperative farming.

We must give effective support to the agricultural trading cooperative movement, and within this, to simple, special groupings for the use of machines, for fruit and vegetable growing, beekeeping, calf rearing, and so forth.   Let both the Party and the state give increased assistance to the formation of new groups and to the development of already existing production groups.   Let these be the schools of cooperation and collective work, of learning the advantages of cooperative farming for individual peasants so that in this way too they can be drawn nearer to the producer cooperatives which our Party continues to regard, as before, the most important tool in the socialist transformation of agriculture.

In the course of developing the producer-cooperative movement, one must most systematically insure the principle of voluntariness.

We must see to it that during the Second Five-Year Plan the already existing, several-years-old, cooperative farms become exemplary socialist large-scale enterprises; their production level should show a steady upward trend, outproducing the private farms by ever greater margins year after year. Much assistance must be given to newly-formed producer cooperatives to overcome their initial difficulties, to lay the foundation of their work so that their production can surpass as quickly as possible the average results of the individual farms. In order to increase the productivity of the producer cooperatives, the assertion of cooperative democracy must be insured in every respect so that members can decide the affairs of their cooperative and establish their own rules in conformity, however, with the sample statute for cooperatives.

It is indispensable for the steady increase in agricultural production that individual farmers also increase their production. Therefore we must insure for them those material conditions by which they can utilize their existing production capacity.

2. Raising the Workers' Standard of Living. During the Second Five-Year Plan the real wages of workers and employees must be increased on an average by at least 25 percent per capita, and during the same period the income in cash and in kind of the peasantry similarly by about 25 percent.

The carrying out of production plans is the firm basis of the further raising of the working people's standard of living also in 1956.

a) In the interest of increasing the well-being of workers and employees this year:

the Central Committee recommends to the Government on the basis of economic results achieved the abolition of peace-loans. This will result in the first place in an increase of the material means of the workers and employees;

the Government should make preparations already this year for the equitable solution—in so far as the economic situation makes it possible—of the most burning questions in connection with old age pensions;

the Central Committee also recommends that the Government make efforts for further improving the supply of the population and to give special care to maintaining the level of the meat supply.

b) In order to increase the security of produce for the working peasantry further steps must be taken to see that the measures affecting the peasantry's relations to the state should be free of bureaucratic obstruction. The pensioning of disabled and old members of cooperatives must be institutionally solved—using the material means of the cooperatives. Steps must also be taken to insure a better supply of industrial goods for the villages, in particular to raise the sale of goods which service production.

c) The measures to be taken for the improvement of the situation of workers and employees will at the same time improve the situation of the intelligentsia too. Moreover, parallel with the democratization of our public life, greater opportunities must be given to intellectuals in their creative work. Respect toward the working intelligentsia should be based on its work and its present behavior. In the future greater scope than hitherto must be given to intellectuals in Party, state, economic, and other fields of community work.

3. Improving Economic Management. The better organization of production and the better meeting of the workers' increased needs demand the gradual elimination of excessive centralization which prevails in economic life. Of course, the effort aimed at developing democratism in economic life must not influence the order and continuity of production.

a) One must bear in mind that the simplification of economic management sets free manpower, the employment of which must be insured. In the view of the Central Committee, a substantial part of the released manpower must find work in the field of production. This, however, must take place in an organized manner. Comprehensive manpower regrouping cannot yet take place this year.

b) With the gradual decentralization of economic life the principle of greater independence of managers from the ministers downwards to factory directors, foremen, and engineers must be observed.

c) Besides maintaining the Leninist principle of one-man management, we must increase the role of the workers in every economic activity of the factory, workshop, and enterprise. We must find ways and means so that more and more people are able to carry out the work of planning, organization, and direction, so that the creative activity of the workers unfolds as broadly as possible.

d) We must gradually improve our wage and premium system so that the workers can be directly interested in economical production, in the quality of production, and in the economical use of raw materials.

e) Besides the significant measures under way, which this year and next will considerably improve the situation, the Central Committee deems it necessary that a thorough and careful examination of the methods of economic management be undertaken now and measures worked out for raising the all-round standard of economic management. At the same time the Central Committee reaffirms that the central direction of production, the centralized method of planning, remains unaltered as the basic principle of economic management, because, aside from the development of the creative energy of the working masses, in it lies one of the principal advantages of the socialist system over capitalism.

4. Further Democratization of State Life. The strengthening and perfecting of the people's democratic state is one of the most important prerequisites for the building of socialism. For this reason our Party must give every support to the further development of our people's democratic regime, to the improvement of the work of the state organs.

The Central Committee states that in its fundamental traits our state system is thoroughly democratic. Our state is a worker-peasant state in which an ever growing role is being played also by the progressive intelligentsia. *In our country the power is in the hands of the working class in alliance with the working peasantry. In the exercise of power the working peasantry too is taking part under the leadership of the working class.* This is the decisive, characteristic feature which makes it different from bourgeois-type states, as it is a thousand times more democratic than those states. Our basic task is to further unfold the democratic contents of our state, increase the role and authority of elected state organs, and include the working people in the state administration.

a) The rights of the National Assembly must be asserted to a greater extent in the most important questions of internal and foreign policy as well as economic and cultural life. The most important measures concerning the rights and duties of citizens must be enacted through thorough and fruitful debates.

Deputies, in accordance with the Constitution, should establish permanent contact with their constituents, keeping them regularly informed of their activities; and let them (the deputies) utilize the experience of their constituents and also their criticism and their suggestions in their work in the National Assembly. It is the task of the ministries and local councils to support the deputies in their work. The constitutional provision according to which the constituents can at any time revoke the mandate of the representative who failed to live up to their confidence must be implemented. In order to make this possible we must change the electoral law; instead of the present system of list-ballot, which does not permit direct contact with the electorate, the single-member constituency system must be introduced.

b) The councils constitute the basis for our democratic state systems. The Central Committee is of the opinion that it must be insured even more explicitly than it was done already in the existing laws that local councils have at their disposal both politically and professionally well-trained workers and financial means and have the scope of authority to discharge the tasks entrusted to them. It must be insured that local councils be able fully to discharge their administrative and managerial tasks so that they can truly lead the economic, cultural, and social life of the villages. Let them insure the active participation and control of the citizens in the exercise of state power and state administration. In this way the work of local council members done in the interest of the electors will become more effective. We have to increase the spheres of authority and of administration of the local council executive committees and the special administrative bodies. The economic and administrative questions which come under the exclusive authority of the local councils must be defined. The ministries and other national bodies must carry out only special direction and control, as well as the harmonization of the tasks of the different regions. In connection with the reorganization of the local councils' work, special attention should be paid to the strengthening of district councils so that in most cases the people should be able to settle their affairs at the local councils.

For eliminating the bureaucratic traits of our state apparatus, for the sake of decentralization, and for the active participation of the workers in the administration, the structure of the state administration must be simplified. This purpose will be served also by a reduction in the number and the reorganization of the counties, districts, and boroughs which will have to coincide with the increase of the local councils' economic independence and authority.

The Central Committee asks the Council of Ministers to submit this question for approval to the National Assembly in the autumn. The creation of new counties, districts, and boroughs must be completed by January 1, 1957.

The Central Committee deems it necessary that the Government should revise the rigid measures affecting the citizens' right to settle in the largest towns.

c) The work of unfolding the democratization of our state life must be coupled with the widest activity of enlightenment aimed at consolidating civic discipline and strict compliance with civic obligations. The strengthening of state discipline must constantly be borne in mind in every phase of broadening democracy and working toward decentralization, and in our further work.

5. Further Consolidation of Socialist Legality. The further consolidation of socialist legality requires important measures in the field of the revision of laws and decrees, as regards the penal law and the administration of justice, improvement in the work of the organs of the Ministry of the Interior, and effective control of these organs.

a) It is a fundamental requirement of socialist legality that in every field of state and social life there be legal rules corresponding to economic and social conditions which are comprehensible to everybody and that these rules be observed.

We have to create a system of laws and decrees embracing the entire life of the People's Democracy and socialism. This work has to be completed with the participation of theoretical and practical experts and the general public. The preparation of the penal code and the civil code must be speeded up and the sphere of jurisdiction and activity of the state authorities must be defined in a clear and easily comprehensible law.

b) In the interest of defending the workers' interests our judicial authorities must continue to be firm and resolute against those who gravely offend the security of our state or socialist legality. In regard to workers who went wrong by committing lesser crimes we must apply educational measures to an ever wider degree. In their entire activity the judicial authorities must systematically assert, in every phase of legal procedure, the socialist principles of the legal stipulations of the penal code:

in their work the judicial authorities must absolutely insure that nobody's guilt is established on the basis of his own admission unless supported by evidence;

in the course of the investigation, detention or remand in custody can be ordered only in exceptional cases, when warrented by circumstances;

for enforcing legality the prosecution must restrict more effectively the measures taken by the state security authorities in connection with criminal proceedings;

the supervision of the Court of Justice by the prosecution must be strengthened, and while proportionately lessening the parallel activities of the Ministry of Justice, at the same time the court decisions must enunciate the directives based on constitutional principles emanating from the Supreme Court of Justice;

the independence of judges must be consolidated. After the territorial reorganization, independent bodies of judges and people's prosecutors must be elected;

in the interest of securing socialist legality and uniformity in legal proceedings the far too wide scope of authority of the military tribunals and military prosecution must be revised and reduced. The sphere of competence of the civil law courts must be gradually widened to include certain important areas of the state administration, such as disputes arising from labor relations, cases involving property rights, pensions, producer cooperatives, and so forth.

c) The Ministry of the Interior has achieved significant successes in the fight against the real enemy, namely those who strove to overthrow the people's democratic regime, against economic wreckers, spies, and saboteurs. The Party and the state, however, must take further steps to eliminate from the organs of the Ministry of the Interior on the field of Party and state control those incorrect views and remnants of inquiry methods which prevail as a result of previous infringements of the law, and to reassert unfailingly the spirit of socialist legality. Proposals to this effect will soon be submitted for approval to the competent Party and state organs.

The basic principle which must be borne in mind in the solution of these problems is that the organs of the Ministry of the Interior when performing their duties must serve the security of the Hungarian People's Republic and its citizens. Every Hungarian citizen must have the rock-firm conviction that he is being protected against infringements of law by our Party, our state, and our entire society.

d) The Central Committee calls the attention of the Party, the state, and judicial and social organs to the increased protection of the rights of the workers. Party organs must regard as one of their important duties to examine, and if possible to rectify, those wrongs as a result of which honest workers have been placed in an unjust and unfavorable situation as a consequence of former distrustful and often bureaucratic and harsh measures.

e) The Central Committee attaches great importance to the unfailing enforcement of socialist legality and to the effective improvement of the work of state security and judicial organs. It regards with confidence the honest efforts of the comrades working in this field and will help them in their important work in the future.

6. Improvement of Ideological Work. In scientific, cultural, agitation and propaganda work the struggle against the remnants of the cult of personality must be intensified, dogmatism must be overcome, and education must aim to insure independent Marxist thinking in the domains of science, culture, and propaganda. At the same time we must struggle against bourgeois ideology and for the socialist education of the working masses.

a) The development of the various branches of science, including that of the social sciences, renders the emergence of creative debates necessary. Only patient and convincing arguments and ideological struggles have a place in these debates. Attacks on Marxism-Leninism or People's Democracy must not, however, be injected into these debates.

The further democratization of the scientific workers' organizations and associations must be promoted. We must insure that social organizations become schools of socialist education and forums of scientific debates. Closer cooperation must be created between our leading economic organs, on the one hand, and the Hungarian Academy of Sciences and scientific associations, on the other hand, inviting the latter to join in the preliminary work on our development plans.

It must be insured that the representatives of science and students can acquaint themselves, according to their material circumstances, with the scientific achievements and periodicals of foreign countries. The popularization and publication abroad of the achievements of Hungarian science must be made possible to a greater extent.

b) In the field of culture the objective must be to insure that books, theaters, films, music, and the arts are playing their socialist educational role to an ever greater extent. A struggle must, therefore, be waged for the assertion of the principles of socialist realism; however, it must also be made possible for progressive trends, which are pointing toward socialist realism, to assert themselves more fully than before. This does not mean, naturally, that the Marxist criticism of their shortcomings will be abandoned. It must also be made possible for the various schools, new trends and endeavors which exist in socialist realism, and for other related trends to assert themselves, thereby enriching the forms of artistic expression.

The scope of cultural and artistic associations must be increased as regards the education of their members and the solution of their problems, thereby insuring the development of democratic life in these associations. The Communist members of these associations will have to play a great and important role. Party discipline among them must be strengthened primarily by means of ideological persuasion.

Simultaneously with the increasing democratization of scientific, artistic, and cultural life the Party's leading role in ideology must be increased with the assistance of Party members who are working in these fields, and with the help of the respective organs of the Party and the state.

c) Agitation and propaganda must be improved very considerably. Particularly great attention must be devoted to propaganda on economic problems.

The press, the radio, as well as agitation and propaganda, can point to successes in developing the creative initiative of the popular masses, in promoting initiative in the criticism of the harmful consequences of the cult of personality, and in bringing into the open the just criticism of the masses. However, neither the press nor the radio have taken up a sufficiently energetic attitude against inimical views often directed against the Party and People's Democracy which have recently cropped up here and there and against demagogy which has been calculated to mislead the masses. Sometimes they even helped to disseminate these erroneous and harmful views.

Therefore, agitation and propaganda in general, and the work of the press and the radio in particular, must improve quickly and definitely. With the help of statistics, the workers must be thoroughly and systematically informed in all domains of our economic life, thus mobilizing them for the solution of the problems of socialist construction.

7. Mass Organizations of the Workers and the Patriotic People's Front. The widening scope of democratization of our social sphere significantly increases the role played by the mass organizations, and the tasks of our Party in regard to the mass organizations. Our Party organizations must devote much greater attention to every mass organization and mass movement of the workers: the Patriotic People's Front, the trade unions, the Union of Working Youth, the Hungarian-Soviet Friendship Society, the farmers' trading cooperatives, sport organizations, and so forth. The work of Communists in the Party cells who are active in these organizations must be improved everywhere. With their help and by their exemplary attitude they must encourage the leading organs of the mass organizations to be spontaneous and militant, to perform their specific tasks in their own spheres of activity, to elaborate proper forms of organization and the content and methods of the mass-work.

The Party must pay special attention to the developing People's Front movement, to the largest and most important organizations of the workers and employees, the trade unions, and the Union of Working Youth, the DISZ.

a) The Patriotic People's Front, which includes the overwhelming majority of the population, manifests in the most pronounced way the alliance between the working class and the other working sectors of the people. The objective of the PPF is to unite, in a creative way, the forces of the workers, peasants, intellectuals, and working men, in other words, of all the progressive patriotic elements of our country. The People's Front must be given the task of striving, first of all, for the consolidation of national and popular unity. Its main sphere of activity consists, therefore, in rallying every peace-loving and patriotic worker behind the peace front. The PPF movement must explain and popularize the measures taken by the Party and the Government in the interest of socialist progress, to make our economy flourish and to improve the people's material, cultural, and social living conditions. Let it educate the workers to have a high sense of duty in the spirit of our patriotic traditions.

The PPF must increasingly help the local councils in discharging their duties, and the local councils should rely to a greater extent on the PPF movement in their work.

It must be insured, to a greater extent than up to now, that every patriotic, democratic, and peace-loving worker, housewife, small-man, student, etc., take an active part in the PPF movement.

It is necessary that a large number of democratically-minded and peace-loving non-Party members, workers, working peasants, intellectuals, and others, regardless of their nationality, general world view, and religious conviction, be elected to the executive boards of PPF organizations.

The Communists must establish good and friendly cooperation with the non-Party members rallied behind the PPF committees and the PPF movement, and employ patient enlightenment and persuasion in the PPF movement. Party members and Party organizations must encourage and promote the development of constructive criticism in the PPF committees and meetings in the elaboration and execution of constructive and useful proposals aimed at advancing village and community life, and consolidating a progressive, constructive, and democratic public spirit. Party members and Party organizations must participate in the work of the PPF committees and in the PPF movement in an exemplary way, thereby demonstrating that the PPF movement is a genuine, great, political movement which unites the working class, the working peasantry, the intelligentsia, and the middle strata.

b) During the past few months unions have taken an increasing share in the efforts to raise output and productivity. They have mobilized the workers more successfully to fulfill production plans, to strengthen order and discipline in the factories, and to take part in the discussions of the Second Five-Year Plan directives. Trade unions must continue to put production to the forefront of their activities, because increased production is the chief prerequisite of the success of the policy to improve the working people's living conditions.

Trade unions must devote particularly great attention to the development of the technical level, to raising the technical standards of industry, and the specialized training of workers.

Trade unions must adopt a more determined and more militant attitude on protecting the interests of the workers, they must fight to insure that collective contracts are respected, they must take bolder initiatives, and they must consistently focus their activity on improving the workers' living conditions.

The trade unions, these non-Party and voluntary democratic mass organizations of workers and employees, are granted, by our Party and Government, every possibility of satisfying the confidence of the workers. The Central Committee expects all responsible state and Party functionaries to put an end to the belittling of the trade unions and trade union work, which is still quite frequently observable. It is the duty of factory Party organizations to encourage and to assist the work of factory trade unions in every respect.

Growing democracy in the factories and places of work requires the inclusion of trade union organs in discussions on problems of management and economic organization to a much greater extent than before, and they must be entrusted to an ever greater extent with the administration of the workers' social affairs.   Trade union leaders and activists must deal conscientiously with the affairs of the workers and must see to it that the relationship between the workers on the one hand and economic and technical managers on the other hand is good and just.

The elimination of exaggerated centralism and the development of democracy also constitutes a key problem in the trade union movement.   This is how they must gradually reduce their by now emancipated apparatus to develop the system of voluntary social work and to fight with determination against ossified bureaucratic methods.

c) DISZ has, of late, improved its organization and its educational activity.   Good initiative has also been taken in the field of production by the Union and the masses of the youth.

We must insure that the hundreds of thousands of young people find in DISZ important possibilities for education, recreation, entertainment, and athletic activities.   DISZ must overcome bureaucratic methods, its leaders must establish close contacts with the masses of young people, they must live among them, and they must become the young people's genuine leaders.   In this way DISZ can render the best contribution to the development of our socialist democracy.

8. Certain Problems of Hungary's Foreign Policy.   The Central Committee regards the continued efforts to safeguard peace and further relax international tension as the basic part of the Party's policy.

Hungary, in fraternal alliance with the USSR, professes identical views with the Soviet Government on problems of foreign policy.   It supports the five fundamental principles regarding peaceful coexistence.   It regards the proposals concerning disarmament and the banning and destruction of nuclear weapons as particularly important. As a sincere demonstration of its desire to relax international tension and to contribute to disarmament, the Central Committee proposes to the Government to reduce the strength of the army by another 15,000 men, and to place the means thus released at the disposal of socialist construction.

The Party and Government support the efforts to conclude a European collective security treaty. They regard the Warsaw Treaty as the pillar of support of our national safety until the establishment of European collective security. They support all efforts to settle the German problem in a democratic way.

It is the unchangeable objective of our foreign policy to make our collaboration with the liberating USSR, China, and other socialist countries ever wider, deeper, and more varied. The fact that we belong to the mighty socialist world system, extending over more than one third of mankind, is our inexhaustible source of strength.

We want to strengthen and deepen our friendly relations and the possibility of fruitful exchanges with Yugoslavia, engaged in building socialism. The Central Committee deems it desirable that discussions should start between the Hungarian Workers Party and the Yugoslav League of Communists with a view to establishing closer, friendly contacts.[20] The establishment of friendly and comradely relations between the two Parties lies in the interest not only of our peoples and our Parties, but also of the world-wide struggle for peace, democracy, and socialism.

Besides further development of our close friendship and cooperation with socialist countries, we want to establish varied economic, scientific, artistic, sport, and other contacts with countries outside the camp of socialist states.

---

[20] See Chapter VI, Document 1.

III. FOR A FIRM LENINIST POLICY
BASED ON PRINCIPLES

It is only now that favorable conditions have been created for building socialism in our country, for developing the democratic substance of the People's Democracy and expanding socialist democracy. The circumstances which hampered socialist democracy have been eliminated.

In the beginning our state was strongly centralized and democracy was limited. The fact that the cult of personality, which is alien to Marxism, gained ground, in theory as well as in practice, was a contributing factor to the limitation of democracy.

Our Party now is engaged in combat against all this erroneous theory and practice.

In the present circumstances of socialist construction, it is especially the correct interpretation of the class struggle that helps our Party to develop correct forms of socialist democracy.

The disclosure, the remedying, and the correcting of the wrongs done to some former Social Democrats promotes the ideological and political unity of the working class and the heroic cooperation of former Social Democrats with Communists. This does not mean that the Party abandons the right to criticize social democratism. It means that it recognizes merits gained in the past, and that in this respect it centers its attention, first of all, on the tasks of the present and the future.

The course of democratization increases the role of the working class, because the active and creative participation of the working masses in the direction of state, economic, and social life becomes greater, and the leading role of the working class in the life of the country will be manifested in new ways.

The strengthening of the worker-peasant alliance is promoted by correctly interpreting the class struggle and reckoning with the emergence of new symptoms. The alliance of the workers and peasants is particularly strengthened by the fact that not only the poor peasants in the villages but also all the peasants in producer cooperatives are firmly supporting the working class, including the medium peasants who have joined producer cooperatives. The lasting alliance of the working class with the medium peasants is being further strengthened by the just reexamination of the cases of those medium peasants who have been wrongly classified as kulaks. Also the PPF movement enhances the working peasantry's confidence in the working class. Furthermore, this confidence is supported by numerous measures which effectively secure the production of the working peasantry. In the future our Party will be guided even more than before by the idea of the lasting alliance of workers and peasants because this alliance is the most solid pillar of our socialist state.

The just measures of our Party have made a deep impression on the intellectuals and experts of yesterday. Now intellectuals are primarily judged by their work. The further education of their sons will be made possible and their living conditions will be improved.

Hostile exploiting classes have ceased to exist in the towns, while in villages the kulaks have been greatly weakened both numerically and economically. Their strength and influence, however, still persist, and although many former exploiters show loyalty to our People's Democracy and take part in productive work, one must not underrate, in the villages, the hostile agitation of a section of the kulaks, particularly as regards the producer cooperatives. Among the remnants of the urban bourgeoisie there are people who play an active part in spreading the propaganda of the imperialist reaction. Therefore we must be vigilant.

The Central Committee states that the building of socialism in our country is progressing amid class struggle and in these days the class struggle has somewhat sharpened. However, the economic and political basis of the class enemy is steadily narrowing with the building of socialism, and its strength is diminishing. Taking this into account, the Party and the Government feel that the building of socialism could be attained without an acute class struggle. The development of the class struggle, however, is to a large extent subject to the activity of the international imperialist reaction. This reaction, after the 20th Congress of the CPSU, increased its activity against the Soviet Union and the People's Democracies. This did not fail to affect its outposts in Hungary: in the first place, the spy organizations (in the first half of this year forty imperialist spies were arrested) and, in the second place, the mood of the remnants of the class enemy. The gravest danger for the people's democratic order today is the imperialist reaction and its agents in this country.

Under these circumstances, the ideological solidity of our Party and the unity of the working classes under the leadership of the Party, of the working class, is of particular importance. It is for this reason that one has to take notice of the fact that recently in a section of the Party, in certain groups of the intelligentsia, and even among the workers and working peasants symptoms of wavering and mistrust toward the Party were manifested.

The responsibility for this undoubtedly rests in part with the mistakes committed by the Party and its leadership; in part it is due to the increasing pressure of the class enemy.

Our Party has done great work in remedying the mistakes committed before 1953. Later, however, particularly in 1955, some of the mistakes committed before June, 1953, were repeated. The March, 1955, Central Committee meeting acted correctly when it pointedly branded right-wing deviationist views. But after the resolution attempts were made to revive certain bad features of the cult of personality and to weaken collective leadership. Certain people tried to reject justified criticism by branding it as right-wing opportunism. All this provided favorable ground for the revival of various sectarian mistakes. This was accompanied by the fact that although the innocence of many comrades who had been arrested, sentenced, and vilified between 1949 and 1952 was revealed, their rehabilitation was delayed and was incomplete. All this led to a certain scepticism and mistrust toward the Party and Party leadership and to a loosening of the ties between the Party and the masses.

The fact that the justified expectations of Party members and non-Party members sympathetic to the Party after the 20th Congress of the CPSU have not been fulfilled, had a similar effect. The March, 1956, resolution of the Central Committee instructed the Party leadership to work out the implementation of the lessons of the 20th Congress adapted to Hungarian conditions. The Politburo began to tackle this task and its decisions, its guiding principles, were on the whole correct. In the carrying out of these decisions, however, there was hesitation and wavering. For such a turn of events the Politburo is responsible, because it failed to lead with sufficient vigor the struggle for the liquidation of the mistakes of the past, for the assertion of the spirit of the 20th Congress under Hungarian conditions, and for the increased democratization of our state, social, economic, and Party life. It was a mistake that the leading organs of the Party did not organize discussions within the Party on the most important problems of the country. Also, the wavering of *Szabad Nep* has created troubles among the Party cadres and workers.

Both sectarianism and right-wing opportunism are deeply rooted in our Party. We have to wage the sharpest and the most systematic struggle against both of them on the ideological-political level for the assertion of the new policy line of the Party.

Sectarianism has manifested and is manifesting itself in the fact that often instead of political enlightenment it employs administrative measures and means; from time to time one needs administrative means, but these cannot take the place of ideological-political enlightenment and struggle. Sectarianism appeared in the form of dogmatic voicing of certain tenets believed to be unassailable due to the absence of thorough and serious debates on political and scientific questions. Sectarianism often manifested itself in one-sided and impatient cadre policy and in the one-sided interpretation of the class struggle not based on an analysis of the prevailing circumstances. Despite Party directives, one often sees, even lately, that in the producer cooperatives the voluntary principle is violated

in certain places.   Sectarianism manifested itself in bureaucratic methods of leadership, and in certain bureaucratic traits
in the state apparatus, in other bodies, and even in the Party
organizations.   It appeared also in the frequently incorrect
relations toward the former Social Democratic comrades and
in the frequent bypassing of these comrades.   It was further
expressed in the sectarian attitude toward the allied working
classes and intelligentsia and their representatives.

By frankly exposing these sectarian mistakes the Party
mobilizes for battle against them because these harm the Party's
relations with the masses, in particular the Party's relations to
the workers.   By overcoming these mistakes one must fight for
the expansion of socialist democracy.

But there are not only sectarian mistakes in our Party. There
are also serious right-wing deviations.   The main representative
of right-wing deviation is Imre Nagy and certain anti-Party or
misguided elements in his entourage.   The Central Committee
reaffirms that in its resolution of March, 1955, it correctly
described the right-wing deviation, and now it states that the
Party has neglected the ideological fight against the reanimation
and manifestations of right-wing deviations.   Consequently at
this point a quick change is imperative.

Moreover, bourgeois propaganda and agitation have become
more lively and, what is more, certain meetings of the Petofi
Circle turned into open forums of anti-Party attitude.   The
latest Central Committee resolution, therefore, correctly
branded certain speakers in the Petofi Circle as being opposed
to the Party and to People's Democracy.   Certain people standing on the ground of bourgeois ideology in criticizing the
mistakes of the Party deny every success of the Party, the
leading role of the Party, the leading role of the working class,
the democratism of the worker-peasant state born in revolution, and demand "full" freedom of the press (that is, freedom
for spreading bourgeois views).   Today one cannot take any
more an open stand before the workers against the socialist
spirit in Hungary.   Therefore, both the petit-bourgeois opportunist and the advocates of bourgeois views refer, in a mislead-

ing way, to the 20th Congress of the CPSU, the "interests of socialism," and to the "process of democratization," and conceal themselves as "disciples of Leninist ideas" and the "executors, in Hungary, of the 20th Congress's resolutions." Those taking a stand against the Party are on the whole unanimous in their efforts to discredit the Party leadership and to disrupt the unity of the Party. This proves the dangerous character of their action.

Therefore the Central Committee warns every Party member and every loyal subject of the People's Democracy to be vigilant. The Central Committee deems it necessary that a keen work of enlightenment be carried out in the face of every hostile view in the press, radio, in the work of people's education, and at meetings for the explanation of the principles of socialist democracy and for the unmasking of the bourgeois and petit-bourgeois, antiworker and antisocialist, pseudo-democratic demands. In this struggle the Party must rely on the working class, the working peasantry, and the solid intellectuals whose faith has not been shaken by mistakes of the past, however great and tragic, because they know by their own experience that the expulsion of the industrialists, the smashing of the landlords' regime, the clearing of the ruins of war, the reconstruction, and the building of socialism have been achieved in our country in struggles of the working masses led by the Party. They experienced a turn for the better in their lives and realized that this was the achievement of the victories of the revolution. The immense cultural revolution has put in the hands of the people newspapers, books and broadcasting for the dissemination of socialist ideas. All this has been realized through struggles of the workers led by the Party. Therefore, the bulk of the workers, even if they criticized the Party and the Party leadership, have not lost faith in the Party during the last months.

We must rely on the working classes in our endeavor to win over the wavering through ideological fight and by eliminating our mistakes. For the attainment of this aim we have to improve, first of all, the ideological work and to intensify all forms of the ideological-political work of enlightenment. For this reason the Party must devote great attention to the theoretical clarification and elaboration of both the internationally valid fundamental principles of socialist construction, as well as its particular forms applicable to Hungary. In ideological questions it must unite the methods of patient enlightenment and persuasion with an uncompromising firmness in principle, with unfaltering loyalty to the teachings of Marxism-Leninism. For the successful carrying out of the ideological-political struggle the Party must have more initiative in bringing up ideological questions, in the overcoming of dogmatism, in the creation of independent Marxist thinking, because bourgeois ideology can be offset only by living, dynamic Marxism, since truth is on the side of living Marxism.

Therefore, one must beware of empty formulas and of arguing whether the right-wing or the left-wing danger is greater, or which one constitutes the principal danger. Under the present circumstances both of them represent a very serious danger for us. The two are often so interwoven that it is not easy to classify whether it is right-wing or left-wing. One should analyze the sectarian and the right-wing symptoms according to the concrete circumstances at any given moment, and take a stand against any anti-Party, anti-Marxist, anti-Leninist symptoms, and, naturally, against any symptoms directed against our Party and State. Any such attack must be repelled by our Party in unity and by a united will.

The Party loyally adheres to the socialist principles of international proletarianism and true patriotism. Under Hungary's specific conditions of building socialism, the Party, in the service of its own people and country, does not lose sight for a moment of the fact that it is ceaselessly strengthening the unity of the socialist camp, its relations with the Soviet Union, the countries of the socialist camp, and the socialist and working class movements throughout the world.

For this reason the Party again intensifies the struggle against any manifestations of nationalism, chauvinism, and anti-Semitism. The Party is strengthening its ties with the Communist Party of the Soviet Union because both the Communist Party of the Soviet Union and the Hungarian Workers Party hold identical views in every ideological question, in the assessment of the international situation, and as regards the perspectives of socialism.

Our Party does not recoil from difficulties and marches bravely forward on the road of democratization, of activization of the working class and popular masses, using fruitful discussions on the tasks before the Party and the people as its greatest lever in the elaboration of its correct policy.

IV. STRENGTHENING PARTY UNITY AND DISCIPLINE

The Hungarian Workers Party has become great and strong, the vanguard of the working class and the recognized leader of the Hungarian people, because the working masses could ascertain through thousands of facts which they experienced daily in their lives that: the Party is the trustworthy advocate and the most consistent champion of their interests; the Party finds the right way even under the most complex circumstances. The Party has the strength and courage to face the most difficult and most delicate problems, whenever they arise in history, in the course of the evolution of society. It eliminates everything obsolete and breaks away from everything that is harmful, that is in the way of the people's progress. It exposes and corrects its own mistakes, in order that it should thereby mobilize the working class and the working masses for new victories. All these qualities originate from the fundamental character of our Party, since the Party is the trustworthy guardian and continuer of the just revolutionary struggle and traditions of the Hungarian working class. Even today amidst numerous complicated problems, it leads with firm hands the great work of building socialism in our country. Worthy of its fighting tradition, the Party even in today's situation finds the correct solution for every burning question.

In our Party, in our country, the Party eliminates from the way of growing democratism every obstacle and eradicates all harmful remnants of the cult of personality and symptoms of bureaucratism.

The courage, strength, and determination of our Party gives a renewed and convincing proof to the working class, to the working people, of the just cause of the Party.

The Central Committee declares:

a) The main task of the Party today is: to strengthen its ideological, political, organizational unity, to forge Party unity of steel-like hardness, which is the greatest guarantee of the Party's success.

In order to consolidate the unity of the Party we must fight completely to eliminate the remnants of the cult of personality from the Party's life, from political, social, and economic life. The Leninist rules of Party life must be restored in every respect. The supreme principle of Party leadership, the principle of collective leadership, must be enforced unconditionally in the Party and on every level of the Party's life. The Central Committee appeals to the Party membership to insure the collective leadership of Party organizations in the entire Party, as the main pillar of the successful work of a Marxist-Leninist Party.

b) Within the organs of collective leadership and in the entire Party decisions must be arrived at after thorough discussion and deliberation in the spirit of courageous criticism and self-criticism, insuring in this way the formation of correct Party policy.

Party democracy must prevail in all organizations and organs of our Party. Every Party member must become conscious of the fact that he has the right and duty to participate in the current discussions in his Party organization, to speak up honestly for his convictions.

But Party life cannot be characterized by discussions only, for the Party is known for its unity in action; therefore, after closing the debates in our Party we must carry out the resolutions passed consistently.

c) Party discipline must be strengthened in accordance with the principles of democracy. The Party is a voluntary fighting alliance, its members are united by voluntary discipline. The principle according to which the lower Party organs must accept the decisions of the higher Party organs, as well as that the minority must obey the majority (after a resolution has been passed) and that it must carry out the resolution even if it disagrees with its content, must be everywhere—where it has been violated—enforced. We must not tolerate any lack of discipline in our Party, any infringement of the Party line, because it weakens the unity of the Party and limits its ability to act. We must enforce Party discipline, based on democratic principles, primarily by persuasion. In case of necessity, however, violators of the principles of democratic centralism must be called in a disciplinary way to account according to the prescriptions of the Organizational Statute.

d) The Party's strength lies, first of all, in the solidarity, experience, and fighting spirit of its cadres. It must be assured gradually that the mistakes committed in the Party's policy toward its cadres, especially toward the old cadres, will be corrected. The principal task today is to forge a strong unity between the old and new cadres, in order that the battle-hardened old and new cadres may fight together for the enforcement of the Central Committee's, the Party's, policy.

The Central Committee demands that every Communist who is working in leading positions in the economic, state, mass-organizational, cultural, or any other field do his utmost honestly and in a disciplined way for the implementation of the Party's policy.

e) The efforts of the Party, and especially the activities of the Party cadres, must be directed, first of all, toward the solution of economic problems and the raising of the well-being of the working people. The cadres of the Party and Party activists must perform their organizational, educational work among the working masses on the spot, and abandon their former bureaucratic methods. In the interest of better economic leadership Communists working in leading positions, and also all cadres of the Party, must consider it their duty to acquaint themselves with the economic problems of their territory, to penetrate into economic questions, and to become specialists in their areas of work.

f) Bureaucratic trends in the work of the Party must be energetically combated.   In its struggle for building socialism the Party must work, first of all, by providing direction, policy, persuasion, and organization, rather than by giving direct orders through administrative channels regarding production and other matters, which should be left to state and economic organs. The Party must regard as its chief task raising the ideological level of Communists, organizational work, enlightenment and education among the workers, and control of economic and state organs.   Party members must provide example in steadfastness in the performance of their duty, thereby convincing the workers by their personal behavior.

g) The strength of the Party lies in the steadfastness and fighting spirit of its members.   The Central Committee of the Party imposes on every Party member the obligation to espouse vigorously the cause of the Party's policy, fight for its fulfillment, implement the resolutions in a disciplined way, and to combat all hostile trends.   The Central Committee feels assured that our Party membership, counting many hundreds of thousands and representing all the laboring classes of the people and, first of all, the working class, will understand and accept the resolutions of the Central Committee and will exert all its efforts for their successful implementation.

Our Party is firmly resolved that it will consistently assert and enforce the fundamental characteristic of the people's democracy, namely, *that it is dictatorship for the suppression of exploiters, but it is a thousand times truer democracy for the working class and the working masses than even the most developed bourgeois democracy.*   In the different fields of state, social, and Party life our duty is *to develop the democracy of the workers, socialist democracy, in order that we may make the widest masses of workers even more conscious and active builders of socialism. Socialist democracy at the same time means that the workers recognize the discipline based on Leninist democratic principles as binding on themselves.*

The Central Committee is convinced that its resolutions will elicit increased creative activity from Party members and the working masses; that their implementation will effectively contribute to the fulfillment and overfulfillment of the people's economic plan and to the raising of the living standard of our working people.

The Central Committee of the Hungarian Workers Party appeals to the working class, the working peasantry, the progressive intelligentsia, to the entire working people: to rally round the Party and the Government; to fight with militant, spirited work for new socialist successes, for the final victory of socialism in our country!   [All italics in *Szabad Nep*.]

CHAPTER IV

THE STRUGGLE FOR "DEMOCRATIZATION" CONTINUES: AUGUST-SEPTEMBER, 1956

One of the final acts of the Central Committee meeting of the HWP was to dismiss General Mihaly Farkas, former Minister of National Defense, from all Party posts, to expel him from the Party, and to relieve him of his military rank. The charge against him was that while in office (from 1948 to 1953) he violated "socialist legality" and had been responsible for much of the harm done to Communists who had been purged in this period.

On July 30 the Government was reshuffled. Gero resigned his post as first Deputy Premier. In his stead Istvan Hidas was elected. Gyorgy Marosan, a former Social Democrat who had been recently rehabilitated, was made Deputy Premier, Imre Horvath was appointed Foreign Minister in lieu of Janos Boldoczki who became the new Hungarian Ambassador in Moscow. The Minister of Education, Tibor Erdei-Gruz, was replaced by Albert Konya, and other changes were also made.

In August, the HWP returned to deal with the problem of intellectuals in Hungary. The August issue of *Tarsadalmi Szemle*, the Party's theoretical journal, printed a resolution of the Central Committee "concerning certain problems of Party policy toward the intelligentsia."

The resolution summed up a variety of existing prejudices against "the old intelligentsia" which harmed the Party in that they deprived the people's order of much-needed expert talent. It noted that the proportion of Party workers with a university education was exceedingly low (4.3 percent in the secretariat of the Central Committee and only 1.7 percent among the first secretaries of urban Party committees). It acknowledged that "excessive teaching of Party history" to the detriment of philosophy and political economy had had an adverse effect on the attitude of intellectuals. Yet, at the same time, few people had had an adequate opportunity to study the Soviet Union at first hand: "Of several hundred students at the Technical University at Budapest there are only 20 who had been to the Soviet Union."

The situation with respect to the new generation of intellectuals was found somewhat more encouraging, but their inadequate educational background, their "political apathy and cynicism, caused partly by the shortcomings of political education at the Universities and partly by the obstacles they encountered in earning a proper livelihood after they graduated," and excessive class consciousness on the part of some members of the new intelligentsia also gave cause for concern.

Based on the foregoing analysis the Central Committee listed some measures designed to improve the situation. The measures included increasing the attractiveness of the Party for intellectuals (the proportion of intellectuals continued to be very low), dispelling some of the fears and misgivings of the old intelligentsia and overcoming the split between the old and new generations of intellectuals, better utilization of the talents of technical experts with opportunities for their advancement, improving cultural exchange with the Soviet Union but also with the West, increasing the availability of foreign scientific journals and information, substantial improvement in the material conditions of many intellectuals, and, finally, "discontinuing the compilation of confidential cadre material on people working in the intellectual professions."[1]

The next round in the skirmishing between the intellectual community and the Party centered around a meeting of the Hungarian Writers' Union on September 17, 1956.

Writers such as Gyula Hay and Geza Losonczy tried to set the tone of the meeting by stating respectively that in literature the meaning of "having turned over a new leaf" (the reference was to the July resolution of the Party) would have to signify the complete freedom of writers, and that certain past Party resolutions should be revised and repudiated and those responsible for the documents should be removed from office.[2]

Responding in behalf of the Party, *Szabad Nep* sought to caution the writers against deepening the split existing within the

---

[1] *Tarsadalmi Szemle*, XI, No. 8 (August, 1956), 29-41.

[2] See, for example, Gyula Hay, "Before the Meeting of the Writers," *Irodalmi Ujsag*, September 8, 1956; also Geza Losonczy's article in *Muvelt Nep*, September 2, 1956.

Party and defended especially the "splendid July resolution" which promised to redress many past errors.[3]

The pronouncements made at the meeting stressed the necessity of "telling the truth." It was in this spirit that Peter Veres gave his presidential address and Geza Kepes his report on the activities of the Writers' Union during the past two years. This spirit was manifest in the address of Lajos Konya who expressed "continuing concern over the fact that even in the implementation of proper measures [on the basis of the July resolution] there is too much procrastination and bureaucratic-sectarian-dogmatic opposition." Gyula Hay reiterated the necessity of "telling the truth." "The meeting will have achieved its aim," said Hay, "if every one of its actions is underlined by the principle that we Hungarian writers, regardless of Party status and differences in philosophical conviction, conclude a stubborn, protective alliance among ourselves to tell the truth."[4]

The election of a new executive board resulted in the ouster of thirteen former members who were regarded as "Stalinists" and their replacement by an equal number of new members, some of whom had only recently been rehabilitated.

In the meantime Erno Gero, First Secretary of the HWP, departed for his annual holiday in the Soviet Union. He left the country on September 8, joined talks with Khrushchev and Tito in the Crimea on September 30, and returned to Hungary following consultations with Messrs. Mikoyan and Suslov on October 6.

On September 9, a delegation of the HWP led by Janos Kadar and including Istvan Hidas, Zoltan Szanto, and Agoston Szkladan departed for China to participate in the Eighth Congress of the Chinese CP.

On September 23, speaking before a committee of the Patriotic People's Front, Gyorgy Marosan, Deputy Premier and member of the Politburo of the HWP, put out the first official feeler for the readmission of Imre Nagy to the Party. Alluding to the "unsettled" case of Imre Nagy, he said that in the view of the Party leaders Nagy's readmission could be secured on certain conditions.

---

[3] See Istvan Friss, "On the Basis of the Central Committee's July Resolution," *Szabad Nep,* September 16, 1956.

[4] For the proceedings of the meeting, see *Irodalmi Ujsag,* September 22, 1956.

On September 28 a resolution adopted by the Central Council of Trade Unions at its ninth plenary session (which was concluded on September 12) was published in newspapers. It followed the pattern of the July resolution of the HWP in demanding greater autonomy of workers' self-government in the factories and advocating a series of economic measures designed to improve the welfare of the workers.[5]

On September 30 the press printed an announcement of the Presidential Council of the People's Republic convoking the National Assembly for October 22, 1956.

---

[5] See *Szabad Nep,* September 28 and 29, 1956.

CHAPTER V

PRELUDE TO REVOLT: THE REINTERMENT OF LASZLO RAJK AND THE REHABILITATION OF IMRE NAGY OCTOBER 3-23, 1956

On October 3 the Central Committee of the HWP announced that it had reached a decision to pay "last respects worthy of militants and revolutionaries . . . to comrades who, as a result of political trials in past years, have been innocently condemned and executed, and who have already been rehabilitated earlier by the Party's Central Committee and reinstated in their Party membership." (*Szabad Nep,* October 4, 1956.)

On October 6, 1956, there took place the ceremonial reinterment of Laszlo Rajk, Lt. Gen. Gyorgy Palffy, Tibor Szonyi, and Andras Szalai, the chief victims of the purge trials of 1949. The deeper meaning of this macabre ritual was conveyed by an editorial in *Szabad Nep* ("The Nation's Painful, Silent Tribute to Its Great Deceased," *Szabad Nep,* October 7, 1956):

> . . . The silent demonstration of the hundreds of thousands of mourners was a pledge not only that we will preserve the pure memories [of the four dead leaders] but will also remember the dark practices of tyranny, lawlessness, slander, and defrauding of the people . . . .
>
> . . . the people stood honor guard at the biers . . . .
>
> The silent demonstration began. Is it possible to give an account of this, on the basis of consecutive impressions of the facts, the events? It is not! . . . No, it is not possible to speak of mourning when we describe the procession [of thousands upon thousands]. People were numbed not only by a deep sense of grief . . . but by burning hatred, by the memory that these comrades, these men were executed as enemies of the fatherland, of the people! We were led to believe—and we were willing to believe—the slanders about you! Forgive us for this, comrades!

On the same day on which tribute was paid to these Hungarian victims of Stalinism, Erno Gero, Janos Kadar, Istvan Hidas, and Zoltan Szanto (the last three were on their way back from the Congress of the Chinese CP) held discussions with A. I. Mikoyan and M. A. Suslov in Moscow. (*Szabad Nep,* October 7, 1956.)

On October 12 the arrest of Gen. Mihaly Farkas, former Minister of Defense, for having violated "socialist legality" was announced.

On October 14, a Hungarian delegation under the leadership of Erno Gero departed to Yugoslavia to formalize the terms of friendly cooperation between the two countries and Communist Parties. On the same day, the reinstatement of the Party membership of Imre Nagy was made public.

1. Letter from Imre Nagy to the Central Committee of the Hungarian Workers Party Seeking Reinstatement, October 4, 1956[1]

HONORABLE COMRADES:

I follow the imperative voice of my Communist convictions and attachment to the Party by discarding personal interest, prestige considerations, and resentment as I am again turning to the Party. In writing this letter I was above all prompted by my anxiety for the unity of the Party and by a desire to be able to work, as soon as possible, in the ranks of the Party and shoulder to shoulder with members of the Party, on the many and arduous tasks of building socialism for the country's prosperity and the peaceful and happy life of our working people, which require every effort of the Party and the firm and loyal stand of every Party member.

At the same time, when the great tasks arising from the July, 1956, resolution of the Central Committee and last but not least the thwarting of the calculations of the enemies of our People's Republic absolutely demand the ideological, political, and organizational unity of the Party, and also on this basis the national rallying of the broadest democratic forces, my unclari-

[1] *Szabad Nep.* October 14, 1956.

fied Party status and the uncertainty steadily growing around this affair aggravate the Party's unity of action and divide the forces of the Party and democracy precisely at the moment when grave economic and political tasks must be solved under the direction of the Party. In such a situation the cause of Party unity is a paramount and decisive question. I wish to establish that I regard Party unity based on the teachings of Marxism-Leninism and the principles of democracy within the Party as the basic conditions for the Party's success. Therefore I would consider it culpable if the struggle around the so-called Imre Nagy affair within the Party were to sharpen and become an obstacle to the strengthening of Party unity and the firm united policy of the Party when this obstacle could be and can be overcome by settling my affairs.

I want to stress emphatically that in the interest of settling my Party status I will do everything in my power that is compatible with my Marxist-Leninist convictions and principles and with my Communist and human honor.

As I have already said in several memoranda, I deem it necessary to restate that

(a) I am in agreement with the Party's main political line, as determined by the resolutions of June, 1953, of the Central Committee and by the Third Party Congress, that industry, agriculture, and the entire national economy should be placed on the foundations of socialism in the spirit of Marxism-Leninism in accordance with the special conditions existing in Hungary;

(b) I am in agreement with the Leninist principle of democratic centralism on the basis of which I recognize Party decisions as binding on me even if I partly or wholly disagree with them;

(c) I am in agreement in principle with those aims of the Central Committee resolution of July, 1956, which lead that Party along the road of socialist democratism in the spirit of the 20th Congress of the CPSU. Although I hold a different opinion of several points of the resolution, I consider the resolution to be binding on me and I will fight for its realization.

I consider it absolutely indispensable that the accusations made in the past in connection with my political and ideological activity should be properly discussed before a leading Party forum in public and should ideological clarification make it necessary, simultaneously with the rectification of the accusations which proved to be unfounded, I for one am ready to admit the truly existing mistakes.

I am convinced that my case must be settled both in the interest of Party unity and the success of the political and economic tasks. I must emphasize this all the more because my expulsion from the Party took place in violation of democracy within the Party and of the Party statutes and was un-Partylike. I was prompted by this conviction when I sent several memoranda to leading Party organizations and when I turned to the Party committee of my former primary Party organization.

On the basis of all this I feel that my place is in the Party, where I have spent nearly 40 years, and in the ranks of which I have struggled to the best of my ability, either with arms in hand, or by work, words, or pen for the cause of the people, Fatherland, and socialism. I ask the Central Committee to examine my Party affairs again and to return my rights of Party membership so that in this way, with the termination of my Party affair, the successful solution of the tasks facing the Party and the country may also be promoted.

With Communist Greetings

Budapest, October 4, 1956   Imre Nagy

2. RESOLUTION ADOPTED BY THE POLITBURO OF THE HUNGARIAN WORKERS PARTY REINSTATING IMRE NAGY, OCTOBER 13, 1956[2]

THE POLITBURO has discussed Comrade Imre Nagy's letter of October 4 asking for readmission to the Party. The Politburo has resolved:

---

[2] *Ibid.*

1—To annul the resolution of November, 1955, expelling Comrade Imre Nagy from the ranks of the Party because the political mistakes he had committed did not justify his expulsion from the Party. The personal bias of Comrade Matyas Rakosi played a considerable part in bringing about the expulsion. Taking all this into consideration, the Politburo restores Party member rights to Comrade Imre Nagy.

2—It recommends that the Central Committee should shortly discuss the still open problems of the affair, and throw light on the mistakes actually committed by Comrade Imre Nagy and on the overstatements and incorrect findings in the previous Party resolution.

These arrangements will make it possible for the Central Committee to clear up and conclusively close the matter in a principled manner.

The readmission of Nagy to the ranks of the HWP elicited favorable comment from the country's press. The agricultural correspondents' section of the National Union of Hungarian Journalists "saluted the decision of the Politburo . . . annulling the disgraceful measure of expulsion" and expressed hope that it would be followed by a "public debate which will clarify the situation." In a telegram to Nagy the correspondents expressed the hope that he would "be able to continue . . . the fight in the course of which he has already done so much for the education of [the] people and for the amelioration of their conditions." The journalists also expressed their "desire to support" Nagy with all their strength.

On October 18, the Minister of Education informed Nagy of his reinstatement in his professorship of agricultural economy at the Karl Marx University of Economic Sciences in Budapest. On October 20 Nagy's regular membership in the Hungarian Academy of Sciences was also restored.

Meanwhile, discussions continued in the Petofi Circle and at other gatherings of university students. Petofi Circles were being formed in several towns, and in Debrecen a Kossuth Circle, formed in June, 1956, with a similar purpose as the Petofi Circle in Budapest, held its first public debate on October 14. The topics discussed at these gatherings were not all of academic or intellectual

character.   On October 17 the Petofi Circle held a debate on the
status of Hungarian agriculture at which the merits and demerits
of agricultural producer cooperatives were thoroughly examined.
(*Szabad Ifjusag,* October 18, 1956, also *Szabad Nep,* October 19,
1956.)   Other topics discussed concerned the problems of technical intelligentsia, the development of atomic energy resources, and
the condition of Hungarian oil fields.

The demands of the university youth with respect to their own
affairs included a reduction in the number of mandatory courses,
the abolition of required study of foreign languages, a reduction
in the number of compulsory courses on Marxism-Leninism,
replacement of a system of para-military activities required of
students in behalf of national defense by wider opportunities for
athletic activities, and, finally, improvements in board and lodging
at university hostels or dormitories.   (*Szabad Ifjusag,* October 18,
1956.)

On October 19 the Government met some of the demands of
the students and promised to consider others.   At an extraordinary
meeting of university rectors, the Minister of Education, Albert
Konya, announced the discontinuation of compulsory Russian language study, proposed expanding the university curriculum from
four to five years (except in the faculties of law and economics)
in order to relieve some of the pressure from the students, promised
a reexamination of national defense activities at the universities in
conjunction with the Ministry of National Defense, and projected
the formation of a "council on higher education" to consider university problems in general.   (*Szabad Nep,* October 20, 1956.)

On October 20 the executive committee of the Party organization in the Writers' Union issued a resolution calling for a new
Party Congress.

3.   RESOLUTION OF THE EXECUTIVE COMMITTEE OF THE PARTY ORGANIZATION IN THE HUNGARIAN WRITERS' UNION[3]

THE LEADERSHIP of the Party organization, at a meeting on October 17, 1956, discussed the Central Committee's circular on the
political situation.   We took note with pleasure of the discussions between the delegations of the HWP and the Yugoslav

---

[3] *Irodalmi Ujsag,* October 20, 1956.

League of Communists, as well as the readmission of Comrade Imre Nagy to the Party, as the first step to a full clarification of his case. We consider these steps suitable to restore popular confidence in the Party.

Following the 20th Congress [of the CPSU] and the July resolutions, a nearly unanimous attitude developed among the people with regard to the crimes and mistakes of the past. But this attitude does not transcend the limits of condemning past negative phenomena. We deem it necessary that after the past has been completely and sincerely cleared up and the inevitable consequences from it have been drawn, a new, positive, forward-looking unity for action should be forged, whose initiator and standard-bearer can be none other than our cleansed Party.

Only a new, democratically elected Party leadership is capable of performing this task. For this reason we ask the Central Committee to schedule the next Party congress in any event no later than three or four months prior to the general elections which are due to be held next year.

Also on October 20, the university students at Szeged broke their official ties with DISZ and founded their own organization, suited to "the needs of university students," under the name of MEFESZ (Hungarian University and Academic Students Association). (*Szabad Nep,* October 21, 1956.) Their example was followed by students at Budapest who met in two extraordinary sessions on October 22, 1956.

On the same day the executive board of the Petofi Circle also held a meeting at which it adopted a resolution listing a number of demands:

1—In view of the present situation in Hungary the leadership of the Petofi Circle suggests that a session of the Central Committee of the HWP should be convened in the nearest possible future. (Comrade Imre Nagy should take part in the preparatory work for this session.)[4]

---

[4] The resolution is not printed here as a document because it was not available as such. The quotation cited here is based on a report of the Hungarian Telegraph Agency (MTI) as checked against the report of the resolution in *Szabad Nep* (October 23, 1956). The portions of the quotation in parentheses represent text which, though transmitted by MTI, was omitted from the *Szabad Nep* version.

2—We consider it necessary that the Party and the Government disclose in all sincerity the economic situation in the country, revise the directives of the Second Five-Year Plan, and work out a concrete, constructive program that is in accordance with the special conditions existing in Hungary.

3—The Central Committee and the Government should adopt every means possible to insure the development of socialist democracy in Hungary by developing the real function of the People's Front, by fulfilling the legitimate political aspirations of the working class, by introducing self-management in factories and a workers' democracy.

4—To assure the prestige of the Party and State direction, we propose that Comrade Imre Nagy and other comrades who fought for socialist democracy and for Leninist principles should occupy a worthy place in the direction of the Party and Government.

5—We propose Matyas Rakosi's expulsion from the Party Central Committee and his recall from other functions. (It is necessary that the Central Committee, anxious to establish tranquillity in the country, should bring to a halt present attempts at Stalinist and Rakosist restoration.)

6—We propose that Mihaly Farkas's case be tried in public in accordance with socialist legality.

7—We propose that the Central Committee revise certain sectarian resolutions—in the first place those of March, 1955, those of December, 1955, and those of June 30, 1956, concerning the Petofi Circle. (We propose that the Central Committee annul these resolutions and draw the necessary conclusions as regards the persons concerned.)

8—Let even the most delicate questions be made public: the balance sheets of our foreign trade agreement (and the plans concerning the utilization of Hungarian uranium).

(9—With a view to consolidating Hungarian-Soviet friendship, let us establish even closer relations with the Party, State, and people of the Soviet Union on the basis of the Leninist principles of complete equality.)

10—We demand that the Central Committee of DISZ take a stand, at their meeting on October 23, on the points of this resolution and adopt a decision on the democratization of the Hungarian youth movement.

The student rallies throughout the country elicited comment from *Szabad Nep,* the central organ of the HWP.

4. EDITORIAL: "NEW SPRING PARADE," *Szabad Nep,* OCTOBER 23, 1956

MEETING follows upon meeting in our universities and our institutions of higher learning. Students of engineering, philosophy, law, and the creative arts are meeting at the universities of Budapest, Pecs, Szeged. These meetings of the youth are taking place in a passionate and stormy atmosphere, resembling a rampaging river overflowing its banks rather than an artificially channeled stream. Is this flood good? Is this fiery enthusiasm good? Let us admit that the past few years have made us forget about this sort of mass expression of opinion. Sectarianism and the Stalinist mistakes have dulled our sensitivity to mass opinion and mass movements which manifest themselves with elemental force, and even today there are those who cannot rid themselves of the old ingrained habits and regard these meetings of the youth with misgivings and distrust. Our Party and its press organ, *Szabad Nep,* align themselves with the youth, approve of these meetings, and wish these well-considered, creative discussions the best of success.

We know very well that youth, and more particularly the university youth, was for years prevented from making its voice heard in national as well as in their own affairs. We know well that DISZ suffered organic shortcomings and, aside from slogans, was incapable of providing the youth with true, socialist substance. During these years much bitterness, many suppressed desires and wants were dammed up in our youth. Much justified dissatisfaction lay buried in the youth, and who can be surprised if this feeling, suppressed for more than half a decade, now bursts forth with elemental force. Those who would want our youth now to express its opinions cautiously and with calm restraint disregard the concrete historical antecedents and the given circumstances as well as the spirit of the Hungarian youth.

The present meetings in many respects resemble the struggles of the Hungarian university and college students right after the liberation. The atmosphere of these gatherings reminds all of us of the university meetings and college discussions of the years after 1945, and today it is clear to everyone that those years bore healthy, good fruit. There are, however, also differences between the current meetings and those held after liberation. One such difference must be emphatically stressed. In the discussions after liberation only a *small portion* of the participating students believed in socialism and possessed a Marxist world view. Immediately after liberation bourgeois reaction still had considerable representation in the universities, and the children of peasants and workers constituted only a small percentage. The picture is today fundamentally different. At the current meetings, the *vast majority of the participants take part as firm believers in socialism.* At these meetings not 5 or 10 percent but a much larger percentage of worker-peasant students are represented, who take their place in the building of a socialist Hungary as proud bearers of the heritage of their fathers.

There is still another circumstance to which we must pay attention. In the years after 1949 the country's political mistakes unwittingly led to an aggravation of the contradictions [differences] between students of working-class or peasant origin and students of intellectual or petit-bourgeois family background. The present meetings are characterized by the fact that students of divergent social origin march forward hand in hand, demanding in unison the reform of university life and the consolidation of socialist democratism. The consolidation of the unity of the youth is one of the results of these meetings, and it is for this reason too that we greet with pleasure the movement of university and college students.

But there are other reasons as well why we warmly greet these meetings. The spokesmen of sectarian politics paid only lip service to the fact that active participation in politics on the part of the youth is in the vital interest of socialism. In practice they did everything to assure that our university and college youth should not think independently, should not use its head, that there should be no possibility for the expression of independent opinion. We, having turned on the mistakes and crimes of the recent past, do not want to pay lip service alone to the stirring of our university youth, but want to align ourselves with them in deeds, by giving them all possible moral and material aid. We can do so all the better since these rallies have condemned in a most decisive way that sort of dabbling in politics which turns against learning and have rejected that sort of public activity which would prejudice the student's studies.

One of the characteristics of the present youth movement is that it combines a struggle for socialist democratism with a fight for better conditions of learning and broader and more scientific information.

The university youth has expressed its political attitude before the broad public. We welcome the position adopted by the university youth. We agree that those who have defiled socialist humanitarianism should be judged publicly. We agree that veteran fighters of the workers' movement who raised their voices against Stalinism even in the past should find a place in the leadership of the Party and the country. We agree that there is no room in the leadership for those who do not want or cannot consistently proceed along the road fixed by the 20th Congress of the CPSU and the July resolutions of the Party.

It would be easier for us to make promises and thus to quiet rising passions for a while. We will not do this. We do not want to mislead the youth. We must speak the truth even if it is, for the time being, unfavorable. At the same time we ask the youth to have confidence in the Party because we want to satisfy every one of its justified demands.

At the student rallies our youth have given proof of serious political maturity. This maturity is demonstrated not only by the fact that they are discussing matters of national policy, mostly confidently and in a healthy spirit, but also by the fact that they are searching for the road leading forward, and for the possibilities of a solution to problems.

Their proposals bear testimony to the deep responsibility which permeates our youth as regards our People's Democracy. The majority of the students stand on the foundations of socialism. Students of law, philosophy, and engineering have often expressed their determination not to allow a wedge to be driven between university students and young factory workers. On the contrary, just yesterday the students of the academy of arts held a common meeting with the young workers of Csepel. It has happened, nevertheless, that on a few occasions at these university meetings a few dim-witted young men have tried to poison the atmosphere by chauvinistic counterrevolutionary slogans. We are proud of the masses of university and college youth for having isolated these troublemakers in a most determined manner and for taking a stand against troublemaking of that kind.

There are people who seem to see a danger of bourgeois restoration in the heated debates of these meetings. These worries we feel have no serious foundation. Those who have attended these meetings have been able to hear and see that our university students have gone into battle not against but for the people's democratic system and for a purified socialism. In order to increase the effectiveness of this struggle and to further the realization of their aims, let us warn our young people to continue to be on their guard, as they have been up to now, lest counterrevolutionary manifestations be made at their meetings. Let them stand up, as they have stood up, against every kind of attempt at restoration.

Let them be on guard under all circumstances lest their democratic and socialist unity be disrupted by some sort of provocation. They must not forget even for a moment that their struggle is being waged to advance the cause of socialist democratism. In the present circumstances every counterrevolutionary utterance left unanswered and every bourgeois provocation becomes grist for the mill of sectarianism.

They must be aware of their great responsibility: if they fight consistently against sectarianism they also fight against the danger of bourgeois restoration. By standing up against bourgeois endeavors they also pull the ground from under the feet of the sectarians.

We welcome the correct aspirations of our university and college students.   We welcome this tremendous and democratic parade of our youth of which we can say, quoting the ever beautiful lines of [the poet Endre] Ady:

> Fire, blood, fever, news, happy transformation,
> Only creative effort burns in your eyes
> Eternal spring, eternal revolution
> Oh, be resplendent ever more resplendent.

CHAPTER VI

THE REVOLT, FIRST PHASE: DEMISE OF THE HUNGARIAN WORKERS PARTY OCTOBER 23-28, 1956

THE EVENTS of the day on which the revolt broke out cannot as yet be fully reconstructed.

The morning issue of *Szabad Nep* continued to highlight the Polish developments by printing a full text of Gomulka's speech before the 8th Plenum of the Central Committee of the PUWP[1] and commenting that "something of historic significance is taking place in Poland these days."

Meanwhile the University students announced plans for a "silent sympathy demonstration" before the Polish Embassy. Demonstrators were to assemble at 2:30 P.M. in front of the headquarters of the Writers' Union.

At 12:53 a decision of the Ministry of the Interior prohibiting the demonstration was broadcast.

At 2:23 P.M. the decision of the Ministry of the Interior was rescinded.

Shortly before 3 P.M. the demonstrators marched to the statue of Sandor Petofi (in Pest)[2]. They sang the Kossuth hymn, displayed Polish flags, and heard the recitation of Petofi's poem which begins, "Rise, Hungarian, the Homeland calls, the time is here, now or never," and ends, "we will never again be slaves."

From the Petofi statue the demonstrators, still orderly, marched to the statue of Jozef Bem, the Polish hero of Hungarian revolutionary struggles. By this time their number had swelled to an estimated 50,000.

In the meantime the communiqué of the Hungarian-Yugoslav talks was read over the radio:

---

[1] See Poland, Chapter V, Document 2.

[2] Sandor Petofi was a Hungarian romantic poet and revolutionary fighter, believed to have met death on the battlefield in Hungary's struggles for independence in 1848-49.

1. COMMUNIQUÉ ON TALKS HELD BETWEEN REPRESENTA-
   TIVES OF THE YUGOSLAV LEAGUE OF COMMUNISTS AND
   THE HUNGARIAN WORKERS PARTY, BELGRADE, OCTOBER
   23, 1956

THE DELEGATION of the Hungarian Workers Party visited
Yugoslavia between October 15 and October 22 at the invi-
tation of the Central Committee of the League of Yugoslav
Communists. The members of the delegation, Erno Gero,
First Secretary of the Central Committee of the Hungarian
Workers Party, and Antal Apro, Andras Hegedus, Janos Kadar,
and Istvan Kovacs, members of the Politburo of the Central
Committee of the Hungarian Workers Party, had talks with
Josip Broz-Tito, Secretary General of the Yugoslav League of
Communists, and members of the Executive Committee of the
Central Committee of the Yugoslav League of Communists.

They also had a series of meetings and talks with representatives of the Central Committee of the Yugoslav League
of Communists and the Socialist Alliance of Yugoslav Working People, with Aleksander Rankovic, Secretary of the Executive Committee of the Central Committee of the Yugoslav
League of Communists; Svetozar Vukmanovic, Vladimir
Bakaric, Lazar Kolisevski, members of the Executive Committee of the Central Committee of the Yugoslav League of
Communists; Dobrivoje Radoslavjevic and Dusan Petrovic,
members of the Central Committee of the Yugoslav League
of Communists; as well as with numerous leaders of political
and social life in Belgrade, Sarajevo, Zagreb, and Ljubljana.

The representatives of the Yugoslav League of Communists
and the Hungarian Workers Party conducted their talks in
a spirit of friendship, frankness, and mutual understanding
and have agreed upon the following:

The representatives of the two parties noted with satisfaction that of late international tension has relaxed, international contacts have widened, and active coexistence between
states has further developed. They believe it necessary to make

further efforts to solve through negotiation such unsolved international problems as disarmament, banning the use of weapons of mass destruction, the establishment of a collective security system, the reunification of the German people in a democratic way, and peaceful settlement of the Suez problem.

In this new atmosphere the authority and the role of the United Nations have increased. By admitting new members, including the People's Republic of Hungary, the United Nations has progressed further along the road of peace. All this contributes toward developing trust and mutual cooperation between various countries.

The representatives of the two parties have agreed that development of cooperation between the Yugoslav League of Communists and the Hungarian Workers Party, as the leading parties struggling in the two neighboring countries to build a socialist society on the principles of Marxism-Leninism, is inevitably necessary. This cooperation will aid in developing the relations between the Federal People's Republic of Yugoslavia and the People's Republic of Hungary, in strengthening friendship between our peoples, in the interest of peace and progress in the world.

Cooperation between the two parties must develop on the basis of complete trust, sincerity, equality, voluntariness, non-interference in one another's internal affairs, and exchange of views, including the freedom of constructive and comradely criticism based on positions of principle and taking into consideration the interests of socialist development. Consistent implementation of these principles will make impossible a repetition of past mistakes which caused serious harm to the workers' movement.

The representatives of the Yugoslav League of Communists and the Hungarian Workers Party have agreed that cooperation in practice be established through personal contacts, exchanges of views and publications, exchanges of delegations, meetings of Party workers, and all other forms which will appear in the course of cooperation and prove useful. The need has also been stressed for wider exchanges of views and study of experiences in the fields of state and social activities. The exchange of the rich experiences of socialist development and their adoption without any imposition, freely, and in a completely voluntary manner offers valuable aid to the cause of socialism in the individual countries.

The representatives of the Yugoslav League of Communists and the Hungarian Workers Party devoted special attention to promoting mutual relations between the two countries. They agreed that they must work for cooperation between corresponding organs, especially in the economic and cultural fields, where wide possibilities exist which have only lately begun to be realized and used. The fact that our two neighboring countries have been traditionally linked by their economic interests and that they are both in the full swing of socialist construction represents a favorable circumstance for a further widening of our economic relations, especially in the fields of industry, agriculture, goods exchange, and communications.

To this end it is necessary to encourage cooperation between the corresponding organs and bodies in order to study all possibilities and to conclude appropriate agreements which will be of mutual benefit. The representatives of the two parties have also emphasized the need for concluding a cultural convention to encourage cultural cooperation.

The Central Committee of the Hungarian Workers Party extended to the Central Committee of the Yugoslav League of Communists an invitation for a delegation of the Yugoslav League of Communists to visit Hungary. The Central Committee of the Yugoslav League of Communists has accepted this invitation.

In the early evening the Politburo of the HWP announced that a meeting of the Central Committee would be called for October 31. The date was subsequently (at 8:22 P.M.) changed to the "nearest future."

At 8 P.M. Erno Gero addressed the nation in a radio speech:

2. Radio Address by Erno Gero, First Secretary of
   the Hungarian Workers Party, October 23, 1956

Dear comrades! Dear friends! Working people of Hungary!
The Central Committee of the Hungarian Workers Party
adopted important resolutions in July of this year. The membership of our Party, our working class, our working peasantry
and intellectuals, our people received these resolutions with
approval and satisfaction.

The essence of the July resolutions was the fact that we
further develop socialist democracy on the basis of Party unity
based on solid foundations in our Party, in state life, in the
field of production, and in our entire society. By rectifying
numerous mistakes of the past and relying on our achievements
we build socialism in our country, and according to our capacity
and possibilities, gradually raise the standard of living of our
working class and nation.

Following the July resolutions the initiative of the working
masses began to develop widely throughout the country. During the brief period that has elapsed since the resolutions were
passed, numerous measures have been taken to implement them.

It goes without saying, however, that the resolutions could
not be fully implemented during the short spell of a few months.
At the same time mistakes, too, have occurred in the course of
their implementation. The July resolutions, furthermore, could
merely indicate the direction and place the main tasks in the
forefront, without providing a solution for all the problems
which confront our country and people. Many of these problems require further thorough examination to find solutions that
best correspond to the real situation of our country, to our
national characteristics, and to the interests of our working
class and people.

The leadership of our Party is firmly resolved to direct—
in the spirit of the July resolutions—the continued building of
socialism, relying ever more widely on our working class; on
our cooperative, and all working, peasantry; on our intel-

ligentsia; and on the millions of our people. It is our resolute and unalterable intention to develop, widen, and deepen democracy in our country, to increase the participation of the workers in running the factories, state farms, and various economic bodies and institutions.

We, of course, want a socialist democracy and not a bourgeois democracy. Our Party and, in our opinion, our working class and people are jealously guarding the achievements of our People's Democracy and will not allow anybody to harm them. We will defend these achievements under any circumstances from whatever quarter they may be threatened.

The main endeavor of the enemies of our people today is to try to undermine the power of the working class, loosen the worker-peasant alliance, undermine the leading role of the working class in our country, and shake our people's faith in their party—the Hungarian Workers Party; to try to loosen the close friendly ties between our country, the Hungarian People's Republic, and the other countries building socialism, in particular between Hungary and the socialist Soviet Union. They endeavor to loosen the relations which link our Party to the glorious Communist Party of the Soviet Union, the Party of Lenin, the Party of the 20th Congress.

They heap slanders on the Soviet Union. They assert that we are trading with the Soviet Union on an unequal footing, that our relations with the Soviet Union allegedly are not of equality, and that our independence must allegedly be defended not against the imperialists but against the Soviet Union. All this is impudent untruth, hostile propaganda which does not contain a grain of truth. The truth is that the Soviet Union not only liberated our country from the yoke of Horthy fascism and German imperialism but even then when our country lay prostrate at the end of the war, she also stood by us and concluded agreements with us on the basis of full equality, and ever since she has been and is pursuing this policy.

There are those who intend to create a conflict between proletarian internationalism and Hungarian patriotism. We

Communists are Hungarian patriots. We used to be patriots in the jails of Horthy fascism, during the difficult decades of underground work and illegality. Our heroes were patriots here at home and in the Spanish Civil War. We profess that we shall do all in our power to build socialism in our country as regards the most important, most fundamental, and most essential problems on a Marxist-Leninist basis in unison with the other countries—while at the same time having regard to the specific conditions prevailing in Hungary, to the economic and social situation of our country, and to Hungarian traditions.

While we loftily proclaim that we are patriots, we also categorically make it plain that we are not nationalists. We are waging a consistent fight against chauvinism, anti-Semitism, and against any other reactionary, antisocial, and inhumane trends and views. We therefore condemn those who strive to spread the poison of chauvinism among our youth and who have taken advantage of the democratic freedom insured by our state to working people to carry out a demonstration of a nationalistic character.

However, even this demonstration will not shake the resolve of the leadership of our Party to continue along the road of developing socialist democratism. We are patriots but at the same time we are also proletarian internationalists.

Our relationship to the Soviet Union and to all countries building socialism is based on the premise that our Parties, taking on the role of leadership in our countries, are inspired by the teachings of Marxism-Leninism, that we are fond of our people and show respect for all other peoples, that we adhere to the principle of fullest equality and noninterference in each other's affairs, but at the same time we also believe in mutual, friendly, and comradely cooperation. We help each other to facilitate the progress of the cause of socialism in our countries and the triumph of the lofty ideals of socialism all over the world.

This was the principle on which the delegation of our Party's Central Committee conducted talks in neighboring and friendly Yugoslavia. It was on this basis that we reached full agreement with the Yugoslav comrades on all those questions which were subject to discussion between the central committees of the two Parties.

We, then, do not want to interfere in the internal affairs of other countries. For us this is a matter of principle. We do not want to interfere in the internal affairs of Poland either, but this cannot in any way mean that we should not follow our own road. We have our own specific problems, our own traditions, our own political and economic conditions. We must determine accordingly our own methods and means in building socialism.

The leadership of our Party deems necessary the further concretization and development of the July resolutions of the Central Committee. For this reason it considers it necessary to examine several important political and political-economic questions of the country so that the building of socialism in our country may become more secure.

Let us proceed more slowly, but preferably let our progress be smooth. Therefore we have to reexamine some important problems in the directives of our Second Five-Year Plan so that when the plan is worked out in final form the uncertainties and tensions which still exist in the directives might be eliminated.

We must also subject our agricultural policy to a thorough examination. We are firmly convinced that socialism represents the only correct path in agriculture. Only that enables us to supply our working class and urban population with enough food, to insure more raw materials for our food industry and light industry, and to reduce prices by large-scale agricultural production in the future. We must defend our socialist achievements in the field of agriculture. We must defend first of all our producer cooperatives.

We must support socialist agriculture, yet at the same time we must insure the fullest voluntariness in the development of the producer-cooperative movement and we must not define in advance in percentages or figures what results we should achieve in the development of producer cooperatives and when these results should materialize. In the first place it is necessary to improve the work of existing producer cooperatives. Internal democracy must also be further developed in producer cooperatives so that the members fully become the masters of the cooperative and the material interestedness of the whole membership and of each member in raising production and crop yields also increases.

Naturally these and other important problems of our country require extremely serious examination. They require that the Central Committee, the supreme representative organ of the Party between two congresses, take a stand on the political, economic, and other problems with which the country is confronted, as well as on the internal problems of our Party.

In view of the importance of the problems that will have to be decided and the urgency of the tasks needing solution, the Politburo has decided to convene, in the next few days, a plenary session of the Central Committee, and to propose to the Central Committee to discuss the political situation and the tasks of the Party, as well as organizational questions. Until such time as the plenary session of the Central Committee can discuss and decide on the above-mentioned problems, and can define the further tasks of our Party, utmost vigilance is required lest hostile elements disturb the efforts of our Party, working class, and working people, and the clarification of the situation.

There has always been great need for Party unity. Without unity our Party would have been unable to defy the murderous terror of Horthy fascism during a quarter of a century. Without the unity of our Party and the working class, people's democracy could not have triumphed in our country, and the working class allied to the working peasantry could not have gained power. This unity, the unity of the Party, the working class, and the working people, must be guarded as the apple of our eye. Let our Party organizations, in a disciplined manner and in complete unity, oppose any attempt at creating disorder, nationalist well-poisoning, and provocation.

Worker comrades! Workers! One has to state frankly that the question now is whether we want a socialist democracy or a bourgeois democracy. Do we want to build socialism in our country or make a breach in the building of socialism and then to fling the gate wide open to capitalism? Will you allow the power of the working class, of the worker-peasant alliance, to be undermined, or will you stand up resolutely, disciplined and in complete unity, together with the entire working people, in defense of the power of the workers and the achievements of socialism?

In addition to great achievements, the performance of the Party leadership had many shortcomings as well. These shortcomings were exposed and corrections were indicated by resolutions adopted by the Central Committee in July, 1953, by the Third Congress of our Party in 1954, and by several subsequent resolutions of the Central Committee, including the July [1956] resolutions. Our future tasks will be determined by the Party's Central Committee on the basis of thorough debate. The results will then be submitted to our Party membership, our working class, and the working people.

With Party Unity for Socialist Democracy! This was the essence of the resolutions adopted by the Central Committee in July [1956]. Our Party leadership is firmly resolved to move ahead irrevocably toward the full development of socialist democracy, guarding our Party's unity with socialist discipline and in the service of our people's nicer, happier future, surpassing the present achievements of our People's Democracy.

Even while Gero spoke the tumult in the streets became aggravated. The focal points of activity were the House of Parliament (where Imre Nagy allegedly talked with a delegation of the demonstrators), the central studio of the Hungarian broadcasting network, and the printing press of *Szabad Nep*. At one or more of these places shooting started and the printing plant of *Szabad Nep* was put out of commission for two days.

At 10:22 P.M. the Politburo of the HWP called an emergency session of the Central Committee to "evaluate conditions and discuss what to do." The session lasted into the early morning hours. It confirmed Erno Gero as First Secretary but bestowed the premiership on Imre Nagy.[3]

3. ANNOUNCEMENT OF THE COUNCIL OF MINISTERS ABOUT THE OUTBREAK OF DISORDERS, OCTOBER 24, 1956

FASCIST REACTIONARY elements have launched an armed attack against our public buildings and have attacked our armed formations. For the sake of restoring order all public gatherings, meetings, and demonstrations are banned until further notice. The armed organs [of the state] have been instructed to apply the full force of the law against all infractions of this order.

> The Council of Ministers of the
> Hungarian People's Republic

4. DECLARATION OF MARTIAL LAW BY THE COUNCIL OF MINISTERS, OCTOBER 24, 1956

ATTENTION, ATTENTION! Announcement: The Council of Ministers of the Hungarian People's Republic has ordered summary jurisdiction throughout the country to be applied against acts designed to overthrow the People's Republic: revolt, incitement, appeal and conspiracy to revolt, murder, manslaughter, arson, keeping of explosives and crimes committed by use of explosives, force applied against official authorities, force against private persons, illicit possession of arms. Crimes falling into the categories of summary jurisdiction must be punished by death. This order becomes valid immediately.

> Imre Nagy
> Chairman of the Council of Ministers[4]

---

[3] The exact circumstances of Nagy's appointment and, more important, the time and manner of his notification are subject to conjecture. According to reports circulated by students and intellectuals a few days after the outbreak of the revolt, Nagy learned of his appointment well after daybreak and then only indirectly when someone called him to inquire if he knew of the government changes that had taken place.

[4] The authenticity of Nagy's signature on this as well as the next document (No. 5) was later (on October 30) denied by the government.

5. Announcement of the Hungarian Government's Appeal for Soviet Military Assistance, October 24, 1956

ATTENTION! ATTENTION!   The dastardly armed attacks of counterrevolutionary gangs during the night have created an extremely serious situation.   The bandits have penetrated into factories and public buildings and have murdered many civilians, members of the national defense forces, and fighters of the state security organs.

The Government organs have not reckoned with the bloody dastardly attacks and therefore applied for help, in accordance with the terms of the Warsaw Treaty, to the Soviet formations stationed in Hungary.   The Soviet formations, in compliance with the Government's request, are taking part in the restoration of order.

The Government is appealing to inhabitants of the capital to keep calm; to condemn the bloody havoc wreaked by the counterrevolutionary gangs and support everywhere the Hungarian and Soviet troops seeking to maintain order.   The liquidation of the counterrevolutionary gangs is the most sacred cause of every honest Hungarian worker, of the people and Fatherland.   At this moment we are concentrating all our strength on that task.

6. A Plea for Order and a Promise of Hope: Proclamation by Imre Nagy to the Hungarian Nation, October 24, 1956

PEOPLE OF BUDAPEST, I announce that all those, who in the interest of avoiding further bloodshed, stop fighting before 1400 [2 P.M.] today and lay down their arms will be exempted from summary jurisdiction.[5]

---

[5] The amnesty was subsequently extended to 6 and then to 10 P.M. It continued to be extended daily until October 28 when a general cease-fire was ordered (see Document 15 in this chapter) and even after that as not all insurgents surrendered their arms.

At the same time I state that with all means at our disposal we will realize as soon as possible, on the basis of the June, 1953, Government program as I expounded it at that time in Parliament, the systematic democratization of our country in every field of Party, state, political, and economic life. Heed our appeal, cease fighting, and secure the restoration of calm and order in the interest of the future of our people and country. Return to peaceful and creative work.

Hungarians, comrades, my friends! I speak to you in moments pregnant with responsibility. As you know, on the basis of the confidence placed in me by the Central Committee of the Hungarian Workers Party and the Presidential Council, I have taken over the leadership of the Government as Chairman of the Council of Ministers. Every possibility exists for the Government to realize our political program by relying on the Hungarian people, under the leadership of the Communist Party.

The essence of this program, as you know, is the far-reaching democratization of Hungarian public life, the realization of a Hungarian road corresponding to our own national characteristics in the building of socialism, and the realization of our lofty national aims, the radical improvement of the workers' living conditions.

In order, however, that we should be able, together with you, to make a start with this work, the first necessity is the creation of order, discipline, and calm. Hostile elements joining the ranks of peacefully demonstrating Hungarian youth have misled many well-meaning workers and turned against the People's Democracy, against the power of the people. The paramount task now facing everyone is the urgent consolidation of the situation.

Afterwards we will be able to agree on every question, since the Government and the majority of the Hungarian people want the same thing. By referring to our joint and great responsibility toward national existence I appeal to you, to every man, woman, youth, worker and peasant, and intellectual to stand fast and remain calm, resist the provocateurs, and help restore order and assist our forces to maintain order. By common effort we must prevent bloodshed and we must not let our sacred national program be soiled by blood.

The Hungarian Government is preparing for peaceful and creative work. The Government is determined not to allow itself to be diverted from the road of democratization and of the realization of the program corresponding to the interest of the Hungarian people as discussed with the broad strata of the people. We want a policy not of revenge but of reconciliation. For this reason the Government has decided that all those who voluntarily and immediately lay down arms and cease fighting, as in the case of the groups which have already surrendered, will not be brought before summary jurisdiction.

Workers, defend the factories and machines. This is our own treasure. He who destroys or loots causes damage to the whole nation. Order, calm, discipline—this is now the slogan. This comes before everything else.

Friends, Hungarians! I will soon expound in detail the Government's program, which will be debated in the National Assembly when it meets soon. Our future is at stake. The great road of progress of our national existence lies ahead of us. Line up behind the Government. Secure peace, the continuation of peaceful and creative work. Make it possible for every worker in our country to work undisturbed for his own and his family's future. Line up behind the Party! Line up behind the Government! Trust, that learning from the mistakes of the past, we will find the correct road for the prosperity of our country.

7. RADIO ADDRESS BY JANOS KADAR, SECRETARY OF THE HUNGARIAN WORKERS PARTY, OCTOBER 24, 1956

WORKERS, COMRADES! The demonstration of university youth, which began with the formulation of generally acceptable demands, has precipitously degenerated into a demonstration against our democratic order and, under this guise, an armed attack has broken out. It is only with glowing anger that we can speak of this attack by which counterrevolutionary reactionary elements have risen against the capital of our country, against our people's democratic order and the power of the working class.

In regard to the rebels who rose with arms in their hands against the legal order of our People's Republic, the Central Committee of our Party and our Government have adopted the only correct viewpoint: Only surrender or complete defeat can await those who stubbornly continue their murderous and, at the same time, completely hopeless fight against the order of our working people.

At the same time, we are aware that the provocateurs, going into the fight surreptitiously, have been able to hide behind the cover of people who lost their orientation in the hours of chaos, and particularly many youths whom we cannot consider as conscious enemies of our regime. Accordingly, now that we have reached the stage of the liquidation of the hostile attack, and with a view to avoiding further bloodshed, we have offered and are offering to those misled individuals, who are willing to surrender voluntarily at request, a possibility of saving their lives and future and returning to the camp of honest people.

The fight is being fought mainly by the most loyal units of our People's Army, by the members of our Internal Security Forces and police, showing heroic courage, and by former partisans with the support of the fraternal and allied Soviet troops. Yet this fight is at the same time a political fight in which our Party and our working class represent the major power.

Communist and working comrades, workers from Budapest and from the provinces, help by every possible means, and last but not least, by means of political mass enlightenment, to defend and to carry to ultimate triumph the struggle that we are conducting in defense of the political power of the working class as well as in the restoration of a peaceful and normal life within the shortest possible time!

In this fight an important task devolves on every Party organization, every Party official, every male and female worker. In defense of the power of the working people, display such firmness and steadfastness so as to prevent those who intend to restore capitalism—even if they carry out the attack under different pleasing slogans—from ever again resorting to such a daring attempt! Defend the Party's premises, our public institutions, as much as your homes and your factories, against every kind of hostile attack and troublemaking! Help to lead those of good intentions, who have been misled, back onto the correct path and help support the measures taken by our armed forces and authorities!

Communist and non-Party workers must be aware of the fact that, by defending the people's democratic order, they are actually defending the structure and foundations of a socialist society. You must be aware of the fact that our Party and our people rely primarily on you.

Comrades, be sure too that our leading Party and state organs, strengthened by veteran and deserving fighters of the labor movement in the difficult hours of the fight, are resolved to solve every problem of life which is awaiting solution with unflagging energy by the further development of the democratism of Party, state, and social life. The path of decisive reforms is open before us. It is upon us and upon you to cleanse and free this path against every counterrevolutionary force.

Today we still live in hours in which we are fighting for the state power of the working people. Yet tomorrow a new era of liquidating all the mistakes of the past and building a peaceful future will start.

Communist workers, men and women of Angyalfold, Csepel, Kobanya, and Obuda, of the other old bastions of the labor movement, and of the old revolutionary city of Budapest, in these difficult hours and days act as the vanguard in the fight for a happier future, for the firm power of the workers, and for a socialist social order! Be vigilant!

Early in the morning of October 25, the Government announced that during the night "the army, internal security forces, and armed workers together with Soviet troops" liquidated the "counter-revolutionary putsch." A short while later the Ministry of National Defense issued an order of the day.

8. Order of the Day Issued by Colonel General Istvan Bata, Minister of Defense, October 25, 1956

ORGANIZED COUNTERREVOLUTIONARIES making use of the students' demonstration on October 23 to promote their vile antidemocratic aims, attempted in Budapest to overthrow our peaceful People's Democracy by armed force.

Men, NCO's and officers of the Hungarian People's Army held their ground with honor in the fighting on October 24 to put down this counterrevolutionary attempt. They proved that even in the most difficult times they are loyal defenders of the power of the people—of the proletarian dictatorship.

In the great battles they inflicted heavy losses on the counter-revolutionary gangs, captured numerous prisoners, and successfully protected the citizens of the capital against destruction and plundering. Together with the forces of internal security and the units of the fraternal Soviet Army they insured, by their self-sacrificing fight, the achievements of our People's Democracy and the power of the people.

I order the soldiers of our People's Army by increased effort and full determination to liquidate finally all counter-revolutionary forces in the capital by noon today, to secure complete calm and order and to assure the normal flow of peaceful and creative activity in our capital. Every soldier of our People's Army must with full vigilance secure the proper supply of the services and prevent any similar counterrevolutionary outbreak. I express my appreciation to every soldier of our People's Army, our internal security forces, and the fraternal Soviet army which is participating in these struggles. Glory be to those who are sacrificing their lives for our people's regime!

Colonel General Istvan Bata
Minister of National Defense
of the Hungarian People's Republic

Also on the morning of October 25 Erno Gero was dismissed as First Secretary of the HWP[6] and Janos Kadar was appointed in his stead.

9. Radio Appeal by Janos Kadar Asking for an End of the Fighting, October 25, 1956

HUNGARIAN WORKERS, dear comrades!

The Politburo of our Party has entrusted me with the post of First Secretary of the Central Committee of our Party in a grave and difficult situation. This is no time to waste words.

The grave situation in which we have become involved is characterized by the fact that diverse elements are mingled in it. The demonstration of a section of the youth which started peacefully and in which the majority of the participants had honest aims degenerated in a few hours into an armed attack against the state power and People's Democracy in accordance with the intentions of antipopular and counterrevolutionary elements who joined in.

It was in this grave situation that a decision had to be made. In complete unanimity the leadership of our Party decided that the armed attack against the power of our People's Republic had to be repelled by every possible means. The power of the working people, the working class, and the peasantry embodied in the People's Republic is sacred to us and must be sacred to everybody who does not wish to reimpose on our people the old yoke, the rule of the capitalists, bankers, and large estate-owners.

This armed attack caused bloodshed, destruction, and serious material damage and will continue to do so until we put a definite end to it with the help of our entire working people.

As it is evident to everybody that the restoration of conditions for peaceful, creative work and order is the paramount interest of the hour, the Central Committee of our Party is turn-

---

[6] Gero, reported to have been subsequently killed by the insurgents, has not been heard of since this time.

ing to the entire nation, in particular to the population of the capital, asking for their support in mastering this task. In the mastering of the tasks the main force, above all, is the resolute, united stand of the entire Party membership and the working class.

Trusting in the joint and united stand of all workers, peasants, and intellectuals, and of every honest patriot, I also ask the youth to withdraw their support from the disturbers of order and have confidence that their proposals will be examined by the leadership of the Party, in harmony with the interests of the nation as a whole, and will be acted upon.

Beyond this the comrades must realize how important it is that every Communist, the entire working class, should act with unshakable unity in these grave hours.

It is the firm resolve of the Party leadership, after the earliest possible restoration of order, to face frankly and without dilatoriness all the burning questions whose solution cannot be postponed. We want to solve these tasks without delay, by deepening the democratic character of our state, Party, and social life, within the limits of realistic possibilities.

Comrades, the Central Committee of the Party recommends to the Government that, after the restoration of order, it should conduct talks with the Soviet Government in the spirit of complete equality between Hungary and the Soviet Union, fraternal cooperation, and internationalism, for a mutually equitable and just settlement of the issues between the two socialist countries.

Workers, Communist comrades, be unflinching and firm. Defend the order of the people's power, our socialist state, the future of the working people.

10. RADIO ADDRESS BY IMRE NAGY PROMISING NEW POLICIES AND AN ADJUSTMENT IN RELATIONS WITH THE SOVIET UNION, OCTOBER 25, 1956

WORKING PEOPLE OF HUNGARY!

During the past few days our country has lived through tragic events. A small number of counterrevolutionaries and provocateurs launched an armed attack against the order of our People's Republic, which a section of the workers of Budapest, because of their bitterness over the country's situation, supported.

This bitterness has been exacerbated by the grave political and economic mistakes of the past, the remedying of which had been made absolutely imperative by the situation prevailing in the country and the general desire of the people. The new Party leadership and the Government under new leadership are resolved to draw the most far-reaching lessons from these tragic events. Shortly after the restoration of order, the National Assembly will be convened. At its session I will submit an all-embracing and well-founded reform program which will touch on all important problems of our national life. The implementation of this program will demand the transformation of the Government and of the revived Patriotic People's Front by rallying the broadest national, democratic forces around them. For the realization of this program the immediate cessation of fighting, the restoration of calm and order, and the uninterrupted continuation of [economic] production are absolutely indispensable. I call on the working people of the country, on every true patriot, to promote this by all the means at their disposal.

As Chairman of the Council of Ministers, I hereby announce that the Hungarian Government will initiate negotiations concerning the relations between the Hungarian People's Republic and the Soviet Union, among other things about the withdrawal of Soviet forces stationed in Hungary, on the basis of Hungarian-Soviet friendship, proletarian internationalism, equality between Communist Parties and socialist countries, and national independence.

I am convinced that Hungarian-Soviet relations built on these foundations will provide solid ground for sincere and true friendship between our peoples, for our national progress and our socialist future. The recall of the Soviet troops whose intervention in the fighting has been made necessary by the

vital interests of our socialist order will take place without
delay after the restoration of peace and order.

The Government will display far-reaching magnanimity in
a spirit of reconciliation and understanding and will not apply
martial law against those who took up arms not meaning to
overthrow our people's democratic regime and who immediately stop fighting and surrender their arms. This applies to
everyone, all youths, workers, and armed forces personnel.

At the same time, in the interest of workers desiring peace
and order, in the defense of our peaceful democratic state order,
the rigor of the law will be applied against those who continue to attack with arms, incite, and plunder. I warn our
working people with particular care against irresponsible disturbers and rumormongers whose harmful activity is one of
the greatest obstacles to restoring peace and calm.

I am filled with deep grief over every drop of blood shed
by innocent working people who fell victim during these
tragic days. Let us cease the tragic fighting and the senseless
bloodletting. Hungarians, friends, comrades! Under the leadership of the Party let us set out along the road of peaceful
and creative work, building a better, more beautiful socialist
future of our people.

11. Appeal by Gabor Tanczos, Secretary of the Petofi Circle, to Restore Order, October 25, 1956

Friends, young Hungarian men and girls! I speak to you on
behalf of the Petofi Circle, the organization which has done so
much during the past few months to fight for true democracy
and for the termination of the shameful personal tyranny of
Rakosi.

We greatly value the enthusiasm which you displayed during the past few days. We respect your true patriotism. We
are quite certain that you have nothing to do with certain
plundering, cruel elements. We know that the mistakes com-

mitted and the wrong leadership of Erno Gero, who has been relieved of his post, have filled many with bitterness and have led them to commit deeds which they had not originally intended.

But now we have good leadership. Janos Kadar, who was put in prison through personal arbitrariness, has become the First Secretary of the Party. Imre Nagy, for whose vindication we have fought together so much, heads the Government. We must start working and studying at last.

No more precious human blood must be shed. We must prepare for better deeds and for the building of a truly democratic Hungary which is socialist in the Hungarian way and is the equal of every other nation. We must achieve a democratic system of schooling, a reform of the universities, and we must improve conditions in student hostels. But we cannot build, give accommodation, raise the standard of living, and educate while guns roar.

Return to your homes, to your parents and student hostels. Trust the Government headed by Imre Nagy, which in the nearest future will begin to realize all that is dear to the heart of the loyal, patriotic Hungarian youth.

Despite appeals the unrest did not abate. On the contrary it spread to the countryside and made rapid headway there.

In the afternoon of October 26, the first workers' councils were formed in Csepel. A short while later the Central Committee of the HWP issued a declaration to the people accepting several of the insurgents' demands.

12. DECLARATION BY THE CENTRAL COMMITTEE OF THE HUNGARIAN WORKERS PARTY, OCTOBER 26, 1956

NOT SINCE the end of two world wars has our country experienced days as tragic as these. A fratricidal battle is raging in the capital of the nation. The number of injured can be estimated to run into the thousands and the dead into the hundreds.

We must put an immediate end to the bloodshed. To insure this, the Central Committee takes the following measures:

1—The Central Committee of the Hungarian Workers Party addresses a proposal to the Presidium of the National Council of the Patriotic People's Front to put a recommendation before the Presidential Council of the People's Republic for the election of a new national Government. This Government shall have the mission of making good without fail the mistakes and crimes of the past. Relying on the whole nation, it will help to meet out people's every legitimate demand, and, with our people's inexhaustible strength, it will create a free country of prosperity, independence, and socialist democracy. The Central Committee, led by Comrade Imre Nagy, will make recommendations regarding the members of a Government to be formed on the broadest national foundations.

2—The new Government shall start negotiations with the Soviet Government in order to settle relations between our countries on the basis of independence, complete equality, and noninterference in one another's internal affairs. As a first step toward this end, Soviet troops will, after the restoration of order, immediately return to their bases. Complete equality between Hungary and the Soviet Union corresponds to the interests of both countries, because on that basis alone can a truly fraternal, unbreakable Hungarian-Soviet friendship be built. It is on that basis that relations between Poland and the Soviet Union are now being shaped anew.

3—The Central Committee deems correct the election of workers' councils in the factories, through the intermediary of the trade union organs. To satisfy the legitimate material demands of the working class, wage increases must be implemented. For this purpose maximum efforts must be made within the limits of our material possibilities, first of all as regards the lower-paid groups.

4—The Government shall grant an amnesty to all those who have taken part in the armed struggle. The only condition is that they should lay down their arms immediately but at the latest by 10 o'clock tonight.

5—The Central Committee and the Government leave no room for doubt regarding their adherence to the principles of socialist democracy, but at the same time they are firmly resolved to defend the achievements of our People's Democracy and will not budge an inch [*sic*] on the issue of socialism. Their program is suitable to rally every honest patriot. The Central Committee is not oblivious to the fact that our People's Democracy still has bitter and desperate enemies and appeals to Communists, Hungarian workers—to the workers first of all—the armed forces, former partisans, the firm protectors of the people's power, to annihilate without mercy those who raise their arms against the state power of our People's Republic if they fail to lay down their arms within the set time limit.

6—Immediately after order has been restored, we shall set about the elaboration of all the changes which must be realized in our people's economy, agricultural policy, People's Front policy, our Party's leadership, and its entire activity in order to permit the principles of socialist democracy to be fully implemented.

By means of an exchange of opinion with all the people, we shall prepare and realize the great national program of a democratic, socialist, independent, and free Hungary. Let the nation's unity and reconciliation replace the tragic era of murderous fratricide! Let the wounds heal which we have inflicted upon ourselves! If we want to live, we must begin a new life. It is up to us alone to see to it that after the horrible tribulations, internal peace, life without fear, productive work that creates prosperity, freedom, the reign of law and justice should be the lot of our people. Long live free, democratic, socialist Hungary!

Budapest, October 26, 1956   The Central Committee of the
Hungarian Workers Party

13. Appeals by the Central Council of Trade Unions
on the Elections of Workers' Councils, October
27, 1956

WORKERS! The wish of the working class has been realized:
enterprises will be managed by workers' councils.[7] This com-
pletes the process of taking over the factories as the property of
the people. Workers, technicians! You can now regard the
enterprises entirely as your own. From now on you manage
them yourselves. The exaggerated central management of the
factories which prevailed up to now will cease, along with the
faults arising from it.

Great responsibility rests with workers' councils. Therefore, you must elect members of workers' councils with great
circumspection and from among the most experienced and best
workers. The new Government will increase the wages of those
with small salaries. The sooner you start production in the
factories and the better our workers' councils will work, the
sooner will it be possible to raise wages, and the higher will the
increases be. Support, therefore, the new Hungarian Government in its efforts for socialist construction in a free, democratic
Hungary.

The Presidium of the
National Council of Trade Unions

HUNGARIAN ENGINEERS and technicians! The new Government of Imre Nagy represents national unity. The new Government will discuss the country's affairs with the people. It

---

[7] Instructions with respect to the creation of the workers' councils
(issued in the evening of October 26) suggested that the method of
election should be decided in each case according to the desires of the
workers. The jurisdiction of the councils was to extend over "questions
of production, administration, and management." The councils were
to decide on the wage structure in accordance with local requirements.
For the day-to-day management of the factories it was recommended
that the workers' councils should elect from among their own members
a directing body of 5 to 15 members which would also be endowed
with the right of firing and hiring workers as well as administrative,
technical, and managerial personnel.

will discuss the reorganization of the people's economy and important technical problems with engineers and technicians. It will never again happen that burning questions are decided without expert advice. The voice of experts will carry great weight in our country from now on. Nothing will push into the background appreciation of and the opportunity of asserting expert knowledge. Support the Government of Hungarian national unity!

The Presidium of the
National Council of Trade Unions

October 27 was a day of relative calm. It witnessed the reorganization of the Government, however, and hasty preparations for a policy statement.

The roster of the Government included, in addition to Imre Nagy, Antal Apro, Jozsef Bognar (Communists), and Ferenc Erdei (former crypto-Communist National Peasant Party leader) as deputy chairmen of the Council of Ministers, Zoltan Tildy (former leader of the Smallholders Party, President of Hungary from 1946 to 1948, when he was removed and kept under house arrest until the spring of 1956) as Minister of State, Imre Horvath (Communist) as Minister of Foreign Affairs, Ferenc Munnich (Communist, veteran of the Spanish Civil War) as Minister of the Interior, Karoly Janza (Communist, Deputy Minister of National Defense since 1950) as Minister of Defense, and Bela Kovacs[8] (former Secretary General of the Smallholders Party, who was arrested by the Soviet police in Budapest in the spring of 1947, disappeared without a trace, and emerged from prison in the spring of 1956) as Minister of Agriculture. The Government also included Gyorgy Lukacs as Minister of Culture, and several other members. (Lukacs, an internationally known Communist writer and theoretician, returned to his native Hungary after 1945. He was eclipsed after 1948 and emerged to prominence again in the spring of 1956.)

---

[8] Kovacs was contacted by Istvan Dobi, President of Hungary, by telephone and asked to join the Government. He gave his consent without knowing the composition or program of the Government and actually did not participate in any governmental activity until the evening of November 1 when he arrived at Budapest from Pecs where he had been recuperating from the effects of nine years in jail.

14. A Perspective on Events: "Faithful to the Truth,"
Editorial in *Szabad Nep*, October 28, 1956

WE DO not agree with those who summarily dismiss the events
of the past few days as a counterrevolutionary fascist attempt at
a coup d'état. We have followed the developments with attention and are fairly well informed about the various trends. On
this basis we establish the following as facts:

The events started with the demonstration of Budapest university and college youth. It would, however, be a very great
mistake to regard this demonstration purely as a youth movement. The young people of Budapest expressed a heartfelt
feeling, a noble and warm passion shared by the whole people.

We must realize at last that a great national democratic
movement has developed in our country which embraces and
welds together our people as a whole, a movement which was
forced below the surface by the tyranny of the past years but
started to burn with high flame when touched by the first
breeze of freedom during the past few months. This movement
expressed the workers' claim to become genuine masters of the
factories. It was in this movement that the human claim of the
peasantry to be freed from the constant material uncertainty of
existence and unwarranted vexations, and to be able to live their
lives as individual or cooperative peasants according to their
inclinations or desires, developed.

This movement was strengthened by the struggle waged by
Communist and non-Party intellectuals for the freedom of creative work and the moral purity of our system. It was love of
country which imparted to this people's movement its greatest
strength, warmth, and its passionate character willing to risk
even death.

The demand for the equality and the independence of the
country is as all-embracing as the mother tongue we speak. It
is an eternal shame that there were Communists even in leading
positions who did not understand the language of their own
people. What has saved the Party's honor is that even under

Rakosi's tyranny there were Communists, in increasing numbers until they gradually became the majority, who as revolutionaries understood the ever faster, restless throb of the nation's heart. They placed themselves at the head of the struggle which leads the country toward socialism on a Hungarian and democratic path.

This passion which carries away a whole nation perhaps once in a century—this passion caught up the university and working class youth of Budapest on October 23 and prompted it to demonstrate. To the mild and mostly correct demands voiced during the demonstrations we must now add one thing: we must determine what factors and who are responsible for the fact that this mighty and patriotic demonstration was soiled by blood and signaled the beginning of the most horrible fratricidal fight. We cannot, as yet, reply to this question, but our people will not rest until they receive a true and clear answer to the question. Let us examine a few facts which may be helpful in assessing the situation without passion and with great objectivity.

On October 23, 150,000 to 200,000 Budapest youths, joined by a goodly number of older people, demonstrated for the fulfillment of just, democratic, and national demands. The demonstrators demanded, among other things, the revision of Soviet-Hungarian relations and their settlement on a basis of complete equality. Dissonant voices mixed with the demonstrators', especially in the late hours of the evening. These voices went beyond the limits of the struggle waged for socialist democratism. We must add, however, that at this stage many university students volunteered to convince the blinded and extremist elements that the struggle was waged not against the regime but for socialist democratism and for insuring national independence.

People were looking forward with great expectations to Erno Gero's radio address at 8 o'clock Tuesday night.[9] The address, however, was a grave disappointment because it

---

[9] See Document 2 in this chapter.

proved that, first, a number of the leaders at that time were unable and unwilling to understand the essential character of the demonstration; secondly, they could not and did not want to draw the proper concrete conclusions from the demonstration. By that time the atmosphere in the street was tense to the breaking point. At various points in the city armed clashes broke out.

It is important to point out that even after this and on the second and third day of the fighting, demonstrators appeared before public buildings shouting such slogans as "We want independence and freedom; we are not fascists." It is also true that looting, on a fairly small scale, was done only by those bad and infamous elements who had wormed themselves into the ranks of the demonstrators. But we were able to see in many places that articles were untouched behind the broken shopwindows.

On the basis of all this we can assert that even after the outbreak of the armed conflict the question was not simply that counterrevolutionaries fought on one side and units loyal to the regime on the other side. The truth is that among the fighting insurgents there were in the beginning a very large number of honest patriots, including Communists, who did not realize up to that time that socialist democracy was adequately guaranteed.

The tragic events cannot blunt our judgment to such an extent as to lose sight of the truth. We cannot regard those university students who come from the working, peasant, and intellectual classes and the young workers who formed the bulk of the insurgents as enemies of our People's Democracy.

We must also note that public opinion received the appointment of Imre Nagy as Premier hopefully. However, the resolution which confirmed Erno Gero in his post of First Secretary poured oil on the fire. But Imre Nagy's statement, Erno Gero's dismissal and the appointment of Janos Kadar as First Secretary, the declaration of the newly formed Central Committee and the inclusion of Zoltan Tildy, Bela Kovacs, Gyorgy Lukacs, and Antal Gyenes, met with the approval of a large part of the masses.

The armed conflict nonetheless continued, but on a lesser and subsiding scale, after Thursday afternoon. The reason for the subsiding of the strength of the resistance was due not exclusively—not even primarily—to the Soviet troops but to the fact that a significant number of insurgents, realizing that the fulfilment of their democratic demands was guaranteed, availed themselves of the opportunity offered by the amnesty after Thursday and laid down their arms. It is characteristic of the mentality of these democratic strata that after laying down their arms several of them joined with Hungarian soldiers and police in restoring order.

A turning point in the situation was also indicated by the fact that the workers began to form workers' councils. They armed a workers' militia who are taking part in restoring order together with the Government forces. We would, however, distort the truth if we kept silent about the fact that bad elements also took part in the demonstration from the very beginning. These committed armed excesses, especially after the fighting started. They took a stand against our People's Democracy. They murdered innocent unarmed people and prisoners, and looted. One of the proofs of this is that there were a number of people with criminal records among the captured, and that a number of former Horthyite officers were also disarmed. These elements had, and continue to have, counterrevolutionary designs. Against these elements, who are still shooting and are thereby endangering the lives of the peaceful population, the full severity of the law must be invoked.

For this reason, in order to avoid bloodshed on a larger scale, we appeal with sober and calm words, not led by vengeful hatred, to those misled or intoxicated elements who are still fighting to cut themselves off from the counterrevolutionaries and rotten elements and to lay down their arms. They may count on the magnanimity of our national Government. But this is the twelfth hour for them to turn back from the road leading to counterrevolution. In Budapest the fighting is nearing an end. Order and calm must be created. Every possibility is at hand for this, for the whole people desires it.

1—The national Government has already fulfilled the essential demands of our people.

2—Further demands, such as the removal of Soviet troops, were adopted by the Government as its own, and it will begin negotiations in this respect parallel with the restoration of order.

3—The many-sided development of prosperity and democracy requires well-considered political and economic measures. For this we need order and calm. Without this we cannot begin, in peaceful days of constructive work, to raise the level of democracy and the living standard.

4—A considerable number of those who are still fighting are in fact threatening our system, though perhaps against their own intentions. Against these we must use every available means, in order to defend our people, our system, our democratic program. To this end the masses which were demonstrating three or four days ago, Hungary's youth, the whole people, the Party, and the new national Government must take the same platform.

5—Our population has had enough of bloodshed and privations. It wants peace and calm. Let our population take an active part in restoring peace and order! That is now the foremost task.

15. ORDER OF THE GOVERNMENT TO CEASE FIRE, OCTOBER 28, 1956

IN ORDER to stop further bloodshed and insure peaceful development, the Government of the Hungarian People's Republic orders a general and immediate cease-fire. It instructs the Armed Forces to fire only if attacked.

Imre Nagy
Chairman of the Council of Ministers

16. RADIO ADDRESS BY IMRE NAGY ANNOUNCING THE FORMATION AND THE PROGRAM OF A NEW GOVERNMENT, OCTOBER 28, 1956

DURING THE course of the past week bloody events took place with tragic rapidity. The fatal consequences of the terrible mistakes and crimes of these past 10 years unfold before us in these painful events which we are witnessing and in which we are participating. During the course of 1,000 years of history, destiny was not sparing in scourging our people and nation. But such a thing has never before afflicted our country.

The Government condemns the viewpoints according to which the present formidable movement is a counterrevolution. Without doubt, as always happens at times of great popular movements, this movement too was used by criminal elements to compromise it and commit common criminal acts. It is also a fact that reactionary and counterrevolutionary elements had penetrated into the movement with the aim of overthrowing the popular democratic regime.

But it is also indisputable that in these stirrings a great national and democratic movement, embracing and unifying all our people, developed with elemental force. This movement aims at guaranteeing our national freedom, independence, and sovereignty, of advancing our society, our economic and political system on the way of democracy—for this is the only foundation for socialism in our country. This great movement exploded because of the grave crimes committed during the past historic period.

The situation was further aggravated by the fact that up to the very last, the [Party] leadership had not decided to break finally with the old and criminal policy. It is this above all which led to the tragic fratricidal fight in which so many patriots died on both sides. In the course of these battles was born the Government of democratic national unity, independence, and socialism which will become the true expression of the will of the people. This is the firm resolution of the Government.

The new Government, relying on the people's power and control in the hope of gaining its full confidence, will at once begin with the practical implementation of the just demands of the people. The Government begins its work in the midst of conditions of unheard-of difficulty. The grave economic situation bequeathed to us by the past has become further aggravated as a consequence of the fighting of the past few days. The next few months facing us will also be very difficult. The Government clearly sees the gravity of the material situation in which our working class, our peasants, and our intellectuals find themselves.

The Government wishes to rest in the first place on the support of the fighting Hungarian working class, but also, of course, on the support of the entire Hungarian working population. We have decided to work out a broad program, in the framework of which we wish to settle old and justified demands and rectify damages to the satisfaction of the working class, among other things on the question of wages and work norms, the raising of minimum pay in the lowest wage brackets and of the smallest pensions, taking into account the number of years worked, and the raising of family allowances.

To help resolve the exceptionally grave housing crisis, the Government will give its utmost support to all state, cooperative, and private construction of homes and apartments. The Government welcomes the initiative taken by workers for the extension of democracy in their enterprises, and approves the formation of workers' councils. With a firm hand the Government will put an end to the serious illegalities which were committed in the movement of agricultural producer cooperatives and during the course of commassation of land. The Government will work out a great scheme to help the development of neglected and retarded agricultural production to revitalize production in cooperative and individual farms and stimulate productive zeal.

The Government will courageously build on young workers, peasants, students, and the university youth, giving them the means of using their initiative in the framework of a cleaner public life. It will take pains to offer them the best material conditions at the outset of their careers. The Government supports those new organs of democratic self-government which have sprung up at the people's initiative and will strive to find a place for them in the administrative machinery. In order to put an end to bloodshed and in the interest of assuring peaceful development, the Government has ordered a general cease-fire and has commanded the Armed Forces not to shoot unless attacked. At the same time it appeals to all those who took arms to abstain from all military operations and to deliver their arms without fail. In order to assure the safeguarding of order and security, new armed forces will be formed without delay from units of the Army, of the police, and of the armed groups of workers and youth.[10]

The Hungarian Government has come to an agreement with the Soviet Government that the Soviet forces shall withdraw immediately from Budapest and that simultaneously with the formation of our new Army they shall evacuate the city's territory.[11] The Hungarian Government will initiate negotiations in order to settle relations between the Hungarian People's Republic and the Soviet Union, among other things with regard to the withdrawal of Soviet forces stationed in Hungary, in the spirit of Soviet-Hungarian friendship and the principle of the mutual equality and the national independence of socialist countries.

After the reestablishment of order we shall organize a new and unified state police force and we shall dissolve the organs of state security. No one who took part in the armed fighting need fear further reprisals. The Government will put proposals before the National Assembly for the restoration of the emblem of Kossuth as the national emblem and the observance of March 15 once again as a national holiday.

People of Hungary!

In these hours of bitterness and strife one is prone to see only the dark side of the past twelve years. We must not let our views become clouded. These twelve years contain lasting, ineradicable, historic achievements which you, Hungarian workers, peasants, and intellectuals, under the leadership of

---

[10] See Chapter VIII, Document 2.
[11] See Chapter VIII, Document 4.

the Hungarian Workers Party brought into being by virtue of hard labor and sacrifice. Our renascent popular democracy relies on the strength and self-sacrifice which you have displayed in our founding labors and which constitute the best guarantee of our country's happier future.

17. THE DISINTEGRATION OF THE HUNGARIAN WORKERS PARTY: DECISIONS REACHED BY THE CENTRAL COMMITTEE OF THE HUNGARIAN WORKERS PARTY, OCTOBER 28, 1956[12]

THE CENTRAL COMMITTEE of the Hungarian Workers Party held a meeting this morning. It discussed the political situation and adopted the following decisions:

The Central Committee approves of the announcement made by the Government of the Hungarian People's Republic today.[13] It appeals to every Party organization, every Party member to promote the implementation of the contents of this announcement.

In view of the exceptional situation which has emerged, the Central Committee transfers its mandate to lead the Party, which it received from the Third Congress [in 1954], to a six-member Party Presidium whose chairman is Comrade Janos Kadar and whose membership includes Antal Apro, Karoly Kiss, Ferenc Munnich, Imre Nagy, and Zoltan Szanto.

The mandate of the Party Presidium is valid until the Fourth Party Congress which should be convened in the shortest possible time. In its work the Party Presidium will rely on the Central Committee and the Politburo.

Meanwhile the voices of the outlying areas where the insurgents met with less resistance than in Budapest began to be heard. One of the loudest was that of the workers' council and student parliament of Borsod County (capital, Miskolc) who formulated their demands in the following terms:

---

[12] See also Chapter VIII, Documents 6, 14.
[13] See the preceding document.

18. APPEAL BY THE WORKERS' COUNCIL AND STUDENT PARLIAMENT OF BORSOD COUNTY, OCTOBER 28, 1956

ATTENTION, ATTENTION! Appeal to the Hungarian workers' councils and freedom fighters, Debrecen, Szeged, Hatvan, Szekesfehervar, Pecs, Szombathely, Gyor, Moson-Magyarovar, Szolnok, Nyiregyhaza, and all workers' councils, members of workers' councils, freedom fighters, and the youth of the country!

In the course of several days of our fight for freedom the unanimous demand of the entire country slowly begins to take shape. Therefore, we workers, students, and armed forces under the leadership of the workers' council and student parliament of Miskolc submit the following proposal:

1—We demand the formation of a new provisional Government fighting for a truly democratic free and socialist Hungary, excluding all ministers who have served under the Rakosi system.

2—This Government can only be created by general and free elections. As this cannot be realized in the present situation, we suggest that Imre Nagy should form a provisional Government containing only the most indispensable ministries. All ministries of related functions should be amalgamated. In the present situation there is absolutely no need for twenty-two Ministers and three Deputy Premiers.

3—The first act of the independent, new provisional Government thus to be created, resting on a coalition of the Hungarian Workers Party and the People's Front, should be the immediate recall of Soviet troops from our country, not to their bases but to their fatherland, the Soviet Union.

4—The new Government should include in its program and fulfill the demands of all the workers' councils, plants, student parliaments of the country. These demands have already been made known everywhere in the press.

5—The new state power shall have only two kinds of armed forces—the police and the regular army. The state security authority [AVH] is to be abolished.

6—Abolition of summary jurisdiction and full amnesty after the withdrawal of the Soviet troops for all fighters for liberation and patriots who have participated in the rising in whatever form.

7—General elections within two months with the participation of several parties.

Let us develop a joint point of view about the above. This point of view appears to be shared by all and is not at all identical with that of the present Government which is relying on a foreign power.

CHAPTER VII

FOREIGN COMMUNIST REACTIONS TO THE HUNGARIAN EVENTS OF OCTOBER 23-28, 1956

1. EDITORIAL: "COLLAPSE OF THE ANTIPOPULAR ADVENTURE IN HUNGARY," *Pravda*, OCTOBER 28, 1956[1]

IN THE PAST FEW DAYS the Hungarian People's Republic has been the scene of events which have attracted public attention in all countries. In reporting these events, the bourgeois press and radio are employing their favorite weapons of slander and fabrications more than ever before.

What happened in Hungary?

Comrade Janos Kadar, First Secretary of the Central Committee of the Hungarian Workers Party, characterized these events in his October 25 radio speech as follows:[2]

Antipopular counterrevolutionary elements transformed within a few hours a loyal demonstration of our youth, whose intentions were for the most part peaceful, into an armed struggle against the people's democratic system. The leadership of our party unanimously decided that all possible measures should be taken to repel the armed outbursts directed against our people's democratic system. The authority of the working people, i.e., of the working class and the peasantry, embodied in the people's republic must be doubly sacred for everyone who does not wish to restore the old yoke over our people—the domination of capitalists, bankers, and big landowners.

Comrade Imre Nagy, Chairman of the Hungarian Council of Ministers, speaking over the radio the same day, also indicated that "a handful of counterrevolutionary instigators staged an armed attack against the regime of our people's republic,

---

[1] Translation reprinted from *The Current Digest of the Soviet Press,* VIII, No. 41 (November 21, 1956), 12-13.

[2] See Chapter VI, Document 9.

and this attack was supported by some sections of the Budapest
working people who were dissatisfied with the situation in Hungary."³   Imre Nagy appealed to the people to defend the
people's democratic system.   The speeches of the leaders of the
Hungarian Workers Party and the Hungarian Government
emphasize the counterrevolutionary nature of the attempt made
against the people's democratic system in Hungary.

This antipopular venture was the result of prolonged subversive activity conducted by the imperialist powers with the
criminal intent of destroying the people's democracies and
restoring the capitalist system in these countries.   While the
countries of the socialist camp fight consistently with all the
power at their command for peaceful coexistence of states with
different social and economic systems, for the reduction of international tension and for the strengthening of international cooperation, the imperialist circles of the United States, England,
Western Germany, and certain other countries are making every
effort to interfere in the affairs of the socialist countries through
provocations, subversive activity, and the organization of a
counterrevolutionary underground.

Who does not recall the incendiary "Christmas Messages"
sent by some politicians from the other side of the ocean which
were open provocational calls to action against the people's
democracies in Eastern Europe?⁴   Moreover, it is well known
that matters are not restricted to such appeals alone.   The

---

³ See Chapter VI, Document 10.

⁴ The reference is to a message of President Eisenhower, broadcast
over Radio Free Europe, which read as follows: "During the Christmas
season I want you to know that the American people recognize the trials
under which you are suffering; join you in your concern for the restoration of individual freedoms and political liberty; and share your faith
that right in the end will prevail to bring you once again among the
free nations of the world." Another message from Secretary of State
Dulles read: "On this first of all Christian holidays I join with the
millions of Americans whose thoughts are with you. We share your
firm faith in God. We look to the future with hope and resolution, confident that freedom and justice shall at last prevail." (See *The Department of State Bulletin*, XXXIV [January 16, 1956], 85.)

United States Congress appropriated more than $100,000,000 for subversive activity against the socialist countries. This money is used to send spies and saboteurs into the people's democracies, to launch balloons filled with incendiary "literature," to print enormous quantities of spurious, provocative leaflets, to conduct an unbridled radio propaganda campaign against the socialist countries, etc. The imperialist intelligence services use every possible opening to expand their net of agents in the people's democracies and try their best to revive and recruit the remnants of the defeated exploiting classes.

The events in Hungary made it crystal clear that a reactionary counterrevolutionary underground, well armed and thoroughly prepared for decisive action against the people's government, had been organized with outside help. This is borne out by the fact that the rebels acted according to a plan laid out in advance and were led by people experienced in military affairs, namely by officers of the Horthy regime. Knowing very well what he was talking about, UP correspondent Francis Cyrus reported October 25 from Vienna: *"The rebels were apparently well armed. This indicates that a well trained and armed underground apparently took advantage of the rising discontent in Hungary to strike a blow at Communist rule."* A correspondent of the Italian news agency Agenzia Nazionale Stampa Associata remarked on his part that *"the rebels are led by men highly skilled and experienced in military tactics."*

These reports speak for themselves. They prove once more that the counterrevolutionary elements were well prepared in advance and that they were waiting for an opportune moment to strike a blow against the people's democratic system.

It is perfectly obvious that people's Hungary has had and still has her difficulties and unsolved problems which were generated by a variety of causes. In the past serious mistakes were made in Hungary in the fields of economic management and of Party and state work, and there were violations of democratic principles and socialist legality. All this was bound to affect the efforts made to improve the material conditions of the working people. A great deal of work is required to root out these mistakes, to eliminate the difficulties, to bring a further rise in the material well-being of the Hungarian people, and to satisfy their demands in the economic and other spheres. The Workers Party and the Government, the working class, the peasantry, and the working intelligentsia of Hungary have sufficient strength and resources to overcome the difficulties faced by the country in her forward march on the path to socialism.

But the enemies of the Hungarian people, for their own selfish interests, tried to use the country's difficulties as a means for destroying the people's government and restoring reactionary rule. They took up arms and skillfully drew into their venture certain elements of the working people who apparently did not understand the direction toward which they were being pushed.

Bourgeois propaganda is now trying to present the working people as the instigators of the armed struggle. But could a single honest person be found who would dare to equate the Hungarian working people with those people who barbarously set the National Museum afire and directed their automatic rifles and machine guns against the firemen and soldiers who tried to save the treasures belonging to the Hungarian people? Who would dare to equate the Hungarian workers with those who burned books in the streets of Budapest, thus recreating scenes of medieval obscurantism and Hitlerite gangsterism?

The Hungarian Government was compelled to use armed force in defending the people's democratic system established by the Hungarian workers in a struggle against the Hitlerite aggressors. Units of the Hungarian army began liquidating the counterrevolutionary rebellion. The Hungarian People's Republic Government asked the Soviet Government for help. In response to this request Soviet troops stationed in Hungary under the Warsaw Pact came to the aid of the Hungarian troops and the Hungarian working people who were defending the people's government.

As Comrade Imre Nagy indicated in his October 25 radio address, the use of Soviet troops in the struggle against the counterrevolution became "necessary to safeguard the vital interests of our socialist system."[5]

The antipopular venture collapsed as a result of the measures taken by the leadership of the Hungarian Workers Party and the Hungarian Government. The people's democratic system was severely tested and has once more reaffirmed its enormous vitality. Radio Budapest announced today the formation on a broad democratic basis of a new national government of the Hungarian people's democracy under Imre Nagy. The new government assumed office immediately.[6]

The Hungarian Government, guided by the desire not to punish anyone who had been misled, proclaimed amnesty for all those who laid down their arms voluntarily.

The workers of the large enterprises in Budapest are establishing committees to maintain order. Life in the city is gradually being restored to normalcy.

The enemy onslaught against the people's democratic system in Hungary evoked a wave of anger and indignation among all those who cherish the cause of socialism.

Trybuna Ludu, the Polish United Workers Party newspaper, comments on the events in Hungary as follows: "Unfortunately, organized counterrevolutionary elements, ready to turn the sentiments of the Hungarian public against the most sacred cause— the cause of socialism—infiltrated the peaceful demonstrations of the Hungarian population. These elements circulated unbridled nationalistic and anti-Soviet demogagic slogans and drew upon the reservoir of the politically backward strata of society. A very dangerous situation resulted which was a threat to the socialist conquests of the Hungarian working people and of the people's system."

"The false and cruel enemy, who up to now had only made plans, threatened, and gathered strength in secret, came out openly against the Hungarian people," wrote *Rude Pravo,* the organ of the Communist Party of Czechoslovakia. "In these

---

[5] See Chapter VI, Document 10.

[6] For the Government's program see Chapter VI, Document 16.

past few days the citizens of the Hungarian capital had a chance to see with their own eyes the bloody face of the enemy of socialism, who started a fratricidal struggle in the interest of aims proclaimed daily behind Western borders."

The Yugoslav newspaper *Borba* pointed out that "certain reactionary and counterrevolutionary elements" exploited the peaceful demonstrations of the Hungarian working people and had resorted to armed conflict "to achieve their antisocialist goals."

The democratic press of other countries sharply condemned the berserk enemies of socialism in Hungary. Pointing out that "counterrevolutionaries and avowed adherents of the former Horthy dictatorship" exploited the situation which arose in Hungary, the American *Daily Worker* declared: "Our State Department, which works hand in hand with émigré groups who have sworn to defeat socialism in Hungary and other Eastern European countries, applauds the actions of these antisocialist forces."

The Hungarian working people, who fought heroically for the establishment of a socialist state in 1918 and who established their own people's rule after the defeat of Hitler's legions, dealt a crushing blow to the schemes of imperialist reaction. They are determined to defend their people's regime and to continue on the path of building socialism.

2. Editorial: "In the Face of the Hungarian Tragedy," *Trybuna Ludu*, October 28, 1956

THE EVENTS in Hungary are shaking the conscience of every honest man in Poland. The fratricidal struggle lasting now for several days and the heavy casualties caused by it have cast a shadow of mourning over our land.

Many of us are asking ourselves the dramatic question: How has it come about that under the conditions of the existence of the people's rule a considerable faction of the Hungarian people has come out armed against this rule?

We repeat: Hungarian people, because although—as it

usually happens in mass movements—irresponsible and, in some cases, reactionary elements joined the action, they do not constitute and cannot constitute the backbone of such long-lasting and intense struggles.

The answer to the question posed should not be sought in the simplified version about "alien agencies," nor in searching for counterrevolution at each step. In any event, each attempt at such an answer—and there was no lack of them after the tragic Poznan events in our country—immediately suggests the next question: How is it possible that alien agencies which should have been isolated and cut off from the nation might have succeeded in mobilizing vast masses for the struggle? There does not exist any logical answer to such a question.

This is no place for a chronicle-like description of events. We are relating above—fragmentarily, by the way—information which we received up to late Saturday night. It seems that on the basis of this information and of the official documents of the Hungarian Party and Government, one may be tempted to sketch, at least, the picture of Hungarian events.

The source of the tragedy must be sought, first of all, in the errors, distortions, and even crimes of the past Stalinist period. The tragic rehabilitation of Rajk and other wrongly killed comrades has disclosed before the entire nation the depth of tyranny to which the former leadership of the Party descended. The shameful dealings relating to Comrade Nagy, the draconian measures against all more courageous criticism, the paralyzing of all tendencies toward democratization, the continuation of Stalinism three years after the death of Stalin and one half year after the 20th Congress, and, lastly, the ignoring of the demands of the masses striving to set friendly, allied relations with the USSR on the basis of sovereignty and complete equality of both partners—all this must have deepened the disappointment, dislike, and even hostility toward an authority the popular character of which had been lost in the eyes of the masses. It was not against the socialist revolution in Hungary that the wave of hostility was growing—just as it was not against the Polish socialist revolution that the working class of Poznan struck during the tragic June days—but against the elements of tyranny acting in the name of the revolution and against the bureaucratic degeneration functioning under the shield of socialism.

To all this should be added [the fact] that the forces of progress and democratic regeneration that have been for a long time persecuted by Rakosi remained paralyzed until July of this year. They were too weak within the leadership of the Party and of the Government to accomplish in time a turn, to force changes, in order that the process of democratization be carried on under the direction of the leading faction of the Party, in close contact with the masses, and in an open clash of views and unmasking of the schemes of the Stalinist groups in the manner in which the historic change of the general line of the PUWP, symbolized by the Eighth Plenum, was brought about.

The conservative Stalinist elements in the leadership hampered the processes of democratization until literally the last moment. A peaceful manifestation of the Budapest youth expressing solidarity with the changes in Poland and proposing similar demands pertaining to Hungary was addressed in sharp and incorrect words by the former First Secretary of the Party, Erno Gero, who, condemning the demonstrators for alleged "reaction," aroused in this fashion even more the already erupting emotions. And when the shooting was already going on, when the first victims had fallen—we don't know at this moment exactly how the tragic events began—even then at the suddenly convened meeting of the Central Committee only halfhearted changes were accomplished, leaving Gero in the capacity of the First Secretary and not introducing any essential change in the program and in the entire leadership. Such halfheartedness and obvious unwillingness [to accomplish] progressive changes kindled the conflagration instead of dampening it.

Thus it had happened. The new Government [headed] by Premier Nagy and the new leadership of the Party headed by Comrade Kadar were faced with accomplished facts: armed battles growing from hour to hour and attacks on public buildings. Finally, action by Soviet units could not help but inflame the situation even further.

The new leadership of the Party and of the Government did from the very beginning all that it could to bring about peace in Budapest. But this was not an easy task. In the heat of the erupting struggles, honest information about the new membership and program of the leadership was not able to penetrate everywhere, and, in general, liaison was not able to function everywhere. In addition, the nuclei of struggle also spread to some provincial centers. The elements of order and pacification made their appearance only when the workers' councils, most often headed by Communists, were created, made contacts with the Government, and transmitted to the rebellious groups information about the real course of events.

There is no time now for a full balance of the Hungarian tragedy. The Hungarian comrades will certainly give such an account when the time comes. But two things are beyond doubt. First, that the abolition of the people's power in Hungary, irrespective of the sources of the explosion, [and irrespective] of the intentions of the participants, would have been not only an awful tragedy for Hungary where, as a consequence, the dictatorship of the landlords and capitalists would have reigned anew, but it also would have constituted a threat to peace. The second thing [which is] beyond doubt is the deep solidarity of our nation with the Hungarian nation and its new leadership headed by comrades Nagy and Kadar, and the full support of their program, which expresses postulates and demands similar to ours, corresponding to the deepest wishes of the masses.

In this difficult tragic moment, our traditional solidarity and friendship for the brotherly Hungarian nation manifests itself not only in the Polish blood which the citizens of Warsaw gave today from their own veins to the wounded of Budapest, but, above all, in sincere sympathy and ardent hope that the Hungarian nation will speedily achieve a peace desired by all and will be able to build in its own land its own model of a socialist society.

3. APPEAL OF THE CENTRAL COMMITTEE OF THE POLISH
   UNITED WORKERS PARTY TO THE HUNGARIAN WORKERS
   PARTY TO END THE FIGHTING, OCTOBER 28, 1956[7]

TO THE FIRST Secretary of the Central Committee of the HWP, Comrade Janos Kadar;

To the Premier of the Government of National Unity of Hungary, Comrade Imre Nagy:

The Central Committee of our Party, our entire Party, and the entire Polish nation are listening with the greatest pain and deep disquiet to the tragic news coming from your country. We are shocked by the shedding of fraternal blood and by the conflagration which are destroying your capital. This is why we ask you to transmit to our Hungarian brothers—members of the HWP, the entire Hungarian working class, the entire Hungarian people, so cordially close to us—the following appeal.

Brother Hungarians!

In these tragic days for you, we hold that we must not remain silent. For centuries our nations have been linked by a common love of liberty. We fought for it, shoulder to shoulder, in the last century against the aggressive monarchs. We fought for it, twelve years ago, against Hitlerite fascism, against the native landlords and factory owners. And even in the past few days we took up—you and we—simultaneously and in solidarity, the struggle for socialist democratization of our countries, for equality and sovereignty in relations between socialist countries.

All this gives us the right to turn to you with an ardent appeal.

---

[7] *Trybuna Ludu*, October 29, 1956.

Brother Hungarians!

Stop the shedding of fraternal blood!

We know the program of the Government of National Unity of Hungary, the program of socialist democracy, of betterment of living standards, of creation of workers' councils, of full national sovereignty, of the withdrawal of Soviet troops from Hungary, of the basing of friendship with the Soviet Union on the Leninist principles of equality.

We are far from interfering in your internal affairs. We judge, however, that this program corresponds to the interests of the Hungarian people, and of the entire camp of peace. It seems to us that all Hungarian patriots, including those who are today on the other side of the barricade, can agree with this program.

We think that only those who wish to turn Hungary back from the road to socialism could reject the program of the Government of National Unity of Hungary.

We appeal especially ardently to the Hungarian working class on which rests the chief responsibility for the fate of the country to defend the people's authority and socialism, to defend the unity of the camp of socialism, dear to you and to us, [based] on principles of equality and sovereignty of all countries.

Brother Hungarians!

You and we are on the same side, the side of freedom and socialism. We call to you: enough blood, enough destruction, enough fratricidal struggle. May peace come to reign in Hungary, peace and unity of the nation so indispensable for the realization of the broad program of democratization, progress, and socialism which has been put forward by your Government of National Unity.

Warsaw, October 28, 1956

> The Central Committee of the
> Polish United Workers Party
>
> Wladyslaw Gomulka—First Secretary CC PUWP
> Josef Cyrankiewicz—member of the Political Bureau
>   of the CC PUWP, Chairman of the Council of Minis-
>   ters of the PPR [Polish People's Republic]

4. Message from the Secretary General of the Yugoslav League of Communists, Josip Broz-Tito, to the
Leadership of the Hungarian Workers Party Urging
an End to Bloodshed, October 28, 1956[8]

DEAR COMRADES,

For several days already the Yugoslav people and the
Yugoslav League of Communists have been following, with feelings of concern and agitation, the reports on the tragic clashes
taking place in the neighboring People's Republic of Hungary.
They deeply regret that the harmful and mistaken policy pursued for many years by the responsible political elements has
caused such difficult general conditions in Hungary. This policy
led to a discrepancy arising between the aspirations of the working people for socialist progress and the activities of the state
and the political leadership, and, finally, to the outbreak of
armed conflict.

The significance of these events extends far beyond the
frontiers of Hungary, for they also directly affect the interests
of international socialist development generally.

The Yugoslav state and political leadership did not and
does not wish to interfere in the internal affairs of the Hungarian workers' movement. However, in view of the significance of the events which have been taking place in Hungary
these past few days and because of its solidarity with the
progressive socialist aspirations and interests of the Hungarian
working people, the Central Committee of the Yugoslav League
of Communists appeals to the Hungarian people to make every
effort to prevent further bloodshed.

The working people of Yugoslavia fully understand the
bitterness of the Hungarian people over the mistakes and
crimes of the past. However, it would be extremely harmful
to the interests of the Hungarian working people and socialism
in general, and for peace among nations, if this justified bitterness were to undermine the faith of working people in socialism

---

[8] *Politika,* October 29, 1956.

and the inevitable development of socialist democracy. The Yugoslav Communists and all the working people of Yugoslavia are confident that the conscious fighters for socialism in Hungary will not permit this, just as they will not permit various reactionary elements to exploit present events for their antisocialist aims. The Yugoslav League of Communists and all working people of our country have a profound admiration for all those progressive people in neighboring Hungary who in these days have made great efforts to turn this tragic struggle into an era of revival and to defend the socialist future of their people.

For this reason the Yugoslav public unanimously hails the establishment of the new state and political leadership and the declaration of the Government of the People's Republic of Hungary of October 28 of this month. The essential parts of the political platform of the new Hungarian political and state leadership, such as the democratization of public life, the introduction of workers' self-management and democratic self-government in general, the settlement of relations between socialist countries on the basis of equality and respect for sovereignty, taking the initiative for negotiations on the withdrawal of Soviet troops, as well as the realistic appraisal of the nature of events in Hungary which has been made in the above-mentioned declaration of the Government, are proof that the policy of the present state and political leadership and the genuine socialist aspirations of the Hungarian working people have merged.

Under such conditions, any further bloodshed would only harm the interests of the Hungarian working people and socialism. It could only serve the aims of reaction and bureaucratic deformation. For that reason the Yugoslav Communists and all working people of Yugoslavia are convinced that the Hungarian working class, which has shown such a high level of socialist consciousness, the Hungarian Workers Party, and the whole of the patriotic Hungarian people will know how to put an end to the fratricidal struggle which could have unforeseeable consequences not only for Hungary but for the international labor movement.

The peoples of Yugoslavia and the Yugoslav League of Communists wish the presidency of the Hungarian Workers Party headed by Comrade Janos Kadar and the Government of Comrade Imre Nagy success in these efforts and are convinced that the militant Hungarian working class, on the basis of the new political platform and firmly linked with its new political leadership, will know how to realize the justified aspirations of the Hungarian people.

For the Central Committee of the
Yugoslav League of Communists

Josip Broz-Tito

CHAPTER VIII

THE REVOLT VICTORIOUS: OCTOBER 29-NOVEMBER 3, 1956

1. *Szabad Nep* TAKES ISSUE WITH *Pravda's* INTERPRETATION OF HUNGARIAN EVENTS, OCTOBER 29, 1956

THE LATEST ISSUE of *Pravda* carries a dispatch from its own correspondent about the events in Hungary entitled "Collapse of the Antipopular Adventure in Hungary."[1] This is an error. What happened in Budapest was neither antipopular nor an adventure. What is more it did not collapse. For five days bombs exploded and machine guns were active, spreading death. For five days this city, torn by fate, shed blood and suffered. But through hundreds of deaths, the ideals of true patriotism and democracy were burning in the fires.

The slogans of socialist democracy were the loudest to be heard and not those of the reaction and counterrevolution. The revolutionary people of Buda and Pest want a people's freedom without tyranny, terror, and fear. They want more bread and national independence. Is this then an antipopular adventure?

What collapsed could indeed be called antipopular. It was the reign of the Rakosi-Gero clique.

The *Pravda* article further states that manifestations of the people of Pest and the revolt were instigated by the subversive work of the British and American imperialists. We can safely say that all 1.5 million inhabitants of Budapest are deeply hurt and insulted by this assertion. In body or in spirit, a large portion of the population of Budapest was present at the demonstrations on Tuesday [October 23]. They sympathized or agreed with the basic patriotic and democratic aims of the great popular uprising.

---

[1] See Chapter VII, Document 1.

The bloody, tragic, but at the same time ennobling fight, lasting five days, was not instigated by some sort of subversive work. It was caused, alas, by our own faults and crimes. The greatest of our faults and crimes was our failure to protect the sacred flame which our ancestors had bequeathed to us—our national independence. What does the Hungarian nation want, asked the youth in March, 1848? The independence of the nation, was the answer given by Petofi and his friends in the first of his twelve points.

Let us at last talk frankly. This is the first answer today too. This is the first demand of the nation. Hungary shall be a free and independent country and will live on this basis in peace and friendship with its neighbor the USSR. This is what we have fought for and this is what we want. This is what writers and journalists—fighting with their pen—want. This is what engineers and workers, peasants and demonstrating students, and the Premier of the country want.

A heavy stone rolled off our hearts when the new Government and new leaders of the Party espoused this demand. From behind the dark clouds the sun is rising, red in color because it is bathed in blood, but it is the sun of liberty and peace.

While we are at it, we must make another comment about the deplorable *Pravda* article. It is true that evil fratricide raged for days. Now, we believe that at last it is over. It will be necessary to punish those who, clinging to their power and fearful for their lives, instigated the fight. Punished must be those who ordered fire on the unprotected [demonstrators] in front of the Parliament. Punished also must be those criminal elements who, freed from prison, jumped on the wave of the revolution.

Yes, it will be necessary to punish, but this is quite different from what the *Pravda* article calls "liquidation." No one could, and now no one wants to liquidate the fight of the Hungarian people. Even if at a high price, this fight has nevertheless borne fruit: the victory of the ideals of freedom. And with this and only with this will it bring at last the silence of arms on a soil bathed in blood; beautiful peace, new beautiful bloodless struggles, and the beginning of our constructive work.

2. ORDER OF THE DAY OF THE MINISTERS OF DEFENSE AND
    THE INTERIOR ON THE REORGANIZATION OF ARMED FORCES,
    OCTOBER 29, 1956

SOLDIERS, POLICEMEN, noncommissioned officers, officers, generals, comrades-in-arms:

On the night of October 28 the radio broadcast the national Government's program which marks the rebirth of our people. The Army and the police accept the Government's program in its entirety as their own and stand entirely at the disposal of the new national Government. We shall do our utmost to ensure that order is restored and peaceful constructive work is resumed so that our national independence and freedom can flourish for the benefit of our people. We order the following:

1—The commanders and the members of the Hungarian People's Army and the police must unfailingly carry out the measures, orders, and instructions of the new national Government. They must show respect toward our people in all circumstances and firm discipline.

2—Among members of the Hungarian People's Army and the police the form of address, commencing today in service, shall be "comrade-in-arms."

3—Until a new badge is introduced to be worn on caps, a ribbon of the national tricolor shall be worn.

We have taken measures for the speedy organization and equipping of the armed formations of the Army, police, workers, and youth militia which are to be established in accordance with the Government declaration.

Detailed instructions for the execution of this measure will be issued in a short time.

Glory to the heroes who have fallen in battle! Forward with the people for an independent, democratic, and socialist

Hungary! Long live the unity of our people, our Army, and our police force!

> Karoly Janza, Minister of Defense, and
> Ferenc Munnich, Minister of the Interior

3. STATEMENT BY THE MINISTER OF THE INTERIOR, FERENC MUNNICH, ON THE REORGANIZATION OF THE POLICE, OCTOBER 29, 1956

IN ACCORDANCE WITH the resolution of the Council of Ministers,[2] I have begun to organize a unified democratic police force.

The most decisive task imposed on the new police organization is the restoration of public order and security as soon as possible, and the guaranteeing of conditions of peaceful work.

The police must prevent every kind of illegal excess, harassing of the population, and other infringements of the law. Measures have been taken to insure that only those who have proved themselves worthy by their attitude and behavior in the past shall be members of the newly organized police force.

I call on every honest Hungarian citizen who wants peace and order to support the police in their effort to restore order and public security.

The organization of the police forces is a national task. I appeal to local organizations to support this work.

The reorganization of the police on a national scale is the exclusive task of the Ministry of the Interior.

> Ferenc Munnich, Minister of the Interior

4. ANNOUNCEMENT OF THE WITHDRAWAL OF SOVIET TROOPS FROM BUDAPEST, OCTOBER 29, 1956

ATTENTION, ATTENTION! Units of the Hungarian People's Army tonight began to replace Soviet troops in the eighth borough of Budapest and will insure the withdrawal of Soviet troops.

---

[2] See Chapter VI, Document 16.

By dawn Soviet troops will evacuate the territory agreed upon with the headquarters of the resisters. At 9 o'clock the resisters will lay down their arms. The replacement and undisturbed withdrawal of Soviet troops are the prerequisites for continuation of Soviet troop withdrawals from the capital during the day, according to the agreed plan for gradual withdrawal from Budapest.[3]

I call on all true patriots to support the Hungarian People's Army in carrying out this task successfully and to the satisfaction of the population of Budapest and the whole country.

Lt. Gen. Karoly Janza
Minister of Defense of the
Hungarian People's Republic

5. PROCLAMATION BY IMRE NAGY ON THE RESTORATION OF A MULTI-PARTY SYSTEM AND A COALITION GOVERNMENT, OCTOBER 30, 1956

WORKING PEOPLE of Hungary! Workers, peasants, intellectuals! As a result of the revolution, which is unfolding with tremendous strength, and the mighty movement of democratic forces, our Fatherland has reached a crossroads. The national Government, acting in complete agreement with the Presidium of the Hungarian Workers Party, has arrived at a decision, vital

---

[3] Despite the announcement, the withdrawal of Soviet troops from Budapest and from the rest of the country did not proceed according to schedule and without confusion. In the morning of October 31 Soviet tanks were still reported in front of the Ministries of the Interior and National Defense and the Soviet Embassy in Budapest. As to the rest of the country, on October 30 Szabolcs-Szatmar announced that at Nyiregyhaza Soviet troops were moving to the center of the country. On October 31 Miskolc reported that at Zahony Soviet troops were pouring into the country, but that at Nyiregyhaza and Szolnok they were leaving. On November 1, Soviet tanks surrounded Hungarian airfields in order to secure air transport for Soviet personnel. It was on that day that Messrs. A. I. Mikoyan and M. A. Suslov were authentically reported to be negotiating in Budapest with the Hungarian Communists. On the same day, too, Imre Nagy issued his first appeal to the United Nations. See Document 12 in this chapter.

for the nation's life, of which I want to inform Hungary's working people.

In the interest of the further democratization of the country's life, the Cabinet abolishes the one-party system and places the country's Government on the basis of democratic cooperation between the coalition parties, reborn in 1945.[4]   In accordance with this it sets up an inner Cabinet within the national Government.   The members of this Cabinet are Imre Nagy, Zoltan Tildy, Bela Kovacs, Ferenc Erdei, Janos Kadar, Geza Losonczy, and a person to be nominated by the Social Democrat Party.[5]   The Government will submit a proposal to the Presidential Council of the People's Republic to elect Janos Kadar and Geza Losonczy as Ministers of State.

The national Government appeals to the headquarters of Soviet forces immediately to begin the withdrawal of Soviet troops from the territory of Budapest.   At the same time, the national Government informs the people of the country that it will begin negotiations without delay with the Government of the USSR about the withdrawal of Soviet troops from Hungary.

I announce, on behalf of the national Government, that it recognizes the democratic organs of local autonomy which have been brought into existence by the revolution, that it relies on them and asks for their support.

Hungarian brethren, patriots!   Loyal citizens of the Fatherland!   Safeguard the achievements of the revolution, safeguard order by every means and restore calm.   No blood should be shed in our country by fratricide.   Prevent any kind of disturbance and safeguard life and property by every means at your disposal.

My Hungarian brethren, workers, peasants!   Stand beside the national Government in the hour of this fateful decision. Long live free, democratic, and independent Hungary!

---

[4] The coalition in 1945 included the Communist, Social Democratic, Smallholders, and National Peasant parties.

[5] Miss Anna Kethly became the Social Democratic representative in the Government.

6. APPEAL BY JANOS KADAR, FIRST SECRETARY OF THE HUNGARIAN WORKERS PARTY, FOR COMMUNIST SUPPORT OF THE NEW GOVERNMENT, OCTOBER 30, 1956

MY FELLOW WORKERS, working brethren, and dear comrades! Moved by the deep sense of responsibility in sparing our nation and working masses from further bloodshed, I declare that every member of the Presidium of the Hungarian Workers Party is in agreement with the decisions reached by the Presidium of the Council of Ministers today. As for myself I can add that I am in wholehearted agreement with the speakers before me—Imre Nagy, Zoltan Tildy, and Ferenc Erdei[6]—acquaintances and friends of mine, my esteemed and respected compatriots.

I address myself to the Communists, to those Communists who were prompted to join the Party by the progressive ideas of mankind and socialism and not by selfish personal interest— let us represent our pure and just ideas by pure and just means.

My comrades, my fellow workers! The bad leadership of the past years has left a legacy of great and serious burdens for our Party. We must fully rid ourselves of this legacy with a clear conscience and courageous, straightforward resolve. The ranks of the Party will break but I am not afraid that the pure, honest, and well-meaning Communists will be disloyal. Those who joined us for selfish personal reasons, for a career or other motives will be the ones to leave. But having got rid of this ballast and the burden of past crimes of certain persons in our leadership, we will fight, even if to some extent from scratch, under more favorable and clearer conditions for the benefit of our ideals, people, compatriots, and country.

I ask every Communist individually to set an example, by deeds, without pretense, examples worthy of man and Communist, in restoring order, starting normal life, in resuming work and production, and in laying the foundations of an ordered life. With the honor thus acquired let us earn the respect of our other compatriots as well.

---

[6] For the speech of Imre Nagy see the preceding document. The other speeches are not printed here.

On October 30 a "revolutionary, military council" of the armed forces was formed. It identified itself with the demands of "the revolutionary councils of the working youth and intellectuals" and asked for "the immediate withdrawal of Soviet troops from Budapest and their withdrawal from the entire territory of Hungary in the shortest possible time." It also vowed to disarm all AVH (internal security forces) troops who "had intimidated the armed forces as well."

On the same day a preparatory commission of Revolutionary Armed Forces Committee, composed of representatives of the armed forces, the police, and armed youth and workers' groups, also came into existence. In the evening of October 30, the Government "acknowledged and confirmed" the formation of this committee and empowered it with the creation of a new army. The authority of the Revolutionary Armed Forces Committee was to cease when a "new government based on the result of secret, general elections takes office."

Also in the evening of October 30, Janos Kadar announced the beginning of the "rebuilding" of the HWP. Meanwhile, revolutionary councils in the countryside continued to voice their demands.

7. DEMANDS OF THE SOCIALIST REVOLUTIONARY COUNCIL OF DEBRECEN, OCTOBER 30, 1956

1. IN THE NAME of the population of Hajdu and Bihar counties we demand that Hungary immediately withdraw from the Warsaw Treaty.[7] We demand the immediate withdrawal of all Soviet troops.

2. We ask the United Nations to deal effectively with the case of Hungary, inasmuch as the intervention of the Soviet Union has made an international issue of our internal affairs.

3. We demand the recall of the Stalinist [Peter] Kos[8] from the United Nations.

---

[7] Mutual defense treaty between the Soviet Union and seven of its European allies (Albania, Bulgaria, Czechoslovakia, East Germany, Hungary, Poland, and Rumania) signed at Warsaw on May 14, 1955. The treaty calls for a joint military command under Soviet Marshal Ivan S. Konev.

[8] Hungary's chief U. N. representative.

4. We recognize the government as provisional until the restoration of peace and order and demand that after the withdrawal of Soviet troops, free, democratic, and secret elections take place in Hungary with the participation of several parties.

5. We ask that our demands be broadcast repeatedly and verbatim by the Kossuth Radio.[9] Until our demands are met, the population of our counties will carry out a sit-down strike.

The workers' council of the revolutionary council of Vas county elaborated on these demands and asked for "guarantees of complete freedom of speech, press, and association as well as for freedom of religion" and the "rehabilitation in the shortest possible time of Prince Primate Jozsef Mindszenty and other ecclesiastical personnel" including their reinstatement in their ecclesiastic functions.

In the evening of October 30, Cardinal Mindszenty was actually freed from house arrest in Felsopeteny where he had been held since shortly after his release from prison in July, 1955. His release was officially acknowledged by the Government on October 31.

8. GOVERNMENT ANNOUNCEMENT OF THE RELEASE AND REHABILITATION OF CARDINAL JOZSEF MINDSZENTY, OCTOBER 31, 1956

THE HUNGARIAN NATIONAL GOVERNMENT wishes to state that the proceedings started in 1948 against Jozsef Mindszenty, Cardinal Primate, lacked all legal basis and that the accusations leveled against him by the regime of the day were unjustified.

In consequence of all this, the Hungarian national Government announces that the measures depriving Cardinal Primate Jozsef Mindszenty of his rights are invalid and, therefore, the Cardinal can exercise, without any restrictions, all his civil and ecclesiastical rights.

Imre Nagy, Premier

---

[9] Hungary's central radio station in Budapest.

During the day, on October 31, former political parties began to reconstitute themselves. The National Peasant Party (under Ferenc Farkas) reappeared and on the following day adopted a new name, that of Petofi Party. Likewise, the Social Democratic Party was re-created as an independent party under the leadership of Miss Anna Kethly, with Gyula Kelemen as secretary general. The Hungarian Independence Party also reconstituted itself, as did the People's Democratic Party and the Smallholders Party. (On November 1 a Catholic People's Party headed by Endre Varga was formed and a Catholic National Association under the leadership of Kalman Papp, Bishop of Eger, began to function.) Also on October 31 the presidium of the Trade Union Council resigned in favor of a temporary executive committee of a new National Federation of Free Hungarian Trade Unions.

In the afternoon of October 31, Imre Nagy addressed a mass rally in front of the Parliament.

9. ADDRESS BY IMRE NAGY, CHAIRMAN OF THE COUNCIL OF MINISTERS, OCTOBER 31, 1956

HUNGARIAN BRETHREN, I speak to you again with deep love! The revolutionary struggle whose heroes you were has won! These heroic days have brought into existence our national Government which will fight for our people's independence and freedom. We will tolerate no interference in our internal affairs. We stand on the principle of equality, national sovereignty, and national equality. Our policies will be built solidly on the will of the Hungarian people.

Dear Friends!

We are living through the first days of our sovereignty and independence. We have removed incredibly great obstacles from our way. We have expelled the gang of Rakosi and Gero from our country. They will answer for their crimes. They tried to smear me too. They spread the lie that I called the Soviet troops into the country. This is base calumny. Imre Nagy, who is a fighter for Hungarian sovereignty, Hungarian freedom, and Hungarian independence, did not call these troops. On the contrary, it was he who fought for their withdrawal.

Dear Friends!

This day we opened negotiations for the withdrawal of Soviet troops from the country and for the renunciation of our obligations stemming from the Warsaw Treaty. However, we ask for a little patience on your part. I believe that the results are such that you can give us your confidence.

Dear Friends!

Line up with us, support us in our patriotic work, in the creation of our country's independence, in the restoration of life, in the beginning of creative work. We would like to ensure that our people should live in peace and calm and should have confidence in the future. We ask you, have confidence in the Government, create order and calm, so that we might implement our broad, democratic program.

Long live the free, independent, democratic Hungarian Republic! Long live free Hungary!

Shortly after he spoke, Nagy received foreign newspapermen. A tape-recorded interview with him was broadcast by the Austrian radio network.

10. INTERVIEW WITH IMRE NAGY, OCTOBER 31, 1956

QUESTION: Do you believe that in your negotiations with the Russians on the withdrawal of Soviet forces from Hungary you will be successful only if this takes place within the framework of all Warsaw Pact nations, or do you believe that Hungary can be a separate case?

Nagy: Yes, I believe so, yes. I do not know exactly what is provided by the Warsaw Pact, but independently, I think, we will be able speedily, I think, to solve this question.

Q: What about the Warsaw Pact now? Are you in it or not?

Nagy: At present, we are in it.

Q: Do you wish to leave the Warsaw Pact, if the Hungarian people desire this?

A: Today we have begun negotiations on this matter and other questions connected with this problem.

Q: Would it be of any help to you if the American, British, French, and the other allies in West Germany would simultaneously offer to withdraw their forces from West Germany in case the Russians are willing to withdraw from Poland, Hungary, Rumania, and the other People's Democracies, and particularly from East Germany? Do you think that such negotiations could take place?

A: I cannot speak for the Polish and Rumanian . . .

Reporter: But in your opinion?

A: When this comes up for discussion we will have to take a stand. We will have to give our opinion on this matter then.

Q: It will now be necessary to reconstruct Hungary economically. Will you apply to the Western Powers for aid in the reconstruction of Hungary?

A: It seems to me that we will have to count on all economic forces to help us emerge from this situation.

Q: Will you continue to recognize the German Democratic Republic?

A: I think so, yes.

Q: Also in the future?

A: It appears to me that this is not up for discussion right now. In our foreign policy we do not want to lean only in one direction, but wish to maintain good and friendly relations.

Q: Also with the German Federal Republic?

A: Well, presently we have no relations. It seems to me that this question, too, is premature. We will have to decide later on.

Q: What will be your future relations with the Soviet Union?

A: Very good, I think. Good diplomatic and friendly relations.

Q: According to the agreement you have now concluded, are the Soviet forces now withdrawing to their original bases in Hungary?

A: At present the forces in Budapest, it seems, have already withdrawn, and have returned to their bases.

Q: In Hungary?

A: Yes, in Hungary. I do not know exactly from where they came.

Q: There are also some Soviet forces which came across the border from other states. Are they also withdrawing to where they came from?

A: I think so, yes. I do not know from where they came, but they will return from where they came.

Q: You said just a few minutes ago that you were put under pressure to bring in the Soviet troops, that it was not you who invited the Soviet troops to move into Budapest. Who invited them?

A: It was not me—that I can say. At that time I was not Premier; I was not a member of the Central Committee of the Party.

Q: How then did the opinion appear that you invited the troops?

A: I do not know. At that time I was not a member of the leadership. It may have been this way: At first it was said it was the Government; and then later on, after 2 or 3 days, I was made Premier, and the masses are unable to differentiate. Two days ago or now, it is all the same to them.

Q: But did you not approve of the invitation to the Soviet troops afterward?

A: No.

Q: Did you say it was necessary for the reestablishment of peace and order, or did you not?

A: No, no, no. I did not say such a thing, and I must say that their appearance has caused much damage.

Q: What will now be the first measures of the Government?

A: It is too difficult to give a government program right here.

Q: But perhaps you can tell us the next step?

A: We have very grave economic problems. The most important problem is to restore order here and to reestablish economic life. Today I talked with the workers delegation from Csepel. They will be able to give you some information.

In the morning of November 1, Imre Nagy received the Soviet Ambassador in Budapest (Andropov) and dispatched a telegram to the Soviet Government asking for immediate negotiations about the withdrawal of Soviet troops.

11. TELEGRAM FROM THE PRIME MINISTER OF HUNGARY, NAGY, TO THE CHAIRMAN OF THE PRESIDIUM OF THE SUPREME SOVIET, VOROSHILOV, ASKING FOR NEGOTIATIONS CONCERNING THE WITHDRAWAL OF SOVIET TROOPS FROM HUNGARY, NOVEMBER 1, 1956

THE GOVERNMENT of the Hungarian People's Republic desires to undertake immediate negotiations in connection with the withdrawal of Soviet troops from the entire territory of Hungary.

With reference to the latest declaration of the Government of the Soviet Union, according to which it is ready to negotiate with the Hungarian Government and with the other member states of the Warsaw Treaty concerning the withdrawal of Soviet troops from Hungary, the Hungarian Government invites the Soviet Government to designate a delegation so that conversations can be initiated as soon as possible.[10]   At the same time it requests the Soviet Government to designate the place and date for these negotiations.

At the same time Nagy, who took over direction of the Ministry of Foreign Affairs, informed the Secretary General of the United Nations of his decisions and asked for Four Power protection of Hungary's neutrality.

12. TELEGRAM FROM THE CHAIRMAN OF THE COUNCIL OF MINISTERS OF HUNGARY, NAGY, TO THE SECRETARY GENERAL OF THE UNITED NATIONS, HAMMARSKJOLD, NOVEMBER 1, 1956[11]

THE PRESIDENT of the Council of Ministers of the Hungarian People's Republic as designated Minister for Foreign Affairs has

---

[10] See Part Four, Chapter I, Document 1.
[11] U. N. Document A/3251, November 1, 1956.

the honor to communicate the following to Your Excellency.

Reliable reports have reached the Government of the Hungarian People's Republic that further Soviet units are entering into Hungary. The President of the Council of Ministers in his capacity of Minister for Foreign Affairs summoned M. Andropov, Ambassador Extraordinary and Plenipotentiary of the Soviet Union to Hungary, and expressed his strongest protest against the entry of further Soviet troops into Hungary. He demanded the instant and immediate withdrawal of these Soviet forces. He informed the Soviet Ambassador that the Hungarian Government immediately repudiates the Warsaw Treaty and at the same time declares Hungary's neutrality, turns to the United Nations, and requests the help of the four great powers in defending the country's neutrality. The Government of the Hungarian People's Republic made the Declaration of Neutrality on November 1, 1956; therefore I request Your Excellency promptly to put on the agenda of the forthcoming General Assembly of the United Nations the question of Hungary's neutrality and the defence of this neutrality by the four great powers.

I take this opportunity to convey to Your Excellency the expression of my highest consideration.

13. RADIO ADDRESS TO THE NATION BY IMRE NAGY PROCLAIMING THE NEUTRALITY OF HUNGARY, NOVEMBER 1, 1956

PEOPLE OF HUNGARY! The Hungarian national Government, imbued with profound responsibility toward the Hungarian people and history, and giving expression to the undivided will of the Hungarian millions, declares the neutrality of the Hungarian People's Republic.

The Hungarian people, on the basis of independence and equality and in accordance with the spirit of the U. N. Charter, wishes to live in true friendship with its neighbors, the Soviet Union, and all the peoples of the world.

The Hungarian people desires the consolidation and further development of the achievements of its national revolution without joining any power blocs. The century-old dream of the Hungarian people is thus fulfilled. The revolutionary struggle fought by the Hungarian heroes of the past and present has at last carried the cause of freedom and independence to victory. The heroic struggle has made it possible to implement, in the international relations of our people, its fundamental national interest—neutrality.

We appeal to our neighbors, countries near and far, to respect the unalterable decision of our people. It is true indeed that today our people are as united in this decision as perhaps never before in their history.

Working millions of Hungary! With revolutionary determination, self-sacrificing work, and the consolidation of order, protect and strengthen our country—free, independent, democratic, and neutral Hungary.

14. THE FORMATION OF A NEW COMMUNIST PARTY: RADIO ADDRESS TO THE NATION BY JANOS KADAR, FIRST SECRETARY OF THE HUNGARIAN WORKERS PARTY, NOVEMBER 1, 1956

HUNGARIAN WORKERS, peasants, and intellectuals! In a fateful hour we appeal to those who, inspired by loyalty to the people and the country and the pure ideals of socialism, were led to a Party which later degenerated to a medium of despotism and national slavery through the blind and criminal policy of the Hungarian representatives of Stalinism—Rakosi and his clique. This adventurous policy unscrupulously frittered away the moral and ideological heritage which you acquired in the old days through honest struggle and blood sacrifice in the fight for our national independence and our democratic progress. Rakosi and his gang gravely violated our national decency and pride when they disregarded the sovereignty and freedom of our nation and wasted our national wealth in a lighthearted manner. In a glorious uprising, our people have shaken off the Rakosi regime.

They have achieved freedom for the people and independence for the country, without which there can be no socialism.

We can safely say that the ideological and organizational leaders who prepared this uprising were recruited from among your ranks. Hungarian Communist writers, journalists, university students, the youth of the Petofi Circle, thousands and thousands of workers and peasants, and veteran fighters who had been imprisoned on false charges fought in the front line against the Rakosiite despotism and political hooliganism. We are proud that you, permeated by true patriotism and loyalty to socialism, honestly stood your ground in the armed uprising and led it.

We are talking to you frankly. The uprising of the people has come to a crossroads. The Hungarian democratic parties will either have enough strength to stabilize our achievements or we must face an open counterrevolution. The blood of Hungarian youth, soldiers, workers, and peasants was not shed in order that Rakosiite despotism might be replaced by the reign of the counterrevolution.

We did not fight in order that mines and factories might be snatched from the hands of the working class, and the land from the hands of the peasantry. Either the uprising secured for our people the basic achievements of democracy—the right of assembly and of organization, personal freedom and safety, the rule of law, freedom of the press, and humaneness—or we sink back into the slavery of the old gentry world and with it into foreign slavery.

The grave and alarming danger exists that foreign armed intervention may allot to our country the tragic fate of Korea. Our anxiety for the future fate of our country leads us to do our utmost to avert this grave danger. We must eliminate the nests of counterrevolution and reaction. We must finally consolidate our democratic order and secure conditions for normal productive work and life—peace, calm, and order.

In these momentous hours the Communists who fought against the despotism of Rakosi have decided, in accordance with the wish of many true patriots and socialists, to form a new Party. The new Party will break away from the crimes of the past once and for all. It will defend the honor and independence of our country against anyone. On this basis, the basis of national independence, it will build fraternal relations with any progressive socialist movement and party in the world.

On this basis, the basis of national independence, does it desire friendly relations with every country, far and near, and in the first place with the neighboring socialist countries. It defends and will defend the achievements of the Hungarian Republic—the land reform, the nationalization of factories, mines, and banks, and the indisputable social and cultural gains of our people.

It defends and will defend the cause of democracy and socialism, whose realization it seeks not through servile copying of foreign examples, but on a road suitable to the historic and economic characteristics of our country, relying on the teachings of Marxism-Leninism, on scientific socialism free of Stalinism and any kind of dogmatism, and on the revolutionary and progressive traditions of Hungarian history and culture.

In these glorious but grave hours of our history we call on every Hungarian worker who is inspired by affection for the people and the country to join our Party, the name of which is the Hungarian Socialist Workers Party. The Party counts on the support of every self-conscious worker who identifies himself with the socialist objectives of the working class. Any Hungarian worker who adopts the above principles and is not responsible for the criminal policy and mistakes of the Rakosi clique can be a member of the Party.

The Party awaits all those who in the past were deterred from the service of socialism by the antipopular policy and criminal deeds of Rakosi and his followers. A preparatory committee has been formed composed of Ferenc Donath, Janos Kadar, Sandor Kopacsi, Geza Losonczy, Gyorgy Lukacs, Imre Nagy, and Zoltan Szanto. This committee is to start organizing the Party, to supervise its operation temporarily, and to convene as urgently as possible a national founding congress of the Party. The Party will publish a newspaper under the title *Nepszabadsag* (People's Freedom).

Workers, peasants, and intellectuals, the new Party, the Hungarian Socialist Workers Party, is prepared to do its share in the fight for consolidating independence and democracy, and is ready to fight for the socialist future of our people. It is clear to us that there has never been so great a need for holding the democratic forces together. We turn to the newly-formed democratic parties, and first of all to the other workers' party, the Social Democratic Party, with the request to overcome the danger of a menacing counterrevolution and intervention from abroad by consolidating the Government.

Our people have proved with their blood their intention to support unflinchingly the Government's efforts for the complete withdrawal of Soviet forces. We do not want to be dependent any longer. We do not want our country to become a battlefield. I am speaking to every honest Hungarian patriot. Let us join forces for the triumph of Hungarian independence and freedom!

> The Executive Committee of the
> Hungarian Socialist Workers Party

On November 2, in the face of continuing reports of Soviet troop movements into the country, the Hungarian Government addressed three verbal notes to the Soviet Embassy in Budapest.

In the first note the Hungarian Government recalled that its proposal of the previous week to begin immediate negotiations for the withdrawal of Soviet troops had met with the approval of the Soviet authorities. Nevertheless, Soviet troops entered Hungary on October 31 and November 1. When efforts to obtain the withdrawal of these troops failed, the Hungarian Government repudiated the Warsaw Treaty and sought status as a neutral country.[12] In order to achieve this the Hungarian Government again reiterated

---

[12] See Document 12 in this chapter.

its wish to open negotiations with the Soviet Union and appointed a delegation headed by Geza Losonczy, Minister of State and member of the preparatory committee of the new Hungarian Socialist Workers Party, and including Jozsef Kovago, Andras Marton, Ferenc Farkas, and Vilmos Zentai, for that purpose.

The second note dealt with the military aspect of the same problem and proposed that a mixed Soviet-Hungarian commission should convene immediately in the Hungarian Parliament in order to prepare the withdrawal of Soviet troops. The Hungarian Government designated Ferenc Erdei, Minister of State, Major General Pal Maleter, Deputy Minister of National Defense, Major General Istvan Kovacs, and Colonel Miklos Szucs as its representatives on the commission.

The third verbal note again protested the movements of Soviet troops which continued on November 2; the troops occupied railway lines and stations on the way and in Western Hungary proceeded in the direction of the Austrian frontier. Accordingly the Hungarian Government deemed it necessary to inform the heads of foreign diplomatic missions of these moves and to call the attention of the U. N. Security Council to these recent developments.

15. LETTER FROM THE CHAIRMAN OF THE COUNCIL OF MINISTERS OF HUNGARY, NAGY, TO THE SECRETARY GENERAL OF THE UNITED NATIONS, HAMMARSKJOLD, NOVEMBER 2, 1956[13]

AS THE PRESIDENT of the Council of Ministers and Designated Foreign Minister of the Hungarian People's Republic I have the honour to bring to the attention of Your Excellency the following additional information:

I have already mentioned in my letter of November 1st that new Soviet military units entered Hungary and that the Hungarian Government informed the Soviet Ambassador in Budapest of this fact, at the same time terminated the Warsaw Pact, declared the neutrality of Hungary, and requested the United Nations to guarantee the neutrality of the country.

---

[13] U. N. Document S/3726, November 2, 1956.

On the 2nd of November further and exact information, mainly military reports, reached the Government of the Hungarian People's Republic, according to which large Soviet military units crossed the border of the country, marching toward Budapest. They occupy railway lines, railway stations, and railway safety equipment. Reports also have come about that Soviet military movements of east-west direction are being observed on the territory of Western Hungary.

On the basis of the above-mentioned facts the Hungarian Government deemed it necessary to inform the Embassy of the USSR and all the other Diplomatic Missions in Budapest about these steps directed against our People's Republic.

At the same time, the Government of the Hungarian People's Republic forwarded concrete proposals on the withdrawal of Soviet troops stationed in Hungary as well as the place of negotiations concerning the execution of the termination of the Warsaw Pact and presented a list containing the names of the members of the Government's delegation. Furthermore, the Hungarian Government made a proposal to the Soviet Embassy in Budapest to form a mixed committee to prepare the withdrawal of the Soviet troops.

I request Your Excellency to call upon the Great Powers to recognize the neutrality of Hungary and ask the Security Council to instruct the Soviet and Hungarian Governments to start the negotiations immediately.

I also request Your Excellency to make known the above to the Members of the Security Council.

Please accept, Your Excellency, the expression of my highest consideration.

Budapest, November 2, 1956

Meanwhile in Budapest, Pal Maleter, one of the leading figures of the revolution who had been appointed Deputy Minister of National Defense on November 1, gave an interview to foreign newsmen in which he noted, among other things, that according to military reconnaissance reports, new Soviet troops had entered Hungary during the past few days. He then went on to say:

The view of the Hungarian army is that we want to live in friendship with all peoples. Our army, however, has weapons, and if necessary it can defend itself against the intruders. In the interest of putting the situation in order, the army supports the national Government of Imre Nagy and Zoltan Tildy. But the army makes its further support of the Government dependent on whether the Government fulfills its promise and renounces the Warsaw Treaty.

Question: What negotiations has the Government entered into so far with this end in view?

Answer: On Wednesday [October 31] Zoltan Tildy conferred with Mr. Mikoyan who promised that troops which are in Hungary on grounds other than the Warsaw Treaty will be withdrawn from the country.

Q: Does this mean that the Warsaw troops will remain?

A: This is out of the question. Tildy has informed Mikoyan that we shall repudiate the Warsaw Treaty in any case, and our Government demanded that negotiations in this respect begin as soon as possible.

Q: What will happen to those troops who are coming to Hungary now?

A: Of course, we shall regard them as being outside the Warsaw Treaty and shall treat them accordingly. I must, however, declare that the people of Hungary are mature enough not to regard tardiness in connection with the promises made by some foreign leaders immediately as an act of provocation. Nonetheless, we shall not lay down our arms before national independence has won complete victory.

The journalists then asked Maleter to speak about the insurrection, the fights, and relations between the insurgents and the Army.

A: This insurrection was not organized by anybody. The insurrection broke out because the Hungarian people wanted peace, tranquillity, freedom, and independence, to which the foreign occupiers replied with weapons. At the beginning of the struggle single groups, independent of each other, attacked the intruders without any sort of weapons, and achieved their successes with the weapons thus obtained. Hungarian youth made its own weapons. . . . [Maleter displayed a modified version of the "Molotov cocktail" of World War II fame, used to burn out tanks.]

Q: Please, tell us something about your part in the battles.

A: In the early morning hours of last Wednesday I received an order from the then Minister of Defense to set out with five tanks against insurgents in the eighth and ninth boroughs, and to relieve the Kilian Barracks. When I arrived at the spot I became convinced that the freedom fighters were not bandits, but loyal sons of the Hungarian people. So I informed the Minister that I would go over to the insurgents. Ever since we have been fighting together and shall not end the struggle so long as a single armed foreigner remains in Hungary.

On November 3 the Government of the Hungarian People's Republic was reorganized. *A group of Communist ministers were relieved of their functions at their own request.* The group included Imre Horvath (Minister of Foreign Affairs), Ferenc Munnich (Minister of the Interior), Karoly Janza (Minister of National Defense), Istvan Kossa (Minister of Finance), Erik Molnar (Minister of Justice), Antal Apro (Minister of Construction), Albert Konya (Minister of Education), Gyorgy Lukacs (Minister of Culture), Mrs. Joseph Nagy (Minister of Light Industry), and others. Several of these Communists had held high Party posts under the Rakosi regime. Some of them (notably Kossa, Apro, Munnich) were to reemerge as leaders of still another government, installed under Soviet auspices the following day, November 4.[14]

At the same time, the Government added a few new members to its roster, among them Miss Anna Kethly as Minister of State, and promoted Pal Maleter to be Minister of National Defense. The Government now had eleven members of whom only three (Imre Nagy, Janos Kadar, and Geza Losonczy) were Communists. Of the rest, Zoltan Tildy, Bela Kovacs, B. Istvan Szabo, Anna Kethly, Gyula Kelemen, Jozsef Fischer, Istvan Bibo, and Ferenc Farkas represented other political parties, while the party affiliation of Pal Maleter was not known.

---

[14] See Chapter IX, Document 3.

CHAPTER IX

SOVIET INTERVENTION: NOVEMBER 4—

At noon on November 3 the mixed Hungarian-Soviet commission met and, upon hearing each other's statements on certain technical questions concerning Soviet troop withdrawal, decided to adjourn until 10 P.M. of the same day.

At 10 P.M. the commission met again.

At 5.20 A.M. on November 4 Imre Nagy issued the following statement:

1. STATEMENT BY PREMIER IMRE NAGY ANNOUNCING AN ATTACK BY SOVIET FORCES ON THE HUNGARIAN GOVERNMENT, NOVEMBER 4, 1956

THIS IS IMRE NAGY, Premier, speaking. In the early hours of this morning, the Soviet troops launched an attack against our capital city with the obvious intention of overthrowing the lawful, democratic, Hungarian Government. Our troops are fighting. The Government is in its place. I inform the people of the country and world public opinion of this.

2. APPEAL BY IMRE NAGY TO THE HUNGARIAN REPRESENTATIVES ON THE MIXED HUNGARIAN-SOVIET COMMISSION TO RETURN TO THEIR POSTS, NOVEMBER 4, 1956

IMRE NAGY, PREMIER of the national Government, appeals to Pal Maleter, Defense Minister; Istvan Kovacs, Chief of the General Staff; and the other members of the military mission who went to the Soviet Army Headquarters at 10 P.M. last night and have not yet returned to return immediately and to take charge of their respective offices.

3. FORMATION OF THE HUNGARIAN REVOLUTIONARY WORKER-PEASANT GOVERNMENT: RADIO APPEAL BY FERENC MUNNICH, NOVEMBER 4, 1956

OPEN LETTER to the Hungarian working nation!

Compatriots, our worker and peasant brethren!

The undersigned, Antal Apro, Janos Kadar, Istvan Kossa, and Ferenc Munnich, Ministers, former members of the Imre Nagy Government, announce that on November 1, 1956 [?], severing all our relations with that Government, we left the Government and initiated the formation of the Hungarian Revolutionary Worker-Peasant Government.

We were prompted to take this responsible act by the realization that the Government of Imre Nagy had come under the pressure of the reaction and become impotent. Within that government we had no opportunity whatever for action, in the face of the ever growing strength of the counterrevolutionary threat menacing our People's Republic, our worker-peasant power, and our socialist achievements with extinction.

Esteemed champions of the working class movement with several decades of service have been murdered—Imre Mezo, the secretary of the greater Budapest executive committee of the Party; Comrade [?] the seasoned fighter of the labor movement in Csepel; Sandor Sziklai, the director of the museum of war history. In addition, other generally esteemed sons of the workers and peasantry have been exterminated en masse.

We could no longer stand by idly as members of the Government, incapable of action, while under the cover of democracy counterrevolutionary terrorists and bandits were bestially murdering our worker and peasant brethren, keeping our peaceful citizens in terror, dragging our country into anarchy, and putting our entire nation under the yoke of counterrevolution for a long time to come.

Hungarian workers, compatriots, worker-brethren, comrades! We have decided that we will fight with all our strength against the threatening danger of fascism and reaction and their murderous gangs. We appeal to every loyal son of our People's

Republic, every follower of socialism—in the first place the
Communists—workers, miners, and the best sons of the peasantry and the intellectuals to support every measure of the
Hungarian Revolutionary Worker-Peasant Government and its
entire struggle for the liberation of the people.

Budapest, November 4, 1956,   Antol Apro, Janos Kadar,
                              Istvan Kossa, and
                              Dr. Ferenc Munnich

4. PROGRAM AND COMPOSITION OF THE REVOLUTIONARY
   WORKER-PEASANT GOVERNMENT ANNOUNCED BY JANOS
   KADAR, NOVEMBER 4, 1956[1]

APPEAL TO THE Hungarian people!
   The Hungarian Revolutionary Worker-Peasant Government
has been formed. The mass movement which started on
October 23 in our country had the noble aims of remedying
anti-Party and antidemocratic crimes committed by Rakosi and
his associates and defending national independence and sovereignty. Through the weakness of the Imre Nagy Government
and through the increased influence of counterrevolutionary elements who edged their way into the movement, socialist achievements, our people's state, our worker-peasant power, and the
existence of our country have become endangered.

   This has prompted us, Hungarian patriots, to form the Hun-
garian Revolutionary Worker-Peasant Government. I am now
giving the composition of the Government: Premier, Janos
Kadar; Deputy and Minister of the Armed Forces and Public
Security Forces, Dr. Ferenc Munnich; Minister of State, Gyorgy
Marosan; Foreign Minister, Imre Horvath; Minister of Finance,
Istvan Kossa; Minister of Industry, Antal Apro; Minister of
Agriculture, Imre Dogei; Minister of Commerce, Sandor Ronai.

---

[1] A translation of this appeal as broadcast by the Moscow radio
appears in the New York *Times,* November 5, 1956, p. 20.

The other portfolios remain unfilled for the time being. These portfolios must be filled, after the restoration of the country's legal order, by representatives of other parties and non-Party persons loyal to our people's democracy, who are ready to defend the achievements of socialism. The newly-formed Government addresses the following appeal to the Hungarian people:

Appeal of the Hungarian Revolutionary Worker-Peasant Government to the Hungarian People: Hungarian brethren, workers, peasants, soldiers, comrades!

Our nation is passing through difficult days. The power of the workers and peasants and the sacred cause of socialism are in danger. So are all the achievements of the past twelve years which the Hungarian working nation, and above all you Hungarian workers, have created by your own hands and by your heroic and self-sacrificing work.

With growing impudence the counterrevolutionaries are ruthlessly persecuting the followers of democracy. Arrow Cross members and other beasts are murdering the honest patriots, our best comrades. We know that many questions are still awaiting solution in our country and that we have to cope with many difficulties. The life of the workers is still far from what it should be in a country building socialism. Simultaneously, with the progress attained during the past twelve years, the clique of Rakosi and Gero has committed many grave mistakes and gravely violated legality.

All this has rightly made workers dissatisfied. The reactionaries are seeking their own selfish ends. They raised their hands against our people's democratic regime, which means that they want to return the factories and enterprises to the capitalists, the land to the big estate owners.

The gendarmes and prison wardens of Horthy and the representatives of the hated and cursed oppressive system have already set out to sit on the neck of the people. If they had won, they would not have brought freedom, well-being, and democracy, but slavery, misery, unemployment, and ruthless fresh oppression. Making use of the mistakes committed during the building of our people's democratic system, the reactionary elements have misled many honest workers and particularly the major part of the youth, who joined the movement with honest and patriotic intentions.

These honest patriots wanted the further democratization of our economic and social life and thus the securing of the consolidation of the foundations of socialism in our country. They raised their voice for the strengthening and flourishing of Hungary so that she would become a free and sovereign state which maintains friendly relations with the other socialist countries. For this reason it is wrong and criminal to accuse them for having taken part in this movement.

At the same time one must not lose sight of the fact that, by utilizing the weakness of Imre Nagy's Government, counterrevolutionary forces are indulging in excesses, murdering and looting in the country, and it is to be feared that they will gain the upper hand. We see with deep sadness and a heavy heart into what a terrible situation our beloved Fatherland has been driven by those counterrevolutionary elements, and often even by well-meaning progressive people, who willy-nilly abused the slogans of freedom and democracy and thus opened the way to reaction.

Hungarians, brethren, patriots, soldiers, citizens!

We must put an end to the excesses of the counterrevolutionary elements. The hour of action has struck. We will defend the power of the workers and peasants and the achievements of the people's democracy. We will create order, security, and calm in our country. The interest of the people and the country is that they should have a strong government, a government capable of leading the country out of its grave situation. It is for this reason that we formed the Hungarian Revolutionary Worker-Peasant Government.

The program of the Hungarian Revolutionary Worker-Peasant Government is as follows:

1—The securing of our national independence and our country's sovereignty.

2—The protection of our people's democratic and socialist system against all attacks. The protection of our socialist achievements and the guaranteeing of our progress along the road of building socialism.

3—The ending of fratricidal fighting and the restoration of internal order and peace. The Government will not tolerate the persecution of workers under any pretext, for having taken part in the most recent events.

4—The establishment of close fraternal relations with every socialist country on the basis of complete equality and non-interference. The same principle governs our economic relations and mutual assistance agreements.

5—Peaceful cooperation with every country, irrespective of social order and form of state.

6—The quick and substantial raising of the living standard of the workers, particularly of the working class. There must be more houses for the workers. Factories and institutes must be enabled to build apartments for their workers and employees.

7—Modification of the Five-Year Plan, the changing of the methods of economic management, taking into consideration the country's capacity so as to raise the population's living standard as quickly as possible.

8—Elimination of bureaucracy and broad development of democracy in the interest of the workers.

9—On the basis of the broadest democracy, worker-management must be realized in factories and enterprises.

10—The development of agricultural production, the abolition of compulsory deliveries, and the assisting of individual farmers. The Government will firmly liquidate all acts of law infringement in the field of the cooperatives and commassation.

11—Securing democratic election of existing administrative bodies and revolutionary councils.

12—Support for retail trade and artisans.

13—The systematic development of Hungarian national culture in the spirit of our progressive traditions.

14—The Hungarian Revolutionary Worker-Peasant Government, in the interest of our people, working class, and country, requested the command of the Soviet Army to help our nation in smashing the sinister forces of reaction and restoring order and calm in the country.

15—After the restoration of calm and order the Hungarian Government will begin negotiations with the Soviet Government and with the other participants to the Warsaw Pact about the withdrawal of Soviet troops from Hungary.

Workers, peasants, intellectuals, youth, soldiers and officers! Support our nation's just struggle, defend our people's democratic system.   Disarm counterrevolutionary gangs.   Organized workers, line up behind the Hungarian Revolutionary Worker-Peasant Government.   Resume work without delay.   Working peasants, defend the land.   Fight shoulder to shoulder with your worker brethren for our common cause, for our people's democratic system.   Working youth and students, do not allow yourselves to be misled.   Your future can be guaranteed only by the people's democracy—defend it.   Hungarian workers, the prerequisite for the realization of our justified economic, political, and socialist aspirations is the defense of the people's democratic power, the restoration of order, the resumption of work and of production.

It is for this that the Hungarian Revolutionary Worker-Peasant Government is fighting and calls to the struggle every unselfish son and daughter of the Hungarian Fatherland. Workers, Hungarian brethren, truth is on our side. We will win.

Budapest, November 4, 1956   Hungarian Revolutionary
                                                        Worker-Peasant Government

The new Government's appeal was followed by a confirmation of Mr. Kos's status as Hungary's representative in the United Nations and a protest against Imre Nagy's request for U. N. action in the case of Hungary.

5. Telegram from the Prime Minister of the Hungarian Revolutionary Worker-Peasant Government, Kadar, to the Secretary General of the United Nations, Hammarskjold, Challenging U. N. Jurisdiction in the Hungarian Case, November 4, 1956

THE HUNGARIAN REVOLUTIONARY Worker-Peasant Government states that the appeal made by Imre Nagy to the U. N. organization requesting that the Hungarian question be discussed in the United Nations has no legal force and cannot be regarded as an appeal sent by Hungary as a state.[2] The Revolutionary Worker-Peasant Government categorically opposes the discussion both by the Security Council and the General Assembly of the above-mentioned question since this question lies exclusively within the competence of the Hungarian People's Republic.[3]

Budapest, November 4, 1956

> Prime Minister of the Hungarian Revolutionary Worker-Peasant Government, Janos Kadar;
> Foreign Minister Imre Horvath.

Meanwhile, Soviet troops were in command in Hungary.

---

[2] See Documents 12 and 15 in the preceding chapter.

[3] Despite the request of the Kadar Government the United Nations General Assembly considered the case of Hungary on several occasions. (A United States resolution introduced in the Security Council, calling on the USSR among other things to desist from any intervention in Hungary, was vetoed by the Soviet representative on November 5.) As stated in a report of the U. N. Secretary General to the General Assembly, dated November 30, 1956 (New York *Times,* December 1, 1956, p. 8): "In a number of resolutions the General Assembly has adopted decisions concerning various aspects of the situation in Hungary and requested action of the United Nations referring thereto. The main decisions adopted have covered the withdrawal of troops from Hungarian territory and related questions, including that of deportations; investigations of the situation caused by foreign intervention in Hungary; and humanitarian activities, including assistance to refugees." In a telegram dated November 12 (U. N. Document A/3341, November 12, 1956), the acting foreign minister of the Government, Istvan Sebes, claimed that "the Hungarian Government and the Soviet Government are exclusively competent to carry on negotiations concerning the withdrawal of the Soviet troops from Hungary" and rejected the General Assembly's efforts at securing the dispatch of U. N. representatives to Hungary as being in violation of Article 2, paragraph 7 of the U. N. Charter dealing with domestic jurisdiction. To date (December 14, 1956) the Kadar Government has refused to accede to requests for U. N. observers or even for a visit of the Secretary General of the U. N. to Budapest.

6. APPEAL BY THE COMMAND OF SOVIET TROOPS IN HUNGARY TO THE HUNGARIAN PEOPLE AND THE OFFICERS AND MEN OF THE HUNGARIAN ARMY, NOVEMBER 5, 1956

THE COMMAND and the soldiers and officers of the Soviet Army in Hungary are speaking to you. We are workers, peasants, intellectuals, and working people, just like you. We are not here to occupy your country. We do not want other people's land. We have enough land and natural resources of our own.

We have taken action at the request of the Revolutionary Worker-Peasant Government. That Government informed us that forces of capitalist reaction were engaged in committing abuses in Hungary, that they wanted to restore the power of large landowners and capitalists, and that they wanted to deprive the workers of their achievements, and the peasants of their land. Fascism had appeared as a real danger.

The Government told us that Imre Nagy's Government did not want to fight against reaction, and this enabled the counter-revolutionary gangs which had gained ground to murder workers and patriots, to ravage, and to plunder. The Government of Imre Nagy had disintegrated and did not actually exist. There was total confusion in the country and antipopular forces were committing abuses with impunity.

In this situation the Hungarian Revolutionary Worker-Peasant Government requested the command of the Soviet forces in Hungary to lend a helping hand in the liquidation of counterrevolutionary forces and in the restoration of order, internal peace, and calm. The command of the Soviet forces and we Soviet soldiers and officers are ready to give this help to our Hungarian brethren.

We respect and appreciate the freedom-loving Hungarian people. It is our firm conviction that the Hungarian people are receiving our help with the same understanding as in 1945, when we liberated them from fascist bondage at immeasurable sacrifices on both our parts.

Hungarian workers, do not believe the slanderers who would like to set the Hungarian people against us. We are your unselfish friends. We are soldiers of freedom and friendship among peoples. We support a just and joint cause.

We appeal to the soldiers and officers of the Hungarian Army to fight with us shoulder to shoulder against the unbridled forces of reaction for freedom and democracy. We appeal to every Hungarian who loves his country to take his share in the common struggle and to promote the safeguarding of people's democracy and the victory of the sacred cause of his country and people.

The Command of the Soviet Troops in Hungary

Under the impact of renewed intervention by Soviet armored power, the Government of Imre Nagy fell.[4]

With the fall of the Government of Imre Nagy, the briefly victorious revolt of the Hungarian people seemed crushed, although fighting on a sporadic scale continued. The restoration of law and order, the effective organization of Hungarian political authority, including the rebuilding of a Hungarian Communist Party, and the resumption of normal economic activities eluded the Kadar regime. The difficulties which it encountered were clearly reflected in the drastic measures to which the Hungarian Government resorted in the second week of December in order to disarm the Hungarian people, many of whom retained firearms, and to break the back of workers' resistance. The Hungarian Government's actions, supported by Soviet motorized detachments and infantry, included the declaration of martial law (on December 9) to come into effect on December 11 against all persons "guilty of murder, arson, robbery, or damaging industrial equipment and all persons illegally in possession of firearms," and the arrest of two leaders of the Budapest Central Workers' Council. The Government also ordered the dissolution of the workers' councils, but without apparent success. The workers responded with a renewed call for a general strike. The Hungarian revolt which was officially crushed on November 4 was still far from being over.

---

[4] Nagy and several of his colleagues found asylum at the Yugoslav Embassy on November 4. They remained there until November 22 when they emerged on the basis of an agreement between Yugoslav and Hungarian officials guaranteeing Nagy and his party safe-conduct. The exact whereabouts of Nagy since then are unknown. Janos Kadar admitted that the terms of safe-conduct had been violated and Nagy had been taken out of the country. Yugoslavia protested Nagy's abduction in notes both to the Hungarian and Soviet governments. (For a translation of the Yugoslav note to Hungary, see the New York *Times*, November 24, 1956, p. 2.)

PART FOUR: *The Repercussions of the Polish and Hungarian Events*

The General Debate Continues, October-November, 1956

CHAPTER I

SETTLEMENT OF RELATIONS BETWEEN SOCIALIST STATES

The Polish and Hungarian events of late October, 1956, induced the Soviet Government to state its policy on relations between the USSR and the people's democracies.

1. DECLARATION BY THE GOVERNMENT OF THE USSR ON THE PRINCIPLES OF DEVELOPMENT AND FURTHER STRENGTHENING OF FRIENDSHIP AND COOPERATION BETWEEN THE SOVIET UNION AND OTHER SOCIALIST STATES, OCTOBER 30, 1956[1]

A POLICY OF PEACEFUL coexistence, friendship, and cooperation among all states has been and continues to be the firm foundation of the foreign relations of the Union of Soviet Socialist Republics.

This policy finds its deepest and most consistent expression in the mutual relations among the socialist countries. United by the common ideals of building a socialist society and by the principles of proletarian internationalism, the countries of the great commonwealth of socialist nations can build their mutual relations only on the principles of complete equality, of respect for territorial integrity, state independence and sovereignty, and of noninterference in one another's internal affairs. Not only does this not exclude close fraternal cooperation and mutual aid among the countries of the socialist commonwealth in the economic, political, and cultural spheres; on the contrary, it presupposes these things.

The system of people's democracies took shape, grew strong and showed its great vital power in many countries of Europe

---

[1] *Pravda*, October 31, 1956. The translation reproduced here is from *The Current Digest of the Soviet Press*, VIII, No. 40 (November 14, 1956), 10-11.

and Asia on this foundation after the Second World War and
the rout of fascism.

In the process of the rise of the new system and the deep
revolutionary changes in social relations, there have been many
difficulties, unresolved problems, and downright mistakes, including mistakes in the mutual relations among the socialist
countries—violations and errors which demeaned the principle
of equality in relations among the socialist states.

The 20th Congress of the Communist Party of the Soviet
Union quite resolutely condemned these violations and mistakes,
and set the task of consistent application by the Soviet Union
of Leninist principles of equality of peoples in its relations with
the other socialist countries. It proclaimed the need for taking
full account of the historical past and peculiarities of each
country that has taken the path of building a new life.

The Soviet Government is consistently carrying out these
historic decisions of the 20th Congress, which create conditions
for further strengthening friendship and cooperation among the
socialist countries on the firm foundation of observance of the
full sovereignty of each socialist state.

As recent events have demonstrated, it has become necessary to make this declaration of the Soviet Union's stand on the
mutual relations of the USSR with other socialist countries,
particularly in the economic and military spheres.

. The Soviet government is prepared to discuss together with
the governments of other socialist states measures ensuring
further development and strengthening of economic ties among
the socialist countries in order to remove any possibility of violation of the principles of national sovereignty, mutual benefit, and
equality in economic relations.

This principle must also be extended to advisers. It is
known that, in the first period of the formation of the new social
system, the Soviet Union, at the request of the governments of
the people's democracies, sent these countries a certain number
of its specialists—engineers, agronomists, scientists, military
advisers. In the recent period the Soviet Government has

repeatedly raised before the socialist countries the question of recalling its advisers.

In view of the fact that by this time the people's democracies have formed their own qualified national cadres in all spheres of economic and military affairs, the Soviet Government considers it urgent to review, together with the other socialist states, the question of the expediency of the further presence of USSR advisers in these countries.

In the military domain an important basis of the mutual relations between the Soviet Union and the people's democracies is the Warsaw Treaty, under which its members adopted respective political and military obligations, including the obligation to take "concerted measures necessary for strengthening their defense capacity in order to protect the peaceful labor of their peoples, to guarantee the inviolability of their borders and territory, and to ensure defense against possible aggression."

It is known that Soviet units are in the Hungarian and Rumanian republics in accord with the Warsaw Treaty and governmental agreements. Soviet units are in the Polish republic on the basis of the Potsdam four-power agreement and the Warsaw Treaty. Soviet military units are not in the other people's democracies.

For the purpose of assuring mutual security of the socialist countries, the Soviet Government is prepared to review with the other socialist countries which are members of the Warsaw Treaty the question of Soviet troops stationed on the territory of the above-mentioned countries. In so doing the Soviet Government proceeds from the general principle that stationing the troops of one or another state which is a member of the Warsaw Treaty on the territory of another state which is a member of the treaty is done by agreement among all its members and only with the consent of the state on the territory of which and at the request of which these troops are stationed or it is planned to station them.

The Soviet Government considers it necessary to make a statement in connection with the events in Hungary. The course of events has shown that the working people of Hungary, who have attained great progress on the basis of the people's democratic system, are rightfully raising the question of the need to eliminate serious defects in the sphere of economic construction, the question of further improving the living standards of the population, the question of combating bureaucratic distortions in the state machinery. However, this legitimate and progressive movement of the working people was soon joined by the forces of black reaction and counterrevolution, which are trying to take advantage of the dissatisfaction of a part of the working people in order to undermine the foundations of the people's democratic system in Hungary and to restore the old landowner-capitalist ways in that country.

The Soviet Government, like the whole Soviet people, deeply regrets that the development of events in Hungary has led to bloodshed.

At the request of the Hungarian people's government, the Soviet Government has granted consent to the entry into Budapest of Soviet military units to help the Hungarian people's army and the Hungarian agencies of government to bring order to the city.[2]

Having in mind that the further presence of Soviet military units in Hungary could serve as an excuse for further aggravation of the situation, the Soviet Government has given its military command instructions to withdraw the Soviet military units from the city of Budapest as soon as this is considered necessary by the Hungarian Government.

At the same time, the Soviet Government is prepared to enter into the appropriate negotiations with the Government of the Hungarian People's Republic and other members of the Warsaw Treaty on the question of the presence of Soviet troops on the territory of Hungary.

To guard the socialist achievements of people's democratic Hungary is the chief and sacred duty of the workers, peasants,

---

[2] See Hungary, Chapter VI, Document 5.

intelligentsia, of all the Hungarian working people at the present moment.

The Soviet Government expresses confidence that the peoples of the socialist countries will not permit foreign and domestic reactionary forces to shake the foundations of the people's democratic system, a system established and strengthened by the self-sacrificing struggle and labor of the workers, peasants, and intelligentsia of each country. They will continue all efforts to remove all obstacles in the path of further strengthening the democratic foundations, independence, and sovereignty of their countries; to develop further the socialist foundations of each country, its economy and its culture, for the sake of an uninterrupted rise in the living standards and cultural level of all the working people; they will strengthen the fraternal unity and mutual aid of the socialist countries to buttress the great cause of peace and socialism.

October 30, 1956

The Soviet declaration was hailed by the people's democracies, Yugoslavia, and the Chinese People's Republic, by the Democratic People's Republic of North Korea and the Democratic Republic of Vietnam.[3] *Scinteia* (November 2, 1956), the central organ of the Rumanian Workers Party, called the declaration "the expression of a typical, socialist policy, a genuine code of righteous international relations between free peoples." *Rabotnichesko Delo* (November 1, 1956), organ of the Bulgarian Workers Party, recalled the liberation of Bulgaria "thanks to the Soviet Union and its Army" and asserted that the "USSR, first and most powerful socialist state, helped and continues to help the countries of the socialist camp in the great process of establishing a new regime and in the deep revolutionary changes which the workers are realizing under the leadership of the Communist and Workers Parties." *Rude Pravo* (November 1, 1956), organ of the Czechoslovak CP, noted that

the declaration . . . does not conceal in any way that it has been necessary to eliminate errors and mistakes made during the

---

[3] For a reaction to the declaration in Poland, see Poland, Chapter V, Document 8.

past period of the widespread cult of personality [but] one very important fact again clearly stands out. . . . The Soviet Union never forced and will never force her friendship and help on nations and countries which do not wish it. . . . The forces of international reaction, completely without sense, are hissing that the Soviet Union is forcing her will on other nations.

The events in Hungary demonstrate the exact opposite. The Soviet forces entered Budapest during the first days of the crisis at the request of the Hungarian People's Government in order to help the Hungarian organs restore order in the city. In the streets of Budapest they gave their lives and shed their blood. The latest events in Budapest have shown, however, that a further stay, in present circumstances, might cause even greater complications and acuteness of the situation. The Hungarian reaction which joined hands with all nationalist elements, as latest reports show, succeeded in gaining its many aims. The Hungarian People's Democracy has been given a most serious shock in its very foundations, and one must have the gravest fears as to its future existence.

It is impossible to give a thorough answer to the question as to the roots of the developments which have occurred in the past few days in Hungary. It is possible, however, to express one indisputable conclusion which is fundamentally valid for the entire international workers' movement, as well as for the relationships among the socialist countries, about which the Soviet Government declaration speaks. Once again it is clear that the strength of the revolutionary socialist movement and the fate of socialism in any given country lie primarily in the fact that every Communist Party bears full responsibility not only for the fate of its own nation and country, but also for the entire movement of ours, for the fate of socialism and Communists.

The Soviet Union did not force her help on any country. This applies to all countries, including the people's democracies. However, only the traitor to his own people can hold, in the present situation, that the help of the Soviet Union to the people's democracies is not necessary.

Under the title "Long Live the Great Unity of the Socialist Countries," the *People's Daily* (November 2, 1956) organ of the Central Committee of the Chinese Communist Party, characterized the Soviet declaration as a highly significant document. It contributes powerfully toward consolidating still further the solidarity of the socialist countries, bringing about a common economic upsurge in the socialist countries, and strengthening the struggle of the peoples of the socialist countries against the aggressive forces of imperialism. The Government of the Chinese People's Republic published a statement on November 1 in support of the Soviet declaration.[4] The press of the people's democracies in Europe such as Poland, Czechoslovakia, the German Democratic Republic, Rumania, Bulgaria, and Yugoslavia have unanimously praised it.

The unity of the socialist countries, headed by the great Soviet Union, is the most important support of the causes of the world peace and human progress. Thanks to their common ideological foundations and the identity of their aims in struggle, the socialist countries have established fraternal relations of mutual assistance and cooperation unparalleled in the history of mankind. . . .

In this respect, the many-sided, immense help given by the Soviet Union to various other fraternal countries and to the people of various countries has played a most prominent role. . . .

The socialist cause is new in man's history. A new cause cannot be immune from errors of one kind or another, owing to lack of experience. There is no exception to this, too, as regards the mutual relations between the socialist countries; there is nothing strange in this. But . . . all the errors made in the mutual relations between the socialist countries can be corrected and eliminated. In fact, past errors have either already been corrected or are in process of correction. Therefore, this kind of thing can never be a pretext for breaking the unity of the socialist countries and friendship with the Soviet Union.

The October 30 declaration of the Soviet Government shows unreserved loyalty by the Soviet Union to the common interests of the great unity of the socialist countries and to the Marxist-Leninist principle of equality of nationalities and the principle of proletarian internationalism. . . .

Serving as instruments for strengthening the unity of the socialist countries, there are not only the socialist economic and political systems of the socialist countries, their principle of working class internationalism, and the Marxist-Leninist principles of their working class parties; there are also the various treaties and

---

[4] See Document 2 in this chapter.

agreements between these countries. The treaty of friendly cooperation and mutual assistance, concluded in Warsaw on May 14, 1955 . . . guarantees to the people of the European countries in the socialist camp that they can safely build a happy life for themselves without becoming isolated and helpless in the face of the aggressive forces of Western imperialism. It guarantees that the countries in the camp of socialism will not be picked off one by one by the forces of Western imperialism and internal counterrevolution which are always hostile to socialism, are scheming to overthrow the socialist countries, and trying to reinstate capitalist and fascist counterrevolutionary regimes there. . . .

The Chinese people have great regard for the people of the socialist countries of Eastern Europe who are building a new life for themselves, for the youth of these countries who are preparing to build a new life for themselves. The people of China hope that their comradely influence can help the cause of socialism in Hungary in its present serious condition, and by positive action they can safeguard the great internationalist solidarity of the socialist countries with the Soviet Union at the center. . . .

. . . the people of China stand firmly inside the Socialist camp headed by the Soviet Union. The friendship between the People's Republic of China and the Soviet Union is forever unshakable, for it affects the most fundamental interests of the 800 million people of the two countries. If these interests were jeopardized, this would in turn undoubtedly jeopardize others.

2. STATEMENT BY THE GOVERNMENT OF THE PEOPLE'S REPUBLIC OF CHINA ON THE DECLARATION OF THE SOVIET GOVERNMENT ON RELATIONS AMONG SOCIALIST STATES, NOVEMBER 1, 1956

THE GOVERNMENT OF THE Soviet Union on October 30, 1956, issued a declaration on the foundations of the development and further strengthening of friendship and cooperation between the Soviet Union and other socialist countries. The Government of the People's Republic of China considers this declaration of the Government of the Soviet Union to be correct. This declaration is of great importance in correcting errors in mutual relations between the socialist countries and in strengthening unity among them.

The People's Republic of China maintains that the five principles of mutual respect for sovereignty and territorial integrity, nonaggression, nonintervention in each other's internal affairs, equality and mutual benefit, and peaceful coexistence should be the principles governing the establishment and development of mutual relations among the nations of the world.

The socialist countries are all independent, sovereign states. At the same time they are united by the common ideal of socialism and the spirit of proletarian internationalism. Consequently, mutual relations between socialist countries all the more so should be established on the basis of these five principles. Only in this way are the socialist countries able to achieve genuine fraternal friendship and solidarity and, through mutual assistance and cooperation, their desire for a mutual economic upsurge.

As the declaration of the Soviet Government pointed out, the mutual relations between the socialist countries are not without mistakes. These mistakes resulted in misunderstandings and estrangement between certain socialist countries. Some of these countries have been unable to build socialism better in accordance with their historical circumstances and special features because of these mistakes.

As a result of these misunderstandings and estrangement, a tense situation has sometimes occurred which otherwise would not have occurred. The handling of the 1948-49 Yugoslav situation and the recent happenings in Poland and Hungary are enough to illustrate this.

Following the Soviet-Yugoslav joint declaration issued in June, 1955, the Soviet Government has again taken note of this problem and in its declaration of October 30, 1956, indicated its willingness to solve various problems in mutual relations on the basis of the principles of full equality, respect for territorial integrity, national independence and sovereignty, and nonintervention in each other's internal affairs and by friendly negotiations with other socialist countries. This important step is clearly of value in eliminating estrangement and misunderstandings among the socialist countries. It will help increase their friendship and cooperation.

The Government of the People's Republic of China notes that the people of Poland and Hungary in the recent happenings have raised demands that democracy, independence, and equality be strengthened and the material well-being of the people be raised on the basis of developing production. These demands are completely proper. Correct satisfaction of these demands is not only helpful to consolidation of the people's democratic system in these countries but also favorable to the unity among the socialist countries.

We note with satisfaction that the people of Poland and their leaders have taken notice of the activities and danger of reactionary elements who attempt to undermine the people's democratic system and unity among socialist countries. We consider it absolutely necessary to take note of this and to differentiate between the just demands of the broadest mass of the people and the conspiratorial activities of an extremely small number of reactionary elements. The question of uniting the broadest mass of the people in the struggle against an extremely small number of reactionary elements is not only a question for an individual socialist country, but one deserving attention by many socialist countries, including our country.

Because of the unanimity of ideology and aim of struggle, it often happens that certain personnel of socialist countries neglect the principle of equality among nations in their mutual relations. Such a mistake, by nature, is the error of bourgeois chauvinism. Such a mistake, particularly the mistake of chauvinism by a big country, inevitably results in serious damage to the solidarity and common cause of the socialist countries. For this reason, leading members and personnel of our government and the people of the entire country must at all times be vigilant to prevent the error of big nation chauvinism in relations with socialist countries and others.

We should at all times carry out education resolutely to oppose big nation chauvinism among our personnel and the people of the entire country. If such an error is committed it should be corrected promptly. This is the duty to which we should pay the utmost attention in order to strive for peaceful coexistence with all nations and to promote the cause of world peace.

3. YUGOSLAV COMMENT: "A DECLARATION," EDITORIAL IN
   Borba, NOVEMBER 1, 1956

THE SOVIET GOVERNMENT'S declaration on relations with socialist countries undoubtedly has great international significance, for it provides a positive basis of principle for the regulation of relations and for the development of cooperation among socialist countries.

The principal significance of this declaration is, above all, the result of three positions which are expressed in it. First, the Soviet Government in its declaration notes openly that there were irregularities and mistakes in relations between the socialist countries so far, "which diminished the principle of socialist equality." Second, the Soviet Government stresses that relations between the socialist countries should be founded on principles of full national independence and equality, and third, the Soviet Government supports in its declaration the point of view that in the building of socialism the specific conditions of every individual country must be taken into consideration.

There is no doubt that only a constant and consistent implementation of these Leninist principles of socialist internationalism can remove all irregularities from the mutual relations between socialist countries and give to socialism a powerful, attractive force. For that very reason special significance is given to the positive decision of the Soviet Government to start solving immediately certain very pressing and sensitive problems in the area of international relations of socialist countries with each other.

The Soviet Government expressed readiness to regulate its economic relations with other socialist countries to their mutual advantage and equality and to do away with every possibility of infringing upon their national sovereignty. At the same time the Soviet Government has shown its readiness to discuss with the socialist countries which signed the Warsaw Pact the question of the stationing of Soviet troops on their territories, keeping in mind the principles of mutual agreement, understanding, and good will in connection with this. The Soviet Government also stresses in its declaration that it has already given instructions to its command to withdraw its troops from Budapest when in the opinion of the Hungarian Government that becomes necessary.

These two decisions of the Soviet Government represent concrete steps in the direction of settling relationships among the socialist countries on the basis of correct principles and will undoubtedly meet with a favorable echo in all the socialist countries. They will have the most direct and positive effect on the situation in Hungary, where the problem of relations between the USSR and Hungary is especially acute.

But this is not all of the international significance of the declaration of the Soviet Government. The decision of the Soviet Government to settle questions of economic cooperation and the stationing of troops with other socialist countries came precisely at the time when aggression has taken place against Egypt with the purpose of destroying its independence and its sovereign rights in regard to the Suez Canal. In such a situation, any reinforcement of democratic principles in the field of international cooperation and the undertaking of positive steps aimed at settlement of relations with other countries in the international community removes dangerous obstacles which stand in the way of peace.

CHAPTER II

THE IMPACT OF SOVIET INTERVENTION IN HUNGARY: RELATIONS AMONG SOCIALIST STATES RECONSIDERED

The impact of the Soviet declaration of October 30 had hardly been absorbed when a new, acrimonious debate—in which the USSR and Yugoslavia were the chief but by no means only participants— got under way. The subject still concerned relations among socialist states.

The debate was precipitated by the Hungarian crisis which had taken two decisive turns between November 1 and 4, 1956. First, the victory of the Hungarian revolution—whose proportions were perhaps not fully appreciated by the Soviet leadership until November 1 when two of its representatives, A. I. Mikoyan and M. A. Suslov, assessed the situation on the spot in Budapest—confronted the "socialist camp" with an unprecedented defection from its ranks of potentially much graver consequence than the split between Yugoslavia and the Cominform had been. For while Tito's Yugoslavia—as indeed Gomulka's Poland—essentially sought sovereignty under Communism, Hungary was clearly bidding for independence from Communism. Under these conditions, saving the "socialist revolution" in Hungary must have appeared as a paramount necessity to the leaders of Communist states. Yet, the second decisive turn in the turbulent Hungarian events, the massive intervention of Soviet military power to crush the revolution, entailed severe repercussions both in the Communist countries and outside them, among public opinion in general and the Communist Parties in particular.

The question of justifying the action of the Soviet Union arose, as did other questions relating to the possible allocation of responsibility for the Hungarian events to sources outside Hungary (and not necessarily lodged in the "imperialist camp") and to the effects of the Soviet Union's handling of the Hungarian crisis on the direction in which its relations with the other socialist states might develop.

The mood of the Soviet Union was revealed in an editorial in *Pravda* which appeared on November 4, 1956, coincidentally with the assault of Soviet troops on the Government of Imre Nagy.

1. EDITORIAL: "BLOCK THE ROAD OF REACTION IN HUNGARY," *Pravda,* NOVEMBER 4, 1956

EVENTS IN HUNGARY ARE attracting the attention of the public in all countries.   The Soviet people, who cherish feelings of friendship for the fraternal Hungarian people, cannot but take to heart the successes and difficulties of the Hungarian workers in their struggle for the development of the country along the road to socialism.

Millions of Soviet people are profoundly sympathetic towaru the desire of the Hungarian workers that their Motherland develop successfully as a free, sovereign, socialist state.

We understand the desire of the workers, peasants, and the intelligentsia of Hungary to raise the living standard of the population and to make full use of the great advantages of the people's democratic order for this purpose.

We understand the just demands for correction of the serious errors committed by the leadership in the past, to overcome completely the consequences of the violation of socialist legality, and to put into practice urgent measures for the further democratization of public life.

At the same time, one cannot but see that, parallel with this healthy aspiration of the working masses, actions of reactionary forces, profoundly alien to the people, appear more and more clearly in the events of the last few days—actions which aim at destroying the socialist conquests of the workers and establishing capitalism in the country.

The antipopular elements, in making use of the errors of the past, are taking recourse to demagogic slogans and, in the guise of the false mask of "fighters for freedom," are attempting to deceive the masses of the workers and to capture them.

One should not, of course, confuse those among the working people, and especially among the youth, who are honestly deluded, with the counterrevolutionary elements which are deceiving them treacherously. These elements are hostile to the people, the interests of the workers are profoundly alien to them, and they hate socialism.

The actions of the reactionary forces in Budapest, as numerous facts convincingly show, are the fruit of lengthy subversive work of the imperialist powers. Nyilasists and Horthyites, who had entrenched themselves in West Germany and Austria, acted with the lavish appropriations of the imperialists. These funds were used to wage an unbridled slanderous campaign against people's Hungary, to send numerous balloons with propaganda literature, to transmit broadcasts, to create and strengthen the reactionary underground.

It is precisely these reactionary forces which are at present creating lawlessness in Hungary, destroying socialist enterprises built by the labor of the people, raiding state and public institutions and editorial offices of newspapers, making bonfires out of books, killing workers, and committing cruel acts of barbarism against Hungarian Communists and progressive public figures.

In the streets of Hungarian towns there are corpses of the tortured, shot, and hanged. Reactionaries who have let themselves go are blowing up monuments to Soviet soldiers who were killed in action for the liberation of Budapest from the Hitlerite hordes.

Reports coming in from abroad show that reactionary forces in Hungary are supported by the imperialist powers. Armed Horthyite officers and all sorts of traitorous émigré rabble are crossing the Hungarian border. The reactionary bourgeois press welcomes with jubilation the news about the actions of counterrevolutionary elements.

The Washington *Post* frankly announces the hopes of the imperialist circles that the victory of reaction in Hungary will radically change the balance of power in the world— that is, that it will strengthen the forces of imperialism and war.

At the request of the Hungarian People's Government, the Soviet Government agreed to bring into Budapest Soviet military units to help the Hungarian People's Army and the Hungarian authorities introduce order in the town. In his radio broadcast on October 25, Imre Nagy, the head of the Hungarian Government, said that bringing in Soviet troops "became necessary for the sake of the vital interests of our socialist order."[1]

However, Imre Nagy, having paid lip service to the danger from the counterrevolutionary instigators, in actual fact proved to be objectively an accomplice of the reactionary forces. This could not but complicate the situation in Budapest and in the whole country.

Bearing in mind that the further stay of Soviet military units in Hungary can serve as a pretext for a still greater aggravation of the situation, the Soviet Government gave instructions to its military command to remove Soviet military units from Budapest. The further course of events has shown that, taking advantage of the direct connivance of the Imre Nagy Cabinet, reactionary forces in Hungary became even more unbridled.

The bloody terror against the workers developed on an unprecedented scale. In these circumstances it became abundantly clear that Imre Nagy cannot and does not want to wage a struggle against the dark forces of reaction. The Nagy Government has virtually collapsed, having yielded its positions to the antipopular elements. Chaos reigns in Hungary.

Economic and cultural life are paralyzed. Industrial enterprises and railroads are out of action. Various kinds of reactionary groups, sheltering behind high-sounding names, loudly proclaimed programs, and demagogic slogans, are pretending to power. For example, it is known that in Gyor Horthyite fascist elements are grouped, who direct the actions of the counterrevolutionary forces.

The peoples of the socialist countries, united by the great aims of the construction of socialism and the noble principles of proletarian internationalism, justly express alarm at the situation in Hungary. Among the workers of the socialist states,

---

[1] See Hungary, Chapter VI, Document 10.

anxiety and legitimate anger against the intrigues of reaction in Hungary are growing.

"We find it painful to see," *Jen Min Jih Pao,* organ of the Central Committee of the Communist Party of China, writes, "that a handful of counterrevolutionary conspirators are taking advantage of the situation in Hungary, are attempting to restore capitalism and fascist terror there so as to breach the unity of the socialist countries in Hungary and to undermine the Warsaw Pact."

"Of late," the appeal of the Polish United Workers Party to the working class and the Polish people reads, "the Hungarian events have entered into a new threatening phase.[2] Reactionary elements ever more obviously are gaining the upper hand. The foundations of the socialist order are being threatened. Chaos and ferment reign throughout the country. Reactionary gangs are carrying out lynchings and are brutally killing Communists. The Polish working class and our entire people are watching the events with special attention. The forces of reaction, which are pushing Hungary toward a catastrophe, meet with resolute condemnation in Poland."

The development of events in Hungary, the organ of the Communist Party of Czechoslovakia *Rude Pravo* stresses, is today characterized by a new step of precipitate retreat from the socialist ideas and from the stable solidarity of socialist countries in the struggle against imperialist intrigues and for the defense of peace. This step was taken by the Chairman of the Hungarian Government, Imre Nagy, by his statement about the immediate repudiation of the Warsaw Treaty by Hungary. The reaction, the paper continues, has openly taken the course of removing Communists from participating in the administration of the country so as to free their hands entirely for a resolute encroachment upon the conquests of the working people of Hungary and upon its fundamental democratic rights.

The workers of Bulgaria have greeted with profound indignation the antipopular act provoked in Budapest by the enemies

---

[2] See Poland, Chapter V, Document 9.

of the Hungarian working class, of peace, and of socialism. In the appeal of the National Council of the *Otechestven Front* addressed to the Bulgarian people it is stated that the enemies of peace and socialism do not at present shy from any means to obstruct the victorious advance of the peoples toward peace and socialism. Hundreds of millions of dollars are being appropriated in the state budgets of the United States and other imperialist countries for subversive activities and terrorist acts against the socialist countries. The Bulgarian people, the appeal says, expresses at this time its fraternal solidarity with the Hungarian working people and its anger and indignation with the wily plans of the imperialists who attempt to lead the Hungarian people off the road to peace and socialism and to discredit their friendship with the peoples of the socialist camp.

Appraising the situation in Hungary, the paper of the Yugoslav League of Communists, *Borba,* remarks that at present different antisocialist forces are raising their heads ever more. They take advantage of the difficult situation in which Hungary found herself and want to turn back the development of Hungary along an antisocialist road.

Scinteia, expressing the opinion of the entire Rumanian people, points out that, learning their lesson from the events developing in Hungary, the peoples of the socialist camp will do all they can to see that the intrigues of the imperialist circles, of all internal and external reactionary forces aimed against the people's democratic order, national independence, and peace suffer defeat. The events in Hungary again and again remind all true fighters for the interests of the working class and all workers for the great cause of socialism of the necessity of increasing revolutionary vigilance, of the sacred duty to stand guard over the socialist conquests of the people and to struggle resolutely and mercilessly against the intrigues of reaction.

The experience of the history of the revolutionary struggle of the working class of Hungary again and again confirms the fundamental theses of Marxism-Leninism about the class struggle, about the fact that the classes of the exploiters do not yield their positions without a battle, that they, these classes, have attempted and will attempt to restore, with the support of imperialist reaction, the bourgeois orders dear to their heart, to lay the yoke of capitalist slavery on the workers and peasants.

It is known how cruelly and mercilessly imperialist reaction suppressed the revolutionary forces of Hungary in 1919, when it succeeded in drowning in blood the young Hungarian republic of workers and peasants. In our time, when fascist reaction is trying to repeat anew the bloody reprisals against the fighters for the cause of socialism in Hungary, the words of the appeal of the great Lenin, addressed to the Hungarian working class in May, 1919, resound with special force.

During those militant revolutionary days, V. I. Lenin pointed out in his article, "Greetings to the Hungarian Workers," the great and responsible tasks of the working class which is called upon to overthrow the exploiters, to suppress their resistance mercilessly, not to allow themselves to be deceived by the false slogans about "freedom," and to be firm in the struggle for the victory of socialism.

The working class and the entire working people of Hungary know well what brought the victory of the counterrevolution to their country in 1919. They themselves experienced the true price of the false slogans about "democracy and freedom," under the cover of which imperialist reaction established the fascist dictatorship of Horthy in the country, linked its fate with the fascist dictatorship of Hitlerite Germany, drew the country into a bloody venture during World War II, and brought it to a national catastrophe.

The workers, peasants, and the people's intelligentsia of Hungary did not labor to restore their beloved country, develop its economy and culture, and build a new life without the domination of the capitalists and landowners so that fascist reaction should now come to power again and so that capitalists and landowners might again lay their hands on all the wealth of the country!

No matter how reaction raves, no matter how it is nurtured by the imperialists, it will not succeed in destroying the people's democratic order in Hungary, for whose creation and strengthening the Hungarian people worked selflessly for more than ten years, having taken their fate into their own hands and having created their national independent people's democratic state.

People's Hungary is living through days which are of a decisive significance for the fate of its further development. The question is: Will Hungary continue along the road of socialist development or will the forces of reaction, which are attempting to restore an order throwing the country back by decades, take the upper hand?

The victory of the democratic forces, under the leadership of the working class, insures true national independence for Hungary, full democratic freedom for the entire people, cooperation on the basis of the Leninist principles of equality, of respect for national sovereignty, and of fraternal mutual assistance with all socialist countries.

Under these conditions alone will people's Hungary be able to achieve a rapid upsurge of its economy and culture and a rise in the well-being of the people, gain worthy authority in international questions, and make its contribution to the cause of the strengthening of peace.

If, however, with the help of deception through false slogans and of armed violence the antipopular elements will triumph, then Hungary will fall inevitably into the clutches of the great imperialist powers, she will lose her national independence for many years to come, and will become a playball of the international machinations of aggressive circles, who are hatching plans for a new war. After having taken power into its hands, reaction will establish a regime of white terror and of harsh suppression of any progressive thought and will retard the development of the national economy and culture.

There cannot be any doubt that the Hungarian people, the working class, all true patriots of Hungary, will find within themselves the strength to crush the reaction and lead the country onto the road of a successful advance toward the realization of the great ideals of socialism.

The struggle of the Hungarian people for the preservation and strengthening of the people's democratic order in a free, independent, socialist Hungary will meet with the unanimous support of the Soviet people, of the peoples of all socialist countries, and of the workers of the whole world.

Block the road of reaction in Hungary! This is the urgent task dictated by the course of events.

2. COMMENT BY THE FOREIGN POLICY EDITOR OF *Tanyug*[3] ON THE HUNGARIAN DEVELOPMENTS, NOVEMBER 4, 1956 [4]

IT IS QUITE UNDERSTANDABLE that our entire public has shown tremendous interest in events in Hungary, from the very first day, when demonstrations broke out in Budapest, to the latest developments characterized by the formation of the Government of Janos Kadar and his speech outlining the Government's policy.[5]

This interest results from the fact that our country is a neighbor of Hungary and that our people are not indifferent to the question of the direction in which events in that neighboring country will develop, a country with whom we had experience, of a negative and positive kind, in the past.

This interest also results from the fact that it is not all the same to Yugoslavia, a socialist community, what the fate of socialist development in Hungary will be.

During the past few days the Yugoslav public has followed with alarm both an increasingly strong tendency of the reactionary forces to gain a dominating role, and the behavior of these forces in the towns, especially Budapest, their killing of innocent people without trial, burning books, and the proclamation of slogans which sounded more and more like a return to the times of Horthy and the times of the "Nyilas".[6]

---

[3] Yugoslav Press Agency.

[4] *Borba*, November 5, 1956.

[5] See Hungary, Chapter IX, Document 4.

[6] Hungarian Arrow Cross Party, patterned after the Nazi Party of Germany. It ruled in Hungary from October, 1944, until the country's liberation in the spring of 1945.

Thus, the justifiable revolt of the people against the policies of Rakosi, Gero, and others started to take a path which was obviously not desired by those forces which are in the majority and who had as their aim the elimination of all the negative developments arising from the past which have obstructed normal, healthy development toward the strengthening of socialism and socialist democracy in Hungary.

Certain forces outside Hungary have obviously contributed to this turn of events, especially the reactionary émigré elements represented by Ferenc Nagy and others who have already started moving into Hungary.

A further increase of these activities would be dangerous from more than one point of view:

From the standpoint of the preservation of peace in this part of the world, in Europe, and in the world in general;

from the standpoint of the development of progressive forces in Hungary;

from the standpoint of the development and fate of socialism and the fate of those positive achievements which have been won in the past by the Hungarian people.

It is obvious that neither the socialist and other progressive forces in Hungary nor those in the rest of the world have looked with approval on such methods of struggle as a means for preserving the basic conditions of further progressive and socialist development in Hungary. But an objective and cold-blooded analysis of developments compels us to consider the entire complex of today's events and to approach the latest situation from a realistic position.

This means:

It is impossible to imagine or to assume that, under existing conditions, a return to the old regimes is possible in Hungary or in the other countries of Eastern Europe. It appears that during recent years this accurate appraisal of developments was accepted by all political elements who took a realistic view of the current situation. The course of events in Hungary has whetted certain people's appetites and provoked wishes tending in the opposite direction, which can, to a large degree, undermine current developments directed toward lessening international tensions.

As fighters for socialism, for active peaceful coexistence and the strengthening of peace in the world, we in Yugoslavia think it is clear, and we have stated it more than once, that there can be no peace, progress, or independence in Eastern European countries except on the basis of socialism. Any attempt to change the position of these countries, to put them on any other basis, as the attempt in Hungary was, can only result in consequences which are neither in the interests of these peoples nor in the interests of the preservation of world peace.

On the other hand, a completely different and more normal development is possible, one which would make possible the strengthening of truly democratic relations, based on true socialist development, and in the interests of the people, of peace, international cooperation, and the relaxation of world tension. Poland is proof of this, because developments in Poland are leading toward the strengthening of socialism, socialist democracy, independence, and relations based on the equality of rights between socialist states and all other countries.

The speech outlining the Government's policy by Janos Kadar, the new Hungarian Premier, promises just this kind of an approach, all the more so if we take into consideration the program of the new Government which satisfies the desires which touched off the revolt of October 23. As far as Yugoslavia is concerned, we cannot but express the hope that things will calm down in Hungary as soon as possible, that the wishes voiced in the speech outlining Government policy obtain complete affirmation and an opportunity to be implemented, and to see conditions established which will effect the regulation of relations between Hungary and the Soviet Union on a new basis, on the basis of the principle of full equality of rights and noninterference in internal affairs. This would create real conditions for the withdrawal of Soviet troops from Hungary and a new situation in which socialist develop-

ment would be based on the efforts and interests of the Hungarian people themselves which would completely eliminate
any possibility of future intervention by other states in the
internal affairs of countries which are building socialism. The
Yugoslav public expects that the Government of Janos Kadar
will act magnanimously and with humanity when bringing
order to the domestic scene in Hungary.

Of course, we look in a negative way on the fact that the
new Hungarian Government had to turn to the Soviet army
for aid.

The first reaction to the latest developments in Hungary
bear the imprint of the muddled situation existing today in the
world in general, and in the area of the Eastern Mediterranean
in particular. Armed intervention in Egypt deprives those who
started this intervention of the moral right to claim that their
attitude toward events in Hungary is made in the name of
objectivity and reality.

Of course, we look in a negative way on the fact that the
new Hungarian Government had to turn to the Soviet army
for aid. The employment of foreign troops to help clean up
a domestic situation runs contrary to positions of principle
upon which Yugoslavia bases her foreign policy and which
must rule in international relations. However, we cannot pass
over the fact that the employment of these troops has been
the result of exactly such a negative development as that to
which we referred to above. The fact remains, we repeat, that
the increased pressure of reactionary forces was rising in
Hungary as well as outside Hungary, which is not only not in
the interests of the Hungarian people and socialism, but is
completely contrary to the current approach taken toward
international relations, a fact which directly endangers world
peace.

We in Yugoslavia look on current events, however tragic
and unpleasant they may be, with confidence in the future.
We are convinced that for many these events will be a lesson and
that the principles and the cause of peace, cooperation based

on equal rights, respect for sovereignty, and noninterference in the internal affairs of other peoples will be confirmed with new vigor.

Official Polish reaction to the Hungarian events was recorded in an appeal of the PUWP and the Government to the nation on November 2, 1956,[7] and in the closing statements of Gomulka's speech at a meeting of Party activists on November 4, 1956.[8]

On November 6, M. A. Suslov, speaking on the occasion of the 39th anniversary of the Bolshevik Revolution, discussed the question of relations among socialist states and the Hungarian events in familiar terms.[9]

On November 8, *Pravda* printed an article by Enver Hoxha, First Secretary of the Albanian Workers Party. The article, written in commemoration of the founding of the Albanian Communist Party in 1941, served as a vehicle for a strong reaffirmation of the closest possible ties between a people's democracy and the Soviet Union. Its tone was, indeed, reminiscent of the canons of subordination to and servile imitation of the Soviet Union which prevailed some years earlier. Its implications could hardly be lost on the Communist leaders of Eastern Europe, especially on Josip Tito, for whose address much of Hoxha's statement seemed to be meant and who, by virtue of his country's past and present relations with Albania, might well have been expected to show particular sensitivity to anything that emanated from the pen of an Albanian leader with the imprimatur of the Soviet Union.

3. ARTICLE BY ENVER HOXHA, "THE FIFTEENTH ANNIVERSARY OF THE ALBANIAN WORKERS PARTY," *Pravda*, NOVEMBER 8, 1956

NOVEMBER 8, 1956, IS THE 15th anniversary of the foundation of the Albanian Communist Party, now known as the Albanian Workers Party. Born during World War II when our country was under the domination of fascist invaders, it grew and

---

[7] See Poland, Chapter V, Document 9.
[8] See Poland, Chapter V, Document 10.
[9] See *Pravda*, November 7, 1956.

matured as a revolutionary Marxist-Leninist party in a grim struggle against internal and external foes.

The great achievements of our people—the liberation of the country, the establishment of the peoples' rule, the radical social-political and economic changes, the successes in the building of a new life and in the economic and cultural development of our country—all these are great services rendered by the Albanian Communist Party, the result of the correct and tried leadership of our Party, which has no higher interest than that of the working class and of all the workers of the country.

Only under the leadership of the Albanian Workers Party and with help of the Soviet Union have the Albanian people, constantly struggling for their independence and freedom, created for the first time in their history a people's rule, are living freely in a sovereign state, and hold their destiny in their own hands.

The Party mobilized, organized, and led our people in the national liberation struggle. The Soviet Army's brilliant victory over Hitler's troops—the common foe of our peoples—promoted a great upsurge in the national liberation struggle, while the final victory of the Soviet Union over fascism brought freedom to our people. Therefore, the Albanian people see in the Soviet Union their glorious liberator and savior, and cherish toward it constant feelings of deep gratitude and ardent affection. The Albanian people and their Party detest and despise all those who, while pretending to be friends of the Soviet Union, are striving, behind a screen of socialist slogans, to abuse and disparage the glorious Soviet Army which has saved mankind from fascism and brought freedom to the peoples. We detest and despise all those who slander the marvelous building of socialist life in the Soviet Union, a brilliant result of the Soviet socialist system.

For our Party the question of political power was, from the very first days of the struggle, the main issue of the people's revolution. With the liberation of Albania, a new order arose over the ruins of the old—the rule of the people, whose foundations had been laid during the national liberation struggle when national liberation councils were formed. The establishment of the people's regime and its constant consolidation created the necessary favorable conditions for the achievement of great successes in the development of a new national economy and for the constant improvement of the living conditions of the working masses. The active participation of the people in elections to central and local bodies of the people's regime and in the administration of the country, and also the creative activity of the popular masses, clearly attest to the inexhaustible force and great vitality of the new popular regime in Albania.

In building the people's democratic system, the Albanian Workers Party has based itself and still bases itself on Leninism. It fought and will continue to fight against all those who, claiming the invention of "new forms" and "organization" of the socialist order, strive to impose them on others and who preach the rejection of the experience and example of the Soviet Union. The example of the Soviet Union is the highest form which our Party and people have followed and will always continue to follow. Our Party and people will also emulate the example of any other country building socialism on the basis of Marxist-Leninist teaching.

Before the war Albania's economy was very backward. The fascist invaders damaged it greatly. After liberation, the Workers Party headed the working masses and directed their efforts to restore the country's economy. With the generous help of the Soviet Union and the friendly people's democracies, our Motherland gained many successes in the building of the foundations of socialism.

The Third Congress of the Workers Party, held in May of this year, summed up the results of the fulfillment of the First Five-Year Plan for the development of the national economy and culture of the republic, and approved directives for a Second Five-Year Plan. Proceeding from the experience and stimulating lessons of the 20th Congress of the CPSU, the Third Congress of our Party elaborated clear-cut and correct decisions based on Marxist-Leninist principles. To non-Marxists these correct decisions were, undoubtedly, not to their taste. Such people would have had our Party bow before the falsehood, threats, blackmail, and conceit of certain elements. However, they miscalculated, for our Party has never bowed and will never bow to injustice and blackmail.

The task of the First Five-Year Plan—the transformation of our country from an agrarian into an agrarian-industrial country—has in the main been fulfilled successfully. During those five years our new industry was created, forming the basis for the development of our entire national economy, for the growth of agriculture, and for a consistent rise in the material and cultural standards of our people. In 1955 the volume of industrial production was nearly 10.5 times as high as in 1938 (in 1956 prices). The output in many branches of industry has increased considerably. For instance, in 1955 17.4 times as much chromium ore was extracted as in 1938; the correspondents for other branches of industry are: coal, 54 times; electric power output, 10 times; mechanical industry output has doubled from 1950 to 1955; light industry output at the end of 1955 was 26 times larger than in 1938.

Many successes, compared with the past, can be claimed by our agriculture. Gross agricultural production in 1955 increased by 37 percent over that of 1950. The area under crop cultivation increased during the same period by 13 percent. New crops most valuable and necessary for our economy, such as cotton and sugar beets, have been established in our country.

On the basis of this growth in industry and agriculture, the living standards of the workers have risen. During the years of the First Five-Year Plan, the country's national revenue increased approximately by 70 percent. The real wages of workers and employees increased during that time by approximately 20 percent, and the revenues of the peasants by nearly 30 percent.

The Second Five-Year Plan set the task of insuring a further industrial development, primarily in the ore-mining industry, through full use of existing production capacities and the seeking out and utilization of internal reserves, and of insuring swift development in agriculture, mainly by reorganizing agricultural production on a socialist basis. On this basis, a further improvement in the material conditions of the people should be insured and their cultural standards raised.

Particular attention was paid, in the decisions of the Third Party Congress, to agriculture. The Congress clearly emphasized that the only way to overcome the backwardness of our agriculture was by the method of collectivization based on Lenin's principle of voluntary agreement. This method finds support among our peasants. While in 1950 there were in Albania 90 agricultural cooperatives, by October 1, 1956, there were 758. While in 1950 the area under cultivation in cooperatives was 5.5 percent of the country's entire arable land, by October 1, 1956, it formed 33 percent. Although our agricultural cooperatives are still young, they had higher harvest yields than individual peasant holdings. The Albanian peasantry is convincing itself through its own experience that collective labor is a source of plenty and well-being. Therefore it follows with confidence the path shown by the Party, the path of building socialism in the village. The experience of the cooperative movement in Albania has confirmed once more the correctness of Lenin's theory of collectivization, which is opposed by the enemies of socialism concealed behind various masks.

The Second Five-Year Plan envisages a further raising of the well-being and cultural standards of the working masses. By the end of the Second Five-Year Plan the country's national revenue should increase by 53 percent compared with that of 1955; the real wages of workers and employees, by 25 percent; and the revenues of the peasants by 38 percent.

The Second Five-Year Plan is a big, militant program whose implementation will enable the country's economy and the people's culture to advance still further. The main aim of this plan is to insure a rise in the people's well-being.

Of course, in spite of the successes achieved, we still have economic difficulties and shortcomings in our work. On the basis of the decisions of the Third Congress, the Party mobilizes Communists and all the people to a struggle to overcome these difficulties and shortcomings, so as to strengthen our economy still further.

In the successful solution of its big problems, the Albanian Workers Party was unremittingly guided, and is still being guided, by Lenin's instructions that the strengthening of the ideological, political, and organizational unity of the Party creates the inexhaustible force of the Marxist-Leninist Party, and that close contacts with the masses and faithfulness to the principles of Marxism-Leninism are the main conditions for elaborating a correct Party line and successfully putting it into practice. Fascist invaders, their minions, and all enemies of the Party strove in every way, from the very first days of its foundation, to inflict blows upon it and to disrupt the unity of its ranks. However, the Party invariably and resolutely repulsed the enemies' onslaughts and, correctly following the immortal teachings of Marxism-Leninism, grew, matured, and strengthened and became the only leading force in the country, enjoying the boundless affection of our working masses.

What was decisive in the over-all strengthening of our Party and its leading role, and also in the elaboration and implementation of its correct line, was the fact that our Party invariably based itself, and will continue to base itself, upon the great experience of the CPSU. The Party considers this experience as the best example of a creative application of Marxism-Leninism. Our Party was able to apply this experience to the concrete conditions peculiar to our country, in the building of the Party, the building of a people's democratic state, and in the building of socialism in Albania. Neither the Party nor our people were ensnared, nor will they be, despite some elements who want to lure Communists and the peoples with their slogans of some brand of "special socialism" or some sort of "democracy" which savors of anything but a proletarian spirit.

Marking the 15th anniversary of the foundation of the Albanian Workers Party, Communists and all the Albanian people express their firm determination to move ahead along the path of building socialism. They are equipped with the clear prospect of socialist construction in Albania and stand more firmly than ever in the ranks of the great and powerful camp of socialism headed by the Soviet Union.

Together with the Party's anniversary the Communists and the Albanian people are celebrating the 39th anniversary of the great October Socialist Revolution, which opened before the Albanian people and the whole of mankind the road to salvation, progress, and happiness. As always, our Party will be guided by the glorious experience of the CPSU founded by the great Lenin, which it has always considered its mother and teacher.

Our Party will always be against those who, making use of the just struggle against the cult of personality carried out by the 20th Congress of the CPSU, are striving to revile Lenin's glorious Party in order to cultivate their own personality. Such —if I may call them so—"comrades" are trying with the aid of so-called socialist slogans to see a mote in another person's eye but do not notice the beam in their own! But true Leninists are not blind. They know how to find a mote in their own eye and to clean the eye, but they also know how to find in another person's eye not only a beam but also a mote. As the Albanian saying goes: "People do not feed on hay," the more so Marxists, who know how to look at things as they really are.

The Party and the Albanian people experience a great, boundless feeling of love for the Soviet Union, for it liberated our country from the yoke of oppressors and has always given us all-round selfless fraternal aid in the building of a new and better life. Friendship with the Soviet Union lies at the basis of a free existence of our people, at the basis of the independence and sovereignty of the Albanian People's Republic. The Albanian people will guard this friendship as the apple of their eye and will constantly consolidate it. There does not exist and never will be enough force in the world to upset it even to the slightest extent! The Workers Party and the Albanian people will continue as before, in close friendship with the Soviet Union, with the great Chinese people, and with the other countries of socialist camp, to fight for the consolidation of peace, for cooperation between peoples, for victory of socialism, for peace throughout the world.

No attempts whatever on the part of their enemies will turn the Albanian people from the path they have chosen. They will continuously consolidate their unity and solidarity around the government of the Albanian People's Republic and around the tried Workers Party, their reliable and devoted leader who leads the country on the path of construction of socialism.

4. ADDRESS BY THE SECRETARY GENERAL OF THE YUGOSLAV LEAGUE OF COMMUNISTS, TITO, BEFORE A MEETING OF LEAGUE MEMBERS, PULA, NOVEMBER 11, 1956[10]

COMRADES,

YESTERDAY I expressed the desire to make use of my stay on Brioni, while I am undergoing medical treatment, to come to you and present to you our outlook upon international problems which are today very tangled.

You read newspapers, but newspapers cannot present everything and completely shed light on it, and particularly there is no light shed in them on the causes of what is today happening in Hungary, as well as in Egypt, where it has come to Israeli-French-British aggression. It is quite a tangled situation today and we cannot say that a certain danger does not exist of major conflicts developing, but the peace-loving forces in the world, to which our country also belongs, have demonstrated in the United Nations that with their persevering and indefatigable efforts they can reduce the possibility of international conflict, and have already helped make it more possible for the world to be able to hope that peace will still be preserved.

---

[10] *Borba,* November 16, 1956.

Above all, I would like to deal with what is happening today in Hungary and what took place in Poland, so that we may have an accurate idea of those events which are very complicated, notably in Hungary, where it came to this, that a large part of the working class and progressive men were fighting in the streets, with arms in their hands, against the Soviet armed forces. When the Hungarian workers and progressive elements began with demonstrations and then with resistance and armed action against the Rakosi method and against further continuation of that course, I am deeply convinced that one could not then speak of counterrevolutionary tendencies. One can say that it is regrettable and tragic that reaction was able to find highly fertile soil there and gradually to divert matters into its own channels, taking advantage for its own ends of the justified revolt which existed in Hungary.

THE ROOTS OF THE EVENTS IN POLAND AND HUNGARY

You are aware, in the main, of the causes which have led to the events in Poland and Hungary. It is necessary that we go back to the year 1948, when Yugoslavia was the first to give an energetic answer to Stalin and when she said that she desired to be independent, that she desired to build her life and socialism in accordance with the specific conditions in her country, and that she was permitting no one to interfere in her internal affairs. Of course, it did not then come to armed intervention, because Yugoslavia was already united. Various reactionary elements were not able to carry out various provocations because we had liquidated their main force already during the People's Liberation War. Second, we had a very strong, united, and monolithic Communist Party, steeled in both the prewar period and during the People's Liberation War. We also had a powerful and steeled Army, and most important, we had the unity of the people which personifies all these things.

Once the truth about our country had been victorious and the period of normalization of relations with the countries which had severed relations with us after the ill-famed resolution had begun, the leaders of Eastern countries expressed the desire that we no longer mention that which had been done to us, that we let bygones be bygones, and we accepted this only in order that relations with those countries might be improved as soon as possible. But you will see later that it is indeed necessary to remind certain people who are again today beginning to slander our country and who stand at the head of Communist Parties in the Eastern countries, and in certain Western countries, of what they had been doing to Yugoslavia during these last four or five years, and even longer, when Yugoslavia had stood entirely alone, face to face with a huge propaganda apparatus, when we had to struggle on all sides to preserve the achievements of our People's Revolution, to preserve that which we had already started to build—the foundations of socialism— in one word, to wipe off the disgrace which they had wanted to inflict upon us by various slanders and to prove where the real truth lay. We should remind them and state that these same men had then accused our country, using every possible means, saying that it was fascist, that we were bloodthirsty men and that we were destroying our people, that our working people were not with us, and so forth. We should remind them, they should remember this and keep this in mind today when they again wish to shift the blame for events in Poland and Hungary onto our shoulders. This perfidious tendency originates in those hard-bitten Stalinist elements in various parties who have still managed to maintain themselves in their posts and who would like to consolidate their rule again and impose those Stalinist leanings upon their peoples and on others. I am going to come back to this later. Just now I wish to tell you only that today we must view the events in Hungary in the light of this whole development.

IT IS A QUESTION NOT ONLY OF THE CULT OF PERSONALITY, BUT OF THE SYSTEM WHICH HAD MADE POSSIBLE THE CREATION OF THE CULT OF PERSONALITY

Because of her desire and on her initiative, we have normalized relations with the Soviet Union. When Stalin died, the new Soviet leaders saw that, thanks to Stalin's madness, the Soviet Union found itself in a very difficult situation, in a blind alley both in foreign and internal policy and in the other countries of people's democracy as well, thanks to his nagging and by forcing his methods on them. They understood where the main cause of all these difficulties lay and at the 20th Congress they condemned Stalin's acts and his policy up to then, but they mistakenly made the whole matter a question of the cult of personality and not a question of the system. But the cult of personality is in fact the product of a system. They did not start the fight against that system, or if they have, they have done so rather tacitly, saying that on the whole everything has been all right but that of late, because Stalin had grown old, he had become a little mad and started to commit various mistakes.

From the very beginning we have been saying that here it was not a question of the cult of personality alone, but of a system which had made possible the creation of that cult, that therein lay the roots, that this is what should be struck at incessantly and tenaciously, and this is the most difficult thing to do. Where are those roots? In the bureaucratic apparatus, in the method of leadership and the so-called one-man rule, and in the ignoring of the role and aspirations of the working masses, in different Enver Hoxhas, Shehus,[11] and other leaders of certain Western and Eastern parties who are resisting democratization and the decisions of the 20th Congress and who have contributed a great deal to the consolidation of Stalin's system, and who are today working to revive it and to continue its rule. Therein lie the roots and this is what must be corrected.

THE MOSCOW DECLARATION IS INTENDED FOR A WIDER CIRCLE
OF COUNTRIES THAN YUGOSLAVIA AND THE SOVIET UNION

As far as we are concerned, we have gone a considerable way in our relations with the Soviet Union. We have improved these relations and have concluded a whole series of economic

---

[11] Mehmet Shehu, Prime Minister of Albania.

arrangements, very useful for us, on very favorable terms, and so forth. Two declarations have also been adopted, one in Belgrade and the other in Moscow.[12] Both declarations should in fact be significant not only in our mutual relations but also in relations among all socialist countries. But, unfortunately, they have not been understood in this way. It was thought as follows: good, since the Yugoslavs are so stubborn we will respect and implement these declarations, but they do not concern the others because the situation there is, nevertheless, a little different than in Yugoslavia. Yugoslavia is an organized and disciplined state. The Yugoslavs have proved their worth because they have succeeded in maintaining themselves even in the most difficult times and in not allowing a restoration of the capitalist system, and so forth, to wit, they are something different from you in the Eastern countries where we brought you to power. And this was wrong, because those same elements which provoked such resistance on the part of Yugoslavia in 1948 also live in these Eastern countries, in Poland, Hungary, and in others, in some more and in some less. During the time that we were preparing the declaration in Moscow on our party relations, mainly on the relations between the Yugoslav League of Communists and the CPSU, this was a little difficult to settle. Here we could not completely agree, but, nevertheless, the declaration was issued which, in our opinion, is intended for a wider circle than Yugoslavia and the Soviet Union. We warned that those tendencies which once provoked such strong resistance in Yugoslavia existed in all countries, and that one day they might find expression in other countries, too, when this would be far more difficult to correct.

You know that Khrushchev was here for a rest.[13] On that occasion, we had talks here and many more in Belgrade. Since I and comrades Rankovic and Pucar were invited to the Crimea, we went there and continued the talks.[14] We saw that it would

---

12 See Part One, Chapter I, and Chapter II, Document 2.

13 Khrushchev arrived in Yugoslavia on September 19, 1956.

14 Tito departed for the Soviet Union on September 27 and returned October 5.

be rather difficult going for other countries, since the Soviet leaders had a different attitude toward other countries. They had certain wrong and defective views on relations with these countries, with Poland, Hungary, and others. However, we did not take this too tragically, because we saw that this was not the attitude of the entire Soviet leadership, but only of a part which to some degree had imposed this attitude on others. We saw that this attitude was imposed rather by those people who took and still take a Stalinist position, but that there were still possibilities that within the Soviet leadership those elements would win—through internal evolution—who stand for stronger and more rapid development in the direction of democratization, abandonment of all Stalinist methods, the creation of new relations among socialist states, and the development of foreign policy in this same direction as well. From certain signs and also from the conversations, we saw that these elements were not weak, that they were strong, but that this internal process of development in a progressive direction, in the direction of abandoning Stalinist methods, was also hindered by certain Western countries, which by their propaganda and ceaseless repetition of the need for the liberation of these countries were interfering in their internal affairs and hindering a rapid development and improvement in relations among these countries. The Soviet Union believes that in view of the fact that this interference in internal affairs has assumed rather extensive proportions through propaganda on the radio, the dispatch of material by balloons, and so forth, unpleasant consequences could result if it left these countries completely and gave them, say, a status such as that enjoyed by Yugoslavia. They are afraid that reactionary elements might then be victorious in these countries. In other words, this means that they lack sufficient confidence in the internal revolutionary forces of these countries. In my opinion, this is wrong, and the root of all later mistakes lies in insufficient confidence in the socialist forces of these peoples.

OUR COUNTRY HAS BEEN ACTING VERY POSITIVELY
AND USEFULLY

When the Poznan affair happened[15]—you know about it—
there occurred among the Soviet people a sudden change of
attitude toward us. They started to grow colder. They thought
that we, the Yugoslavs, were to blame. Yes, we are to blame
because we live in this world, for being such as we are, for
having created a Yugoslavia such as she is, because her acts
reverberate even beyond our country. Even if we did not desire
it, our country still acts, and she does so very positively and
usefully. Thanks to the fact that there still remained in
Poland, in spite of all persecutions and Stalinist methods of
destruction of cadres, a hard core of leaders with Gomulka at
their head who at the Eighth Plenum managed to take matters
strongly in their own hands,[16] boldly to put their stamp on the
new course, that is, the course toward democratization, toward
their full independence, but also for good relations with the
Soviet Union, resolutely to offer resistance to interference in
their internal affairs—thanks to this, reactionary forces in
Poland could not make themselves heard, although these forces
certainly did exist and had hoped that they would be able to
rise to the surface as a result of a clash between Communists.
Thanks to the mature reasoning and attitude of the Soviet
leaders, who stopped interfering in time, things have been
stabilized considerably in Poland at present, and are developing
quite well.

I cannot say that this positive development in Poland,
which is very similar to ours, has met with much joy in the
remaining countries of the "socialist camp." No, they criticize
it secretly and among themselves but to some extent openly
as well. Among these countries Poland did not even meet
with as much support as she found among the Soviet leaders,
who had agreed to such an attitude of Poland's. Among those
various leading personalities in some countries of the "socialist

---

[15] See Poland, Chapter II.
[16] See Poland, Chapter V.

camp," and even among some Communist Parties in the West,[17] Poland did not meet with understanding because Stalinist elements are still sitting there.

When that would-be professor of history holds a lecture in France and says that Yugoslavia is a sly agent of imperialism, when men are sitting in the Communist Party of France who at such a tragic and difficult time also come out with such a grave accusation before hundreds and hundreds of people, can this constitute a guaranty that the cause of socialism will develop correctly in the future? It cannot. For such excesses of such irresponsible and decadent elements the leaders of that Party are to blame. Or, for instance, when such a would-be Marxist as Enver Hoxha, who only knows how to utter "Marxism-Leninism" and not a word more, writes an article about Yugoslavia, without reference to her but hitting out at Yugoslavia and Poland,[18] he resolutely condemns the tendencies of one's own path and development in accordance with the specific conditions and even goes against that which Khrushchev and other Soviet leaders have recognized—that there are specific roads to socialism. Such a type has dared not only to slander and stand up against Yugoslavia and still another great socialist country, but to strike even at the Soviet leaders themselves. Such Stalinist elements believe that men will be found in the Soviet Union of a Stalinist brand who will uphold them and help to maintain them on the backs of their people. This, comrades, is fatal.

When we were in Moscow there also was talk of Poland and Hungary and other countries. We said that Rakosi's regime and Rakosi himself had no qualifications whatever to lead the Hungarian state and to bring about inner unity, but that, on the contrary, their actions could only bring about grave consequences. Unfortunately, the Soviet comrades did not believe us. They said that Rakosi was an old revolutionary,

---

[17] The reference is particularly to the French CP, which took a much more rigid stand on developments both in Poland and Hungary than other Communist Parties.

[18] See the preceding document.

honest, and so forth. That he is old, this is granted, but that
is not enough. That he is honest—this I could not say, inasmuch as I know him, especially after the Rajk trial and other
things. To me, these are the most dishonest people in the world.
The Soviet comrades said he was prudent, that he was going
to succeed, and that they knew of no one else whom they could
rely upon in that country. Just because our policy, both state
and Party policy, is opposed to interference in the internal
affairs of others, and in order not again to come into conflict
with the Soviet comrades, we were not insistent enough with the
Soviet leaders to have such a team as Rakosi and Gero eliminated.

GERO DIFFERED IN NO WAY FROM RAKOSI

When I went to Moscow, there was great surprise that I
did not travel via Hungary. It was precisely because of Rakosi
that I did not want to do so. I said that I would not go through
Hungary even if it would have meant making the journey three
times shorter. When increasingly strong dissatisfaction began
to rise to the surface in the ranks of the Hungarian Communists
themselves, and when they demanded that Rakosi should go,
the Soviet leaders realized that it was impossible to continue
in this way and agreed that he should be removed.[19] But they
committed a mistake by not also allowing the removal of Gero
and other Rakosi followers, who had compromised themselves
in the eyes of the people. They made it a condition that Rakosi
would go only if Gero remained. And this was a mistake,
because Gero differed in no way from Rakosi. He pursued the
same kind of policy and was to blame just as much as Rakosi
was.

Well, comrades, what could we do? We saw that things
were not going as they should. When we were in the Crimea,
Gero "happened" to be there and we "accidentally" met him.[20]
We talked with him. Gero condemned the earlier policy and
said that it had been a mistake, that they had slandered Yugo-

---

[19] See Hungary, Chapter III.
[20] Gero joined Soviet and Yugoslav leaders for talks on September 30.

slavia; in short, he heaped ashes on his head and asked that good relations be established, promising that all previous errors would be corrected and that the old policy would never be used again. We wanted to prove that we were not vindictive and that we were not narrow-minded, and so we agreed to have talks with Gero and a delegation of the HWP which was to come to Yugoslavia. We wanted to establish relations with the Hungarian Workers Party because we hoped that by not isolating the Hungarian Party we could more easily influence that country's proper internal development.

However, matters had already gone pretty far, a fact which we did not know, so that Gero's coming to Yugoslavia and our joint declaration could no longer help. People in Hungary were absolutely against the Stalinist elements who were still in power, they demanded their removal and the adoption of a policy of democratization. When the Hungarian delegation headed by Gero returned to their country, Gero, finding himself in a difficult situation, again showed his former face. He called the hundreds of thousands of demonstrators, who at that stage were still only demonstrators, a mob, and insulted nearly the whole nation.[21] Just imagine how blind he was and what kind of a leader he was. In such a critical moment, when all was in turmoil and when the whole nation was dissatisfied, he dared to fling the term "mob" at people among whom a huge number, perhaps even the majority, consisted of Communists and youth. This was enough to ignite the powder keg and to bring about the explosion. Thus the conflict began.

IT IS A GRAVE ERROR TO CALL UPON FOREIGN TROOPS TO TEACH ONE'S PEOPLE A LESSON

There is no point now in investigating who fired the first shot. The Army was called out by Gero. It was a fatal mistake to call the Soviet Army at a time when the demonstrations were still in progress. It is a great mistake to call in the Army of another country to teach a lesson to the people of that

---

[21] See Hungary, Chapter VI, Document 2.

country, even if there is some shooting. This angered the people even more, and thus a spontaneous revolt broke out in which the Communists found themselves, against their will, together with various reactionary elements. The reactionary elements got mixed up in this uprising and exploited it for their own ends. Are there not plenty of Horthyites there? Who has reeducated them? Could Rakosi be expected to have reeducated them? We all know that Horthy had large fascist forces in Hungary, those "Arrow Crossists", various other reactionary elements, the adherents of Ferenc Nagy, and so forth. In short, there were a large number of people who were not for Communism, who were not only against Rakosi but against socialism in general. And all this got mixed into the uprising. These reactionary forces did not dare raise their heads earlier, regardless of all the calls for an uprising from the outside, regardless of the aid which they got from abroad, nor did they have the strength or the courage to rise as long as they thought that the Party was united and monolithic. But as soon as they saw that the Party had split and that a huge section of the Party membership had risen against Rakosi's clique and the remnants of the past, they immediately intervened.

These reactionary forces revealed their true faces very quickly, within two or three days. Since in the general national revolt against everything which had happened in the past the then-existing leadership showed no desire to remove elements which disgusted the Hungarian people and to proceed along a truly Hungarian road of socialist development with all its internal peculiarities, events moved rapidly in the other direction, and the reactionaries began to dominate more and more. The justified revolt and uprising against a clique turned into an uprising of the whole nation against socialism and against the Soviet Union. And the Communists who were in the ranks of the rebels willy-nilly finally found themselves in a struggle not for socialism but for a return to the past, as soon as the reactionaries took matters into their own hands. Against their own will they found themselves in such a situation.

Was it now possible to prevent this? It seems that it was already late. Had Nagy's Government been more energetic, had it not wavered this way and that, had it stood firmly against anarchy and the killing of Communists by the reactionary elements, had it offered decisive resistance to the reactionaries, perhaps matters would have taken a correct turn and perhaps there would nor have been any intervention by the Soviet Army. And what did Nagy do? He called the people to arms against the Soviet Army and appealed to the Western countries to intervene.

In the West this intervention was made full use of. It was exploited by the imperialists who could hardly wait to attack Egypt. They attacked it precisely in this phase of the Hungarian tragedy and attacked it hoping that the Soviet Union would be too preoccupied and would not be able to intervene against this aggression. Thus renewed fighting broke out in Hungary. Soviet troops were reinforced. Nagy fled[22] and a new Government was set up. I can say to you, comrades, that I know these people in the new Government and that they, in my opinion, represent that which is most honest in Hungary. They were persecuted under Rakosi, they were in prisons and stand sincerely for a new kind of development. And the very program announced by Kadar, which you have read, proves this. But Soviet intervention weakens that whole program and the Government itself is in a very serious position.

ON SOVIET INTERVENTION IN HUNGARY

The question may now be asked whether Soviet intervention was necessary? The first intervention was not necessary. The first intervention, coming at the invitation of Gero, was absolutely wrong. The second mistake consisted in the fact that the men responsible, instead of waiting for the second intervention, did not do at once what they did later on, when the second Soviet intervention took place, that is, form a new Government

---

[22] Nagy found refuse at the Yugoslav Embassy in Budapest from November 4-22, 1956.

and issue a declaration. Had they first created a new Government and issued such a declaration, the worker and Communist elements would probably have separated themselves from the reactionary elements and it would have been easier to find a way out of this critical situation.

Before I deal with the second intervention of Soviet troops, I must say that the situation in Hungary assumed such proportions—and you have read a great deal about it—that it was clear that there would be a terrible massacre, a terrible civil war, in which socialism could be completely buried and in which a third world war could break out, because the Soviet Government could not tolerate interference from the West and the return to power of the Horthyites and the old reactionaries.

What did these reactionary elements do? I have already stated that they showed their true faces very early. It became clear that even among the top positions they were assuming more and more power as soon as they ordered that the word "comrade" could no longer be used, that the red star should be taken down. This became clear the moment a Communist could not say that he was a Communist or he would be done away with, and also by the fact that Communists were being hanged. Had there been only one such incident and had they hanged some member of the police who was known for his ill deeds, it might be said that this was the result of a spontaneous revolt of a group of people. But there was a general massacre. In Soprony they hanged twenty Communists. They caught people in the streets and killed them if they wore tan shoes because the police wore tan shoes. They broke into homes and killed Communists. All this was done by the wild fascist and reactionary mobs.

Nagy's Government did nothing to prevent this. It continually cried over the radio and kept calling for help instead of fighting against this and showing in some way the will to put a halt to the massacre of Communists and progressive people. Instead it issued a manifesto, that is, a declaration in which it renounced the Warsaw Pact, proclaimed its independence, and so forth. As if that was the most important thing at the moment. As if its withdrawal from the Warsaw Pact meant something.

Many people are now asking why the second Soviet intervention took place. It is clear, and we have said so and will continue to say it, that we are against interference and the use of foreign armed forces. Which was now the lesser evil? There could be either chaos, civil war, counterrevolution, and a new world war, or the intervention of Soviet troops which were there. The former would be a castastrophe and the latter a mistake. And, of course, if it meant saving socialism in Hungary, then, comrades, we can say, although we are against interference, Soviet intervention was necessary. But had they done everything that should have been done earlier, there would not have been any need for military intervention. This error was, unfortunately, a result of their idea that military power solves everything. And it does not solve everything. Just look how a barehanded and poorly armed people offers fierce resistance when it has one goal—to free itself and to be independent. It is no longer interested in the kind of independence it will gain, in whether there will be restored a bourgeois and reactionary system, but only that it should be nationally independent. It was this idea that prevailed among the people. Naturally, I can now say only that the first thing was the worst that could have happened and the second, the intervention of Soviet troops, was also bad, but if it leads to the preservation of socialism in Hungary, that is, to the further building up of socialism in that country, and to peace in the world, then one day this will become a positive thing, provided that the Soviet troops withdraw the moment the situation in that country is settled and quiet.

We said this to the Soviet comrades. We concealed nothing. The Soviet comrades stated that their troops would then leave. It should be borne in mind that the Soviet Union, too, is now in a very difficult situation. Their eyes have now been opened and they realize that not only are the Horthyites fighting but also workers in factories and mines, that the whole nation is fighting. Soviet soldiers go unwillingly, with heavy hearts. Therein lies the tragedy.

After my report, you can ask questions because I have perhaps not made everything clear. But you can rest assured that we have never advised them to go ahead and use the army. We never gave such advice and could not do so even in the present crisis. In this grave situation we can tell them nothing except that they should take care to correct their old mistakes. That is the crux of the matter. Therefore, we should combat those rumors in our country which see in the Soviet intervention a purely interventionist act. That is not correct. I, comrades, am deeply convinced of this.

I am deeply convinced that the bloodshed in Hungary and those dreadful sacrifices made by the Hungarian people will have a positive effect and that a little light will reach the eyes of the comrades in the Soviet Union, even those Stalinist elements, and that they will see that it is no longer possible to do things in this way. It is our tragedy—the tragedy of all of us—that socialism has been dealt such a terrible blow. It has been compromised. And do you not recall, comrades, that we often said that such methods would only compromise socialism? We did say it. I would not like us now to beat our chests and to take pleasure in all this and say, "We told you so."

EVENTS IN HUNGARY WILL PROBABLY MARK THE LAST TRAGEDY

In connection with this tragedy I want to say one thing—that these irresponsible elements in the various Communist Parties who are still in power thanks to Stalinist methods, that they are very poor support on the side of the Soviet Union if they advise it to act according to their ideas. I think that inside all these Parties there are honest Communists who see much further than these various Stalinists. They see much further. And if they want the situation there to improve not in the manner of Hungary but rather in a peaceful, Communist way, then they must criticize negative things and listen a bit to the voice of the masses, the voice of the Party members, and the entire nation. Because, if these prophets and advisers continue acting in a destructive way and if they find it necessary to do nothing but slander our country, to continue flinging mud at us, then, of course, socialism will still have a difficult time ahead of it. Yugoslavia stands so firmly on its own legs and has up to now withstood so many blows that these slanders from abroad will not make her deviate from her path. Although we are not as yet fully satisfied with our internal development, we will endeavor to make our people as satisfied as possible and, such as we are and such as we shall be, we will increase our efforts to prevent such prophets and advisers from succeeding in their plans, which are directed toward halting the process which began in 1948 in Yugoslavia, and is now continuing in Poland, and we will not allow them to divert this process onto a Stalinist track.

On one occasion I said to the Soviet comrades that this would have happened even if Stalin had not died, that this could have happened even more easily were he alive. They did not deny this. We cannot assume the right to tell them to do things this way or that, we can only point out the mistaken and negative results which may be caused by this or that act of theirs. I believe that the events in Hungary will probably be the last tragedy necessary to jolt the Soviet comrades and leaders who are still blind to this in other countries into doing everything in their power to prevent such a situation as now prevails in Hungary from arising in other countries as well.

In some countries and parties of Eastern Europe certain leaders are saying that this cannot happen to them, that they have a strong organization, a strong army, a powerful police force, that their membership is already informed of everything, and that everything is under control. Gero said the same thing, and Rakosi, too. And what good does it do them? None at all if they do not change the methods which they have used and if the people one day revolt. Now they are reaping what they were sowing from 1948 onward. They sowed the wind and are reaping the storm. (*Long applause.*)

THE OUTLOOK FOR OUR DEVELOPMENT AND IMMEDIATE TASKS

The events in Hungary have also stimulated somewhat various elements who still exist in our country. There are not many of them, but they babble a lot. Some of them indulge in wishful thinking, hoping for trouble in order to profit by it. I never said that we have liquidated and reeducated all the Ustashi,[23] Chetniks, and those bigoted Vatican adherents. I always said that only the unity of the people will prevent them from attempting anything and achieving anything in our country. More than ever, the unity of the people and Party is necessary today, but not because we are afraid that anything could happen in this country, for Yugoslavia is still not the same as Hungary or any other country. We have carried out our revolution through the shedding of our blood, through the liberation struggle, and have cleaned our house thoroughly during the revolution. There is no such danger for us.

I will not say that our people are completely satisfied and that everything in our country is as it should be. Nor am I satisfied myself. But conditions are quite different in Yugoslavia; there is a perspective in our country, and working people in Yugoslavia are more and more productive in their labors. What does not yet satisfy me? You will remember, comrades, that I made a report last year in which I pointed out the necessity to change the course of our investment policy. I profoundly believed that the people who run our economy would take this to heart and that we should first and foremost really devote attention to the living standards of our people. In this regard a certain turning point has been reached, a certain stabilization in the market has been achieved, and the rapid rise in prices has been halted, the rise which threatened inflation, but all I expected has not been done. We have now decided to suppress again, even more energetically, the tendency to build and build. We must now see to it that the living standard is improved and that the defences of our country are also

---

[23] Terrorist and underground formations of the interwar and wartime periods.

strengthened. These two things have priority and we shall take care of them. That much I wanted to say about it.

I would now like to say something about various elements which exist in our country. They think like this: "Now riots have occurred in Hungary, the Horthyites as well as the Vatican and others will come to power there, and here is a chance for us." In their opinion, Yugoslavia will again be cut off and encircled and they will be able to act more easily in it. There are still such elements but I say that they are very much mistaken. For in our Party there are not 800,000 members—Gero said their Party had that many, and hearing this I looked at him a little doubtfully—but we have something over 600,000 Party members, cadres who have been steeled in the revolution and in struggle and who have not joined our Party along with various upstart elements or other tendencies, but are bearing on their shoulders the burden of building our country. They will always know in time how to prevent anybody from trying to undermine our country. We are a country in which there exists the League of Communists with over 600,000 members and the Socialist Alliance of Working People[24] with seven million members.

These seven million people are conscious builders of socialism, they have their program and know what they are aiming for. These seven million people can always give the word if they see that it is no longer possible to go this way any further, if they think that we can no longer invest such large funds in capital construction, or if this or that is necessary. Of course, nobody has the right, neither I nor the whole of our leadership, to oppose such a desire on the part of our people— namely, that our country be built at such a rate as is possible today. You know, comrades, when you are daily confronted with such questions, when you look and see that this or that factory, if built, would tomorrow produce such results that there would be an immediate improvement in the situation, when you then see that only a few millions of capital investments

---

[24] The Yugoslav version of "National Front."

would be necessary in order to ensure so much more production, when you only see this, then the other thing—our man—fades away a little. You see only the factory and not the man.

It is clear that we are still in a difficult situation. We have a considerably unfavorable balance in foreign trade, which continues to increase despite the fact that during the last year and a half we have concluded rather good agreements, first of all with the Soviet Union for a considerable loan under very favorable terms at 2 percent interest. Secondly, we have concluded an agreement on the payment of reparations by Germany. The Czechs canceled, that is, equalized 100 million dollars, while debts with Hungary will be settled in keeping with her possibilities. These agreements have eased the situation in the field of construction. Finally, we have wheat and raw materials on credit from America to a value of about 100 million dollars. Our situation is not as difficult as some would wish to make it. There will be food and bread. In our country the market is a little unorganized since people devote too little attention to the problem of assuring that it is sufficiently provided with supplies even though very favorable conditions exist throughout the entire country. Take Belgrade, for instance, a city which has the Pančevački Rit farms close by and where there are excellent conditions for growing vegetables. There are many districts and other communes where huge quantities of consumer goods could be prepared for the market, but they are not being prepared. Today, for example, vegetables are being transported from Ljubljana to Kopar. What kind of a policy is this since we know that Kopar formerly supplied Trieste. There are a number of such things in our country which cannot be considered as favorable.

WE MUST HELP THE CURRENT KADAR GOVERNMENT

Comrades, I have digressed somewhat from the subject about which I was speaking. I wanted to tell you that, viewing current developments in Hungary from the perspective of socialism or counterrevolution, we must defend Kadar's present Government, we must help it. We must help it because it is in a very difficult situation. We must combat all those elements which now, in an irresponsible way, throw all the blame on the Russians. Yes, the Soviet comrades are responsible because they failed to see and correct earlier the errors of the Rakosi regime, for not having made it possible for those men to come to power whom the working class and the entire people trusted. For one cannot impose a leader on a people; that is impossible.

In Poland the situation has become stabilized, but not entirely. The same elements are acting there, too, the elements which are against good relations between Poland and the Soviet Union. You know that those Poles who have reactionary leanings hate the Russians and the Soviet Union. It is necessary to lead the Polish people away from reaction which hates not only the USSR but also socialism as such. For the working class and Communists in Poland have a broad horizon, a wide outlook, and know that they can get support from the Soviet Union. For example, without the support of the Soviet Union, the Poles would hardly be able to defend the Oder-Neisse border, which the Germans never recognized and which will again be the subject of their claims. In brief, what is needed here is mutual aid and support.

Likewise, it is necessary that we act in closest contact with the Polish Government and Party and help them as much as we can. Together with the Polish comrades we shall have to fight such tendencies as may crop up in various other parties, whether in the Eastern countries or in the West. Comrades, this struggle will be difficut and long, for what is actually involved is whether the new trend will triumph in the Communist Parties—the trend which really began in Yugoslavia and was supported by a considerable number of factors originating in the decisions of the 20th Congress of the Communist Party of the Soviet Union. Now the question is, will this course be victorious or will the Stalinist course again prevail. Yugoslavia must not withdraw into her own shell, she must work in every direction, but not by undermining these countries from within, which would result in negative excesses, but in the ideological field, through contacts and talks, and thus to insure the victory of the new spirit. One should not refrain from criticizing what is bad in those parties. You have read the article in *Borba* which, in my opinion, is not bad as a first article, but it is not sufficient, and still more must be written about it. It is the duty of you Communists and leaders who work in the field to explain this to our members. I think that you will agree with my statements. (*Prolonged applause.*)

ON AGGRESSION AGAINST EGYPT

Now permit me to refer briefly to the aggression which has taken place against Egypt. You have read about our position in the United Nations and the statement which I made in connection with that aggression, and you also read our newspapers. But I would like to go a little further back. When I met Nasser for the first time, on my return voyage from India,[25] he gave me an exact account of all their difficulties in Egypt, which is an underdeveloped country without industry, with a very low standard of living, and without any strong internal organization —a party on which one could rely. Nasser said that the leaders of Egypt are soldiers who have taken power into their hands to serve their people, to create freedom for them, and to defend their independence. When he was setting forth all these difficulties, they really seemed almost insurmountable to us. Later, the second time we visited Egypt and Cairo,[26] we talked again and saw that these difficulties were enormous. But we observed that the people in that country had started to awaken, that they had started to acquire national consciousness, a people which had previously been suppressed and dormant due to prolonged occupation and the colonial activities of the British and French. We realized that Nasser and his team could rely on the people in the execution of their difficult tasks, under the condition that there be peace.

I openly expressed to Nasser my fears that I was hardly able to believe the imperialists would leave them in peace and that

[25] In February, 1955.
[26] In December, 1955.

he should take care not to offer them any possibility, not even the slightest pretext, to interfere in the affairs of the East. Of course I could not tell him in detail what he should do, but could only indicate the danger which lay ahead. I told him he should know that the imperialists are men without scruples, that they have not yet renounced their aspirations, that they consider Egypt, which is the strongest state in that part of the world, the most dangerous threat to imperialist and colonial possessions in Africa and Asia, and that the strong upsurge and development of Egypt might tempt the imperialist and colonial powers to block its efforts toward progress. It was our view, and I expressed it to Nasser, that they should first strengthen the country internally, that they should create an internal political organization, a strong and firm army, that they should raise themselves economically, endeavoring to get credits wherever they can, and straightaway let the people see something as a result of the new authority of the state, to let them feel a certain improvement. These were our suggestions and proposals which they readily accepted.

During our first meeting Nasser already told us that he would have to nationalize the Suez Canal, since Egypt, an independent country, could not tolerate foreign administration of its own territory. Of course, they had full rights to nationalize it, and only the right moment had to be chosen. When the nationalization of the Suez Canal took place, the great colonial powers, England and France, reacted sharply, there were threats of armed attack to prevent nationalization. But thanks to the United Nations, this first threat of war was averted. It was decided to conduct negotiations and to settle this problem by peaceful means. Despite this, there was staged a sudden aggression. Egypt was first attacked by Israel and then by England and France. The entire aggression was probably planned jointly, and the moment of attack was chosen when the deplorable events in Hungary took place. The confusion in Hungary was welcomed by them because they had already prepared themselves. England and France used Israel's aggression as a motive, saying they must safeguard the Suez Canal.

ISRAEL SHOWED THAT IT WAS AN INSTRUMENT
OF THE GREAT POWERS

This was typical aggression which did not differ in any
way from earlier classical aggressions on the part of the colonial
powers. It is precisely the same. The men who brought about
this aggression are today repenting, in my opinion, because
they did not succeed. First, they imagined they would destroy
Egypt in a few days and depose Nasser; second, they thought
that such a state of mind reigned in the world that people
would not interfere, and that the United Nations would not
condemn them because they would get a majority in that organization. But they miscalculated. The opposite happened.
Egypt was not ruined, although it suffered great losses; its
army fought well and the interventionists did not succeed in
occupying the whole of the Suez Canal, although they are still
fighting. The Egyptian people did not depose Nasser, as
Eden expected. In England itself, the Laborites took a very
sharp stand against the aggression and the Government's policy.
In the United Nations, the vast majority condemned this act of
aggression and the creation of an international police force
for Egypt is now under way, for which we have also offered
our own contingent. That is, the Egyptians themselves have
requested this, and most probably we, too, will send a contingent from our army.

This time Israel showed that she was an instrument of the
great powers and that as such she constituted a danger to peace.
It is true that there exists a terrible opposition to Israel among
the Arabs because nearly a million and a half Arabs have been
expelled from that part of the world and these people now
live under terribly difficult conditions. Egypt and other Arab
countries did not want to conclude peace nor give a guarantee
that they would respect Israel as a state, that is, they did not
recognize her. They still refuse to recognize her, but this
does not give Israel the right to undertake aggression. This
does not give them such a right under any condition, as the
English and others would like it to appear. Whether the

Arabs will recognize Israel depends a great deal on peaceful talks and on persuasion, on the solution of all outstanding problems which have been hanging in mid-air since the truce. What is here most tragic, in my opinion, is that the French Socialists have disgraced themselves and shown again that they are faithful servants of the circles which are trying to retain the old classical forms of colonialism at all costs. They will never wash this stigma from their faces. By means of the aggression against Egypt they wished to settle not only the Algerian question but also to reap benefits in other Near East countries. They believed that this conflict would spread to other Arab countries and that they might thus strengthen their colonial positions. The English thought that after the occupation of the Suez Canal they would be in a firmer position in the East, that after the destruction of Egypt their interests in the Middle East would be secured. It is tragic that this aggression received the support of the majority of deputies in the French Assembly. Only the Communists and a small section of the Socialists were against it. This is very tragic.

And this, comrades, compels us to be cautious. For it has turned out that the upholders of so-called Western democracy, France and England, are for peace, justice, and democracy only in words, while actually they are hotbeds which can lead to extreme reaction and aggressive undertakings if an opportunity presents itself. I am convinced that the unfortunate French people will have to pay dearly one day precisely because of this policy which is pursued by the French Socialists, headed by Guy Mollet.

We wished to help the French on the Algerian question. We told Nasser that we considered it difficult for the French to leave Algeria and that it would be a good thing to find some solution in a union between France and Algeria. When we visited France,[27] we said the same thing to the French leaders. "Instead of spending a billion francs every day for the army which you are maintaining in Algeria, give one half of that sum

---

[27] In May, 1956.

for the improvement of the living standards of those people, for the construction of roads and other projects, and the Algerian people will have nothing against you, will not be against a solution in the form of a union with France. Instead of spending a billion francs a day, and that is thirty billions a month, you would be better off following that path." Some French leaders admitted this was correct while others said that the prestige of France was at stake. They have their prestige now! They have disgraced themselves before the whole world. The whole world condemns the act of the French Government, the act of aggression.

YUGOSLAVIA IS VERY ACTIVE AND ACTS IN A POSITIVE WAY IN THE UNITED NATIONS

Comrades, things have not yet been clarified. It is still not clear what they are planning and how far they will go. I doubt that the whole affair with the international police will run smoothly. The English will probably wish to see part of their army remain in Egypt as police, which is impossible both under the United Nations statute and because they are aggressors. They cannot stay in Egypt. Egypt would never agree to this, nor would any honest person. They can always find a motive to continue their aggressive actions. The fact that the Soviet Union took up this problem so forcefully startled them a little and compelled them to think.

More than ever before we must direct all our forces today toward preserving peace. Yugoslavia is very active and acts in a positive way in the United Nations. For our part we shall do everything in our power for the preservation of peace in the world. The vast majority of peoples do not want war. If anyone in the world values peace, I think it is our people who desire it in order to be able to build a better life in peace. We have suffered enough, we have shed enough blood in the last and in previous wars, and have reason enough to fight with all our might for the preservation of peace in the world. But this matter has now passed beyond our boundaries.

Our country is united, strong, and monolithic. There exists only the question of improving the life of our people as much as possible. Our unity, our monolithic character, coolheadedness, consideration of the gravest world events without becoming nervous, and levelheaded judgment are important for us. We must not permit the babbling of various doubtful elements. The people from below, the masses, must silence them and prevent them from sowing discord.

If anything is unclear to you, we are always at your disposal, we can always explain the situation to you. It is clear that there are sometimes things which cannot be told. You should not think that I said everything today, because I have not been able to do so. But one thing I can tell you, namely, that what I have not told you also is of great importance, and that it is in a great measure positive. Yugoslavia today plays a role in the world which is reckoned with. In order that she should continue to play this positive role, I think we must continue the policy which we have consistently followed until now and preserve the strength which we have today.

This, comrades, is what I wanted to tell you. I have set forth, briefly, the basic outline and the most important things which I thought could be useful to you in explaining the issues while doing your work in the field.

Tito's speech made on November 11 was not released to the public until November 16. It evoked a sharp rejoinder in the pages of *Pravda*.

5. ARTICLE: "TO CONSOLIDATE FURTHER THE FORCES OF SOCIALISM ON THE BASIS OF MARXIST-LENINIST PRINCIPLES," *Pravda*, NOVEMBER 23, 1956

THE EVENTS IN Hungary, where the counterrevolution succeeded in going into action to attack socialist achievements and the people's democratic order, have evoked a deep response in the minds and hearts of all people who hold the interests of socialism dear.

In all the countries of the socialist camp the intrigues of reaction have been unanimously condemned. The press of the Communist Party of China has published articles which are inspired with a spirit of proletarian internationalism, and which have attracted general attention by the depth of their Marxist-Leninist analysis of the Hungarian events. The speeches of the leaders of the Communist Parties of France, Italy, and other countries have shown the unanimity of views in the ranks of the world Communist movement on the question of the events in Hungary. The Communist Parties of capitalist countries are manfully fighting against the debauch of reaction.

Events in Hungary show that the reaction for its anti-popular purposes tried to exploit the accumulated grievances of the working masses who were justly demanding an improvement in the leadership of the country and in the standard of life of the population.

There is no doubt that in the Hungarian events the former state and Party leadership of Hungary, headed by Rakosi and Gero, are to blame, for in solving problems of socialist construction they committed gross mistakes both in general political questions and in the field of economic policy and cultural development.

The leadership of the Party headed by Rakosi and Gero became estranged from the Party masses and the people and did not know the mood of the working class, the peasantry, and the intelligentsia.

The crudest violations of legality were committed in the case of Rajk and a number of other cases in which many honest Party and state workers suffered innocently.

In the economic field serious miscalculations were made:

A considerable part of the means was earmarked for the building of new large enterprises that were beyond the powers of a small country like Hungary.

A fast rate of industrialization which is correct under conditions in the Soviet Union was mechanically adopted in Hungary. Large enterprises were built after a set model, without regard to economic conditions and without adequate provisions for raw materials.

The former Party and state leadership of Hungary mechanically copied the experience of the Soviet Union in the field of industrialization despite the fact that the leaders of the Hungarian Workers Party were repeatedly given comradely advice not to do this.

The planning of economic development should have proceeded from the concrete conditions of Hungary, and account should have been taken that not every country needs to develop all branches in industry within its boundaries, since it can rely on all the other socialist countries.

More means should have been expended on the development of agriculture and on increasing the production of consumer goods, which would have made it possible to improve steadily the living standards of the population.

The road taken by the Soviet Union, creating its own powerful industry within a short space of time, was conditioned by the Soviet Union then being the only country of socialism in a capitalist encirclement.

Our people had to endure great self-denial and the mobilization of means in order to develop heavy industry as the most important guarantee of the country's independence and as a basis for the development of its economy.

The whole course of history proved that we had taken the correct road. If this had not been done the Soviet country would not have been able to resist Hitler Germany in the war and to destroy fascism.

Mistakes were also made in Hungary in matters of Party construction, and this led to a weakening of the Party. The Hungarian Workers Party had more than 900,000 members, in a country with a population of 9,000,000. The doors of the Party were opened to all who wished to join, and, hence, all sorts of people joined it. The workers joined it because it is their Party, because the working class can maintain, consolidate, and develop its conquests only if it creates and strengthens this Party. But the Party was also flooded by petit-bourgeois elements; people alien to the Party, careerists who wanted to exploit it for their own ends, rushed into the Party.

The Party leadership did not pay due attention to selecting for the Party the truly best people and did not do enough work in educating the cadres and all members of the Party in the Marxist-Leninist spirit and in the spirit of international workers' solidarity.

For this reason, when difficulties arose the Party was unable to cope with the complicated situation in the country and could not rally the advanced forces of the people for the fight against reaction.   More than that, the Party itself proved to be dis-organized.

The leadership of the Hungarian Workers Party did not sufficiently respect the national peculiarities of the country.

During the ten-year development of the people's demo-cratic order it was undoubtedly possible to educate people and to promote them to positions of leadership in the Party and government to a greater extent than had been done.

Practices were tolerated which hurt the national self-respect of the Hungarian people.

Thus a start was made to introduce a military uniform resembling the Soviet uniform.

But each nation has national traditions and customs which must be respected.   There is no need for everybody to have his hair cut to the same pattern.   After all, does the same army haircut and the same system of markings in schools prove the unity and international cohesion of socialist countries?

These of course are repugnant measures of no good to any-body which to a lesser or greater extent offended Hungarian national feelings.

After the 20th Congress [of the CPSU] Rakosi proved unable and unwilling to head the movement for reform, and, on the contrary, in opposition to the views expressed by the majority of Party members, declared that the policy pursued by the Hungarian Workers Party so far had been completely cor-rect and needed no improvement whatsoever.

This caused serious dissatisfaction in the Party. The Party leadership, without a clear political line, did nothing to settle past mistakes definitely and in a short time.

It should be added that for several months there was open propaganda in Hungary against the Party and the Government in the press, among a section of the literary people, students, and so on.

Along with justified criticism of the leadership, this propaganda carried more and more nationalistic and chauvinistic slogans, advocating a return to bourgeois democracy and appealing to antisocialist sentiments, frequently under the mask of opposing "the Yugolsav path to socialism" to the path followed by the entire socialist camp, including the Soviet Union.

The Rakosi-Gero leadership was not giving any rebuff to these negative sentiments and proved unable to base its actions on the proletarian party organizations where at that time healthy internationalist attitudes still prevailed.

The leadership of the Party and Government displayed a lack of vigilance; they failed to recognize both the growth of justified dissatisfaction of people as well as ever widening diversionary, conspiratorial activity of counterrevolutionary elements.

Under such circumstances, dissatisfaction became increasingly bitter until finally it led to street demonstrations in Budapest on October 23.

A section of the workers joined in the demonstrations with the good intention of expressing their justified dissatisfaction caused by the mistakes of the former leadership. But this elemental dissatisfaction was exploited by counterrevolutionary forces.

It has now been proved beyond any doubt that the counterrevolutionary elements had been organized in advance, that they had a military command center, that they had their forces ready and in position for carrying out a putsch, that they had men assigned to capture arsenals, that they had selected objectives to be attacked, that they had organized means of transportation for delivering and distributing arms at previously selected places. That is why the bloody events in Budapest, instigated by the provocational actions of the fascist-Horthyist bands, took place.

Western bourgeois newspapers write quite openly that the Hungarian events had been carefully prepared by reaction for a long time, both inside the country and from the outside, and the skillful hand of the conspirator could be felt everywhere from the very beginning. Allen Dulles, the chief of the American intelligence service, said frankly that "we had known" about the Hungarian events beforehand. A correspondent of the West German newspaper *Welt am Sonntag* writes about one of the rebels: "The first thing I saw on him was the German Iron Cross order." The newspaper *France-Soir* states that the American radio stations, broadcasting "appeals to the rebels, had done a great harm" in Hungary. The same newspaper admits that "the most reactionary and clearly fascist elements" played a leading role in the Hungarian events.

In order to block the actions of these antipopular elements and to restore order in Budapest as quickly as possible, the Hungarian Government addressed itself to the Soviet Government with the request for help by the Soviet troops stationed in Hungary in accordance with the Warsaw Pact. The actions of the Soviet troops and their participation in the restoration of order curbed the activity of the reactionary forces and forced them to retreat.

But as soon as the Soviet Government, at the request of the Imre Nagy Government, ordered its troops to leave Budapest, the counterrevolutionary forces started a cruel massacre of Communists, of public and political figures, and of supporters of the people's democratic system.

Many facts show that Irme Nagy pursued a double-faced policy. On the one hand he announced that the entry of the Soviet troops into Budapest was necessary in order to suppress the counterrevolutionary forces, on the other hand he encouraged the active resistance of the counterrevolutionaries and remained in touch with them.

Not encountering determined resistance on the part of Imre Nagy's Government, the counterrevolutionaries got hold of arms, created armed gangs which then received aid from the imperialist states, and dictated their conditions to Imre Nagy's Government.

Imre Nagy's Government had practically no power in the country. It sat in the Parliament building and conferred with the people through the microphone.

And during that time the fascist-Horthyist gangs murdered whomever they chose, seized progressive leaders in the streets, hanged them or cut their heads off.

Within seven or eight days the Imre Nagy Government was reshuffled several times, and every day it slipped more and more to the right.

Imre Nagy's Government became a cover for the activities of the counterrevolutionary forces. The conspiratorial military center was able to exert increasing pressure on its activities.

Under those circumstances the best men of the country, men like comrades Janos Kadar, Ferenc Munnich, and Gyorgy Marosan, members of Imre Nagy's Government, broke away from that Government. The new Government—Janos Kadar's revolutionary Government of workers and peasants—decided to put an end to the blood bath, stand up to the reactionary fascist forces, and to ask the Soviet Union for help.

Under such conditions the Soviet Union's decision to come to the aid of Hungary's revolutionary forces was the only correct decision to take.

A socialist state could not remain a passive spectator in face of the bloody orgy of fascist reaction in the People's Democratic Hungary.

When everything in Hungary becomes calm, when life returns to normal, the Hungarian working class, peasantry, and intelligentsia will undoubtedly better understand and correctly evaluate our actions.

We consider that we have fulfilled our international duty in helping the Hungarian working class in their struggle against

the counterrevolutionary machinations. We have brought sacrifices in this struggle only to preserve the socialist conquests
of the Hungarian working class and of the whole working
people, so that they would be able to continue their develop
ment, to lead their own life, and to build their independent and
sovereign socialist state.

We shall remain in the future friends of the working people
of Hungary in the struggle for our common cause: for the victory of socialism, for the construction of a new society, and for
the consolidation of peace. Our Party considers it its duty to
support the Hungarian Socialist Workers Party in its work of
implementing the revolutionary principles of Marxism-Leninism.

When order has been restored in Hungary and its Government considers that the presence of Soviet troops is not necessary, the Soviet Union for its part will under no circumstances
insist on its forces remaining there.

Among foreign reactions to events in Hungary, Comrade
Tito's recent speech at Pula attracts one's attention.[28]

In his speech he devoted much space to the events in
Hungary and pointed out correctly that counterrevolutionary
elements had played a provocatory part in them.

Very soon [Tito said], after two or three days, these reactionary
forces showed their real face. In the face of a nationwide indignation against everything which had been done in the past, the leadership of that period did not show any desire to remove the elements
which had caused the indignation of the Hungarian people or to
follow a genuinely Hungarian path to socialism, with all the specific
conditions of the country. As a result, events soon took a different
turn, and reaction asserted its rule more and more.

Comrade Tito gave a striking characterization of the Imre
Nagy Government:

The Nagy Government did not do anything to avert such a state
of affairs. It was constantly shedding tears over the radio and
calling for help instead of combating it and showing its determination to prevent the murder of Communist and progressive people.

---

[28] See the preceding document.

If the Nagy Government had been more energetic, if it had acted energetically against anarchy and the murder of Communists by reactionary elements, if it had put up a determined resistance against reaction and so on, it is possible that the events would have followed a correct road and perhaps it might not have come to the intervention of Soviet troops.

But what did Imre Nagy's Government actually do?

It called the people to arms against the Soviet Army and addressed itself to the Western countries asking them to intervene.

The events in Hungary, as Tito pointed out, assumed such dimensions that it became clear that a terrible massacre and a terrible civil war would take place there, and that this could lead to the final end of socialism and to a third world war. Although we are against intervention, Tito declared, the Soviet intervention was necessary. This, evidently, is a correct evaluation of the Hungarian events.

But in the same speech Tito calls the aid of Soviet troops to the Hungarian Government "an error" and says: "We never advised them to resort to help by the army." It is impossible to term such a position consistent and corresponding to reality. It is now completely clear to all that without this aid the counter-revolution could have won in Hungary and that a fascist-Horthyist regime would have been established. Consequently, the aid of the Soviet troops was a necessary and unavoidable step.

It is known that the help shown by the Soviet Union to the working people of Hungary in their struggle against counter-revolution called forth the approval of brotherly Communist Parties and of the workers of the socialist countries.

Reflecting the point of view of the Communist Party of China, the newspaper *Jen Min Jih Pao* wrote:

The position of the Soviet Union in relation to the Hungarian events is a completely correct position of proletarian internationalism. The Soviet Government and the Soviet people have no reason to look on with folded hands when the Government of Hungary, representing the will and national interests of the people, appeals to the Soviet Union for aid and when the Hungarian people would have become slaves of fascism unless the Soviet Union stretched out its brotherly hand in answer.

The fate of socialism in Hungary was being decided in the past few weeks. If a fascist Hungary had appeared in the center of Europe, the political situation of a number of countries of Eastern and Central Europe would have changed significantly, and the international situation of the whole European continent would have undoubtedly worsened.

The events in Hungary were the first great sortie during the entire postwar period, a sortie that has showed that the threat of facism has not yet passed. Under these conditions all adherents of socialism must display ideological unity, strict vigilance, and a principled approach in tackling problems relating to the Hungarian events.

All the more surprising are some propositions in Tito's speech which in no way contribute toward a rallying of the adherents of socialism, or to a correct understanding of a number of important problems of the international situation and of the current tasks of the world Communist movement.

To begin with, Tito's speech, along with some correct evaluations of the Hungarian events, contains others which are bound to arouse justified objections.

Here, look [Tito said to his audience], how strongly a people can resist, with naked hands and badly armed, if they are driven by one goal: to free themselves and to be independent. They don't care any more what kind of independence this would be and whether the bourgeoisie and the reactionary system will be restored in the country, provided they will be nationally independent. This was first and foremost in their minds.

In the first place, Comrade Tito patently exaggerates when he speaks in this case of "the people"; secondly, Marxism-Leninism teaches us a different mode of analysis of phenomena of this order.

If part of the workers are indifferent whether they come under the yoke of exploitation, under the cover of false slogans of "freedom and independence," whether their country is converted into a tool of the great imperialist powers, or whether they are plunged into a new war, as the fascist-Hitlerite Horthy clique did with Hungary in 1941-44, this means that this part of the working class fell in the trap set by reaction.

This would mean, consequently, that the masses go not toward freedom and independence but in a diametrically opposite direction, toward enslavement and loss of independence.

Marxism-Leninism requires that in analyzing social phenomena one must always answer the direct question: which classes stand to gain from one or another development, the interests of which classes are served by one or another public activity of people? It is true that considerable strata of the working people were drawn in the whirlpool of events in Hungary. History knows many cases when the national feelings of the masses have been aroused, inflamed, and utilized by reactionary forces against the vital interests of the people.

In his speech Comrade Tito dealt with another important international question—the aggression of England, France, and Israel against Egypt.

This is a most typical aggression [he said] that in no way is different from the former classical aggressions of the colonial powers. Israel [Tito continued] showed itself this time to be a weapon of the great powers and, as such, she is a threat to peace.

The most tragic thing in my opinion [the orator noted] consists in the fact that the French Socialists disgraced themselves and again showed that they are the most faithful servants of the circles that try, at any price, to maintain the old classical forms of colonialism. . . . And this teaches us, comrades, to be careful because it shows that the carriers of the so-called Western democracy—France and England—are for peace, justice, and democracy only in words, but in reality they are sources from which can spring extremely reactionary and aggressive actions if opportunities for this are presented.

From this correct evaluation one conclusion should follow—that is, the necessity of heightening the vigilance and unity of all peace-loving peoples.

Speaking about the Hungarian events, Comrade Tito makes a number of critical remarks addressed to the Communist Party of the Soviet Union. Special attention should be paid to these remarks. We, evidently, are not against criticism.

The Moscow Declaration states as the common opinion of the CPSU and of the YLC [Yugoslav League of Communists] that our cooperation will be based on friendly criticism and on a comradely exchange of opinions on questions of dispute between our Parties. We have, on our part, had no reason to renounce this decision. But the critical remarks of Comrade Tito attract our attention because they are made in a tone such as had almost disappeared in the recent period.

Let us take the basic proposition put forward by Tito with regard to the Soviet system. He insistently emphasizes that "the cult of personality is really the product of a definite system." He states that one must speak about "the system that guaranteed the creation of a cult of personality."

In actual fact, the cult of personality was in glaring contradiction with our whole Soviet socialist system. We were able to carry out the struggle against the cult of personality and to achieve great success in eliminating its consequences in the shortest time only on the basis of our political and economical system.

The Soviet socialist system, created by our working class in alliance with the peasantry, by all the working people of the Soviet Union, and by the Communist Party, has been tested by the experience of history. The basis of the invincible might of the Soviet socialist system consists in the fact that it is based on socialist forms of ownership of the instruments and means of production. The Soviet social system is a real people's society. In our country the exploiting classes have been fully liquidated; the moral and political unity of society has been created and made permanent. The alliance of the working class and of the peasantry has been further strengthened and the indestructible friendship of all the peoples of the USSR has been forged in the struggle for socialism.

This is the result of life's verification of our system; the creation in a short historical time of a mighty industrial socialist power, of a country with an advanced socialist agriculture in conditions of hostile capitalist encirclement, when not only were we not given any material aid from abroad, but when, in the course of decades, a persistent, open and covert economic, political, and ideological struggle against the first country of socialism was waged.

After a series of object lessons, even the enemies of the Soviet Union have no reason to doubt the reality of this result. The enemies of socialism tried to test the strength of our system in the most extreme furnace of war. The Soviet political and economic system, created by the peoples of our country under the direction of the Communist Party, has withstood with honor this most difficult test. The victory of the Soviet Union in World War II had a universal historical significance. It saved the peoples from fascist enslavement, opened the way to and created favorable conditions for the construction of socialism in a number of countries.

The Soviet system has shown its might in the restoration of an economy ruined by war, when we not only could not count on foreign aid, but gave aid ourselves to the young people's democratic states.

The strength of our system lies in its collectivism and in its profound socialist democracy. The Soviet system is the union of millions and millions of workers of city and country in the name of the great goal of the construction of a new society. The glorious deeds of the Soviet people are before the eyes of all. Quite recently hundreds of thousands of people were united in the great crusade on the virgin lands at the call of the Party and they obtained great results under difficult conditions.

All this, of course, does not mean that we do not have any inadequacies. There are such, and we subject them to sharp and direct criticism, carrying on systematic work toward eliminating them.

Our inadequacies were revealed at the 20th Congress of the Party and there was shown also the correct road to overcome them. Nobody can deny that our Party and the Soviet Govern-

ment is persistently and substantially realizing the greatest measures for raising the living standards of the workers, for strict
observance of revolutionary legality, and for the further development of socialist democracy.

So stand matters with the Soviet system, which would not
be destroyed by war, by economic blockade, or by the various
machinations of the enemies of socialism. It would not, of
course, be destroyed either by the cult of personality, because
this system, the socialist system of the dictatorship of the proletariat, has as its basis the alliance of the working class and of
the collective farm peasantry, having been called into life by
the laws of the historic development of society, and being the
embodiment of the creative energies of the masses of millions
of working people.

How else, in this case, can Tito's remarks about our system
be interpreted if not as an attempt to cast a shadow over the
system of social life of the Soviet people? Are we not forced
to ask whether this is not a repetition of the previous attacks on
the Soviet Union that were fashionable in the past, when the
relations between the USSR and Yugoslavia were getting worse
and worse?

The Yugoslav people and the Yugoslav League of Communists can apply any forms and methods they want in building socialism. But is it correct to disparage at the same time the
socialist system of other countries and to exalt their own experience, advertising it as the universal and the best method?

It is impossible not to see that the thought appears ever
more often in the Yugoslav press that "the Yugoslav road to
socialism" is the most correct and even the only possible road,
almost for all the countries in the world. At the same time
they do not talk about the positive sides and attainments of
socialist construction in other countries. Such a position
reminds one of the old saying, "Without us even the sun does
not rise!"

The creative diversity within the common path of socialist
development is determined in different countries by concrete,
objective conditions.

Notable experience in socialist construction has been gained by the great Chinese People's Republic. Working in complex historical conditions, the Chinese Communist Party marked a great contribution to the theory and practice of building a socialist society.

The world Communist movement may properly pride itself on the ability of the Chinese comrades to discover and successfully implement new methods of solving the most complicated problems in the life of hundreds of millions of people. However, the Chinese comrades always maintain that they are far from claiming that their methods of socialist construction are universal, although these methods have fully justified themselves in their country.

The wisdom of the leadership of the Chinese Communist Party finds its expression in the fact that they do not oppose the experience of building socialism in their country to the experience of other countries, being able to utilize the experience of all socialist countries for the successful solution of the tasks of building a new society in China.

Much that is unique in the solution of different questions of building socialism is possessed also by the European people's democracies. The experience of economic and cultural development in Poland, Rumania, and Albania, the experience of cooperative agriculture in Bulgaria, the significant attainments in the development of industry and agriculture in Czecho-slovakia—all this and much else enriches the treasury of experience in the creation of a new social structure.

In Yugoslavia there are also particular forms of socialist construction. New methods and techniques for administration and economic management are being tested in practice.

The workers' councils in Yugoslavia appeared comparatively recently. Each year of their existence correctives are introduced into their functioning, but some positive aspects of this form are already apparent. It is impossible to say this about another innovation that has produced negative effects, namely, some measures in the field of planning, which have weakened the planning system of the Yugoslav economy and have strengthened the influence of market relations which the Yugoslav press has admitted.

There can be no doubt that good experience will always find its adherents and followers if it withstands the test of time and gives positive results. Conversely, it is ridiculous to take offense at other countries if one method or another applied in one country is considered unsuitable for another.

What are the advantages of the "Yugoslav road to socialism" about which Yugoslav authors speak? In answering this question, the authors of Yugoslav press articles usually refer to one innovation or another of a political character.

But socialism—the new social structure—presupposes the reconstruction of the economy, which is the basis of all social life. This reconstruction has begun in Yugoslavia, but, as the Yugoslav comrades themselves know well, much still remains to be done to complete this reconstruction.

It is known that in Yugoslavia's economy agriculture plays a great role, but nonetheless, in the area of grain production the prewar level still has not been attained and, unfortunately, the victory of socialist relations in agriculture is still distant. It is known also that the annual deficit of wheat in Yugoslavia is approximately 600,000 to 650,000 tons.

It is completely evident what great significance the aid received from capitalist states, in particular the U.S.A., has for the economy of Yugoslavia. As a result of the situation that arose, Yugoslavia, in the course of a number of years, had the possibility of exploiting the aggravation of contradictions between the imperialist and socialist countries.

But if a vital part of its economy is aid from capitalist countries, then it is impossible to recognize that such a road has any special advantages. All countries in the socialist camp can hardly reckon on such aid. They cannot build their policy on the assumption of aid from the imperialists.

Consequently, such a road cannot in any case be universal. It is known that the imperialist circles have given aid to Yugoslavia not because they are sympathetic to socialism or to the building of socialism in Yugoslavia. The politicians from the imperialist camp have admitted that any means to sow and inflame discord among socialist countries may enter into their plans. It is impossible to forget for a minute that the enemies of socialism want to sow discord in the cooperation of socialist countries by every means, and to weaken the connections between them.

In his speech Comrade Tito puts forward the slogan of the "independence" of socialist countries and of Communist Parties from the Soviet Union and from the Communist Party of the Soviet Union.

However, it is known to everybody that the Soviet Union does not demand any sort of dependence or subordination from anyone. This was said with all force in the decisions of the 20th Congress of the Communist Party of the Soviet Union. This position was once more reaffirmed in the declaration of the Government of the USSR of October 30, 1956, "On the Principles of Development and the Further Strengthening of Friendship and Cooperation between the Soviet Union and Other Socialist States."[29]

Our Government is correcting the past errors that existed in this direction with all decisiveness. Of this there is testimony in the experience of our relations during the last years with Yugoslavia. We boldly acted to wipe out all errors of the past relationship with Yugoslavia, not caring about any considerations of prestige, being first to extend the hand to the Yugoslav Government and to the League of Communists.

Nobody can deny that for its part the Communist Party of the Soviet Union has done and is doing all that is necessary to place relations on the basis of Marxist-Leninist ideology in the interest of strengthening cooperation with the brotherly people of Yugoslavia and in the interest of the struggle for peace and socialism.

While giving a generally positive evaluation of the development of Soviet-Yugoslav relations and of agreements concluded

---

[29] See Part Four, Chapter I, Document 1.

between the USSR and Yugoslavia, Tito reproaches the Soviet leaders for not wishing to spread the principles fixed in these relations to other socialist countries. This strange and entirely farfetched allegation is needed by Tito to accuse the Soviet Union of "insufficient confidence in the socialist forces of the countries of people's democracy."

These allegations are refuted by facts.

There is the Belgrade declaration and the joint statement of the governments of the USSR and of Yugoslavia regarding Soviet-Yugoslav relations, and there is also the declaration about the relations between the Yugoslav League of Communists and the Communist Party of the Soviet Union.[30] There is the declaration of the Government of the USSR about the bases of the development and further strengthening of friendship and cooperation between the Soviet Union and other socialist states.

There is the joint statement in connection with the conversations between the delegation of the Central Committee of the Communist Party of the Soviet Union and of the Government of the Soviet Union and the delegation of the Central Committee of the Polish United Workers Party and of the Government of the Polish People's Republic.[31]

These documents reflect the Leninist principles of the relations between socialist states; yet Comrade Tito all the while continues to speak about some supposed "Stalinist Course" in relation to the countries of people's democracy.

Already before the 20th Congress, in connection with the consideration of Soviet-Yugoslav relations, the plenum of the Central Committee of the Communist Party of the Soviet Union of July, 1955, unanimously adopted the following decision, in which it is said:

In all our relations with the countries of people's democracy, and also with the brotherly Communist and Workers Parties, the Soviet and Party organs and all our workers abroad must be strictly guided by the Leninist principles of socialist internationalism: full

---

[30] See Part One, Chapter II, Document 2.
[31] See Poland, Chapter V, Document 11.

equality, respect for national sovereignty, and taking account of the national peculiarities of each country. Soviet Communists must serve as an example in carrying out the principles of proletarian internationalism, as is fitting for the representatives of a multi-national socialist country where, on the basis of Marxist-Leninist theory, the national question has been fully solved.

The historic experience of the Soviet Union and of the people's democracies shows that, given unity with respect to that which is most important and basic in the cause of guaranteeing the victory of socialism, different forms and methods for deciding the concrete problems of socialist construction can be applied in different countries, depending upon historic and national peculiarities.

As is known, the 20th Congress of the Communist Party of the Soviet Union paid much attention to the questions of the correct relations—based upon the principled positions of Marxism-Leninism—between our Party and all other brotherly Communist and Workers Parties.

To speak now, after the 20th Congress, about supposed "Stalinists" in the Communist Party of the Soviet Union who are supposedly trying to subordinate brotherly parties, means simply to close one's eyes to the policy that the Communist Party of the Soviet Union is actually carrying out in relation to the socialist countries.

This policy is based on the principles of full equality, respect for territorial integrity, state independence, and sovereignty and noninterference in each other's internal affairs, and it is permeated by the spirit of strengthening friendship between peoples and by the spirit of proletarian socialist internationalism. This policy is permeated by concern for strengthening the friendship, brotherly cooperation, and unity of all countries of the socialist camp and concern for strengthening peace in the entire world.

What does Comrade Tito call for in his speech? To go it alone? But it is permissible to ask: What does this road promise, what advantages does it offer the socialist countries? There are no such advantages.

There can be nothing useful for the cause of building a socialist society in the appeal to break with other socialist states and to withdraw from the friendly family of socialist countries. The most important conditions for the success of our great cause are faithfulness to the great banner of socialist internationalism and the unity and solidarity of all fighters for socialism.

In the light of the requirements of socialist internationalism, the tone with which Comrade Tito considered it possible to speak about Communist Parties and their leaders is bound to cause surprise. He includes, without any basis, all leading figures of the brotherly parties, both from the West and the East, who do not agree with his point of view, among the "Stalinists," attributing to them the most negative features.

About them he uses no other term than "inveterate Stalinist elements" and "irresponsible elements in different Communist Parties." Similar attacks directed at Communist leaders abound in the entire speech delivered in Pula.

Choosing as the theme for his speech the question of the mutual relations among Communist Parties, Tito in reality did not conduct a comradely polemic. He did not debate, but rather abused various leaders of the Communist and Workers Parties. The speech was not at all delivered in the tone of a conversation or a debate on an equal basis with proper respect for differing opinions. However, there was no basis for talking about "Stalinists" and "Stalinism" inasmuch as our Party, as well as other Communist Parties, has fought and will fight for the revolutionary principles of Marxism-Leninism.

The disparaging attitude reflected in the speech toward such a country as Albania and its leaders is particularly impermissible. Speaking about the Albanian comrades, Tito used rude and insulting expressions. At the same time, it is known that the Yugoslav leaders often speak in defense of the thesis of the equality between large and small peoples and of the right of each to have their opinion and to support it. Usually they insist that nobody can claim a monopoly on the definition of truth.

But here, hardly had Comrade Enver Hoxha written an article that did not please the Yugoslav comrades, and they throw abuse at him.[32] It is possible that the article could have been written differently. But why may Comrade Hoxha not have his own opinion, the right to criticize, that the Yugoslav comrades claim?

In his speech Comrade Tito did not only clearly interfere in the affairs of the Albanian Workers Party. He intruded as unceremoniously into the affairs of the French Communist Party and also the affairs of other Communist Parties, including the affairs of our Party. He tried, without giving the others the right of appeal, to give an evaluation of the internal situation in these Parties, and the activities of their leaders.

"The election of leaders," wrote the organ of the French Communist Party, *L'Humanite,* "is the internal affair of each party, and foreign intervention in this affair, may, as the past has shown, only bring harm to the workers' movement as a whole."

It is impossible not to agree with this justified remark.

After all that has been said, it is not surprising that Comrade Tito's speech was met with joy in bourgeois circles abroad. We may remember here the words of the veteran figure of the workers' movement, August Bebel, who recommended that one think about what one is doing if one is praised by the enemy. Our opponents are hastening now to the conclusion that this speech will be the cause of serious differences between the Soviet and Yugoslav Communists and will lead to the worsening of Soviet-Yugoslav relations.

To whom is it not clear that in the general interests of the Communist Parties it is impermissible to inflame disputes, to go over to mutual attacks, to return to the atmosphere of differences that, thanks to mutual efforts, belongs to the past?

The higher interests of the cause of the working class and of socialism imperatively require the attainment of mutual understanding and the elimination of all that can bring negative solidarity of the forces of socialism on the basis of Marxist-Leninist principles.

---

[32] See Document 3 in this chapter.

The cooperation of the Communist Party of the Soviet Union and of the Yugoslav League of Communists, as is shown in the declaration "On the Relations of the Yugoslav League of Communists and of the Communist Party of the Soviet Union," must be based on complete voluntariness and equality, friendly criticism, and the comradely character of the exchange of opinions regarding questions of dispute between our Parties.

It is known that in the past incorrect views inconsistent with Marxist-Leninist theory on some important questions of socialist construction prevailed among some of the leaders of the Yugoslav League of Communists and that deviations from the principles of proletarian internationalism took place.

In undertaking the rapprochement with the Yugoslav League of Communists, our Party realized that the attainment of a unity of views regarding important ideological problems would require a long time, inasmuch as there were and still are differences between the Communist Party of the Soviet Union and the Yugoslav League of Communists on a number of ideological questions.

For its part, the Communist Party of the Soviet Union will continue its policy of cooperation between our Parties on a principled Marxist-Leninist basis in the interests of the brotherly peoples of the USSR and Yugoslavia, and in the interests of the defense of peace, democracy, and socialism. We are convinced that currently disputed questions must also be considered and cleared up in a quiet, friendly atmosphere by means of a comradely exchange of opinion.

The Communists of the Soviet Union, like the Communists of all countries of the world, are aware that in conditions where reaction is carrying out a merciless campaign against the forces of socialism and democracy, when the imperialist and fascist elements in many countries are conducting furious attacks against Communists and are trying to introduce divisions in the international movement, a further consolidation of all the forces of socialism on the basis of Marxist-Leninist principles of socialist internationalism is necessary.

The *Pravda* editorial, of course, was not the last word in the debate. The Yugoslav position was further defined by Edward Kardelj, Vice President of the FPRY, in a speech before the National Assembly on December 7, 1956.

Meanwhile, articulate public sentiment in Poland over the Hungarian events ran high and considerably ahead of the cautious attitude taken by the Polish Government. On December 10 and 12 anti-Soviet riots and demonstrations were reported in Szczecin and Poznan. On December 17, an agreement governing Soviet troop dispositions and movements on Polish territory was concluded at Warsaw.

Under the pressure of events, the relations between the Soviet Union and the East European people's democracies were undergoing swift, almost daily reappraisal. The pattern of settlement which might emerge from the turmoil of Hungarian and Polish developments could not at this time be estimated.